United Nations Conference on Trade and Development

The Competitiveness Challenge: Transnational Corporations and Industrial Restructuring in Developing Countries

United Nations
New York and Geneva, 2000

Note

UNCTAD serves as the focal point within the United Nations Secretariat for all matters related to foreign direct investment and transnational corporations. In the past, the Programme on Transnational Corporations was carried out by the United Nations Centre on Transnational Corporations (1975-1992) and the Transnational Corporations and Management Division of the United Nations Department of Economic and Social Development (1992-1993). In 1993, the Programme was transferred to the United Nations Conference on Trade and Development. UNCTAD seeks to further the understanding of the nature of transnational corporations and their contribution to development and to create an enabling environment for international investment and enterprise development. UNCTAD's work is carried out through intergovernmental deliberations, technical assistance activities, seminars, workshops and conferences.

The term "country" as used in this study also refers, as appropriate, to territories or areas; the designations employed and the presentation of the material do not imply the expression of any opinion whatsoever on the part of the Secretariat of the United Nations concerning the legal status of any country, territory, city or area or of its authorities, or concerning the delimitation of its frontiers or boundaries. In addition, the designations of country groups are intended solely for statistical or analytical convenience and do not necessarily express a judgement about the stage of development reached by a particular country or area in the development process.

The following symbols have been used in the tables:

Two dots (..) indicate that data are not available or are not separately reported. Rows in tables have been omitted in those cases where no data are available for any of the elements in the row;

A dash (-) indicates that the item is equal to zero or its value is negligible;

A blank in a table indicates that the item is not applicable, unless otherwise indicated.

A slash (/) between dates representing years, e.g., 1994/95, indicates a financial year;

Use of a hyphen (-) between dates representing years, e.g., 1994-1995, signifies the full period involved, including the beginning and end years.

Reference to "dollars" ($) means United States dollars, unless otherwise indicated.

Annual rates of growth or change, unless otherwise stated, refer to annual compound rates.

Details and percentages in tables do not necessarily add to totals because of rounding.

The material contained in this study may be freely quoted with appropriate acknowledgement.

UNITED NATIONS PUBLICATION

Sales No. E.00.II.D.35
ISBN 92-1-112503-0

Foreword

> "Globalization is a process that can still be steered and shaped by human beings according to human values. ... Rather than reconcile themselves to the need to adapt themselves to a supposedly unmodifiable global system, developing countries must strive to shape it according to their own development needs at their own pace and in line with their own strengths and weaknesses. This process will, of necessity, go hand in hand with the struggle to integrate themselves successfully into a transformed and more open economic system. ... It is not the amount and pace of international integration that counts but its quality."

> Rubens Ricupero, Message to UNCTAD X, Bangkok, February 2000

This study is a contribution to the debate on how developing countries are facing the competitiveness challenge, and coping with globalization. It traces the role that foreign direct investment (FDI) has played in developing the garments, colour television receivers and automobile industries of Argentina, Brazil, Costa Rica, the Dominican Republic, Malaysia, Mexico, Morocco and Thailand. It also compares the role that FDI has played in Chile and Zimbabwe as these countries developed their natural-resources-based industries. The study's particular advantage is that the analysis straddles three levels: the micro-level effect on individual firms; the meso-level impact on the industry; and the responses at the macro level, namely the policies adopted by developing country governments. It therefore allows a comprehensive view of the interlocking needs of firms, industries and the macroeconomy.

Many developing countries have embarked on a process of industrial restructuring using international investment to integrate into the global production chains that characterize the current economic system. Over the past 15 years, three industries have stood out as especially dynamic in this respect: garments, consumer electronics and the automotive industry. These are industries registering significant shares in world trade flows, and high rates of growth in both trade and investment. Increasingly, they are organized as integrated global production systems in which transnational corporations (TNCs) source from a variety of affiliates, supplier firms and locations.

On the other hand, commodity trade and natural-resources-based processing are the more conventional sectors for integration into global markets via FDI and the activities of TNCs. Historically, commodities have been a more problem-ridden market, marked by cyclical fluctuations in world prices and perennial obstacles against upgrading into the export of processed products.

World trade and investment patterns are driven by three interdependent processes. The first is one where, for political, historical or geographical reasons, economic ties between the home country of a TNC and a developing host country are strong, inducing a bundling of FDI flows to that destination. The second one is where TNCs create global production chains, using affiliates in different locations to produce components of a "world product", driven by comparative advantage and economies of scale. A third variant is trade-regime-related, where preferential access to a particular host or third market triggers investment flows: the influence of the economics of regional trading blocs such as ASEAN, the European Union, MERCOSUR and NAFTA are obvious cases in point.

As a combined result of these processes, a number of developing countries have emerged as FDI-based export platforms in the course of the last decade. Some assemble imported intermediate products for re-export, others process and manufacture for regional markets, while the most sophisticated exporters are manufacturing high-quality products for world markets.

Viewed from the development perspective, the issue is to what extent a developing country can tap into the globalizing economy and benefit from FDI and international trade in a sustainable manner. This depends, among many other factors, on the role that TNCs assign to their affiliates in developing countries in the global production chain; to what extent and on what terms they source from local enterprises and take root in the host economy; and whether they rely on local technological capacities and develop the skills of management and labour in the host countries.

TNC activities have a direct bearing on competitiveness and affect industrial development and upgrading. As commercial enterprises, TNCs base their choices and decisions on short- and long-term criteria of profitability. Competitiveness at the firm level is their prime rationale. For developing countries, on the other hand, macroeconomic growth, international competitiveness, and economic and social development are the prime objectives. Accordingly, developing country governments need clarity and decisiveness regarding the elements of their own macroeconomic and development goals. Their FDI-related policies need to be part of a greater scheme of development strategies. They can use FDI as an instrument to upgrade competitiveness and thus cope with the pressures of globalization, but government policy-making needs to be the linchpin. Moreover, governments need to analyze the sectors, industries and types of production most attuned to their development needs and vision. Ideally, they negotiate – at least in the case of major projects – the position assigned to them in the global strategies of TNCs when they deal with potential incoming FDI. FDI flows, the role of TNCs and the impact on competitiveness of developing countries also depend on the evolution of the international trading system and shifts in market access, in turn requiring policy-making and negotiating at the multilateral level.

The findings of this publication give cause for caution – they illustrate the vulnerability of the industries under review and the difficulties that countries have faced in becoming competitive. They do, however, also give cause for optimism: where governments have had policies in place to anchor international trade and investment in their domestic economies, globalization has opened an avenue to competitiveness and economic development.

Preface

This publication is the result of extensive surveys undertaken in a sample of affiliates and domestic firms in selected industries in ten developing countries, as well as a review of the complex literature on the subject. The United Nations Centre on Transnational Corporations (UNCTC), in New York, and subsequently UNCTAD's Division on Investment, Technology and Enterprise Development, in Geneva, conceptualized and coordinated the research as part of their continuing work on the role of foreign direct investment in development. In addition to the research and on-site surveys, two seminars contributed to analysing the findings in depth.

A large number of experts in academia and in the United Nations Secretariat contributed to this publication. Many of the co-authors and experts who prepared case studies and sectoral analyses are based in developing countries. Each author's contribution is reflected in the table of contents. Karl P. Sauvant, Padma Mallampally and Zbigniew Zimny provided conceptual and thematic guidance. Jörg Weber managed the project from 1994 to 1998, and organized several conceptual and methodological meetings. From 1998, Gabriele Köhler was responsible for substantive advice and technical project management, and saw the study to its completion. Paul Stephenson and Kumi Endo undertook copy editing, and Rikkert van Assouw prepared the index. Production of the volume was carried out by Irenila Droz, Florence Hudry and Jenifer Tacardon, with support from Fernando Krichilski and Maria Lourdes Pasinos. It was desktop-published by Teresita Sabico. Diego Oyarzün designed the cover.

The case studies and analyses were funded by the Interregional Project on Transnational Corporations and Industrial Restructuring in Developing Countries (TC-INT/93/A50) sponsored by the Government of Denmark. The advisory role of Henrik Schaumburg-Müller and the financial contribution by the Government of Denmark are gratefully acknowledged.

Glossary

ADEFA	Asociación de Fábricas de Automotores de Argentina (Argentine Automobile Manufacturers Association)
AFTA	ASEAN Free Trade Area
AICO	ASEAN Industrial Cooperation Scheme
AMIA	Asociación Mexicana de la Industria Automotriz (national automobile producers' association of Mexico)
ANFAVEA	Associação Nacional dos Fabricantes de Veículos Automotores (national automobile producers' association of Brazil)
ASEAN	Association of Southeast Asian Nations
ATC	Agreement on Textiles and Clothing
BBC	Brand-to-Brand Complementation
BEFIEX	Benefícios Fiscais à Exportação (Brazilian Fiscal Benefit for Special Export Programme)
BOI	Board of Investment (Thailand)
BUILD	BOI Unit for Industrial Linkage Development (Thailand)
CACM	Central American Common Market
CAD	computer-aided design
CAN and CANPLUS	Competitive Analysis of Nations (computer software of ECLAC)
CBU	completely built-up units
CEDOPEX	Centro Dominicano de Promoción de las Exportaciones (Export Promotion Center of the Dominican Republic)
CEM	contract electronics manufacturing
CKD	completely knocked-down
DL 600	Decree Law 600 (Chile)
ECLAC	Economic Commission for Latin America and the Caribbean
EPZs	export processing zones
ERP	effective rate of protection
ESAP	Enhanced Structural Adjustment Programme
ESCAP	Economic and Social Commission for Asia and the Pacific
EU	European Union
FDI	foreign direct investment
FOB	free on board
FTAA	Free Trade Area of the Americas
G7	Group of Seven
GATT	General Agreement on Tariffs and Trade
GDP	gross domestic product
GSP	Generalized System of Preferences
HICOM	Heavy Industry Corporation (Malaysia)
HTS 9802	Heading 9802 of the United States Harmonized Tariff Schedule
IFZ	Industrial Free Zone (Dominican Republic)
IMF	International Monetary Fund
ISI	import-substitution industrialization
ISO	International Standardization Organization (quality standard)
JICA	Japan International Cooperation Agency
JIT	just-in-time (delivery of inputs)
JTC	Joint Technical Committee for Local Content (Malaysia)
LC	local content
LG	Lucky Goldstar
LTA	long term arrangement
MERCOSUR	Southern Common Market (Mercado Común del Sur)
MFA	Multi-Fibre Arrangement

MIGA	Multilateral Investment Guarantee Agency
MITI	Ministry of International Trade and Industry (Japan)
MNE	multinational enterprise
MTI	Ministry of Trade and Industry (Malaysia)
NAFTA	North American Free Trade Agreement
NIE	newly industrializing economy
OBM	original brand-name manufacturing
OECD	Organisation for Economic Co-operation and Development
OEM	original equipment manufacturing
OPIC	United States Overseas Private Investment Corporation
PCB	printed circuit boards
PTA	Preferential Trade Area for Eastern and Southern African States
QS9000	Quality System 9000 (quality control standard)
R&D	research and development
RTZ	Rio Tinto Zinc
SECOFI	Secretaría de Comercio y Fomento Industrial (Mexican trade and industrial promotion agency)
SITC	Standard International Trade Classification
SMEs	small and medium-sized enterprises
TCL	textiles, clothing and leather
TDRI	Thailand Development Research Institute
TNC	transnational corporation
TQM	total quality management
TRIMs	Trade-Related Investment Measures Agreement of the WTO
TV	television
UDI	Unilateral Declaration of Independence (Zimbabwe)
UN	United Nations
UNCTAD	United Nations Conference on Trade and Development
UNESCO	United Nations Educational, Scientific and Cultural Organisation
UNIDO	United Nations Industrial Development Organisation
USAID	United States Agency for International Development
USITC	United States International Trade Commission
VAT	value-added tax
WTO	World Trade Organization

Table of contents

Boxes

Tables

Annex tables

Figures

Chapter I

Competitiveness, restructuring and FDI: an analytical framework

1.1 Introduction

Rapid technical progress is driving sweeping changes in the global economy. It is so broad and far-reaching that some see the emergence of a new technological paradigm transforming the productive system (Freeman and Perez, 1988). This paradigm offers a cornucopia of productive knowledge, with immense scope for raising incomes, employment and welfare. It is also an irresistible force for globalization. By reducing transportation and communication costs, it links economies in closer, tighter webs. It facilitates the integration of production under common ownership (of transnational corporations), allowing access to capital flows, world markets, skills and technology. Its productive potential induces Governments to liberalize trade and investment policies. This policy shift is assisted – sometimes induced – by the international community, which is fashioning new rules of the game to facilitate increased trade and capital flows, promote the enterprise sector and protect property rights.

The emerging system is changing the location of production and innovation and, thus, national patterns of comparative advantage. Moreover, technical progress is creating new forms of industrial organization and management and altering relations between productive and other sectors, in particular, research institutions, universities and the information transmission sector. All this calls for new skills and work specialization. There are many ways in which the new paradigm differs from previous paradigms. According to Esser et al. (1996, p. 1), it is characterized by a "new pattern of competition ... marked by knowledge- and technology-based competitive advantages; competitive advantages based on inherited factor endowments are losing their significance" and the "emergence of new organizational structures characterized by less hierarchic concepts... . The firms are embedded in dense technological and productive networks (industrial clusters, industrial districts, business alliances, long-term contractual arrangements with suppliers)". The same authors go on to say: "Radical technical change gives rise to both a restructuring of old industries and a creation of new ones and to substitution processes that see traditional raw materials being edged out by new ones... In the political sphere, the new pattern of competition requires active policies aimed at shaping new industrial locations. Their formulation and implementation is based on cooperative approaches that focus on the know-how provided by firms, science and the public sector (policy networks), in this way complementing the policy mechanism." The system is immensely productive. It is also enormously demanding (World Bank, 1999). Enterprises in developing countries are facing far more competitive environments in this fast-moving technological world. To survive and compete, they have to restructure their activities, facilities and skills. Restructuring needs to take place *within* firms, to raise their ability to compete, *across* firms to shift resources from those unable to compete to those that are, and *geographically*, from uncompetitive to competitive regions and countries.

This is a study of the impact of foreign direct investment (FDI) on industrial restructuring in selected industries in some developing countries. The focus is on how FDI affects the ability of economic actors – directly, foreign affiliates, and indirectly, local firms or the economy at large – to compete better in a globalizing world, primarily by raising, upgrading and diversifying exports. It is, in brief, about the impact of transnational corporations (TNCs) on the industrial competitiveness of host countries, an issue of growing concern in the developing world.

1.2 Concerns with national competitiveness

Governments have long worried about national competitiveness. Initially, this preoccupation was more manifest in the mature industrialized countries than in developing countries. The European Union, the Organisation for Economic Co-operation and Development (OECD), and UNCTAD have published several studies on this subject.[1] Many developed countries established high-level committees to deal with competitiveness, often reaching across ministerial divisions to devise appropriate policy. The United Kingdom Cabinet Office's White Paper on competitiveness (1996) expressed this concern succinctly:

> "Improving competitiveness is central to raising the underlying rate of growth of the economy and enhancing living standards. Achieving this means removing the impediments to investment in machines, people and ideas and improving the efficiency with which resources are used throughout the economy, not just in those sectors directly involved in international trade. It means giving people the freedom to grasp new opportunities. It involves benchmarking all our activities against the best of our competitors to see how well we are doing compared to them and what we can learn from them.
>
> The need to improve our competitiveness is not imposed by Government, but by changes in the world economy. Improving competitiveness is not about driving down living standards. It is about creating a high skills, high productivity and therefore high wage economy where enterprise can flourish and where we can find opportunities rather than threats in changes we cannot avoid" (p. 10).

With widespread liberalization, this concern has spread to policy makers in many developing countries: the restructuring of industries to face international competition, the upgrading of domestic technological and other capabilities, and their attractiveness as sites for production and investment by TNCs, have become a major focus of development policy.

The trend towards globalization of production, facilitated by falling transport and communications costs exposes countries to much greater competition than at any time in the

---

[1] See, for instance, European Communities (1994), OECD (1994) and UNCTAD (1995). There are many studies of United States, European and Australian industrial competitiveness: see, among others, DTI (1998), Hughes (1993), Scott and Lodge (1985), CBI and LBS (1994), Competitiveness Policy Council (1993), Irish Competitiveness Council (1998), and Australian Business Foundation (1997).

past. The failure to keep up with changing technologies imposes far greater penalties. It is hardly surprising, then, that Governments of developing countries worry about how their industrial sectors will fare in this challenging world, and how to harness globalization as a force for upgrading and export growth rather than for devastation and de-industrialization.

Competitiveness is often confused, wrongly, with maintaining low wages. While low-cost labour provides an excellent launching pad for the initial export of simple manufactures by developing countries, countries cannot grow if their competitive edge remains low-wage, unskilled labour. True competitiveness requires that economies continue to produce more goods for international markets as wages rise and the phase of labour-intensive exports is complete.[2] Thus, competitiveness over time means upgrading simple labour-intensive activities to make higher-quality products that yield greater value-added, and so sustain higher wages. It means diversifying from these into more complex activities that offer a broader base for production and building capabilities. And it means deepening local technological and organizational skills over time to handle more advanced functions (say, from simple assembly to adaptation and improvement, new product design, innovation and basic research). The process of longer-term industrial restructuring should comprise all these elements if it is to lead to sustained benefits.

There is thus an important distinction to be drawn between *static* and *dynamic* competitiveness. Static competitiveness competes on the basis of received endowments such as low-cost labour or natural resources. These are the starting points for export growth, but they lose their edge as technologies change or incomes rise. In dynamic competitiveness the productive sector retains its edge in international markets as wages grow and new technologies and demand patterns emerge. Restructuring for industrial competitiveness means moving from static to dynamic sources of cost advantage in manufacturing industry, not cutting wages to retain a market position in labour-intensive exports. In essence, this means moving within activities to more complex products and processes and across activities from low to high value-added industries.

Restructuring entails that countries move up the technological ladder in both existing and new activities. This is not just a matter of adopting more capital-intensive technologies in response to rising wages (moving smoothly along a given production function), as textbook economics may suggest. This gives the impression that restructuring is an automatic and costless process of responding to market signals. This impression can be misleading, since there are complex learning processes involved, calling for technological effort, skill building, networking and using new organizational forms. These processes can be costly, prolonged and uncertain; in developing countries they tend to face widespread market and institutional failures. It may also involve moving backwards and forwards along the "value chain" of production, diversifying in related activities on the basis of existing competencies. In general, it necessitates the shift in the industrial structure from simple to complex activities, in particular those that offer greater scope for technological advance and more spillover benefits to related activities. Without such a structural shift, developing countries may just stay in a

---

2 Reinert (1995) used the case of Haiti, which has the lowest production cost for baseballs, to illustrate that this would not lead to Haiti being described overall as a very competitive economy.

low-growth path; it is only countries that manage a sustained structural transformation that achieve long-term competitive industrial growth.[3]

As noted, restructuring in the current context poses difficult challenges. Protected activities become exposed to extremely intense and demanding competition: as a consequence, industries are obliged to introduce new and often much larger-scale technologies. What is more, industries have to operate at "best practice" efficiency, often with new modes of organization. All this is very different from the post-war decades, when technological and managerial slack could be tolerated. New competitors or new technologies often overtake existing comparative advantages. Restructuring is thus no longer a discrete process of adapting to a once-for-all increase in competition or change in technology, but a continuous one of flexibly responding to very rapid change: it is developing the capacity to adapt continuously to technical change.

FDI is relevant to restructuring in several ways (see UNCTAD, 1995). As one of the main manifestations of globalization and a carrier of new technologies, it provides both opportunities and threats to developing host countries. The opportunities arise from the benefits that TNCs can bring in terms of financial, technological and human resources – the main ones are access to state-of-the-art technologies and to large markets overseas. The threats arise from the competitive pressures they exert on domestic enterprises and from their own strategies, for instance, by exploiting static advantages in host economies and not upgrading these dynamically, or by choosing to use intermediate inputs from abroad rather than from potential local suppliers. Much also depends on the nature of the activity and the endowments and policies of host countries.

1.3 Influences on competitiveness and restructuring

Industrial competitiveness is affected by a large number of factors. The ultimate agent for building competitiveness and undertaking industrial restructuring is the individual firm, which responds to signals from the product and factor markets surrounding it to obtain, master and adapt technology, improve upon it over time, and produce and market its products. The influences, at this level, on whether and how firms invest in building up their competitive capabilities can be simplified into three main sets – the incentive structure, the factor markets on which firms draw, and the institutions with which they interact (figure 1.1). Each of these has three sub-determinants (many more could be added but the purpose here is to provide a simple schema). There is a potential role for policy in improving competitiveness. Each "market" that the firm operates in can suffer from deficiencies and failures, giving the wrong signals, providing inadequate inputs or support or failing to respond at all to its needs. Governments can help by remedying these market failures and coordinating individual firms' efforts where necessary (see Lall, 1996, for a discussion of the theoretical issues involved).

---

3 On the possibility of such "multiple equilibria" and the need to shift across them, see Rodrik (1996) and Stiglitz (1996). On the historical analysis of the growth process as the move across specific activities, see Reinert (1995).

All this concerns competitiveness at the individual enterprise level. "Industrial restructuring" includes this but goes further, to cover the improvement of competitiveness at the industry, sector, regional and national level. The policy concerns are similar. Governments have to ensure that industrial activities as a whole face a combination of incentives that stimulate the adoption of relevant new technologies and support efforts to master, adapt and improve upon these technologies. They have to assist the factor markets that provide the finance, skills, information and marketing support that competing requires. They have to help in setting-up or improving the institutions that are necessary for these markets to function. And they have to coordinate investment decisions across activities where market forces by themselves are unable to provide adequate information (Stiglitz, 1996). In the long term, countries manage this process with different degrees of success, with different roles played by their Governments; however, the evidence suggests that recent successes, for instance in Asia, have involved a significant role for government policy.

Figure 1. 1. Triangle of national competitiveness

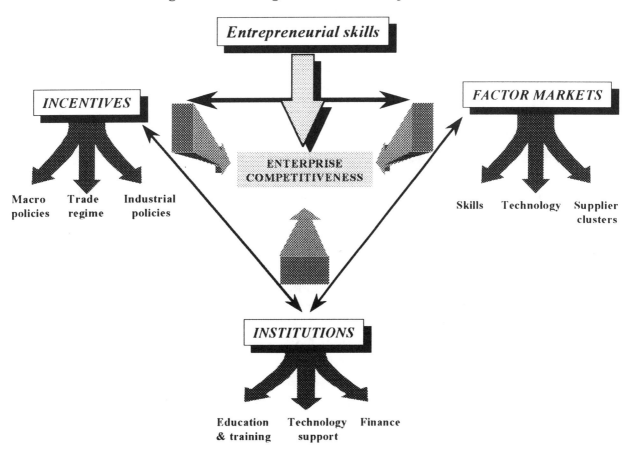

Source: UNCTAD.

The process of industrial restructuring has many components, involving elements of broad macroeconomic policy and infrastructure as well as those more specifically concerning firms themselves. This report focuses on the latter set, which are broken down into four components:

- physical investment;
- human capital investment;
- technology upgrading;
- improved supply linkages.

Physical investment is generally an important element of restructuring to the extent that new plant, equipment, buildings and so on are needed to improve competitiveness. Upgrading of productivity can take place without adding to investment, by improving skills, organizational routines or the use of existing technologies; however, more sustained improvements would require new facilities or technology with "embodied" components in the form of physical investment.

Human capital investment is also generally required in the industrial restructuring process. While some necessary skills can be hired directly from labour markets, many that are specific to the technologies being used have to be created in-house, by training and on-the-job learning. The need for skill upgrading rises with the complexity of new technologies that may be introduced. With the growing pace of technical change, moreover, firms have to invest increasingly in continuous re-training of their employees to keep abreast of their competitors. Human capital creation can mean both an increase in the total amount of training as well as a change in its content – traditional training methods or curricula may be inappropriate to restructuring needs in a liberalizing economy.

Technology upgrading is an essential component of restructuring for competitiveness. Such upgrading can take place with existing facilities and equipment, for instance by improving quality or maintenance, lowering costs, changing product design or speeding delivery; or it can involve purchasing new technologies (with new equipment and skills). The more radical the restructuring process, the greater the technological upgrading involved; however, the extent of local effort required can vary. Where technologies are highly embodied in the equipment (as with process industries), the upgrading may not require a great deal of local technological effort. In contrast, where there is a great deal of tacit knowledge and coordination involved (as with metal working), it may take long periods of learning and technological activity. In more advanced firms, technology upgrading may involve launching or increasing research and development (R&D) into new products and processes, since simply mastering existing technologies may not yield sufficient competitive advantage to cope with world-class competitors.

Improved supply linkages refer to raising productivity by establishing more or closer relations with local suppliers and subcontractors. This includes greater transfer of technology or skills to local suppliers to raise their quality and efficiency; the fostering of a network of suppliers who can provide the needs of just-in-time production; closer collaboration with vertically related firms in technology development; or strengthening relations with local consultants and technology institutions. The strengthening of the local supply base is an increasingly important part of building competitiveness in a globalizing world. It is necessary, not just to improve the quality and efficiency of production but also to raise local content, capture greater spillover benefits and promote small and medium-sized enterprises.

These four categories of restructuring activities are addressed in the case studies of this volume. TNCs influence each type of restructuring in economies where they establish affiliates. Where possible, and applicable the case studies provide evidence from interviews on the nature of this influence.

1.4 Globalization and shifting competitive advantages

The three most relevant features of the globalization process this study is concerned with are: (a) industrial relocation; (b) increased international competition in manufactured trade; and (c) the knitting together of the international economy through FDI.

The economic structure of industrialized countries has moved towards the services sector as competitiveness in many manufacturing industries has eroded with rising wages and changing technologies. Many industries have had to be pruned, restructured or closed down. By 1995, manufacturing contributed less than a third of GDP in industrial economies; at the same time, there was a significant relocation of industry to developing countries (UNIDO, 1996). The growth and pattern of international trade in manufactured products illustrates clearly the nature of the relocation process. Take, for instance, the structure of imports of the mature industrialized countries. In 1995, manufactures contributed over three-quarters of all OECD imports, up from 55 per cent in 1980.[4] In the period 1980-1995, 47 of the 50 most dynamic imported products were manufactures (at the SITC three-digit level). Of these, 32 were from six technologically advanced and dynamic industries such as computers, other electrical machinery, electronic equipment, chemicals, automotive products and non-electrical machinery. The 50 products also included less technologically advanced products such as garments, which, while technologically relatively stable, were undergoing a process of massive relocation from high- to low-wage countries.

The intensification of international competition is shown by changes in import market shares of the OECD countries (table 1.1). Over the period 1980-1995, the share of OECD imports of manufactures from developing countries as a whole practically doubled, from 10.8 to 19.7 per cent of the total, while industrialized countries lost market shares correspondingly.

Table 1.1. Market shares in OECD imports of manufactures, 1980-1995
(Per cent)

Country/region	1980	1995	Percentage change 1995-1990
OECD countries	85.4	75.4	-12
Developing Asia	7.9	16.2	105
Latin America	2.1	3.4	67
Africa	1.3	0.8	- 41
Central and Eastern Europe	1.3	1.1	- 16
Total CAN data base	98.6	97.0	
Others	1.4	3.0	

Source: ECLAC, CANPLUS.

---

[4] Figures reached using the CANPLUS computer software on international competitiveness developed by the Economic Commission for Latin America and the Caribbean (ECLAC).

The largest gains took place in Asia and Latin America. In the six dynamic industries, Western Europe and North America both lost market shares (-11.9 and -3 per cent respectively), while Japan gained (2.2 per cent). In the developing world, the four "Asian tigers" took the largest increase in market share (3.7 per cent), followed by China (2.7 per cent), the four "new tigers" (2.4 per cent), and 25 Latin American countries (2.3 per cent).[5]

Who were the individual winners and losers? The winners and losers, defined as the 10 countries that gained or lost one-half of a percentage point or more of OECD imports of manufactures between 1980 and 1995, are shown in table 1.2. The winners are mainly Asian developing economies (China, Singapore, Malaysia, the Republic of Korea, Thailand, Taiwan Province of China and Indonesia), and a few others (Mexico and Spain). The "losers" are all developed OECD members (Germany, the United States of America, Belgium/Luxembourg, France, the United Kingdom, Italy, the Netherlands, Sweden and Switzerland). The countries with the largest market shares lost ground in industrial exports to a group of challengers from the developing world, mainly from Asia.[6]

The prime movers of the globalization process were TNCs. These companies are, in general, domestic firms that transformed into TNCs in the course of industrialization and, more recently, globalization. By 1998, some 60,000 TNCs with 500,000 foreign affiliates accounted for world sales of $11 trillion and assets of almost $15 trillion. FDI in that year came to $640 billion, and it was highly concentrated. In most investing ("home") countries, the top 25 investors controlled over one-half of the outward FDI stock. The 100 largest TNCs (by external assets) control one-fifth of the global foreign assets and one-third of TNC sales. These firms originate in a small group of industrialized countries: the United States (35 per cent), Japan (16 per cent), the United Kingdom (11 per cent), Germany (13 per cent), France (10 per cent), the Netherlands (7 per cent) and others (8 per cent). They concentrate on a few activities: automotive, petroleum/mining, electronics, chemicals, food products and others (UNCTAD, 1999a). Interestingly, the main home countries were losing world export market shares while their TNCs were expanding production overseas, expanding activities overseas and restructuring their domestic manufacturing.

Globalization has, of course, meant a rapid expansion of FDI flows. From an average annual outflow in the order of $170 billion in 1987-1992, total FDI increased to over $640 billion in 1998. As a proportion of gross domestic product (GDP), FDI more than doubled from 5 to 12 per cent, and of gross fixed capital formation from 4 to 8 per cent. A substantial share of FDI flows were for mergers and acquisitions rather than greenfield investments, especially in the industrialized countries, indicating the nature of the restructuring process in particular industries. FDI flows also changed in destination. Developing countries accounted for 17 per cent of inflows in 1985-1990, and 26 per cent in 1998. Within the developing world, FDI was heavily concentrated in Asia (about 51 per cent in 1998) and Latin America (43 per cent in 1998). The five principal recipients of FDI accounted for almost 60 per

---

[5] The four "Asian tigers" are Hong Kong (China), Singapore, the Republic of Korea and Taiwan Province of China. The four "new tigers" are Indonesia, Malaysia, the Philippines and Thailand.

[6] This topic is taken up for the cases of developing Asia and Latin America in Mortimore, Bonifaz and Duarte de Oliveira (1997).

Table 1.2. Winners and losers in world trade in manufactures, 1980-1995
(Per cent)

Economy	OECD import market shares			Manufactures as per cent of the country's exports to the OECD
	1980	1995	Change 1980-1995	
10 winners	**15.8**	**26.6**	**10.7**	**87**
China	0.5	4.3	3.8	88
Mexico	0.7	2.1	1.4	76
Singapore	0.5	1.5	1.0	92
Malaysia	0.4	1.3	0.9	79
Spain	1.4	2.1	0.7	77
Republic of Korea	1.5	2.2	0.7	93
Thailand	0.2	0.9	0.7	70
Taiwan Province of China	1.8	2.4	0.6	92
Indonesia	0.1	0.6	0.5	49
Japan	8.7	9.2	0.5	98
9 losers	**65.5**	**53.6**	**-11.8**	**82**
Germany	16.2	12.8	-3.3	89
United States	13.0	11.3	-1.7	81
Belgium/Luxembourg	5.3	3.8	-1.5	83
France	7.7	6.6	-1.1	79
United Kingdom	6.6	5.6	-1.0	80
Italy	6.3	5.4	-0.9	89
Netherlands	4.1	3.4	-0.7	63
Sweden	2.6	2.0	-0.6	85
Switzerland	3.0	2.4	-0.6	84

Source: ECLAC, based on the CANPLUS computer programme.
Note: Winners and losers are classified as having gained or lost market shares in OECD manufactures imports.

cent of all inflows to developing countries during 1998: China (27 per cent), Brazil (17 per cent), Singapore (4 per cent), Thailand (4 per cent) and Mexico (6 per cent). Thus, a significant part of industrial expansion by TNCs focused on a relatively small group of host countries, though others were also involved (for many of these even low levels of TNC participation by global standards meant significant changes in their industrial and export structures).

For most developing countries, integration into the production systems of TNCs took the form of foreign affiliates, in one out of three cases via the acquisition of local companies. For some developing countries with strong local enterprises, however, association with TNCs took the form of inter-firm agreements between local and foreign firms (through subcontracting, original equipment manufacture or joint ventures) or strategic partnerships (co-production, use of common components or modularization).

1.5 TNCs and industrial restructuring

As noted above, TNCs can play an important role in industrial restructuring. By virtue of their size, technological prowess and internalized markets for skills, capital, technology and brands, they offer access to investible and human resources, technology and supply linkages. Moreover, in activities where their production networks dominate world trade, their presence can make it easier to enter markets and achieve competitiveness. In those activities where scale economies are important, TNCs can offer the resources to reach minimum efficient sizes by aiming production at export markets if domestic markets are insufficient to support economic plants. The international location and integration of TNC production facilities has been one of the main forces behind recent shifts in competitiveness and industrial restructuring.

However, direct TNC involvement is only one of several possible means of upgrading and restructuring industrial activities in developing countries. Each of the factors critical to competitiveness may be available from other sources, or from TNCs themselves (by non-equity-based contracts). Capital can be obtained through a variety of channels other than direct investment; technology can be purchased in non-FDI forms, created locally or imitated; skills can be generated locally or recruited directly. In fact, some economies with impressive industrial records (Japan, the Republic of Korea and Taiwan Province of China) have relied on domestic enterprises to drive industrial and technological growth. This required the Government to play an important role in guiding, coordinating and stimulating investment and factor market responses. The activities of other countries that relied on FDI have also not been of a laissez-faire nature. The best industrial performers in this group were those where Governments adopted policies to target, guide and utilize TNCs rather than wait passively for market forces to guide investment. TNCs would invest in new technologies and upgrade their affiliates because the local skill, technology and institutional base was improving sufficiently to make these new activities and functions viable.

Industrial restructuring is thus the outcome of several factors. Given the initial level of industrial development (and assuming sound macroeconomic and investment policies), it results from the interplay of TNC activity and strategies with host country public policies on trade, investment, factor markets and institutions. The host country may adopt different strategies to using the resources offered by TNCs, ranging from a passive open-door approach, through proactively targeting and directing TNCs, to controlling their entry to build up local capabilities. In essence, the impact of TNCs depends on how their internalized transfers of capital, technology and skills build on, and in turn affect, the development of local markets and capabilities (Dunning, 1993). The effects may be positive or negative.

This section considers briefly the existing state of knowledge on the positive and negative effects of FDI on developing host countries.[7] Not all the issues raised here were investigated in the country studies presented in this volume, but the discussion is designed to "set the stage".

---

[7] For a comprehensive analysis, see UNCTAD (1999a).

1.5.1   TNCs and product markets

What effects do TNCs have on trade, competition and export performance in the host country? Trade and competition policies of host economies interact with FDI. The policy framework affects the entry and composition of foreign investments. Foreign investors in turn influence the policy regime. The presence of globally integrated TNCs can induce governments to liberalize more readily, and to open up inward-looking economies to import competition and export promotion. Much depends on the nature and strategies of the TNCs concerned. Those searching for low-cost locations to serve world markets, or processing local resources for international markets, are much more likely to press for liberal trade regimes than those that are aiming primarily at local markets. This applies particularly to large firms with globalized operations, which benefit from international integration of production and services. These are TNCs that are pursuing the deep or complex integration of their activities in host countries (UNCTAD, 1993). In a world that is rapidly opening up anyway, TNCs may appear to be a marginal direct influence. However, their indirect impact, as the engines of globalization, is likely to be very strong – host countries look to TNCs to ease their liberalized economies into international activity.

TNCs also affect the domestic market structure. The beneficial impact is that new entry, in particular of efficient firms, raises the intensity of competition and forces incumbents to improve or exit. The competitive spur that TNCs provide is one of their most important advantages to previously sheltered industrial structures. However, the impact of large affiliates (backed by the resources of their parent firms) on local market structures and enterprises has long been debated. It is feared that TNCs, with their financial and other competitive advantages, may use aggressive entry tactics, cause growing market concentration and stifle local entrepreneurship. In many host economies, especially those with small domestic markets, FDI is in fact often associated with higher levels of concentration. However, it is premature to draw definite conclusions from this. The rise in concentration may reflect the realization of scale economies rather than anti-competitive behaviour by TNCs. Moreover, concentrated domestic market structures in countries with open trade regimes and the possibility of foreign investment entry have a different economic implication than similar structures in relatively closed economies: markets are far more contestable in the former than in the latter. Nevertheless, predatory conduct always remains a risk – and calls for stringent competition policies. According to UNCTAD:

> "... in a globalizing and liberalizing world economy, the number of actual or potential entrants into foreign markets increases. This gives rise to a greater potential for competition in markets regardless of their geographical scope. Entry barriers are less the outcome of government policies and more associated with costs and know-how or technological advances. Thus, despite the openness of the world economy to new competitors, entry barriers may lead to increased concentration (followed perhaps by increased market power). On balance, the effects of liberalization and globalization on market structure and competition depend substantially on industry characteristics influencing market

contestability. But in certain industries, especially those in which integrated production holds efficiency gains for firms, TNCs can play an important role in the process" (UNCTAD, 1997a, p. 179).

For that reason, UNCTAD has recommended that countries establish review procedures for certain mergers and acquisitions to ensure that they result in improved market performance, especially from an efficiency perspective (UNCTAD, 1997a; UNCTAD, 1999; UNCTAD, 2000).

What is the impact of a strong foreign presence on the development of local entrepreneurship? While TNCs can stimulate the growth of local suppliers and provide a competitive spur to local firms, Governments legitimately worry about whether an open-door policy will lead to advanced industries falling under foreign-owned control when some at least could remain in local hands. The argument is related to that for infant industries: given the high costs, risks and duration of building up competitive capabilities in advanced industries, domestic firms may not be able to develop without an initial period of protection from foreign entry. The "infant entrepreneur" argument may have a sound theoretical basis. Some developing countries have built up domestic enterprises in advanced activities by restricting direct foreign entry and subsidizing the growth of local firms. The Republic of Korea is a classical example of the use of selective trade and FDI interventions to develop their giant *chaebols,* some of which are among the leading TNCs from the developing world. However, the argument has also been misused to prop up inefficient domestic firms with close ties with policy makers, resulting in inefficient, incompetitive production.

Are there any economic reasons to prefer domestic to foreign ownership of dynamic industries? There may be, if local firms are more prone to strike supply, technological and other linkages in their home economies than do foreign firms, and if the retention of corporate decision-making in the home country has benefits. In developed countries, TNCs tend to retain their most vital and technologically advanced functions in the home country, particularly in large countries like the United States (Porter, 1990). This clearly offers dynamic benefits to the home country and may deprive developing countries of an opportunity for more advanced R&D. But restricting foreign ownership in advanced industries may mean slower or more limited *access* to new technologies and markets. Local firms can gain access to new technologies by other means, including licensing them from TNCs, but licensing tends to become more difficult and expensive as technologies grow more advanced and as the firms become competitive threats to innovators. The promotion of local ownership in technologically dynamic industries requires that sufficient domestic skills and technological effort can be mustered to substitute for foreign licences. Not all developing countries can claim to meet this condition.

As far as export promotion is concerned, one of the main advantages that TNCs offer is the possibility of participation in their global supply networks and direct access to their sales channels and brand names. A significant and growing proportion of world trade, especially in sophisticated manufactures, takes place within TNCs, between different affiliates. In a large number of vertically integrated activities, TNC participation may be the only way for new entrants to access export markets. In other activities, especially those with strong product differentiation, TNCs offer an avenue to overcome the entry barriers that can hold back exporters which lack established marketing outlets or brands.

However, TNCs may not always be more export-oriented than domestic firms. Much depends on the country and industry, the capabilities of local firms and the level of technology used in export activity. TNCs can increase exports substantially from host countries with FDI-friendly policies, outward-looking trade regimes and efficient labour and appropriate infrastructure. Their contribution is likely to be lower in simple assembly activities where local firms offer comparable levels of efficiency. For instance, a substantial proportion of clothing exports from the developing world comes from domestic enterprises subcontracting to foreign importers and retailers. The TNC contribution is likely to be greater in activities with advanced technologies or integrated production systems spread over different countries (by intra-firm trade). This is where they have the greatest strengths in terms of innovation, production know-how and skills, and internal markets they can coordinate efficiently. The most dynamic export item from developing countries in recent years has been electronics products. Much of this has come from assembly operations in South-East Asia, and more recently Mexico, as part of tightly-knit TNC operations where different functions are spread in line with costs and skills in different locations.

Developing countries can succeed in complex industrial exports without going through TNC networks if they are able to build the necessary indigenous base of technological capabilities. Even the early Asian newly industrializing economies (NIEs) relied on technologies imported or copied from TNCs, though, as noted, their own R&D became increasingly important as buying new technologies grew more difficult. Their exports depended heavily on original equipment manufacture (OEM) arrangements with TNCs. Under these arrangements they made electronics and other products to specifications provided by TNCs, which sold the products under their own brand names (Hobday, 1995). OEM arrangements gave TNCs greater flexibility and access to low-cost efficient suppliers; it gave the exporters access to new technology and saved them the costs of export marketing. However, OEM arrangements in advanced products have taken root only in countries with well developed local capabilities – in others, like Malaysia, similar products are exported by foreign affiliates. Not many developing countries have the technological base to replicate the autonomous export success of economies such as the Republic of Korea and Taiwan Province of China. Moreover, the new international rules of trade and investment make it more difficult for others to mount the kinds of strategies used by them. This suggests that much of the growth of sophisticated exports in the future will be situated in or around TNC systems – some of them headquartered in NIEs whose enterprises have built up advanced capabilities.

The benefits of TNC-driven export activity are highly concentrated. In general, the bulk of the developing world's manufactured exports come from a handful of countries. In 1996, just 12 economies accounted for over 90 per cent (Lall, 1998). These economies were China, the Republic of Korea, Taiwan Province of China, Singapore, Hong Kong (China), Malaysia, Indonesia, Thailand, the Philippines, India, Mexico and Brazil. In many of these, TNCs played significant export roles. TNCs do account for large proportions of exports from other developing countries, but the values involved are small. In many cases, TNC- manufactured exports are driven by the availability of low-cost labour. Some dynamic upgrading has certainly taken place, but not in all host countries: the ones that succeeded best are those where the Government undertook to raise the quality of factor inputs and to induce investors into more complex activities. In others, the technological level of TNC export activity has tended to stagnate. The case studies will highlight some of these differences.

1.5.2 Factor markets

TNCs can benefit host countries by improving three vital ingredients of competitiveness: technology, local suppliers and skills.

Technology: The main benefit that developing host countries expect from TNCs is access to advanced technology and their ability to implement new technologies effectively (with the entire package of skills, capital and marketing that makes them commercially viable). With the rising costs and scale of frontier innovation and the growth of strategic alliances in high-tech activities, it is becoming increasingly difficult in many activities to obtain new technologies without direct participation by TNCs. Moreover, with the growing liberalization of FDI regimes, the rising cost of innovation is leading many TNCs towards greater internalization of technology transfer. In activities with economies of scale and the need to integrate production across many countries, even the deployment of less innovative technologies requires such participation. In general, FDI provides the fastest and most effective way to deploy new technologies in developing host countries. As the number of TNCs grows and their origins diversify, the range of technologies offered also increases. Growing competition among TNCs can improve the terms on which host countries can obtain technology, potentially strengthening the advantage of FDI as a source of technology transfer, if Governments use their bargaining power effectively.

However, there are two possible drawbacks of FDI technology transfer. First, TNCs tend to transfer the results of innovation but not the innovative capabilities, which are centralized in advanced industrialized countries, mainly in their home countries. This results in a truncation of the process of technology transfer, and can relegate developing host countries to lower levels of technological activity (even when their industrial capabilities have reached a level when, as in many NIEs, they are able to efficiently undertake advanced R&D work). There is certainly a powerful argument that developing countries that have been able to build up the most powerful innovative bases have restricted internalized technology transfer via TNCs precisely in order to allow national enterprises to develop their infant innovative capabilities.

The second possible drawback is that TNCs may transfer the technology that is appropriate to the static factor endowments of host economies and not their dynamic endowments. Thus, they may invest in simple assembly technologies and move on to lower-cost locations when wages rise; it is not in their economic interest to invest in the creation of the high-level skills that would make more complex technologies viable. How widespread this practice is cannot be judged from the available evidence, since both cases have been observed. In some countries, rising wages have led to more capital-intensive processes while in others investors have relocated elsewhere. Even in countries where processes have been upgraded, however, it is commonly found that little R&D activity is located in the host economy: the process of deepening technological capabilities is not clearly promoted by FDI.

Domestic suppliers and linkages: TNCs can be powerful sources of demand for the output of local suppliers and subcontractors, and can raise their capabilities and quality to international levels more effectively than links among domestic firms by transmitting technical or market information, skills, finance and other forms of assistance. Under import substitution regimes, many large countries forced the pace of local content by imposing time-bound rules, albeit not always efficiently. "Tigers" like the Republic of Korea and Taiwan Province of China, for example, did use them effectively by ensuring that supplier capabilities were able to match world levels and were geared to their export effort (Lall, 1996). However, local content provisions are now under the purview of the Uruguay Round Agreements. TNC linkages are being increasingly driven by pure cost and efficiency considerations. As a result, TNCs are changing their sourcing patterns and raising local content in countries that have capable supply clusters, while lowering it elsewhere. They are also often rationalizing regional patterns of sourcing to get fewer components from particular countries but on larger scales. This is leading to second-round effects on FDI patterns, as TNC home-country suppliers set up affiliates near their principals to meet this need for efficient local content.

The evidence suggests that TNCs have strong, but often very uneven, effects on the development of local suppliers in host countries. As with FDI flows themselves, there appears to be growing concentration on locations that are industrially advanced and able to meet the rigours of world competition without substantial additional cost and effort. Other locations may well receive FDI but may not gain much by way of local depth and linkages.

There are differences in terms of the organization of global production, for example, between producer-driven and buyer-driven networks. Producer-driven commodity chains are those in which large, usually transnational, corporations play central roles in coordinating production via backward and forward linkages. This is most characteristic of capital- and technology-intensive industries, such as automobiles, aircraft, semiconductors, and electrical machinery. Buyer-driven chains are those in which large retailers, brand-named merchandisers, and trading companies play a central role in shaping decentralized production in a variety of exporting countries, often developing countries. This pattern of industrialization is typical of relatively labour-intensive consumer goods, such as garments, footwear, toys and housewares (Gereffi and Koreniewicz, 1994).

There also appear to be differences by home country of the investor. Japanese investors have been particularly criticized for sticking with traditional suppliers (though this seems to be changing with greater international experience and under host government pressures). United States investors have been more amenable to developing local suppliers (though they are more likely to retain majority or full ownership of their own affiliates).

Governments have a significant role to play in terms of institutional support focusing on upgrading the capabilities of domestic suppliers and with regard to promotional programmes combining public and private resources to accelerate linkage development (FIAS, 1995).

Skills: The gaining of competitiveness in most new technologies requires a more highly skilled workforce at all levels of the enterprise. What is more, it needs different kinds of skills and work attitudes: "multi-skilling", teamwork and flexibility, rather than simply people trained in traditional ways to do routine production line tasks. The pace of technological change also raises the need for constant retraining of the workforce, and many developed countries are now emphasizing the central role of "lifetime education" to maintain an efficiency and innovation edge. Of course, different economies have very different skill needs, as figure 1.2 shows. What is incontrovertible is, however, the need to invest in skills: *all* economies constantly need to upgrade their human capital stock to sustain industrial competitiveness.

Figure 1.2. Human capital and industrial development patterns

Level/pattern of industrial development	Human capital profile	
	Skills	Technological capabilities
Low levels, mainly simple assembly and processing activity for domestic market	Literacy, simple technical and managerial training. Practically no in-firm training except informal on-the-job learning.	Ability to master assembly technologies, copy simple designs, repair machines, but many activities operate well below world best practice levels of technical efficiency.
Intermediate level, with export-oriented activities in light industry, some local linkages in low-tech products	Good secondary & technical schooling and management financial training. Low base of engineering and scientific skills. In-house training mainly by export-oriented enterprises. SMEs have low skill levels.	World-class assembly, layout, process engineering and maintenance in export oriented industries. In others; capability to undertake minor adaptations to processes and products. Little or no design/ development capabilities. Technology institutions weak.
Deep industrial structure but mainly inward-oriented; technological lags in many activities	Broad bur often low quality schooling, vocational and industrial training. Broad engineering base. In-house training lagging. Training institutes de-linked from industry. Management and marketing skills weak. SMEs have some modern skills.	Process mastery of capital and skill intensive technologies, but with inefficiencies. Considerable backward linkages, significance adaptation of imported technologies. Little innovation, low linkages with universities and technology institutions.
Advanced and deep industrial structure, with many world-class activities, own design & technology base	Excellent quality schooling and industrial training High levels of university trained managers, engineers and scientists. Training institutes responsive to industrial needs. Large investments in formal and informal in-firm training . SMEs have high skill levels and competence.	Ability to monitor, import and adapt state of art advanced technologies. Good design and development capabilities in sophisticated technologies. Deep local linkages with suppliers, buyers, consultants, universities and technology institutions.

Source: UNCTAD.

The contribution of TNCs to skill development is potentially large. Many foreign affiliates in developing countries pay higher wages to employees than local counterparts, and invest more in training. They tend to be more aware of emerging trends in training and the need for new forms of skill creation; they are able to use state-of-the-art training materials and techniques; and their training is oriented to global markets (UNCTAD, 1994, 1999a). Several large TNCs have set up training facilities to ensure that their need for specialized skills is fully met. Examples include Intel and Matsushita in Malaysia. Such training can, in principle, have spillover benefits if, for example, employees leave, join local firms or set up their own facilities. Furthermore, the presence of advanced manufacturing TNCs also attracts a host of foreign investors in modern services, which create valuable new skills in finance, marketing, accounting, shipping and infrastructure.

Nevertheless, host countries cannot rely on TNCs to meet their broader or emerging skill needs. TNCs use the technologies that are appropriate to local education levels and train mainly to create efficient operators of such technologies – they tend not to invest in creating the skills needed for higher levels of technologies as these emerge. Such investments are generally more expensive and long-term, and here it is educational institutions that have to meet the needs. In other words, the upgrading of the general skill level and provision of high-level specialized training is something that host countries have to do for themselves. Indeed, such upgrading itself can be used to attract higher-quality inward FDI and to induce existing investors to move into more complex activities.[8] Moreover, TNCs from the developed world tend to concentrate in industries with more advanced technologies, leaving a wide range of simpler activities in which skill creation has to depend on local firms. TNCs from other developing countries do enter into simple labour-intensive activities, but these tend not to invest heavily in training. In essence, industrial enterprises, however attuned to training, cannot replace the education and training provided by the national education system, and this remains a vital area of host government policy.

Organizational change is as much a part of competitiveness today as technological progress proper; indeed, many new, flexible and information-based technologies could not be used efficiently without accompanying changes in organization and management. Enterprise hierarchies are tending to become "flatter"; there is much more interaction and cooperation between vertically linked firms in the value-added chain; networking and information-sharing are becoming more vital for achieving the full economies of specialization and innovation; flexible automation and just-in-time techniques require teamwork and multi-skilled workers.

As with skill creation, TNCs can make a valuable contribution to the upgrading of management and organization systems in host countries, with beneficial spillover effects on local firms (suppliers, buyers and competitors). This has been particularly noted for Japanese TNCs investing in other OECD countries, but it is also true of developing host countries where foreign investors have often triggered the adoption of modern management techniques.

---

[8] On how the Government of Singapore used skill creation to induce upgrading by TNCs in the hard disk drive industry, see Wong (1997).

Nevertheless, the introduction of new organizational techniques has a life of its own. It is pursued independently by local firms, who learn about them overseas and use consultants to help them: the introduction of just-in-time, total quality control and other systems now has a momentum unrelated to FDI inflows. One important source of improving quality management has been the increasing use of ISO 9000 systems; ISO certification is increasingly becoming a *sine qua non* of all export activity to the developed world and is likely to spread to intra-developing country trade.

To sum up: this review confirms that it is very difficult to evaluate the effects of TNCs on host developing economies in general, and on industrial competitiveness and restructuring in particular. What is clear is that TNCs, as they lead a processes of technological advance and integration of production systems across countries, are bound to assume increasing importance in industrial development. What is also clear is that some of the restrictive FDI policies used by developing countries in the era of import-substitution were not conducive to their industrial growth and competitiveness; few analysts would disagree with the proposition that the greater openness to FDI observed today can enhance efficiency. Within this broad consensus, however, there is room for differences of opinion on how FDI can and should be used in the national interest. This debate is very different in spirit and content from that which took place some two decades ago, showing greater acknowledgement of the contributions that TNCs can make to host countries' economic development.

The main impact of TNCs on industrial competitiveness is related to their advanced technologies and skills, access to capital and final product markets, and participation in globalized systems of production and exchange. With the shrinking of economic space and economic liberalization, these become increasingly significant for industrialization in host developing countries. Moreover, the growing synergy between industry, services and infrastructure (particularly those concerning the generation and transmission of knowledge) and the rapidly increasing role of TNCs in these sectors, implies that participation in international economic life requires adaptation in policies and rules. Many local firms in developing countries are becoming transnational themselves, and are striking alliances with major players directly. There is a convergence over time of FDI policies across countries (though differences still exist in the interpretation and application of rules), and intensifying competition in attracting TNCs.

However, TNCs do not have a uniformly beneficial effect on developing host economies. Their role is context-specific, varying by industry and technology, and by the level of industrial and entrepreneurial development of the host country. These effects can be highly concentrated by both sector and destination. Therefore, Governments need to intervene in the FDI process, to maximize the beneficial impact on their economies, to induce better-quality inward investments, to foster the growth of national enterprises and capabilities, and to guard against potential negative impact. Thus, both theory and practice provide strong grounds for a proactive role for the host Government.

1.6 Attracting FDI

Figure 1.3 shows schematically the main economic determinants of FDI in developing countries. It also illustrates that there is a two-way relationship between FDI and competitiveness. While TNCs can improve host economy competitiveness, the competitiveness of the economy is also one of the most important factors in attracting more, and better-quality FDI. Thus, improvements in the competitiveness of the host economy are becoming an important tool for FDI promotion. With growing globalization, better information on economic conditions and a convergence of FDI incentives across host countries, the process of attracting FDI has become more professional and sophisticated. In the most effective FDI promotion agencies, efforts are increasingly targeted by activity and investor, with detailed follow-up services and surveys on investor perceptions and satisfaction (Wells and Wint, 1990). Incentives are shifting away from general front-loaded benefits such as across-the-board tax holidays to performance-based measures.

Figure 1.3. Determinants of FDI in developing host countries

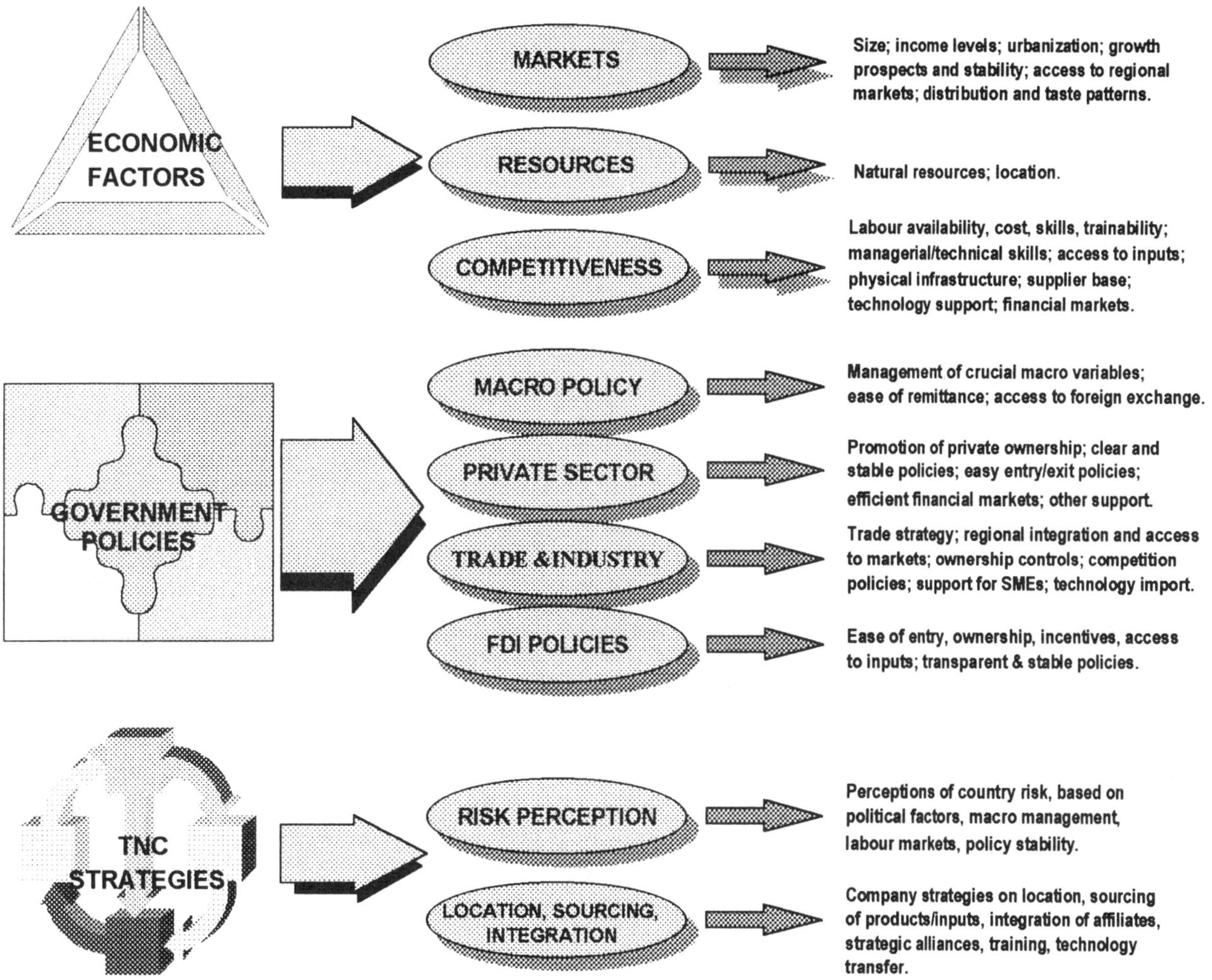

Source: UNCTAD.

As part of this evolving approach, Governments are tailoring their factor markets and investment conditions to the needs of particular investors, backing this up by offering grants in addition to fiscal benefits (grants are used much more in the developed than the developing world). For instance, Ireland's success in attracting FDI into electronics has been due largely to its ability to create a skilled human resources base to allow TNCs to set up efficient world-class plants there, and to target the world's leading electronics firms. Singapore and Malaysia have used a similar approach. Costa Rica recently has experienced success with targeting Intel: it has attracted a major semiconductor assembly and testing plant to Latin America in the face of intense competition from larger, more industrialized countries (Spar, 1998). This illustrates the mutual feedback between FDI and competitiveness strategies.

1.7 TNC strategies

The pattern, extent and impact of FDI on competitiveness depend not just on the circumstances and policies in host countries, but also on the strategies pursued by TNCs. There are differences between firms from a given home country, as well as some national differences in the attitudes of TNCs, and some of these show up in the country studies below. This section considers some recent general trends in TNC strategies that may affect industrial competitiveness. (For an elaboration, see UNCTAD, 1993.)

There is an emerging process of "deep integration" in TNC operations in sophisticated services, high-technology industries and in engineering activities with significant scale economies. This stands in contrast to traditional strategies of stand-alone affiliates and "simple integration", in which only part of the production chain is integrated (figure 1.4). Traditional strategies still predominate in many industries in which TNCs operate, and there are large differences between firms in their attitudes to integration; however, it is the emerging trends that are worth noting.

It can be argued that it is in the most dynamic industries that deep integration strategies are gaining at the expense of more traditional strategies (UNCTAD, 1993). There are many reasons for this, most of them to do with technological change and intensifying competition. This change may have sweeping and important implications for the international economy, at a time when many developing countries are choosing to participate more fully in trade and investment.

"Transnational corporations are pursuing complex integration strategies in response to competitive pressures in the expectation of greater efficiency. The overall size of the integrated international production system that is emerging is difficult to gauge, but a number of indications suggest the emergence of transnational corporations that are visibly global in their operations in industries such as automobiles, microelectronics, consumer electronics, household appliances, office machinery, instruments, pharmaceuticals and financial services... . In these industries, the value-added chain is, in whole or in part, geographically fragmented; but the individual functions of the chain, whether internalized or externalized, remain under the control and coordination of the major transnational corporations. In these industries, the leading firms have — or strive to have — a direct presence in each of the three Triad members. Within those areas, production and distribution are being rationalised and restructured, particularly where, as in the case of the European Union, internal barriers to the flow of factors, as well as intermediate and final products, are being dismantled. In the process, the nature of the world economy is undergoing a profound change: from being a collection of independent national economies linked primarily through markets, the world economy is becoming, for the first time, an international production system, integrated increasingly through numerous parts of the value-added chain of production."[9]

What are the implications of this emerging structure for the location and sourcing decisions of TNCs in developing countries? "The result is a broader range of opportunities for host countries to attract TNC activities, but also higher requirements in terms of human resources and infrastructure as well as open frameworks for trade and investment" (UNCTAD, 1993, p. 174). This can have favourable implications for the development of competitiveness in the host economies concerned.

Figure 1.4. Types of integration between parent firms and affiliates of TNCs

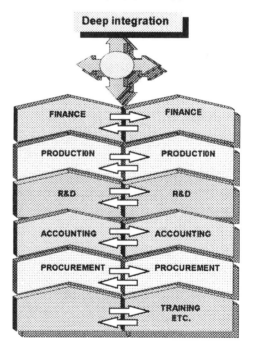

Shallow integration	Deep integration
INTER-FIRM ARM'S LENGTH TRADE IN GOODS AND SERVICES BASED ON DIVISION OF LABOUR BETWEEN INDEPENDENT PRODUCERS	INTER- AND INTRA-FIRM EXCHANGE OF GOODS, SERVICES, & PERSONNEL BASED ON DIVISION OF LABOUR AND AS PART OF INTEGRATED PRODUCTION, WITH COMMON GOVERNANCE OF TNCs OVER MOST FUNCTIONS

Source: UNCTAD, 1993.

---

[9] UNCTAD (1994, pp. 144-145). The "Triad" refers to three groupings of developed economies: the United States and Canada, Europe and Japan.

However, as with some of the other skill and technological benefits noted in the previous section, it is likely that relatively few developing countries will be involved in deep integration into TNC global networks. Most are not, and the unequal spreading of integration may render the weaker economies even more peripheral to the emerging system. In an open trade and investment system, the ability to attract TNC production, increase exports, create local linkages and foster greater training for local employees would depend on making all these profitable by providing efficient factor markets. To quote UNCTAD:

"Those developments make it more important than ever for developing countries to build up their own human and physical infrastructure. In addition to providing the basis for industrialization and development of the domestic economy, it would allow national enterprises to join up with transnational corporations on a more equal basis. It would raise the quality and sophistication of the FDI a host country could attract, and would strengthen the prospects for technology acquisition. It would also enable host developing countries to build up supplier capabilities that are sometimes a precondition for the location of multinational enterprise activities and which, moreover, add to the economic and technological spillovers from foreign affiliates. The building up of such capabilities has been an essential feature of developing countries, including those in Asia and Latin America, that have succeeded in restructuring both their international and domestic production sectors towards higher-value-added activities (UNCTAD, 1993, p. 177).

These trends in technology, investment, competitiveness and TNC strategies appear to be mutually reinforcing, leading to the uneven pattern of FDI flows that recent years have witnessed. The liberalization of FDI policies will certainly help the less-developed countries to attract TNCs, but by itself it is unlikely to even out and dynamize the process of foreign investment and competitiveness development.

TNC strategies have important implications for the case studies in this volume. It is possible, for instance, that affiliates in the same host country, or in different countries, are given different resources to upgrade their capabilities according to the perceptions and tactics of their parent firms. For this reason, the case studies collect and analyse information on relations between parent firms and affiliates and on how the latter fit into emerging global TNC strategies.

1.8 Methodology of case studies

The case studies presented in this volume illustrate divergent outcomes of industrial restructuring. Each case study describes the background to the industry, notably the pattern of world competition and the role of TNCs. The studies consider the policy framework for FDI in the host country and provide information on inflows and the structure of foreign activity in industries.

They report the findings of interviews with firms in terms of the impact of TNC activity on industrial restructuring, exploring four main areas: physical investment, human capital investment, technology upgrading and supplier linkages. The presentations vary by country, depending on the information and data available. The objective of these case studies is to draw out pertinent policy implications for industrial restructuring and TNCs.

1.9 Choice of countries and industries

Eight countries were selected to illustrate the impact of TNCs on restructuring in industrial activities, and to reflect the differences observed among countries and regions:

- Chile
- Costa Rica
- Dominican Republic
- Malaysia
- Mexico
- Morocco
- Thailand
- Zimbabwe

The analysis is organized around the following four industries:

- **the colour TV industry,** analysed for Malaysia, Thailand and Mexico (chapter 3);
- **the automotive industry**, examined in Mexico, Argentina and Brazil, and Malaysia and Thailand (chapter 4);
- **the garment industries** in Costa Rica, the Dominican Republic and Morocco (chapter 5); and
- **natural resource-based industries** in Chile and Zimbabwe (chapter 6).

These industries were selected as they represent different types of technology:
- Relatively simple labour-intensive technologies (garments);
- Resource-based activities using a mixture of simple to complex technologies;
- Skill- and scale-intensive engineering technologies (automobiles); and
- R&D-, skill- and scale-intensive electronics technologies (TV receivers).

Several of the countries are active across the whole range of technologies, but the study focuses on special aspects of their industrial development. The spread of industries studied is fairly broad, so as to be of relevance to most developing countries. They also capture a range of technological aspects and TNC activity. The selected industries, with the exception of the natural resource-based ones, are among the most dynamic in world trade, and three – excepting garments – are those in which the 100 largest TNCs typically have significant presence. These industries are central to the globalization process, and the accelerated restructuring and intensified competition that accompany it.

24

The nature of TNC participation differs by activity, host country and the level of technology deployed in the countries. TNCs offer more to competitiveness and restructuring in some activities than in others, and the way that developing countries can take advantage of the resources offered by TNCs varies according to their initial endowments, strategies and location. The international strategies of TNCs vary within a given industry, according to their perceptions of the technological and competitive challenges facing them, and their reactions to the national policies and strategies of host countries. As a consequence, their impact on host developing countries differs largely, as do the policy implications for these countries. The four case studies aim to analyze these different implications; the final chapter synthesizes the implications of the case studies for policy.

Chapter 2

Economic background to the case studies

This chapter outlines the background to the eight developing economies covered in this study, presenting their export performance and competitiveness, patterns of international specialization, trends in inward FDI and their position regarding two important determinants of competitiveness, namely, human capital and technological activity.[1]

2.1 Background on trade performance

2.1.1 Total values and market shares

The manufactured export performance of the eight countries over the period 1980-1995 is shown in table 2.1, with some Asian NIEs included for comparison. The largest exporter of manufactured products in absolute terms (including *maquiladora* exports) is Mexico, followed by Malaysia and Thailand; the other countries are much smaller international players. In terms of growth rates, the highest increase is recorded for the whole 15-year period by Malaysia. In the period 1990-1995, Mexico has the lead with a massive 38 per cent annual increase, followed by Malaysia and Thailand, with 30 per cent and 23 per cent respectively. On a per capita basis, the largest exporter by far in the group is Malaysia, with Thailand and Mexico some distance behind.

Table 2.1. Export performance in manufacturing, 1980-1995
(Dollars and per cent)

Economy	Value of exports (Dollars)			Rates of growth (Per cent)			Exports per capita 1995 (Dollars)
	1980	1990	1995	1980-1990	1990-1995	1980-1995	
Chile	790	1 218	2 729	4.4	17.5	8.6	195
Costa Rica	241	379	862	4.6	17.9	8.9	278
Dominican Republic [a]	275	426	1 034	4.5	19.4	9.2	148
Malaysia	2 156	13 403	49 340	20.1	29.8	23.2	2 505
Mexico	5 970	11 754	58 862	7.0	38.0	16.5	652
Morocco	576	1 961	2 737	13.0	6.9	10.9	101
Thailand	1 706	15 083	42 281	24.4	22.9	23.9	729
Zimbabwe	184	470	759	9.8	10.1	9.9	70
Taiwan Province of China	17 849	62 600	104 302	-	10.7	12.5	4 967
Republic of Korea	15 898	61 787	117 573	14.5	13.7	14.3	2 642
Singapore	13 947	47 659	108 277	13.1	17.8	14.6	37 337

Sources: World Bank trade database and UNCTAD *World Investment Reports, various issues.*

[a] Exports were calculated from shares in OECD country import markets.

---

[1] The financial crises in 1997-1999 in several Asian and Latin America economies have altered trade flows, but the overall trends remain unaltered.

Table 2.2. Market shares in OECD countries, 1980-1995
(Per cent)

Country	1980	1985	1990	1995
Chile	0.23	0.21	0.27	0.28
Costa Rica	0.07	0.07	0.08	0.10
Dominican Republic	0.08	0.09	0.09	0.12
Malaysia	0.67	0.68	0.71	1.21
Mexico	1.26	1.77	1.50	2.09
Morocco	0.15	0.14	0.17	0.18
Thailand	0.30	0.35	0.66	0.99
Zimbabwe	0.03	0.05	0.04	0.03

Source: ECLAC, CANPLUS.

Table 2.2 and figure 2.1 show the evolution of market shares of the eight countries in OECD destination markets. OECD market shares serve as an indicator of competitiveness in the world's largest and most demanding export markets. However, for the Asian countries the regional market is taking on increasing significance, because of the lowering of trade barriers and the growing integration of production across national boundaries by TNCs. The final sales may in fact be to OECD countries, but appear as imports from other countries. The largest share in 1995 is held by Mexico, followed at some distance by Malaysia and Thailand. The latter has about a third of its exports going to countries of the Association of Southeast Asian Nations (ASEAN).

Figure 2.1. Evolution of market shares in OECD countries, 1980-1995
(Per cent)

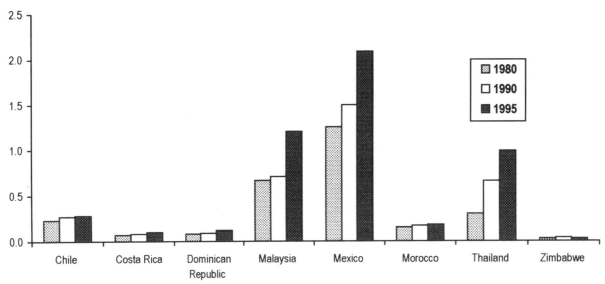

Source: ECLAC, CANPLUS.

In terms of evolution over time, Thailand and Mexico registered the largest increases in the 1980s, while the other countries saw modest increases. In the first half of the 1990s, the Mexican market share jumped visibly. Zimbabwe's share declined by 0.01 per cent.

2.1.2 Technological basis of competitiveness

The analysis of the technological basis of export growth can reveal the industrial structures underlying the international competitiveness of the sample countries.[2] One way to do this is to break down manufactured exports by technological category (Pavitt, 1984), and to observe how market shares have changed for the countries studied.

There are interesting differences in patterns of growth in trade. Annex table 2.1 lists the 50 fastest-growing world exports over the period of 1980-1995. These products accounted for 40 per cent of total global manufactured trade in 1995 (up from 28 per cent in 1980), and their rate of growth in the period 1990-1995 (13.1 per cent compounded) was some 5 percentage points higher than for all manufactured products. The top four products, accounting for as much as 20 per cent of the total, are all electronics products. In addition, there are several other electrical, electronic and advanced chemical products among the 50 products – these are all high-technology products, based on significant R&D efforts, and with close relations with the science base. Such products dominate recent growth in world trade: technology intensity and demand growth seem to be the main motive forces in recent export expansion.

The growing role of technological factors in competitive advantage can be further illustrated using the OECD technological classification (OECD, 1987). Total world exports are grouped into the five categories shown in table 2.3, which gives their values, shares and growth rates. Science-based and differentiated products together comprise what are conventionally considered high-technology products. The largest categories in world exports are scale-intensive products (such as metallurgical, automobiles and most heavy process industries), but differentiated products (sophisticated machinery) are very close behind, followed by labour-intensive products.

Table 2.3. World exports of manufactures, by OECD technological category
(Billions of dollars and per cent)

Technological category of products	Value 1995	Distribution (Per cent)	Rates of growth (Per cent)		
			1981-1990	1991-1995	1981-1995
Resource-intensive	555.8	14.5	7.4	6.6	7.1
Labour-intensive	802.0	21.0	9.9	7.6	9.1
Scale-intensive	870.2	22.8	7.8	7.0	7.5
Differentiated	859.2	22.5	8.4	8.6	8.4
Science-based	733.7	19.2	12.6	13.3	12.9
Total	**3 820.9**	**100.0**	**8.8**	**8.5**	**7.3**

Source: ECLAC, CANPLUS.

[2] There is a large literature on the relationship between technology, technological capabilities and competitiveness. For a sample see Ernst, Ganiatsos and Mytelka (1998), Kumar (1999), Lall (1990, 1996), Mortimore (1995), Porter (1990), and UNCTAD (1999).

The highest rates of growth are recorded by science-based products: these show the highest acceleration in growth in the 1990s as compared to the 1980s. Differentiated products also increased their growth rate. The other product categories suffered a deceleration in their growth rates: the increasing significance of technology in the growth of trade is evident.

The technological breakdown of the 50 fastest-growing manufactured exports shows this more strikingly: 9 per cent of such exports were resource-intensive, 17 per cent labour-intensive, 10 per cent scale-intensive, 26 per cent differentiated and 39 per cent science-based — nearly 65 per cent of these products are in the "high-technology" category. In terms of growth, in 1990-1995 the highest rates were for science-based products (16 per cent), followed by differentiated (12 per cent), scale-intensive (12 per cent), resource-intensive (11 per cent) and labour-intensive (10 per cent) products.

However, it must be recognized that the fast-growing exports also include less technology-intensive products, many of which are important to the sample countries. There are labour-intensive manufactures like garments, toys, plastic products and simple metal manufactures, whose growth is largely due to a relocation of production facilities (from high- to low-wage countries) within a slow-growing structure of demand. There are also resource-intensive products like glass, rubber or wood products, where export growth is due to the better exploitation of the resource base, technological change and fast-growing demand in user industries or in consumer markets.

What sorts of exports are the sample countries specialized in? To gauge this, a technology-based classification organizes exports under four broad headings: resource-based and low-, medium- and high-technology.[3] This classification was further refined by sub-dividing the last three into two groups each, distinguishing specific sets of industries that are of particular significance in manufactured trade. The full list of technological categories is shown in box 2.1. These categories were applied to the exports of each country to OECD countries for 1980-1995, using the COMTRADE data in the ECLAC CANPLUS programme (Mortimore, 1995).

Annex table 2.2 gives the list of groups of products for each category; table 2.4 summarizes the findings for the export structures (as percentages of total exports) of each country. Let us consider the relative patterns by each major technological category.

> **Box 2.1. Technological categories of exports**
>
> **Resource based**
> **Low-technology**
>   Textile, clothing and footwear cluster
>   (SITC 611-2, 651-9, 831, 842-8 and 851)
>   Other low-technology products
> **Medium-technology**
>   Automotive cluster (SITC 713, 781-6)
>   Other medium-technology products
> **High-technology**
>   Electronic/electrical cluster (SITC 751-9, 761-4)
>   Other high-technology products
>
> *Source*: Lall, 1998.

---

[3] For a detailed discussion of the methodology, see UNCTAD (1999a, p. 230).

**Table 2.4. Export structure of selected developing economies,
by technological category of products, 1980-1995**
(As a percentage of total exports)

Economy	Year	Resource intensive	Low-technology			Medium-technology			High-technology		
			Total	Textile Cluster	Other	Total	Automotive cluster	Other	Total	Electronic cluster	Other
Chile	1980	49.0	0.8	0.1	0.7	48.1	0.0	48.1	0.3	0.0	0.2
	1985	53.9	1.5	0.2	1.3	40.9	0.0	40.9	0.2	0.0	0.2
	1990	55.9	2.8	1.4	1.4	38.5	0.1	38.5	0.1	0.0	0.1
	1995	67.7	3.3	0.8	2.4	26.8	0.1	26.7	0.1	0.0	0.1
Costa Rica	1980	91.2	6.2	5.3	0.9	0.3	0.0	0.3	1.5	0.1	1.3
	1985	80.9	13.9	11.6	2.4	1.4	0.0	1.4	3.0	0.3	2.7
	1990	66.6	27.3	22.9	4.4	1.4	0.1	1.4	3.7	0.2	3.5
	1995	60.4	30.3	25.9	4.4	2.3	0.0	2.3	5.8	0.3	5.5
Dominican Republic	1980	62.3	25.2	11.4	13.8	1.7	0.0	1.6	1.6	0.0	1.6
	1985	44.9	37.8	23.3	14.5	1.7	0.0	1.7	2.3	0.3	1.9
	1990	22.0	61.3	44.7	16.6	1.4	0.0	1.4	9.2	0.6	8.6
	1995	14.9	67.1	55.6	11.4	1.7	0.0	1.7	12.6	0.4	12.2
Malaysia	1980	69.0	6.0	3.5	2.5	10.0	0.0	9.9	14.4	1.5	12.8
	1985	61.4	7.7	5.1	2.6	5.8	0.1	5.7	23.8	4.3	19.5
	1990	42.4	15.2	8.9	6.3	6.5	0.6	5.9	34.9	16.1	18.7
	1995	19.3	14.9	6.9	8.0	7.0	0.6	6.4	56.9	34.5	22.4
Mexico	1980	67.2	7.2	3.0	4.1	10.2	2.3	7.9	11.6	5.5	6.1
	1985	58.2	8.3	2.3	6.0	15.1	8.6	6.5	15.7	6.9	8.8
	1990	34.3	13.3	3.9	9.5	23.8	14.5	9.2	25.3	10.6	14.7
	1995	20.4	16.1	5.6	10.5	29.1	19.4	9.7	30.6	13.3	17.3
Morocco	1980	78.8	14.4	13.3	1.1	5.5	0.3	5.1	1.0	0.1	0.9
	1985	63.1	23.2	21.8	1.3	11.1	0.4	10.7	2.2	0.3	1.2
	1990	48.1	37.4	36.0	1.4	11.4	0.49	10.9	3.9	0.4	3.6
	1995	37.2	44.5	42.7	1.8	10.6	0.4	10.2	7.4	0.3	7.1
Thailand	1980	59.8	22.8	11.8	11.0	14.5	0.0	14.4	2.9	0.1	2.8
	1985	54.2	30.4	17.5	12.9	7.4	0.	7.3	7.2	0.8	6.4
	1990	35.8	39.8	20.0	19.8	6.3	0.7	5.6	17.8	10.5	7.2
	1995	28.1	33.5	16.1	17.3	7.5	0.7	6.8	29.4	19.4	10.1
Zimbabwe	1980	52.4	35.6	0.7	34.9	11.3	0.0	11.3	0.2	0.1	0.1
	1985	56.8	25.2	3.6	21.6	13.1	0.0	13.0	0.5	0.2	0.3
	1990	49.8	25.9	5.9	20.0	16.4	0.1	16.3	0.6	0.2	0.4
	1995	56.8	27.9	9.7	18.2	12.5	0.0	12.5	0.6	0.1	0.5
Memorandum items: export structures of four Asian tigers and G7											
Asian NIEs [a]	1980	6.2	63.0	42.9	20.2	9.2	0.5	8.7	17.8	11.2	6.6
	1985	4.2	56.8	37.7	19.1	9.7	0.8	9.0	27.5	17.0	10.5
	1990	2.0	46.8	27.7	19.1	11.6	2.5	9.1	38.8	26.5	12.4
	1995	1.7	31.5	15.1	16.4	15.0	5.1	9.9	51.3	33.2	18.2
G7 countries [b]	1980	22.4	21.6	6.0	15.6	39.1	14.9	24.2	14.8	5.8	9.0
	1985	18.0	19.3	5.4	13.9	40.8	18.2	22.6	19.1	8.8	10.3
	1990	14.9	20.5	5.3	15.2	40.8	16.7	24.2	21.6	8.9	12.7
	1995	13.6	19.3	4.6	14.7	41.1	17.3	23.9	23.2	9.1	14.1

Source: ECLAC, CANPLUS.
[a] Hong Kong (China), Republic of Korea, Singapore and Taiwan Province of China.
[b] Canada, France, Germany, Italy, Japan, United Kingdom and the United States.

Figure 2.2. Shares of resource-based exports to OECD
(Per cent of exports)

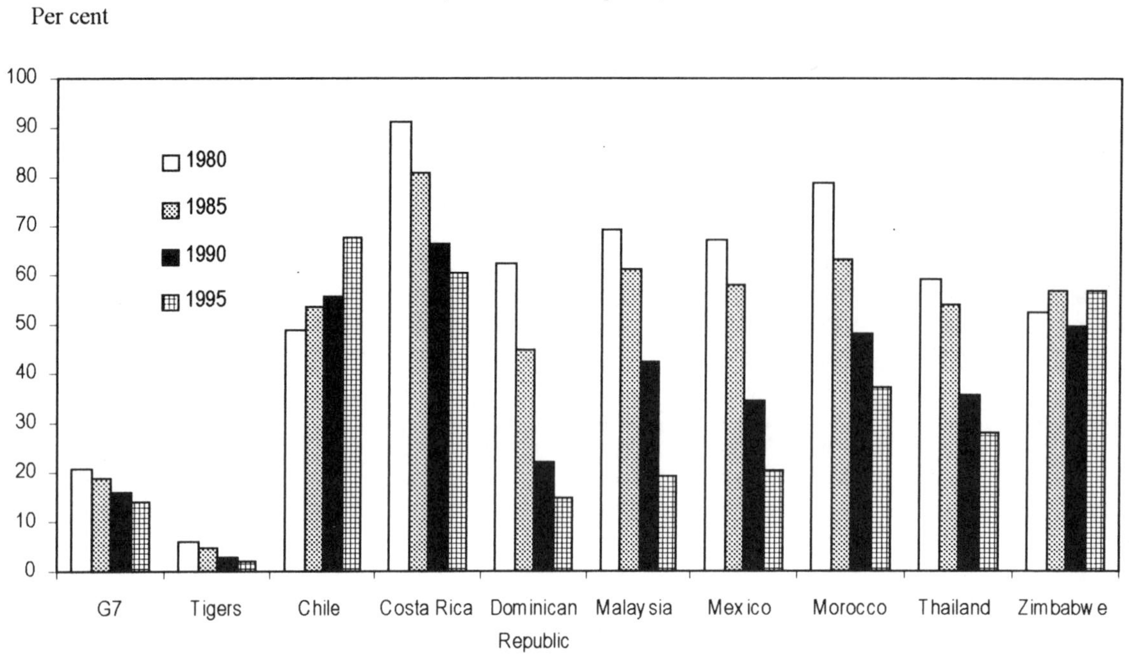

Per cent

Source: ECLAC, CANPLUS.

Resource-intensive exports. This category includes primary products as well as processed exports that are highly dependent on natural resources. As figure 2.2 shows, the highest share of resource-based exports in 1995 is that of Chile, followed by Costa Rica and Zimbabwe. These shares have fallen for all economies in the sample except for Chile and Zimbabwe – the countries used in the case studies to illustrate restructuring in natural resource-based industries. However, almost the whole of Chile's-medium-technology exports, which consist mainly of refined local copper, are essentially resource-intensive, with the downstream manufacturing of final products undertaken mainly in the developed countries. The trade classification system places it in a different category and gives a somewhat misleading impression that Chile is engaged in technologically complex export activity. If processed copper is classified as a resource-based export, the total share of such exports rises to nearly 95 per cent – a case *par excellence* of natural-resource dependence. However, this is not to downplay the significance of the industrial activity that does take place in Chile: the refining of primary copper is a very capital-intensive process industry, and its processing of agro-based products has undergone substantial technological upgrading in recent years (Pietrobelli, 1998).

The other sample countries show a more conventional pattern of export growth for developing countries, that is, the share of resource-intensive products falls with rising industrial development. The sharpest declines (of around 50 percentage points) are for the Dominican Republic, Malaysia and Mexico. The G7 countries, with the most mature and settled export structures, start with a relatively low level which gradually declines further (reaching 14 per cent by 1995); only the Dominican Republic approaches this level among the sample countries. The "Asian tigers", which are all resource-scarce countries, start with very low shares which fall further over the period, stabilizing at around 2 per cent in the 1990s.

Low-technology exports. These largely comprise the labour-intensive products which most developing countries use when they embark on export-oriented industrialization. With industrial maturity, their share tends to decline as rising wages and technological competence lead to more complex exports (as in the G7); however, other factors also affect their share in some cases. Figure 2.3 shows the findings for the countries in our sample, the Asian tigers and the G7 countries. The Dominican Republic and Morocco have the highest and fastest-growing share of low-technology exports. Costa Rica follows a similar pattern. Chile is at the other extreme, with very small shares of low-technology products throughout the period. Malaysia and Mexico show a similar evolution, with more complex exports growing mainly due to the influence of processing operations of TNCs. Thailand starts with a higher share, which fluctuates as it draws in electronics TNCs. These countries have relatively low domestic industrial capabilities, but benefit from the globalization of some complex activities where labour-intensive processes can be "separated" and economically located elsewhere. By contrast, in Hong Kong (China), the Republic of Korea and Taiwan Province of China (not shown in the figure), the fall in the low-technology share is a reflection of growing domestic capabilities (Lall, 1996); however, a broad base of low-technology exports continues to provide nearly a third of their export earnings. In the G7 countries, low-technology exports remain at around 20 per cent; this significant and stable share suggests that countries can retain competitiveness in these activities even with high wages if they are able to upgrade technology, product quality, design and skills. In fact, the case study on the garments industry (chapter 4) suggests that reaching the top-quality segments of labour-intensive activities may actually be more difficult than upgrading capabilities in apparently more complex activities.

Figure 2.3. Shares of low-technology exports in total exports to OECD
(Per cent of exports)

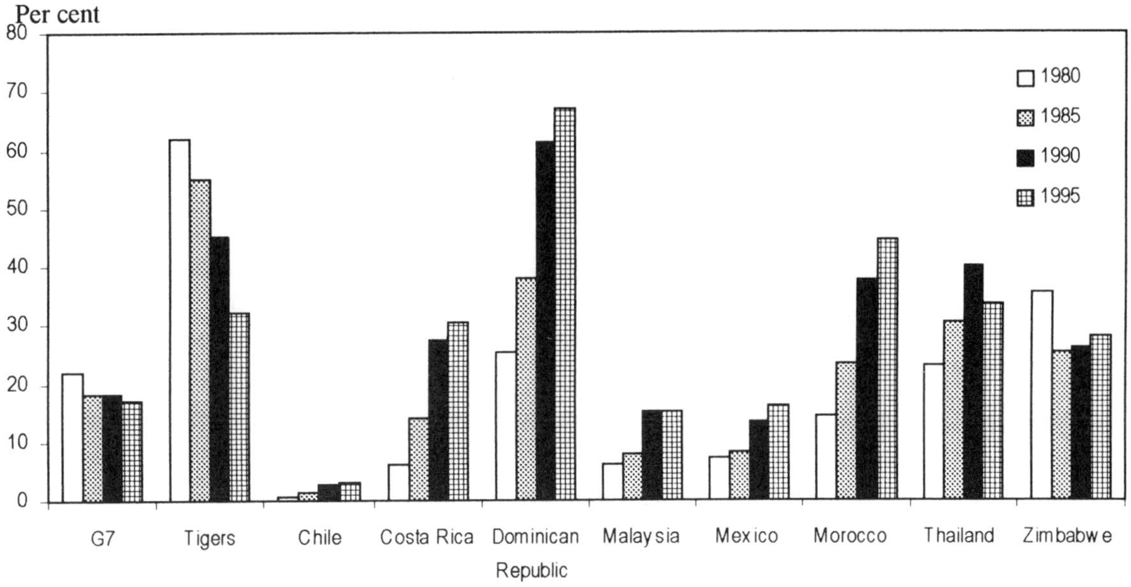

Source: ECLAC, CANPLUS.

31

Exports from the textile cluster have been important to export growth in many developing countries. It is thus interesting to chart their shares for six of the countries in the sample for which these are significant (figure 2.4). The growth of low-technology exports in Costa Rica, the Dominican Republic and Morocco is driven by this cluster – garments are the main product involved. Thailand and the Asian tigers also retain significant but declining shares of exports from the cluster (which also includes footwear and textiles). The cluster provides around 5 per cent of G7 exports; several industrialized countries remain major clothing exporters, specializing in high-quality products and the design-intensive stages of the process.

Figure 2.4. Share of textile, garment and footwear exports
(Per cent of exports)

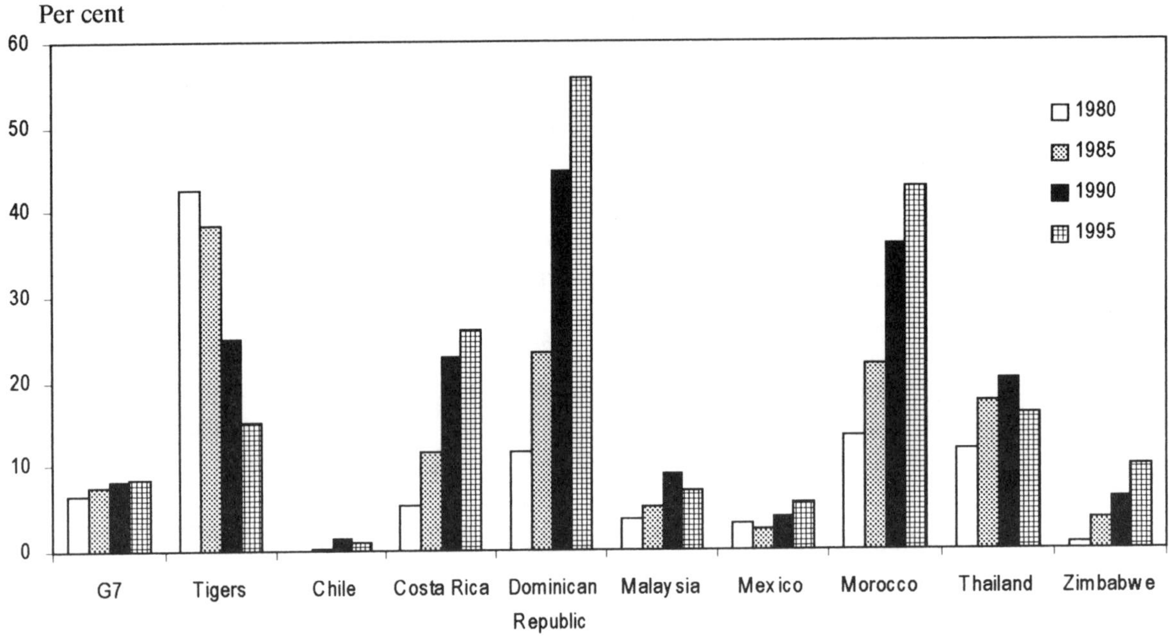

Source: ECLAC, CANPLUS.

Medium-technology exports. These exports generally involve complex skill- and capital-intensive technologies that do not change very rapidly or involve high levels of R&D, as in large-scale process industries like chemicals and engineering activities like automobiles or (standardized) machinery. While competitive advantage in some such products rests on a natural resource base (as in the case of copper products, noted earlier for Chile), in general their inherent technological complexity means that reaching world competitiveness requires specialized technical and organizational skills, experience and technological effort. In particular, medium-technology engineering products are extremely linkage-intensive, calling for a diverse and efficient base of suppliers and subcontractors; exports of these products tend to arise after long periods of industrial development.

Figure 2.5 shows the evolution of export shares for these products. The high share of medium-technology exports by Chile is, as noted, explained by copper. Mexico's rapid rise in medium-technology exports is driven largely by the growth of automotive exports to the United States market by TNCs (after considerably upgrading the capabilities built up during a lengthy period of import substitution), and by the growing competitiveness of heavy process industries in chemicals, glass, cement and metallurgy. The high and rising share of medium-technology products in G7 exports illustrates the significance of industrial maturity and the long learning processes involved in gaining competitiveness in these activities. The Asian tigers are also gaining competence in these exports, but still lag well behind the G7.

Figure 2.5. Share of medium technology exports
(Per cent of exports)

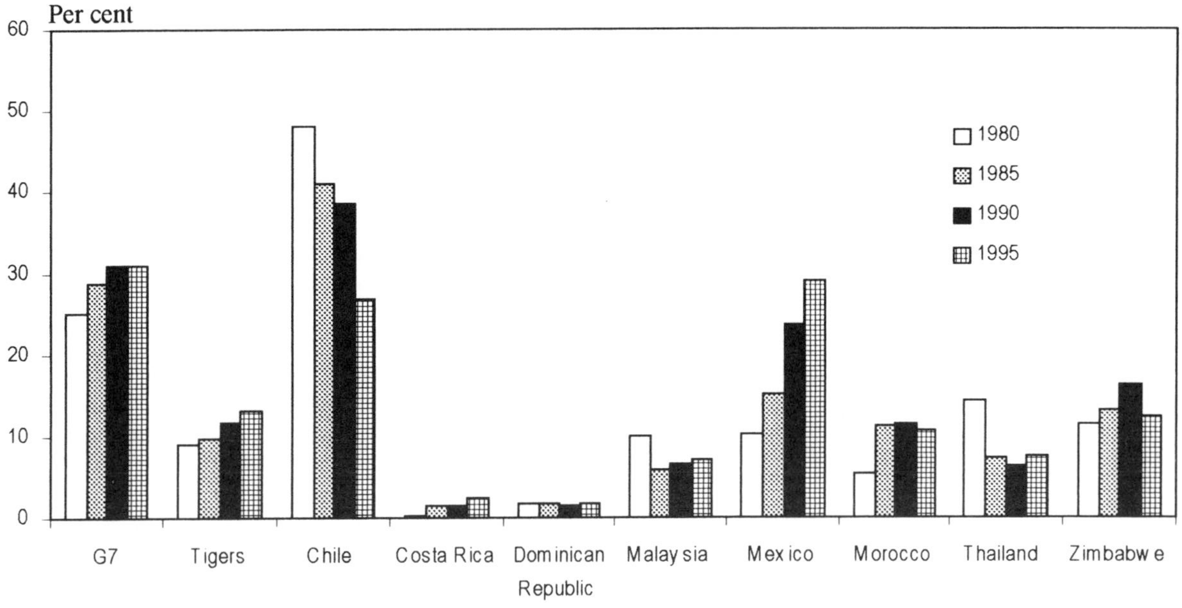

Source: ECLAC, CANPLUS.

Zimbabwe makes a relatively strong showing in medium-technology exports; this is traceable to its diverse and fairly well-developed metal-working industry which was built up during its long period of economic isolation in the 1970s. Currently, Zimbabwe's exports of engineering products are directed mainly to neighbouring African countries (though not to South Africa); its industry lacks the capabilities to compete in more advanced markets, to which it exports resource- or labour-intensive products. TNCs play a relatively small role in such exports, and their future growth may be threatened as its neighbours develop their own capabilities or expose their markets to competition from Asia (Lall et al., 1997). Morocco's exports in this category consist mainly of chemical products and simple automotive components for the European market; its own engineering sector is not sophisticated.

It is interesting to note the weak position of Malaysia and Thailand in medium-technology products, despite their strength in more sophisticated high-technology exports. This is due to their specialization in the labour-intensive assembly stages of TNC electronics production (with low levels of local content). Their domestic engineering sectors remain relatively underdeveloped, certainly by the standards of the industrialized countries that are the main investors and export markets.

Figure 2.6 shows the shares of automotive products in the exports of Malaysia, Mexico, Thailand, the Asian tigers and the G7 countries. It illustrates graphically the striking, and possibly unique, role played by auto TNCs in boosting manufactured exports from Mexico (see chapter 5). It also shows the enduring and important role of these products in G7 trade. The Asian tigers have an increasing but small share of auto exports, but this understates their significance for the Republic of Korea because the other Asian tigers have low or zero exports of auto products. Malaysia and Thailand have relatively small exports here; the former exports the indigenous Proton cars and the latter auto parts under the aegis of TNCs. The implementation of special rules for the automotive industry in regional integration schemes, such as the North American Free Trade Agreement (NAFTA), the Southern Common Market (MERCOSUR) and ASEAN, is resulting in significant restructuring and relocation in that industry.

High-technology exports. These are products like electronics, complex machinery and fine chemicals, with high rates of product and process innovation based on costly R&D and, increasingly, close links with the underlying science base. They require a strong base of scientific and technological skills, an advanced supporting infrastructure of educational and technology institutions, and a highly developed supplier base. However, many high-technology engineering products have stages of production that require relatively simple labour-intensive assembly operations; these can be economically relocated to low wage areas in much the same way as low-technology activities like garments.

Figure 2.6. Shares of automotive exports
(Per cent of exports)

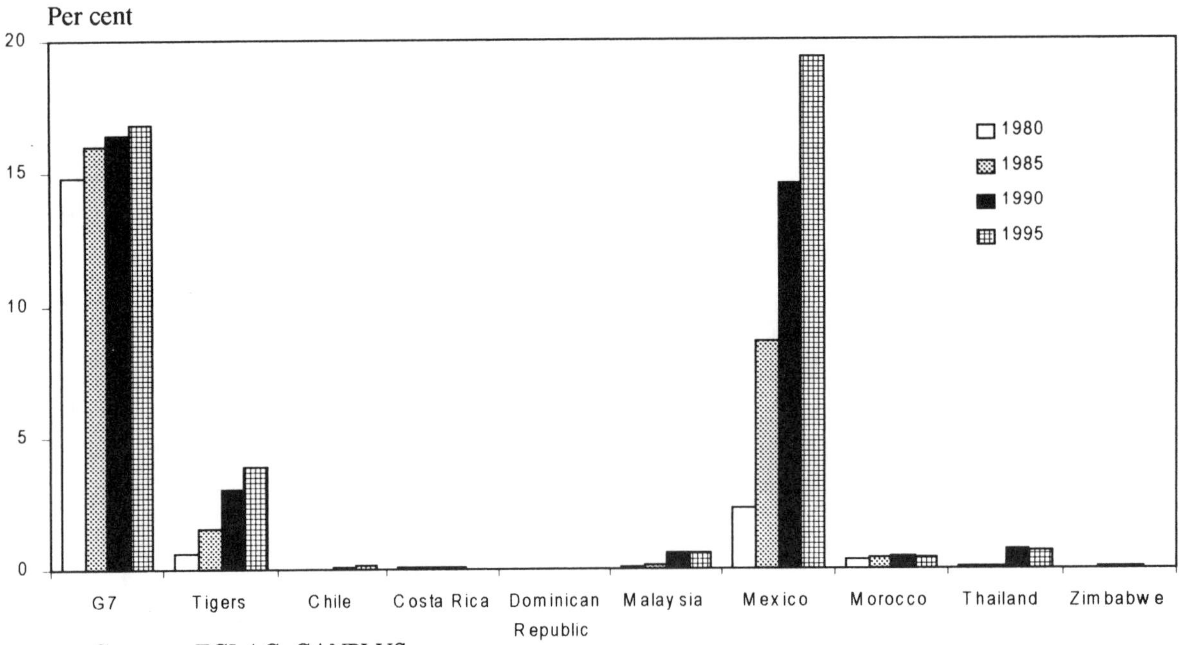

Source: ECLAC, CANPLUS.

It is this relocation that has been the engine of high-technology export growth from many developing countries – the move from simple assembly to more value-added processes is much more difficult. Some countries, like Malaysia, have changed process technologies to use state-of-the-art automated facilities and have mastered some low-level design functions, but not the more advanced stages of product or process innovation. The only developing economies that have fostered the whole technological spectrum in local enterprises in high-technology industries are the Republic of Korea and Taiwan Province of China; Singapore has been able to induce TNCs to undertake the most complex processes but not to localize the innovation process there.

Figure 2.7a and 2.7b shows the shares of high-technology and electronics products. Malaysia has the highest share of both high-technology and electronics exports in the sample, because of its lead in the TNC networks for the assembly of semi-conductors, consumer electronics and other electronics products. Its share is the second highest in the world, after Singapore (which is highly specialized in advanced producer electronics). Malaysia is followed at some distance by Mexico and Thailand; none of the other sample countries are significant exporters of high-technology or electronics products.

Figure 2.7a. Total high technology exports
(Per cent of exports)

Figure 2.7b. Electronic exports
(Per cent of exports)

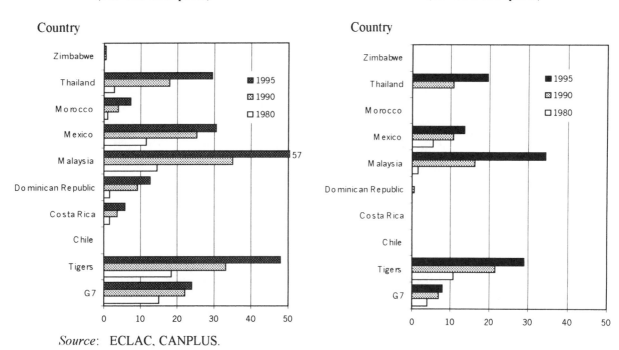

Source: ECLAC, CANPLUS.

High-technology exports by the Asian tigers differ by country (Lall, 1996). Singapore is predominantly reliant on TNCs, while the Republic of Korea and Taiwan Province of China are driven by domestic companies, with the support of an impressive base of technological activity and investments in human capital (see below). Hong Kong (China) specializes in relatively simple high-technology exports and undertakes very little R&D. Interestingly, the Asian NIEs have a much higher share of high-technology exports than the G7 – this is due to the broader, more industrial and mature base in the G7 countries, with a higher weight of medium-technology activities.

2.1.3 Conclusions

The analysis of the trade data shows striking differences between the patterns of export growth across industries by technological characteristics and between sample countries in industrial competence and specialization. The drivers of recent export growth and competitiveness have increasingly been complex technology and technological differentiation rather than the possession of natural resources or low-cost labour. This has not precluded a rapid growth in the exports of some resource- or labour-intensive products, which have enjoyed a rise in final demand or a shift in production from high- to low-wage economies (within a slowly growing final market). Nor has it prevented highly industrialized countries from retaining a significant position in the trade of such products, in the case of labour-intensive technologies, by moving into high-quality, design-based products and very skill-intensive processes. However, it is clear that industrial development and income growth are associated with the use of more advanced technologies and skills. The main caveat to this generalization is that many low-income countries without a significant technology or skill base have also become major exporters of "high-technology" products – where TNCs have relocated relatively simple labour-intensive processes within these industries.

The sample countries differ greatly in the technological pattern of their export competitiveness for manufactured products. There are many reasons for these differences, including size, levels of industrial development, resource endowments, skill base and government policies on FDI, trade and industry. All these affect the impact of TNCs on industrial restructuring: by the extent of foreign participation in the industrial sector, the structure and strengths of the industrial sector itself, the openness of the sector to trade and globalization, and the availability and quality of the skills, technology and infrastructure that facilitate restructuring. Different groups of countries illustrate different levels of technology embodied in exports:

- *Chile* is the most striking case of competitive advantage based on natural resources, with up to 95 per cent of its manufactured exports to OECD countries arising from agro-industries (including fishery and forestry) and copper processing. This is not to say that there is no technology or skill involved; both forms of processing have been based upon considerable technological and human resource development. However, the export structure is vulnerable to slow growth and technological substitution that generally threatens primary exporters.

- *Costa Rica* and the *Dominican Republic* are small economies that have moved from a dependence on simple primary exports to manufacturing via export-processing-zone activities, particularly in garment assembly. Their industrial base remains fairly undeveloped, and their main advantage, apart from low-cost labour, is proximity and access to the United States market. In fact their main advantage is created by special trade privileges granted by the United States.

- *Malaysia* provides an example of a resource-rich country that has moved quickly into manufactured export production and within that from simple to complex products, with one of the highest ratios in the world for high-technology electronics exports. It has enjoyed considerable inflows of FDI. Its domestic industrial and technological base is relatively weak, but the export-oriented sector has increased local content over time and struck some local linkages; there has been some upgrading of the technology content of operations from assembly to low-level design and engineering.

- *Mexico* has a large industrial sector with a long history of import substitution in heavy industries like automobiles and intermediates. With recent liberalization   and integration into the North American economy, it has enjoyed a massive inflow of FDI which has restructured its industrial sector and spearheaded export growth in a range of medium- and high-technology industries. In the 1990s it has experienced one of the world's highest rates of manufactured export growth, led by automotive and electronics assembly products, the former with deep local integration and the latter only recently emerging from the simple assembly stage.

- *Morocco* follows a similar pattern to Costa Rica and the Dominican Republic, but with respect to the European rather than the United States market. Its industrial structure is relatively under-developed, but specialization in labour-intensive assembly for high-income neighbour markets has allowed its competitiveness to grow in a narrow range of activities. As with Costa Rica and the Dominican Republic, however, the long-term sustainability of its export growth is not assured, because the special access that allows it to fend off competition from lower-wage countries is due to be phased out.

- *Thailand* presents a similar profile to that of Malaysia, but with a lower level of electronics development and a greater emphasis on labour-intensive products. As with Malaysia and Mexico, its export activities are largely driven by TNCs, but it also has a strong indigenous industrial sector in traditional activities. It recently commenced on an ambitious programme for its automobile industry.

- *Zimbabwe* has a surprisingly diversified (albeit low-technology) industrial base compared to its neighbouring countries, though it remains primarily dependent on resource-intensive exports. Its base of engineering capabilities is good in comparison with the immediate developing region but not with the rest of the world. Its labour-intensive exports have not taken off despite fairly low wages because of its inability to attract export-oriented FDI into manufacturing, a characteristic it shares with the most of the countries in the region.

2.2 Main factor markets affecting competitiveness

2.2.1 Human resource base

There are several approaches to examining the human resource base. The first is to compare "raw" labour costs, which can be approximated by labour costs in the garment industry. Table 4.4 in chapter 4 shows this for a large range of developed and developing countries, allowing most of the sample countries (indicated in bold) to be located on the world scale; Chile is missing since it is not a significant garment exporter.

The highest labour costs in the sample are for Costa Rica, followed by Mexico, Malaysia,[4] the Dominican Republic, Morocco and Thailand; the lowest labour costs are recorded for Zimbabwe. This ranking does not correspond in any intuitively plausible way with export specialization: Costa Rica with the highest labour costs also has one of the highest levels of dependence on labour-intensive exports. Conversely, Malaysia is the most technology-intensive but does not pay the highest wages.

Raw labour is not, of course, the most important element of competitiveness as far as human resources are concerned. The level of skills of the work-force is far more important, especially as far as modern manufacturing activities are concerned. It is difficult to measure the skill levels of national labour forces, since much of skill creation takes place on the job, by informal training and learning. What is possible is to measure workers' levels of education. The most readily available data pertain to enrolments in the three different levels of education. (But these data are also subject to qualifications because of differences in completion rates, quality of teaching, equipment provided and the curriculum content and relevance.)

Table 2.5. Enrolment and literacy ratios, 1980 and 1995
(Per cent)

| Country | Enrolment by education level | | | | | | Literacy |
| | Primary | | Secondary | | Tertiary | | |
	1980	1995	1980	1995	1980	1995	1995
Chile	109	98	53	70	12	27	95.0
Costa Rica	105	105	48	47	21	30	94.7
Dominican Republic	118	97	42	37	19 [a]	..	81.5
Malaysia	93	93	48	59	4	7	83.0
Mexico	115	112	46	58	14	14	89.2
Morocco	83	73	26	35	6	10	42.1
Thailand	99	98	29	37	13	19	93.5
Zimbabwe	85	119	8	45	1	6	84.7

Source: UNDP, 1995; UNESCO, 1997.
Note: Enrolment rates are expressed as percentages of the relevant age groups. Literacy rates are percentages of the adult population.
[a] 1985.

Table 2.5 shows gross enrolment ratios, as percentages of the relevant age groups, and relative literacy rates for the adult population for the sample countries for 1980 and 1995. All the countries except Morocco have virtually universal primary enrolment and levels of literacy exceeding 80 per cent. At the secondary level, the best enrolment ratio is for Chile, at 70 per cent of

---

[4] Chile would come slightly below these countries if per capita income rankings were used as a guide to wages.

the age group; the lowest are observed in the Dominican Republic, Thailand and Morocco. At the tertiary level, the highest enrolment is for Costa Rica, with Chile close behind; the lowest is for Zimbabwe followed by Malaysia. Mexico is the only country at this level registering a decline in enrolment levels. It is worth noting the relatively small human capital bases of the two Asian countries, despite their specialization in high-technology exports – reinforcing the earlier conclusion that they are concentrated in the simpler processes in these activities. In addition, it is known that both face severe human capital shortages when upgrading within these activities (see Lall, 1995).

It is useful to look at tertiary level enrolments in science and technology subjects as an index of high-level technical manpower, and vocational training enrolments as one of lower technical skills. Table 2.6 shows tertiary technical enrolments in sample countries, some NIEs and selected OECD countries, as a percentage of the total population (not of the age group, as table 2.5). The Latin American countries in the sample have the highest figures. The lowest level of technical training is in Zimbabwe; this reflects the late start, in its region, of tertiary education – university enrolments in Zimbabwe are second highest in sub-Saharan Africa after South Africa. The two South-East Asian economies register less than half the average values of the Latin American countries. In Morocco, most technical graduates specialize in science rather than engineering, which is likely to be more relevant to industrial technology. The other sample countries turn out more engineers than scientists.

Table 2.6. Tertiary-level students in technical fields
(Numbers and percentage of population)

Economy	Natural science		Maths and computing		Engineering		Total	
	Pupils enrolled	Per cent of population	Pupils Enrolled	Per cent of population	Pupils Enrolled	Per cent of population	Pupils enrolled	Per cent of population
Chile	8 577	0.06	..	..	85 483	0.61	94 060	0.67
Costa Rica	706 000	0.02	5 373	0.18	6 281	0.21	12 259	0.41
Dominican Republic	4 791	0.07	6 315	0.09	13 095	0.20	24 201	0.38
Malaysia	8 776	0.05	4 557	0.02	12 693	0.07	26 026	0.14
Mexico	42 457	0.05	97 575	0.11	221 867	0.26	361 899	0.42
Morocco	71 143	0.28	./.	..	1 051	0.00	72 194	0.28
Thailand	39 045	0.06	./.	..	51 949	0.09	90 994	0.15
Zimbabwe	1 799	0.02	399	0.00	4 718	0.05	6 916	0.06
For comparison:								
Republic of Korea	81 222	0.18	171 147	0.38	437 537	0.98	689 906	1.55
Taiwan Province of China	16 823	0.08	32 757	0.16	179 094	0.86	228 674	1.09
Japan	59 030	0.05	20 891	0.02	488 699	0.39	568 620	0.46
France	304 093	0.53	./.	..	50 845	0.09	354 938	0.62
Germany	310 435	0.39	./.	..	389 182	0.49	699 617	0.88
United Kingdom	105 983	0.18	76 430	0.13	219 078	0.38	401 491	0.69
United States	496 415	0.19	525 067	0.20	801 126	0.31	1 822 608	0.70

Sources: UNESCO, 1997, and World Bank, *World Development Reports*, various years.
Note: ./. indicates that the number is not separated from other technical subjects.

None of the sample countries matches the performance in high-level technical skills of the Republic of Korea and Taiwan Province of China, which now are ahead of the main OECD countries in investment in training scientists and engineers (in particular the latter). Chile matches the levels reached by France and the United Kingdom. Mexico turns out large absolute numbers of engineers, undoubtedly a vital input into its medium-technology and some high-technology export-oriented operations. These comparisons, simplified as they are, again bear out the weak relationship between factor endowments and the pattern of export specialization (at least in terms of crude export data): the exact nature of the technology in which a country specializes is clearly the relevant variable, and crude export data cannot show this. Moreover, the operations of TNCs cut across competitive advantages given by endowments, and government policies (or the lack thereof) on technology development and upgrading can make an enormous difference to the pattern of exports.

The lead is again taken by Chile, with nearly 2 per cent of its population enrolled in vocational training. It is followed at some distance by Mexico, and Thailand. These data do not, as noted, capture the importance of skill creation for industrial employees; in fact, the relevance of vocational training as a means of enhancing industrial competitiveness may also be in doubt. Nevertheless, as they stand, the data suggest that the pattern is very similar to that for high-level technical education, and show the same weak relationship with export competitiveness.

Table 2.7. Vocational training enrolment, 1980 and 1990
(Number and per cent)

Country	Year	Population (Millions)	Pupils enrolled	Per cent of population	Year	Population (Millions)	Pupils enrolled	Per cent of population
Chile	1980	11.1	169 129	1.52	1990	13.2	255 396	1.93
Costa Rica	1980	2.2	2 254	0.10	1993	3.3	2 710	0.07
Dominican Republic	1980	5.4	22 898	0.42	1985	6.4	21 156	0.33
Malaysia	1980	13.9	18 031	0.13	1990	17.9	30 691	0.17
Mexico	1980	69.8	491 665	0.70	1990	86.2	792 481	0.92
Morocco	1980	20.2	10 106	0.05	1989	24.5	16 537	0.07
Thailand	1980	47.0	297 114	0.63	1990	55.8	444 218	0.80
Zimbabwe	1980	7.4	734 000	0.01	1988	9.3	11 104	0.12

Source: UNESCO, *1997.*

2.2.2 Inward foreign direct investment

This section gives background data on inward FDI into the sample countries, to supplement the analysis of TNC involvement in specific industries in the case studies below. Table 2.8 sets out UNCTAD data for 1985-1996.

Table 2.8. Foreign direct investment inflows,1982-1996
(Millions of dollars)

Country	1985-1990 Annual average	1991	1992	1993	1994	1995	1996
Chile	700	523	699	809	1 773	1 695	3 140
Costa Rica	100	178	226	247	298	396	410
Dominican Republic	87	145	180	91	132	271	160
Malaysia	1 054	3 998	5 183	5 006	4 342	4 132	5 300
Mexico	2 618	4 762	4 393	4 389	10 972	6 963	7 535
Morocco	83	317	422	491	551	290	400
Thailand	1 017	2 014	2 114	1 730	1 322	2 003	2 426
Zimbabwe	-10	3	15	28	35	43	47

Source: UNCTAD, FDI/TNC database.

The largest recipient of FDI, among the countries over the period and studied, is Mexico, followed by Malaysia in 1992-1993, Chile and Thailand. Zimbabwe suffered net outflows over much of the 1980s, but has recovered since 1991. The other three countries have moderate FDI inflows.

2.2.3 Technological effort

There is no good quantitative measure for total technological effort, since this comprises a broad and diffuse set of activities. Formal R&D is the only form of technological effort that is measured across countries, though definitions may vary and it comprises only one end of the spectrum of technological activity. Table 2.9 shows two broad measures: numbers of scientists and engineers in R&D; and spending on R&D in total and by productive enterprises as a percentage of gross national product (GNP), as well as in dollars per capita.

Table 2.9. R&D employment and expenditures
(Number, value and per cent)

Economy	Scientists and engineers in R&D Year	Total number	Number per million of population	R&D Expenditures Year	Total R&D as per cent of GNP	By productive enterprises as per cent of GNP	Per capita R&D (Dollars)
Chile	1988	4 630	364	1994	0.8	0.14	38.6
Costa Rica	1992	1 722	555	1986	0.3	0.02	4.4
Malaysia	1992	1 633	87	1992	0.4	0.17	11.3
Mexico	1984	16 679	217	1989	0.2	0.01	4.0
Thailand	1991	9 752	173	1991	0.2	0.02	2.6
Republic of Korea	1994	117 486	2 636	1995	2.8	2.38	272.0
Taiwan Province of China	1991	34 387	1 669	1993	1.7	0.92	214.6
Singapore	1994	7 086	2 512	1994	1.1	0.66	153.6

Source: UNESCO, 1997; Taiwan Province of China Council for Economic Planning and Development.
Note: Data for Dominican Republic, Morocco and Zimbabwe are not available

None of the sample countries invests significantly in R&D, when compared with the Asian tigers – technological leaders in the developing world. In terms of employment of scientists and engineers per million population, Costa Rica takes the lead, followed by Chile and Mexico. Malaysia has the lowest number in the sample, with only 3 per cent of the level in the Republic of Korea; the comparable figure for Costa Rica is 21 per cent.

In terms of total R&D expenditures, Malaysia, Costa Rica and Mexico share the bottom places; Chile is in the lead with 0.8 per cent. In comparison, the Republic of Korea spends 2.8 per cent of GNP on R&D, one of the highest figures in the world; even Singapore, despite its high dependence on imports of TNC technology, spends 1.1 per cent. The bulk (80 per cent or more) of total R&D spending is financed by the Government in all sample countries except for Malaysia (where the proportion is under 60 per cent); R&D by productive enterprises does not reach 0.2 per cent of GNP for any of them. Many observers would regard industry-financed R&D as the most relevant indicator of technological activity relevant for competitiveness, and here comparison with the Asian tigers shows the technological weakness of the sample economies much more starkly. The best-performing of the sample economies, Malaysia, does not exceed 6 per cent of the figure for the Republic of Korea. The lowest comes to only 0.7 per cent. In terms of per capita R&D spending, the highest figure is that of Chile ($39) and the lowest that of Thailand (a mere $2.6 dollars). The former is 14 per cent of that in the Republic of Korea, the latter only 1 per cent.

It is again evident that formal technological effort bears little relationship with the technological complexity of manufactured exports in the sample countries. The reasons have been noted above: these countries are implementers of technology, often at a relatively simple level. Moreover, technological effort is needed for all kinds of manufacturing activity, not just high-technology exports. Thus, Chile's effort goes into supporting its resource-based activities; the more high-technology export structure of Thailand does not have indigenous technological content apart from efficient operation. This raises questions about the long-term sustainability of export growth. Some of these issues will be raised in the case studies presented in this volume.

Chapter 3

The colour TV receiver industry

3.1. Introduction

The electronics industry encompasses a wide range of activities, which can be subdivided into the following groups: electronic components, consumer electronics, computer hardware, computer software, communication equipment and industrial electronics. The more sophisticated segments, such as semiconductors, are largely located in industrially advanced nations, simpler ones like consumer electronics are spread widely around the globe, with developing countries playing a significant role. There is considerable scope for geographically separating the labour-intensive stages of the production process and siting them in countries with low-cost and abundant labour and welcoming FDI policies. [1] This chapter focuses on a large consumer electronics subsector – the colour TV receiver industry – in Malaysia, Mexico and Thailand. From the early 1980s, the manufacture of colour TVs shifted significantly from developed to developing countries, driven by fierce competition among the leading consumer electronics TNCs. The three countries selected for study are among the principal recipients of FDI in this activity.

Section 3.2 reviews recent production and consumption patterns in the industry. It discusses recent location strategies of the main TNCs, showing how they have incorporated developing countries into their global production networks. Sections 3.3 and 3.4 focus on the experience of Malaysia, Mexico and Thailand, assessing the impact of FDI on production, industrial restructuring and international competitiveness. Most of the information in this section is based on studies of foreign affiliates in the TV receiver industry in the countries concerned. [2]

3.2. Overview

3.2.1 Production and consumption patterns

The production of consumer electronics has traditionally been fairly concentrated. [3] Even now the production sites are still mainly in the developed countries (table 3.1), with Japan, North America and Western Europe together accounting for 68 per cent of worldwide production in 1992. However, in recent years a few developing countries have become important producers. Developing Asia accounted for nearly a quarter of world production by 1992; the category "all others" includes other developing countries, led by Mexico.

---

[1] Four-fifths of semiconductor production was located in the United States, Japan, Western Europe and the Republic of Korea in 1996. The corresponding figure for consumer electronics production was 60 per cent (Dicken, 1998, p. 357).

[2] See Yew (1997) for a full report about the Malaysian interviews and Carrillo, Mortimore and Alonso et al. (1997) for the Mexican interviews. The interviews in Thailand were carried out by Mortimore.

[3] "Consumer electronics" as a sector is generally defined to include the following categories: colour and monochrome TV receivers, radio receivers, video cassette and audio recorders, record players, hi-fi equipment (tuners, amplifiers), pocket calculators and electronic games (Dicken, 1998, p. 354).

Table 3.1. Production and consumption of consumer electronics products, by region, 1992

(Billions of dollars and per cent)

Country or region	Production		Consumption	
	Value	Composition	Value	Composition
Western Europe	13.9	18.1	24.1	33.8
North America	6.6	8.6	22.4	31.5
Japan	31.6	41.3	13.4	18
Developing Asia	17.9	23.3	5.7	8
All others	6.6	8.6	5.5	7.7
Total	76.6	100	71.1	100

Source: Yearbook of World Electronics Data 1994.

The OECD countries are the main consumers, though their share is decreasing over time. The major growth in those countries occurred in the 1960s and 1970s, when the product was new and its prices fell as a result of technological changes and growing volumes of production. TVs are now a mature product, with relatively few first-time buyers. New demand comes mainly from replacement purchases, from households acquiring additional sets and from technological upgrading (advanced features such as remote controls, teletext, wide screens or high-definition). The greatest potential for growth now lies in the middle- to higher-income developing countries. Even so, Western Europe, North America and Japan together still absorb over 80 per cent of total production. Thus, the main production sites in developing countries are mainly geared to export to developed countries.

Table 3.2. Principal suppliers of OECD imports of TV receivers, 1980-1996

(Per cent)

Country	Share in OECD imports, 19951996	Percentage change in share, 1980-1996
Mexico	20.7	>10 000
United Kingdom	9.7	175
Malaysia	7.9	>10 000
Germany	6.8	-70
France	5.7	957
Spain	5.3	1 585
Thailand	4.9	4 524
Belgium/Luxembourg	4.8	-31
Japan	4.6	-73
Austria	4.1	18
Top ten	74.5	*N.A.*
All others	25.5	N.A.

Source: ECLAC CANPLUS.

Table 3.2 ranks producers of completely built-up TVs by their share in OECD imports in 1995-1996. Mexico comes first, Malaysia is third and Thailand seventh. Together, these three developing countries account for one third of OECD imports, and have expanded their market shares rapidly since 1980, largely at the expense of producers in the developed countries.

Table 3.3 shows import shares in North America, Western Europe and Japan. Suppliers from developing countries have made more headway in the North American and Japanese than in European markets. The North American market is now primarily supplied by Mexico, with Malaysia, Thailand and China in a "second league". The Japanese market is supplied increasingly by Asian developing countries: Malaysia, Thailand and China.

**Table 3.3. Principal sources of imports of colour TV receivers into North America,
Western Europe and Japan, 1980-1996**

(Per cent)

Rank	North America			Western Europe			Japan		
1995-1996	Source economy	Per cent market share	Per cent change 1980-1996	Source economy	Per cent market share	Per cent change 1980-1996	Source economy	Per cent market share	Per cent change 1980-1996
1	Mexico	63.5	9,773	United Kingdom	17.4	251	Malaysia	29.5	>10 000
2	Malaysia	11.7	>10 000	Germany	12.4	-62	Thailand	19.8	>10 000
3	Japan	7.4	-72	France	10.5	1 251	Republic of Korea	16.7	-37
4	Thailand	5.3	>10 000	Spain	9.7	2 056	Singapore	10.2	187
5	United States	4.4	-56	Belgium/	8,6	-14	China	9.8	>10 000
6	China	2.1	>10 000	Austria	7.5	50	Taiwan Province of China	4	-92
7	Republic of Korea	1.8	-92	Japan	3.8	-67	United States	3.3	-53
8	Canada	1.1	-78	Turkey	2.8	2 826	Philippines	3.2	9 166
9	Singapore	0.4	-87	Nether-lands	2.5	-40	Mexico	2.1	2 948
10	Taiwan Province of China	0.3	-99	Republic of Korea	2.2	-33	Belgium/ Luxembourg	0.7	-21
Top 10		98.0			77.4			99.3	
Others		2.0			22.6			0.7	
TOTAL		100			100			100	

Source: ECLAC CANPLUS.

- = loss of market share during 1980-1996.

The three mature NIEs (the Republic of Korea, Singapore and Taiwan Province of China) are also important suppliers to Japan, but they are losing shares to other developing Asian countries (partly because their own producers are relocating there). Western Europe continues to be supplied mainly by countries that are members of the European Union.

3.2.2 *The increasing dominance of Japanese TNCs*

The growing role of developing countries as exporters of TV receivers has been driven by the activities of TNCs. Among these, Japanese firms are especially strong, accounting for 55 per cent of world production (table 3.4). Seven of the eleven principal consumer electronics TNCs are Japanese, and account for almost three-quarters of total consumer electronics sales by those eleven firms. In Japan they constitute 99 per cent of consumer electronics production, in Europe 27 per cent and in the United States 20 per cent.[4] Philips (Netherlands) is the only non-Japanese TNC among the five "first division" companies. The other three big non-Japanese competitors are "second division" firms, Thomson (France), and Samsung and LG Electronics from the Republic of Korea.

[4] The Japanese presence in European and American markets was a reaction to the restrictive trade policies designed to protect local producers from emerging Japanese competition in the 1960s and 1970s. The trade restrictions induced Japanese producers to set up local "completely knocked down" (CKD) operations, or, after the Government of the United States imposed a minimum requirement of 50 per cent local content, assembly of imported loose components (Zampetti, 1996, p. 243).

**Table 3.4. Principal transnational corporations in
the consumer electronics industry, 1991**
(Billions of dollars and per cent)

Company	Sales electronics		Foreign sales as per cent of total sales
	Products	Share	
Matsushita (Japan)	36.6	19.4	48.0
Toshiba (Japan)	26.6	14.1	29.0
Hitachi (Japan)	25.2	13.4	24.0
Philips (Netherlands)	23.8	12.6	94.4
Sony (Japan)	23.0	12.2	75.0
Total first division	*135.2*	*71.7*	..
Thomson (France)	12.6	6.7	69.0
Mitsubishi (Japan)	12.5	6.6	21.0
Sharp (Japan)	9.7	5.2	50.0
Samsung (Republic of Korea)	7.1	3.8	58.0
Sanyo (Japan)	6.1	3.2	41.0
LG (Republic of Korea)	5.0	2.7	51.0
Total second division	*53.0*	*28.2*	..
Grand total	188.2	100.0	..

Source: "The electronic business international 100",
Electronic Business, Dec. 1992, pp. 84-85.

The dominance of Japanese TNCs has its origins in the period after the Second World War when the Government of Japan designated consumer electronics as a "strategic" sector, supporting its firms and protecting the domestic market from imports. This allowed Japanese firms to import and use the technology of major Western companies, especially RCA (United States) and Philips (Netherlands). However, they went much further, revolutionizing the industry by combining economies of scale, regional specialization, lean production techniques and design improvement driven by heavy R&D investments. This gave them considerable cost and quality advantages *vis-à-vis* their major European and United States competitors. By the mid-1990s, Japan's productivity in consumer electronics was estimated to be 15 per cent higher than that of major firms in the United States, and 28 per cent higher than Germany's producers (McKinsey Global Institute, 1993, p. 15).

The consumer electronics industry is characterized by a high degree of divisibility in production processes as well as high minimum efficient scales in some processes.[5] Japanese firms established large-scale component plants and linked them tightly by just-in-time procurement. Their networks included plants under their own management as well as a host of independent and semi-independent component suppliers operating on subcontract and original equipment manufacture (OEM) arrangements. The success of these networks was driven by continuous improvements in design through sustained R&D expenditures: R&D by the leading Japanese TNCs is now approximately 5 to 7 per cent of turnover. Superior design, component quality and low production cost became the main competitive assets of Japanese producers. By the early 1980s, Japanese models, using integrated circuits more intensively, required up to 30 per cent fewer components than sets built in Europe or the United States (Dicken, 1998, p. 364).

---

[5] The production process consists of three principal stages. The *design stage* is highly research-intensive. The *manufacture of components* (especially of television cathode ray tubes) is highly capital-intensive, and subject to high economies of scale and high minimum efficient scale of production. The optimal production scale for TV tubes is approximately 1 million units per year, compared with only 400,000 units for complete sets. The *assembly stage* is the most labour-intensive and lends itself most to employment of large numbers of low-skilled workers (Dicken, 1998, p. 364).

The strategies employed by the Japanese TNCs are summed up in a recent report on the globalization of the consumer electronics industry:

"An extensive network of procurement relations links the major consumer electronics companies. Some of them have established a series of component production facilities and/or international purchasing offices in the Asia-Pacific region. Again Japanese companies have spearheaded the process. For example, through co-operating firms, a Japanese company can procure resistors made in Korea, condensers made in Chinese Taipei, transformers made in Hong Kong (China), magnetic heads and integrated circuits made in Malaysia and TV cathode-ray tubes made in Singapore, and assemble them in Singapore or Malaysia for markets in Asia, the United States or Europe. ... A particularly intense form of collaboration between companies, which gives rise to large flows of trade in components, is represented by the 'Original Equipment Manufacturer' (OEM) arrangements. OEMs build products to their customers' specifications for sale under their customers' label. ... OEMs in turn sometimes subcontract part of the manufacturing process. As a result, the origin of consumer electronics products becomes increasingly more difficult to ascertain. Subcontracting, also known as contract electronics manufacturing (CEM), has grown very intensely and is projected as a US$22 billion global business by the mid-1990s. It is quite important also for the consumer segment. Industry leaders, such as Sony and Matsushita, are making use of CEM as part of their global strategies to foster international competitiveness" (Zampetti, 1996, p. 228).

Japanese TNCs, driven by a relentless search for efficiency and cost reduction, have built up extensive production and procurement networks spanning the Asia-Pacific region. A new inter-country division of labour is emerging in which the location of the sub-processes primarily depends on international differences in costs and skill and infrastructure endowments.

3.2.3 Emerging opportunities for developing countries

The internationalization of TV production in the developing world has gone through several phases. Simplified, these were as follows:

- The first stage of TV manufacture in developing countries, before the advent of TNC networks, was during the period of import-substitution in countries such as Argentina, Brazil, India and Malaysia. This stage was aimed primarily at the domestic market and promoted by tariffs, import quotas and overvalued local currencies. TNC affiliates or joint ventures played an important role in some of these countries; while others promoted national champions. Some countries remained at the final assembly level, but others were able to build up local content. Competitiveness in international markets was not an objective during this phase. The leading concern was that the industry should help save foreign exchange and contribute to industrial growth. Instruments such as local content requirements, domestic ownership shares, local staff training and participation of local personnel in management were widely used. It is important for this study to see the extent to which the physical and human capacity built up during this phase helped countries to develop their national industry and enhance competitiveness.

- The next stage saw TNCs locate TV assembly operations designated for export in developing countries. As inward-oriented strategies gave way to more openness to trade and foreign investment, the attraction to foreign investors shifted from protected markets to accessing competitive factors of production, mainly low-cost labour. In the first instance, relatively small-scale, technically less demanding, labour-intensive processes were moved to low-wage countries. Prior import substitution was not necessary to attract such activities. However, this does not mean that the import-substitution phase did not contribute to the development of subsequent export-oriented ventures. For instance, in Malaysia and Thailand, companies were able to build on local supplier capabilities and infrastructure that had been developed during import substitution.

- A few developing countries were able to move to the next stage, setting up "regional *assembly* centres". Initially these consisted of assembly plants, characterized by long production runs using relatively unsophisticated, standardized technologies, designed for export to neighbouring countries. Their competitive advantage still lay in low labour costs, attractive incentives for foreign investors and (in some cases) trade preferences in developed country markets. The production of the complex skill- and R&D-intensive items remained concentrated in Japan and Western Europe, the main regional manufacturing centres, and to some extent in the Republic of Korea.

- The next phase was the introduction of "*regional manufacturing* centres". While these original competitive advantages remained important in TNC location decisions, in the 1980s the competitive position of their home countries began to deteriorate due to rising wage costs and/or appreciating currencies.[6] Increasingly, TNCs looked for sites with *skilled* low-cost labour, a well-developed local supplier base and efficient modern infrastructure, not merely in the form of roads, electricity, ports and railways but also in telecommunications and finance. From a corporate perspective, the aim was to use such sites as part of integrated TNC production systems, supplying components or "completely knocked down" (CKD) kits to the surrounding region, and manufacturing more sophisticated models and components. The prerequisite for regional manufacturing (as opposed to assembly) centres was the possession of advanced manufacturing and supplier capabilities.

- The final stage in the TNC production network is that of the "*global manufacturing* centre". This requires world-class capabilities for the full manufacture of TV receivers, including design and development. In global manufacturing centres, local content of production typically exceeds 80 per cent, not because of local content *regulations*, but because of local competitive *advantages*. Advanced local R&D

---

[6] The yen continued to appreciate *vis-à-vis* the United States dollar until April 1995. Thereafter it began a gradual depreciation.

capabilities and a good supply of technical manpower would be important elements of comparative advantage. Such centres become the hub for the production of CKD kits for distribution to regional assembly centres serving the three major developed country markets, and serve as regional or even global staff training centres for TNCs. The first signs of a move towards the development of global manufacturing centres in a few developing economies are becoming apparent, but there is still some way to go.[7]

These trends present important opportunities to developing countries. However, there is nothing automatic about the process by which countries progress from one phase to the next. Although there are important shared interests between TNCs and host countries, there are also tensions at every stage. For example, many TNCs may be content to tap the traditional advantages of developing countries, such as low-cost labour or trade preferences available to them in major destination markets. Some may prefer to source from internal sources, import from home-country companies or induce establishment of local affiliates of home-country suppliers, rather than establish links with local companies that require coaching to bring them up to required standards. Much depends on the ability of national policy makers to formulate coherent policies to induce the TNCs to take the desired decisions, make the necessary investments, transfer the requisite technology and skills, and graduate affiliates in developing countries to regional assembly or regional manufacturing centres.

This is difficult for host-country Governments, for various reasons. First, the requirements for success vary at each phase of the industry's development: policy makers must be informed of potential diverging interests to formulate policies. Second, policy makers must be fully aware of the changes in markets and technologies that shape TNC internationalization strategies. Third, there is intense competition among developing countries for FDI, which limits the scope for policies to deepen national industrialization processes. The case studies on Mexico, Malaysia and Thailand explore these issues in more depth.

3.3. FDI in Mexico, Malaysia and Thailand

Mexico, Malaysia and Thailand have been major recipients of FDI in the past decade. As table 3.5 shows, Mexico's share of total FDI inflows into the Latin American and Caribbean region fluctuated between 19 and 38 per cent between 1985 and 1996, with an estimated $12.1 billion in 1997. Malaysia and Thailand's FDI flows are also large, with Malaysia's share in total Asian FDI (excluding China) ranging from 10 to 28 per cent and Thailand's from 5 to 11 per cent in 1985-1997, and amounting to $3.8 billion and $3.6 billion in 1997, respectively.

---

[7] For example, some firms have begun to relocate some of their R&D efforts to developing host countries, although the quantitative impact on the global distribution of R&D activity is still quite limited (Reddy, 1997).

Table 3.5. FDI inflows into Mexico, Malaysia and Thailand, 1985-1997

(Millions of dollars and per cent)

Country/region	1985-1990[a]	1991	1992	1993	1994	1995	1996	1997[b]
Total Latin-America and Caribbean (LAC)	8 145.0	15 356.0	17 611.0	17 247.0	28 687.0	31 929.0	43 755.0	56 138.0
Of which:								
Mexico	2 618.0	4 762.0	4 393.0	4 389.0	10 973.0	9 526.0	8 169.0	12 101.0
Per cent of total LAC	32.1	31.0	24.9	25.4	38.3	29.8	18.7	21.6
Total Asia, excluding China	10 838.0	18 630.0	18 495.0	23 703.0	26 892.0	31 537.0	39 211.0	41 623.0
Of which:								
Malaysia	1 054.0	3 998.0	5 183.0	5 006.0	4 342.0	4 132.0	4 672.0	3 754.0
Per cent of total Asia excluding China	9.7	21.3	28.0	21.1	16.1	13.1	11.9	9.0
Thailand	1 017.0	2 014.0	2 114.0	1 804.0	1 322.0	2 002.0	2 286.0	3 600.0
Per cent of total Asia excluding China	9.4	10.7	11.4	7.6	4.9	6.3	5.8	8.6

Source: UNCTAD, 1997 and 1998, annex tables B.

[a] Annual average.

[b] Estimates.

3.3.1 Mexico

Between 1982 and 1997, more than $80 billion of FDI entered Mexico.[8] Manufacturing was the most important destination, accounting for a little over half of the accumulated stock.[9] Most of the accumulated stock by the end of 1995 was of North American origin (59 per cent from the United States and 2.5 per cent from Canada). European countries provided most of the rest. In contrast to the two Asian countries discussed in this chapter, Japanese investments in Mexico were relatively small (less than 5 per cent), although the TV industry differs from this pattern.

The growth in FDI in Mexican manufacturing in recent years can be traced to significant changes in the policy environment. There was a shift from inward- to outward-oriented industrialization in the 1980s. FDI regulations became more favourable to investors. Perhaps most importantly, the conclusion of the North American Free Trade Agreement (NAFTA) in 1994, given the proximity of the North American market, served as a major draw to investors.[10] Before 1989, the Law to Promote Mexican Investment and to Regulate Foreign Direct Investment took a very restrictive stance towards FDI, prohibiting FDI in several

---

[8] Estimate based on information provided by the Foreign Investment Directorate of the Mexican Ministry of Commerce and Industrial Development and data from table 3.5.

[9] Other important target sectors have been tourism and other services such as telecommunications.

[10] "Into the spotlight: a survey of Mexico", *The Economist*, 13 February 1993, p. 3.

sectors[11] and limiting it in others.[12] It also made authorization contingent upon foreign investors' ability to meet designated national development goals.[13] There were specific regulations on FDI in important sectors (such as the automotive, pharmaceutical, computer and electronics industries) and restrictive rules governing the transfer of technology. This investment regime gave the Mexican authorities a high degree of discretion over the activities of foreign investors.[14] These restrictions were eliminated or reversed completely by the new interpretation of the law in 1989 and the promulgation of a new law on foreign investment during the 1990s. The latter introduced automatic authorization and slashed restrictions and sectoral limitations, preparing the ground for the new rules that were to come into effect under NAFTA in 1994.

The Mexican law on export processing operations along the border with the United States (the *maquiladora* programme) formed a major element in the new investment regime. Although this programme had existed since 1965, it was only after the peso was devalued in 1985 and 1994 that it began to take off, aided by the adoption of a more liberal stance on FDI and trade policies. The *maquiladora* programme allows for duty-free imports into free-trade zones or in-bond operations provided that the output is exported. It became the preferred mechanism by which foreigners took advantage of low-cost Mexican labour while avoiding FDI restrictions.

FDI in Mexico was encouraged by production-sharing provisions of the United States Harmonized Tariff Schedule (HTS 9802, for short). Production sharing occurs when parts made in the United States are shipped to other countries for assembly; the assembled goods are then returned to the United States for further processing or packaging and distribution. Duty is charged only on value added outside the United States (USITC, 1997a, p. 1-1). This tariff provision was enhanced by NAFTA provisions, which progressively eliminated United States and Canadian duties and quotas on imports from Mexico and permitted local content to share in the free market access.[15]

This regime has significantly raised FDI-driven exports. To illustrate:

- Mexico's *maquila* exports accounted for 47 per cent of Mexican exports by the end of 1996. They were the second most important source of foreign exchange (after oil), and the most dynamic component in exports. In addition, they were the most important source of new employment. The number of *maquila* companies increased from 620 in 1980 to 2,400 in 1996, employment in those companies from 124,000 to 752,000, and their value added from $772 million to $6,140 million. After the

---

[11] Petroleum, basic petrochemicals, electricity, transportation, radio and television, gas distribution and forestry.

[12] Minerals, petrochemical by-products and auto parts.

[13] Examples of such criteria were: complementarity to national investment; positive balance-of-payments effect; employment generation in general, and of Mexican technicians and administrative personnel specifically; use of Mexican products and parts; diversification of investment sources; avoidance of monopolist market positions; positive technological contribution; positive production, price and quality effects.

[14] Export processing industries were practically the only activities exempted from such restrictions.

[15] As part of the NAFTA agreement, the *maquiladora* programme is scheduled for abolition on 1 January 2001. The major effect of this will be that the components needed for Mexico's export-assembly that currently enter the country duty-free will become dutiable if they are imported from countries other than the United States and Canada.

devaluation of the peso in 1994, *maquila* exports grew by 18 per cent in 1995 and 15 per cent during the first half of 1996.

- Assembly in Mexico is now an important competitive strategy for many United States producers of labour-intensive articles. Mexico is the most important supplier country under the HTS 9802 tariff mechanism, with a trade value in 1995 of around $25 billion.[16]

- In 1995, the combined "NAFTA value" of Mexican exports was $10.5 billion.

As a result, Mexican exports to the United States almost doubled in a very brief period of time: from $40.7 billion in 1992 to $79.5 billion in 1995. Seven-eighths of this entered the United States by way of the HTS 9802, NAFTA, or the two combined.[17] This export boom was driven almost exclusively by FDI.

The colour TV receiver industry benefited in a major way from these changes in Mexico's trade and investment regime. Production expanded from 1.7 million units in 1987 to over 18 million units in 1996. An important cluster for export production of colour TV receivers was established in Tijuana, just across the border from San Diego and close to the port of Long Beach (California). The drive came almost wholly from foreign investors. However, it differed from most other industries making use of the HTS 9802 and NAFTA mechanisms in that United States TNCs did not dominate it.

Its expansion was a direct result of changes in the industry in the United States. By the mid-1980s, most United States TV producers had been pushed out of the industry by European and Japanese TNCs. Thomson purchased the TV facilities of General Electric and RCA, Philips acquired the Sylvania and Magnavox trade marks, and Matsushita purchased Quasar. European TNCs with production facilities in the United States had a combined market share of about 34 per cent in 1990. There also emerged a group of fast-growing Japanese TNCs with a roughly similar market share. This latter group began to invest heavily in Mexico's Tijuana cluster. In addition, LG Electronics (Republic of Korea) purchased the Mexican operations of Zenith, the last independent United States TV producer.

Japanese TNCs in Mexico were very successful in the United States market with colour, projection and high-definition TVs. Their success prompted TNCs from Europe and the Republic of Korea to invest in similar operations, mainly in another major *maquila* cluster in Ciudad Juarez. A number of new investments were made recently, mainly by Asian TNCs,

---

[16] Other important source regions were South-East Asia, which supplied $8.6 billion worth of assembled semiconductors, and the Caribbean Basin, which supplied $4.5 billion in the form of assembled garments. Official data apparently understate Mexico's share of the total by about $10 billion (USITC, 1997a, pp. 1-6).

[17] United States importers can register a good simultaneously under HTS 9802 and NAFTA, using the former for its United States-origin content, while registering the remaining portion of the entry's value under NAFTA's reduced tariff rates. Since the sum of the individual NAFTA and HTS trade flows ($44 billion and $25 billion, respectively), is greater than the value of total imports ($59 billion), it is obvious that the practice has given rise to a certain amount of double counting.

to increase and modernize production and to adapt to NAFTA rules of origin.[18] Since the end of 1994, Asian investors have pumped in more than $1 billion of new investments into the industry, in both the Tijuana and Ciudad Juarez clusters. The Republic of Korea led the effort with $650 million, followed by Japan with $400 million. As a result of the Korean inflows, the Ciudad Juarez cluster has reached approximately the same capacity as the Tijuana cluster (table 3.6). However, the Japanese-dominated Tijuana cluster remains more dynamic, and has been termed the "TV-set capital of the world" (Darlin, 1996, pp. 111-2). Of a total expected TV production of 25 million units in the near future,[19] Tijuana companies could supply at least 9 million (table 3.6).

These investments suggest that market shares in the United States market will come to resemble the pattern in other consumer markets, with Japanese and Korean companies progressively displacing other producers. The dominant position of Asian producers is evident from table 3.6.

Table 3.6. Principal companies in the Mexican TV industry, end of 1996

Company (Year of entry)	Country of origin	Models assembled	Annual production capacity (Units)
Group 1: The Tijuana cluster			
Sony (1985) *	Japan	Sony	3 000 000
Samsung (1988) *	Republic of Korea	Samsung	1 850 000
Matsushita (1980) *	Japan	Quasar, Panasonic, National	1 500 000
Sanyo (1982) *	Japan	Sanyo	1 100 000
Hitachi (1986) *	Japan	Hitachi	900 000
JVC (1996)	Japan	JVC	700 000
Group 2: The Ciudad Juarez cluster			
Thomson	France	GE, RCA	not known
Philips	Netherlands	Magnavox, Sylvania	not known
LG Electronics	Republic of Korea	Zenith, Goldstar	not known
Daewoo	Republic of Korea		not known
Orion	Republic of Korea		not known
Estimated total annual capacity of all companies			18 000 000

Source: UNCTAD.

Note: Interviewed companies are marked with an asterisk.

---

[18] In particular, companies are trying to reduce dependence on components and parts from Asian sources which will become dutiable after the scheduled abolition of the *maquiladora* programme in 2001. See also the discussion of the impact of the changes in the trade rules on the Mexican economy in section 3.4.1.

[19] Estimate by Juan Elak, President of the Mexican Business Council for International Affairs, as quoted in *Business Mexico*, June 1997, p. 3.

3.3.2 Malaysia

Malaysia adopted an outward-oriented strategy in the second half of the 1980s, earlier than most developing countries. Its Industrial Master Plan of 1986-1995 emphasized private-sector-led growth with an emphasis on manufacturing. FDI inflows fluctuated from 12 per cent of gross fixed capital formation in 1970-1990 to 25 per cent in 1991-1993 and 12 per cent in 1994-1996 (UNCTAD, 1998a). By 1986, the share of foreign affiliates in total domestic sales of manufactures was 41 per cent (UNCTAD, 1996, pp. 121-122). Malaysia increased its share of FDI to all developing countries from 4 per cent in 1984-1989 to 7 per cent in 1990-1995 (ESCAP, 1998, p. 18). By the end of 1992, there was over 19 billion ringgit (approximately $7.5 billion) of FDI registered in fixed assets. Most of this had come from Asia and the Pacific, particularly Japan (37 per cent), Singapore (15 per cent), Taiwan Province of China (7 per cent) and Hong Kong, China (5 per cent). Of the non-Asian investors, Western Europe accounted for 16 per cent and North America for 11 per cent.

FDI in Malaysia concentrated heavily in the electrical and electronic equipment sector (38 per cent of the total stock in 1992).[20] In 1990, over 90 per cent of the fixed assets in this industry were foreign-owned, up from 68 per cent in 1970 (Rasiah, 1995, p. 176). Japan accounted for 17 per cent of the total FDI stock in the industry in 1992, making it the biggest single investor in this industry. In turn, this industry constituted almost half of total Japanese FDI in Malaysia. Matsushita, one of the biggest consumer electronics TNCs, is the largest foreign investor in Malaysia. The electronics industry also accounts for 59 per cent of United States FDI, 57 per cent of FDI from Taiwan Province of China, and 48 per cent of FDI from Hong Kong, China.

This large foreign presence owes much to a dynamic export-processing sector that was allowed to develop separately from the rest of Malaysia's economy. Efficient management, good infrastructure, low-cost English-speaking labour and a liberal regime for trade and capital provided a hospitable environment for FDI. The Government also provided foreign investors with generous incentives, including export benefits, pioneer status (income tax exemptions), investment tax credits, licensed manufacturing warehouses, labour utilization benefits, location benefits and an accelerated depreciation allowance.[21] The Government placed certain limits on the extent of foreign ownership, depending on export performance and the nature of the products manufactured for the domestic market.[22] Moreover, Malaysia imposed capital controls in September 1998, to prevent massive outflows of foreign capital in connection with the Asian financial crisis. The restrictions are now being relaxed. A summary of Malaysia's FDI policy regime (until September 1998) is given in table 3.7.

---

[20] Less important destination sectors for FDI were petroleum products (9 per cent), non-metallic mineral products (7 per cent), chemical products (6 per cent), textiles and garments (6 per cent) and food products (5 per cent).

[21] For details of Malaysia's FDI policy regime see ESCAP (1995).

[22] Up to 100 per cent foreign ownership is allowed if an enterprise exports 80 per cent or more of its output irrespective of whether it competes on the domestic market with local producers. An enterprise exporting 50-79 per cent is allowed 100 per cent foreign equity if it invests $50 million ringgit (about $20 million) or more in fixed assets or implements projects which have at least 50 per cent value added, and if it does not compete with local manufacturers in the domestic market. The investment rules also allow for 51 per cent foreign ownership if an enterprise exports 51-79 per cent of its production, and 30-51 per cent foreign ownership if it exports 20-50 per cent of its output (ESCAP, 1995, pp. 115-118).

FDI in Malaysian industry has contributed significantly to its investment rate, and to its export and employment growth. The country almost doubled its investment rate (from 20 to 36 per cent of GDP) and its export share (from 42 per cent to 83 per cent of GDP) from the 1960s to the period 1991-1994 (UNCTAD, 1996, p. 110). The manufacturing sector was the engine of this success. Its share in GDP rose from 9 per cent in 1960 to 32 per cent in 1994. The share of manufactures in total exports jumped from 10 per cent in 1970 to 82 per cent in 1994. The electrical and electronic equipment industry became the leading manufacturing sector, accounting for 27 per cent of manufacturing output in 1991 (up from 2 per cent in 1970), 21 per cent of fixed assets (from 4 per cent) and 31 per cent of employment in manufacturing (from 2 per cent) (Rasiah, 1996, p. 176). It generated 64 per cent of all manufactured exports and 45 per cent of total exports in 1994, and was the country's largest foreign exchange earner. It grew particularly rapidly in the 1980s: from 1981 to 1992, the number of companies rose from 208 to 530 and employment from 80,000 to 287,000. Within the electrical and electronics industry, consumer electronics accounted for 39 per cent of output, 45 per cent of value-added, 36 per cent of fixed assets and 35 per cent of employment.

Table 3.7. FDI policy regime in Malaysia

Aspect of FDI policy	Description
Access	All sectors open to FDI; some states do not allow landholding by foreign companies.
Ownership	Foreign equity participation linked to proportion of output exported; 100 per cent allowed in projects exporting 80 per cent or more of their output.
	In domestic market-oriented production, 100 per cent equity is allowed for only five years.
Approval	Process greatly simplified since 1988.
	Central Coordination Centre on Investment (later renamed Advisory Services Centre) set up in 1988.
Fiscal incentives	Tax holiday.
	Investment tax allowance.
	Tax deductions for R&D, training, re-investment, etc.
Exchange control	Until 1998.
	No control of transactions on current account.
	Repatriation of profits, dividends, royalties and sale proceeds of assets freely permitted.
	Very limited restrictions on capital account.
Performance requirement	Extent of foreign ownership linked to export.
	For certain incentives, local content guidelines apply.
Other relevant aspects	Free access to domestic credit.

Source: ESCAP, 1998, p. 10 and p. 105.

TV production was one of the most dynamic activities in Malaysia's consumer electronics sector in the 1980s and 1990s. Between 1981 and 1994, production grew from 158,613 units to 7.7 million units (of which 7.2 million were for export). However, the production of TV sets had started long before Malaysia's export-oriented phase. Matsushita set up a plant for colour TVs in 1965, assembling kits imported from Japan. It added a facility in 1972 for the production of relatively simple TV components, and another in 1987 for more complex components such as device yokes and flyback transformers. Sharp entered in 1968 with Roxy to assemble colour TVs. Other early entrants during import-substitution were

Toshiba, Philips and Sanyo, which began assembly through a Malaysian assembler (Syarikat Hitec). Production during this phase concentrated on the domestic market.

The three export operations that currently dominate Malaysian TV production were established during the late 1980s. All were new facilities with no link to the previous import-substitution plants. In 1988, Sony set up a huge integrated export operation called SBN, which produces major components (device yokes, flyback transformers and tuners) in-house, with an annual production capacity of 3 million units. In 1989-1990, Matsushita established MTV, an export-oriented colour TV plant, and MMEC for cathode ray tubes. The former has a capacity of about 1 million units, the latter of over 6 million tubes. In 1990 Sharp set up a new export-oriented plant, separate from the old Roxy plant, whose output was sold in the domestic market. The new plant currently has a capacity of about 2.6 million units. Sharp intends to phase out TV production in the Roxy plant, because it can compete better by meeting domestic demand from its export operation. Roxy will concentrate on the production of other consumer products such as refrigerators and vacuum cleaners. Together, the TV production facilities owned by Sony, Matsushita and Sharp account for about two-thirds of total Malaysian production. They are all highly competitive operations operating with world-class technology of a manufacturing rather than an assembly nature.

During the 1990s, the principal consumer electronics TNCs from the Republic of Korea, LG Electronics and Samsung, entered the Malaysian market for colour TV receivers. In contrast to the Japanese firms, both opted to contract Malaysian companies to assemble their products, and to concentrate on gaining market share in the *domestic* market. In 1996 the three big exporters simultaneously dominated the domestic market, with a share of 30 per cent for Matsushita, 30 per cent for Sony, and 16 per cent for Sharp. Samsung's market share stood at 6 per cent, and LG Electronics' at 5 per cent. Interestingly, Samsung set up its own plant to manufacture cathode ray tube with an annual capacity of about 6 million units, similar to Matsushita and Chung Hwa (Taiwan Province of China). Thus, the two new entrants had distinct strategies: Samsung primarily entered as a supplier of critical components while LG Electronics merely "tested the water" by way of local assembly. Some basic data about the current major producers in Malaysia's TV receiver industry are given in table 3.8.

3.3.3 Thailand

Foreign direct investment has played a significant role in Thai economic growth, though not as marked as in Mexico and Malaysia. FDI inflows were 4.5 per cent of gross fixed capital formation on average in 1986-1996 (UNCTAD, 1998a). Nearly 440 billion baht (about $17.6 billion)[23] of FDI was received, mainly from the four Asian NIEs and Japan (table 3.9). Most of this (36.8 per cent) flowed into the manufacturing sector, especially into the electrical and electronic equipment industry, which received 13 per cent of the total.[24] By 1986, 49 per cent of total manufacturing sales were generated by TNC affiliates (UNCTAD,

---

[23] Converted at the 1995 exchange rate of $1 = 24.97 baht, i.e. before the sharp devaluation of the baht in 1997.

[24] Other important destination sectors were trade and services (20.1 per cent), construction (10.0 per cent) and finance (7.1 per cent), and others (26.9 per cent).

1996, p. 122). However, foreign firms' activities were less deeply rooted in the local economy, in terms of local content, than in economies such as Malaysia and Singapore. Imports of parts as a share of exports of finished electronics products was still over 60 per cent in the 1990s (UNCTAD, 1996, pp. 120-121).

Table 3.8. Principal companies in the Malaysian TV industry, end of 1996

Company (Year of entry)	Country of origin	Models assembled	Annual production capacity (Units)
Group 1: Large-scale export operations			6 600 000
Sony (1988) *	Japan	Sony (Triniton)	3 000 000
Sharp (1968, 1990) *	Japan	Sharp	2 600 000
Matsushita (1965, 1989) *	Japan	Panasonic, National	1 000 000
Group 2: Medium-sized foreign firms			720 000
Hitachi	Japan	Hitachi	350 000-400 000
Funai	Japan	Funai, Symphonic Schneider	350 000-400 000
Group 3: Small and medium-sized national assemblers			1 800 000
Silver	Malaysia	Contract	Between 50 000 and
Makang	Malaysia	Contract	600 000 units each
Syarikat Hitec	Malaysia	Contract (Mitsubishi, JVC,) Philips,Toshiba	
Video Plus	Malaysia	Contract	
Setron	Malaysia	Contract (Sanyo, Goldstar)	
E. Coast Electronics	Malaysia	Contract (NEC)	
Estimated total annual capacity of all companies			9 150 000

Source: UNCTAD.

Note: interviewed companies are marked with an asterisk.

The Thai Board of Investment (BOI) has played an important role in channelling FDI to priority sectors, trying to get "the correct mix of productive labour, strategic location, investment incentives, and political stability".[25] The stock of FDI receiving BOI investment incentives reached 140.5 billion baht (approximately $5.6 billion) in 1995, and was primarily of Japanese and Asian NIE origin (table 3.9). BOI is the principal agency providing incentives to investors in Thailand, operating on the basis of the 1997 Investment Promotion Act and its

Table 3.9. Distribution of Thailand's FDI by major source countries

(Per cent)

Source economies	Total FDI inflows 1970-1995 (Per cent)	FDI stock receiving BOI incentives, 1995 (Per cent)
Hong Kong (China), Singapore, Taiwan Province of China	30.6	21.1
Japan	29.7	43.1
United States	16	6.9
Western Europe	12.7	9.2
Other	11	19.6

Source: UNCTAD (1996).

---

[25] Board of Investment (1997, p. 10).

precursors. It promotes projects that strengthen industrial and technological capability, use domestic resources, create employment opportunities, develop basic and support industries, earn foreign exchange, contribute to the economic growth of regions outside Bangkok, develop infrastructure, conserve natural resources and reduce environmental problems. It does this by fiscal and other incentives, including investment guarantees, import protection, permits, tax incentives, additional incentives for companies operating away from Bangkok,[26] and additional support for export operations (Board of Investment, 1996a).

There are significant foreign ownership restrictions in Thai manufacturing (Board of Investment, 1996a, pp. 11-14).[27] These date back to the 1970s and 1980s when the Government, under pressure from big business groups, actively regulated industries by means of discretionary policies (Pasuk and Baker, 1998, pp. 83-85). While trade and FDI policies have been liberalized substantially since the late 1980s, Thai nationals must own 51 per cent of shares of foreign companies whose production is mainly for the domestic market.[28] Majority foreign ownership is permitted in companies that export over half of their production, and 100 per cent foreign ownership (i.e. foreign subsidiary status) is permitted if at least 80 per cent of production is exported. Consequently, only a third of the value of the BOI-promoted FDI stock belongs to foreign subsidiaries. The remaining two-thirds constitute investments in joint ventures. For the firms receiving BOI incentives, the Alien Business Law restricts the level of foreign ownership.[29] However, many restrictions are currently being revamped and liberalized, in part because they are seen to be in conflict with WTO norms. Further changes are under way in response to the IMF restructuring package adopted in the course of the Asian financial crisis of 1997/1998.

Since 1992, the BOI Unit for Industrial Linkage Development (BUILD) has encouraged the growth of supporting industries by providing information about subcontracting to large producers, as well as to buyer firms seeking to source in Thailand. It also helps small and medium-sized Thai companies achieve standards required in subcontracting arrangements, and provides matchmaking services for firms seeking specific components or raw materials in the country. Its incentives cover some sectors relevant to electrical and electronic equipment, for example, fabricated metal products and electronic connectors from metal or plastic components. The success of this endeavour is, however, reportedly mixed.

Thailand's economic performance was impressive until the crisis of mid-1997. Investment was 41 per cent of GDP in 1991-1994 (up from 22 per cent in the 1960s), and the share of exports in GDP was 37 per cent (up from 16 per cent). The per capita GNP growth rate was the fastest in the world in 1985-1994. Industrialization was at the heart of this

---

[26] The aim is to induce companies to locate outside Bangkok, or even outside Greater Bangkok. Certain incentives are conditional upon the zone of location.

[27] These restrictions are subject to case-by-case exemptions, especially when it concerns direct involvement in technological development.

[28] Except those located outside Bangkok and its bordering areas.

[29] However, United States firms can claim exemption under the Treaty of Amity and Economic Relations between Thailand and the United States (Board of Invesntment, 1996b, pp. 28-30).

dramatic economic expansion. The manufacturing sector increased its share in GDP from 22 per cent in 1980 to 30 per cent in 1996. The share of manufactures in total exports jumped from 32 per cent in 1980 to 82 per cent in 1995. The share of the electrical and electronics industry in total manufacturing was 9 per cent in 1994, and its exports accounted for 21 per cent of total exports in 1995 (Board of Investment, 1996c).

FDI as a proportion of gross fixed capital formation rose from 2 per cent in the 1970s to 5 per cent in the 1990s (UNCTAD, 1996, p. 122). However, from the late 1970s to the late 1980s its role was relatively limited. During the first years of the export boom that resulted from the depreciation of the baht against the yen (i.e. after 1985), local companies and joint ventures were the main engines of growth. Foreign investors, led by Japan and Taiwan Province of China, began to flood in from 1987 onwards, driven by a search for low-cost production sites in the region as the yen and other East Asian currencies continued to strengthen.[30] The macroeconomic effects of this became visible in the 1990s, when TNCs began to overtake local firms that had been the early movers in several important industries (Pasuk and Baker, 1998, pp. 31-38). The TV industry is a good example of this development.

The production of colour TV receivers expanded from 500,000 units in 1986 to 6.1 million units in 1996, of which 4.6 million were exported. As in Malaysia, TV assembly in Thailand began in the 1960s and 1970s during the import-substitution era. Taking advantage of import protection, seven foreign firms (Mitsubishi, Philips, Sanyo, Singer, Hitachi, Toshiba and Matsushita) and one national firm (Tanin Industrial) started assembling CKD kits, primarily for the local market. By 1986, four-fifths (400,000 units) of total TV production in Thailand was directed to the domestic market. Five of the seven foreign companies were organized as joint ventures, and two as foreign subsidiaries. Most firms also produced a range of other electrical and electronics consumer products.

From 1987 onwards, nine foreign firms (World Electric, JVC, Tatung, LG Mitr, Samsung, Sharp, Sony, Thomson and NEC) set up export-oriented assembly plants. Four were joint ventures and five were subsidiaries. By the end of 1996, 18 foreign companies were assembling colour TV sets (table 3.10). The national firm, Tanin, is now extinct; while it had initially succeeded in exporting monochrome TV receivers under an OEM arrangement and with some own component production, it could not graduate into colour TVs, either with its national brand or as a subcontractor. There is one new national assembler, TVI. The high number of joint ventures (10) in the table reflect BOI restrictions on foreign investment in firms aiming at local markets.

There are three principal groups of assemblers. The first consists of three very large exporters, the second of medium-sized plants that also export a sizeable proportion of their output, and the third of smaller firms that sell mostly on the domestic market. All plants in the first two groups, except two medium-sized producers (National Thai and Sanyo), were established during the second wave of FDI after 1987. Together, these plants account for over 90 per cent of total production capacity in the industry. In contrast, the firms in the third

---

[30] FDI inflows slackened in the early 1990s but accelerated again in 1993 as the yen began to move upwards again (Pasuk and Baker, 1998, p. 36).

group were set up in the 1960s or 1970s, with the exception of the Samsung plant. There has been a dramatic reorientation in the industry, away from production for the local market towards export markets. This reorientation is still underway, because several of the firms that sell more than half of their total output domestically are restructuring to expand capacity and compete better not just in the national market but also in international markets.

Table 3.10. Principal companies in Thailand's TV industry, end of 1996

Company (Year of entry)	Country/territory of origin	Foreign share	Annual production capacity (Units)
Group 1: Large-scale export operations			4 200 000
Thomson (1990)	France	Subsidiary	More than 1 000 000 units
World Electric (1988)	Japan	Subsidiary	each
JVC (1989)*	Japan	Subsidiary	
Group 2: Medium-sized firms, production mainly for export			
NEC (1991)	Japan	Joint venture	3 200 000
Sony (1988)	Japan	Subsidiary	Between
Sharp (1992)*	Japan	Joint venture	400 000 and 750 000
LG Mtr (1987)	Republic of Korea	Joint venture	units each
National Thai (1970)	Japan	Joint venture	
Tatung (1990)	Taiwan Province of China	Subsidiary	
Sanyo (1969)	Japan	Joint venture	
Group 3: Small and medium-sized firms, production mainly for domestic market			700 000
Hitachi (1970)*	Japan	Joint venture	Less than 200 000 units
Samsung (1989)*	Republic of Korea	Joint venture	each
Philips (1967)*	Netherlands	Subsidiary	
Toshiba (1969)	Japan	Joint venture	
Mitsubishi (1964)	Japan	Subsidiary	
Singer (1960)	Netherlands	Joint venture	
Others: without full information			not known
Distar (1992)	Republic of Korea	Joint venture	
Tri-Star (n.d.)	not known	not known	
TVI (1993)	Thailand	Not applicable	
Estimated total annual capacity of all principal companies			8 100 000

Sources: UNCTAD, based on Board of Investment of Thailand and the Brooker Group.
Note: Interviewed companies are marked with an asterisk.

3.4. FDI, restructuring and competitiveness

The growth of the TV receiver industry in Mexico, Malaysia and Thailand has been due to the expansion and relocation strategies of a few large TNCs, which dominate worldwide production in an industry characterized by keen competition and fast technical progress. They use leading-edge technologies and strive for continuing improvements through R&D, organizational improvement, human resource development, investment in new equipment, and upgrading their supplier base. Potentially, therefore, they can make a substantial contribution to local industrial upgrading and restructuring, and to enhancing the international competitiveness of the host countries. This section investigates the evidence for any such impact in the three developing economies under review. We use data from interviews with some of the local subsidiaries of leading TNCs,[31] supplemented by information from secondary sources.

Since the plants were primarily export-oriented, it would be expected that their operations positively affected manufactured exports by the countries concerned. However, on their own, such data are rather shallow indicators of host-country competitiveness. Additional data are needed to reveal the effects on local economic development. Section 3.2.3 outlined a range of possibilities with respect to the depth of TNC involvement in the local economy. The least favourable one is that of the regional assembly centre, where TNCs are merely using a developing country as a low-cost site for their assembly activities. In such cases, export growth is the result of low-wage assembly without local linkages or long-term commitments to the host country. Import content tends to be very high because of the absence of a developed local supplier base, reducing the positive effect of exports on the balance of payments of the host country. This stage may seem a necessary first step towards deeper integration of the foreign investors in the local economy; however, there are no automatic mechanisms to ensure greater "rooting" over time, and it is possible for countries to remain in this first phase. In this case, the benefits for the host country are likely to remain limited.

The scenario with the maximum positive impact on local industrial development is when a host economy serves as a global manufacturing centre. Here, TNCs make a long-term commitment to the site, with significant investments in modern technology, local human capital development, local technology development and transfer, nurturing of backward linkages, and the strengthening of local suppliers.

The impact of TNCs on the economies of the three countries discussed here lies somewhere between the minimum and maximum impacts. In this section we try to determine the impact of TNCs on the three economies, and to the assess the integration of TNC operations in national industrialization processes. We first assess the macroeconomic effects on a country's export balance and market share. We then look at the following indicators of impact: human capital formation; technology acquisition, transfer, development and diffusion; and the building of local supplier networks.

3.4.1 Mexico

3.4.1.1 Setting and competitive performance of the industry

The impact on Mexico's manufactured exports of recent FDI in the TV industry is easy to demonstrate: by 1995-1996, Mexico had become the largest supplier of colour TV

---

[31] The companies marked with an asterisk in tables 3.6, 3.8 and 3.10.

receivers to OECD countries (table 3.2). Its market share was more than twice that of its closest competitor (the United Kingdom). These exports predominantly emanated from the TNC plants operating in the two *maquila* clusters, Tijuana and Ciudad Juarez. Exports by the industry contributed in a major way to the spectacular growth of Mexico's manufactured exports. Electronic goods took a 13 per cent share of total manufactured exports, second to automotive products (the biggest example of a TNC-dominated industry) with 20 per cent. These are the industries in which Mexico has the highest import market shares in OECD countries (over 3 per cent each).

The dominant position of Mexican TV exports to OECD countries stems from its very large market share (64 per cent) in North America. Its market shares in Western Europe and Japan are much lower (table 3.3).[32] This is related to the various trade regulations and the *maquiladora* programme described above. An indication of the importance of NAFTA is that the "NAFTA value" of television receivers amounted to $724 million in 1995 (i.e. 6.9 per cent of the total NAFTA import value). The North American market was captured quickly. In just four years (from 1992 to 1995), exports of TVs, video monitors, cathode ray tubes and associated products to the United States grew by 49 per cent from $547 million to $814 million (6 per cent of all exports to that market in 1995). Mexico's share in the total TV imports by the United States grew from 41 per cent in 1990 to 69 per cent in 1996, well ahead of Malaysia (12 per cent), Japan (7 per cent) and Thailand (5 per cent).[33] The establishment of NAFTA undoubtedly contributed to this.

The four subsidiaries from Japan and one from the Republic of Korea in the Tijuana cluster that were interviewed for this study (firms marked with an asterisk in table 3.6) confirm these trends. Four of the five asserted that they had gained export market share between 1990 and 1995, and all five had done so between 1985-1990. Interestingly, this was not only due to the North American market; one firm (Sony) also exported to several other global locations, while two others (Samsung and, to a lesser extent, Hitachi) are now also developing Mexico as a base for export to Latin America. Before 1990 there were no local sales, even though in-bond assemblers were allowed to sell up to 50 per cent of their output on the domestic market. In the mid-1990s, domestic sales ranged from 2 per cent (Sanyo) to 14 per cent (Samsung), a sign of diversification away from the leading western markets. Dynamic developing-country markets (including the host country's own) are beginning to assume importance, although the growth of the Mexican domestic market experienced a setback due to the 1994 peso devaluation and the consequent decrease in real incomes and demand.

The five subsidiaries play a dominant role in their respective TNC networks. Four of the five companies considered their role in the international strategy of their parents to be "very important". This was so in 1985-1990, and has remained unchanged during the rapid

---

[32] As we have seen in section 3.3.1, in the Western European market Mexico does not even rank among the top 10 suppliers.

[33] Information from ECLAC's MAGIC software. The *import* market share (69 per cent) should not be confused with the *total* market share mentioned earlier (60 per cent).The latter refers to Mexico's share in *total* United States sales (i.e. sales from domestic sources and imports together).

expansion period of 1990-1996. Initially, the main aim of the strategy was to gain market share in the United States (and later also Canada) by using a proximate low-wage site. Access to the United States market was critical, not only to the success of the subsidiaries operating in that site, but also to the global success of the TNCs as a whole. This forced the subsidiaries to work towards productivity improvement, and access to the United States market was closely linked to high productivity.

3.4.1.2 *Human capital formation*

With their rapid expansion, these companies have been major generators of local employment. Together, they employed 10,148 persons in 1995, against 1,139 in 1985. During the 1970s and 1980s, TNCs in the *maquiladoras* were often criticized for not transferring useful skills to their employees (Bustamente, 1983, pp. 224-256; and Fernandéz-Kelly, 1983). This is changing. Though the sample companies still employed mainly low-wage unskilled workers, they are making great efforts to upgrade the labour force's skills. Human resource development is listed as the second most important source of productive efficiency improvement (after technological upgrading, considered below). It is especially important for operating modern automated production processes, undertaking local R&D and applied engineering for design – activities which they have recently begun to undertake – and integrating backwards into the assembly and manufacture of more complex components (see also below). The Mexican content of more complex operations such as R&D in new TV designs and quality control has increased, which is crucial as the intensely competitive North American market requires increasingly complex, better-quality and more sophisticated products with new features.[34]

Human capital formation involves training workers and quality-control staff, the employment of more skilled labour, and the implementation of changes in work organization (such as job rotation, to expose workers to a wider range of tasks and give them a broader perspective on operations). Every new employee is exposed to formal training for an average of 45 hours. Personnel with qualifications receive more – 74 hours in the case of technicians and 68 in the case of skilled labour. The average skill level of the TV labour force is rising. Technicians and engineers now represent over 5 per cent of total staff, and 4 per cent are supervisors. In addition, around 22 per cent of the production workers are skilled (up from 12 per cent in 1980 and 20 per cent in 1985). In 1975, 5,924 technicians and professionals were employed in the export-processing manufacturing industries of Tijuana. By 1995 this figure had risen to more than 10,000. The companies are no longer the "screwdriver plants" of one decade ago which were based exclusively on low-wage unskilled labour.

The majority of technical centres, institutes and universities are oriented towards satisfying the demand of the in-bond assembly industry in their technical and electronics engineering courses (Carrillo, 1991). This was initially done on an informal basis. Recently agreements have been prepared between television firms and local technical education colleges and universities with a view to adapting certain parts of the curriculum to the needs

---

[34] See "The Tijuana triangle", *The Economist*, Manufacturing Survey, 20 June 1998, pp.15-16, for details about human capital formation in the Sanyo plant in Tijuana.

of the firms. Moreover, their students are provided with workplace experience, and qualified graduates are offered employment.

3.4.1.3 Technological development

The companies interviewed consider that proprietary technology is the single most important determinant of their competitiveness. Their core technology (both product and process) is considered world-class. There has been a rapid increase in automation. The number of programmable units (mostly computer-controlled machine tools and computers) more than doubled in the period 1990-1995. In addition, some of the firms had introduced robots and automated equipment for shop-floor transportation. Within the production process (which includes the receipt of inputs, their assembly into finished products and the handling of inventories) the firms had an average of 160 automated units per plant in 1990. By 1995 this figure had risen to 335.[35]

In view of the need to continuously improve productive efficiency and to provide new product features for the United States market, continuous technological improvement is vital. So is quality management: four companies had obtained ISO 9002 certification by 1995, and the fifth company was preparing to apply for it. Some of the firms were also working towards ISO 9000 certification to ensure international environmental standards.

All five firms interviewed considered that technology transfer was vital to improving international competitiveness. The most common mechanism for the acquisition of new technological knowledge is informal transfer within the TNC network. In the selection of new product technology the subsidiaries are highly dependent on their parent companies. Technology transfer is not confined to engineering knowledge about products and processes; new management concepts in the form of (mainly Japanese) organizational practices are also crucial for productivity and quality.[36] The adoption of multi-tasking and the use of work teams, more flexible production lines and quality control circles have improved quality, productivity and labour relations.

Traditionally, local innovation through an affiliate's own R&D and design was very weak. However, it is gaining in importance. Four of the five firms now carry out R&D activities locally, and two are involved in the design of components or equipment. The average expenditure on R&D was 5.4 per cent of the total manufacturing cost and there was an average of eight engineers devoted to R&D. One company, for example, had an R&D collaboration agreement with a leading Mexican private university, the Centro de Enseñanza Técnica y Superior (CETYS). In addition to formal R&D, the applied adaptation of process technology to local conditions (especially different specification of inputs) was prevalent. There was considerable adaptation in plant design, quality and product technology, though very little in managerial technology (especially in marketing).

---

[35] The same tendency is noted in "The Tijuana triangle", op. cit.
[36] Other studies have also documented the recent implementation of automated technology and innovative organizational practices such as JIT and TQM. For relevant references see Sargent and Matthews (1997, p. 1669).

On the whole, interviewees' responses to questions, about human resource development and technological improvement indicate that the firms are gradually moving into increasingly complex operations. Even though their main activity is still assembly based on low-cost labour-intensive activities, they are gaining greater technological responsibility in the international strategy of their parents. Local product design, quality improvements and more complex assembly, manufacture and R&D are beginning to assume importance. There are already cases in which the entire manufacturing process (with the exception of the cabinets and the circuit boards) is handled by the subsidiaries themselves. Clearly, one can no longer characterize these operations as simple assembly processes.

3.4.1.4 Building local supplier networks

The development of local supplier networks is where the TNCs have made least progress. The lack of backward linkages to local as well as foreign-owned firms based in Mexico has long been a significant shortcoming of Mexico's *maquiladora* programme. Mexican content of colour TV receivers was only 0.6 per cent in 1990. This is partly due to HTS 9802, which penalizes increased Mexican content in assembly-based exports to the United States by charging duty on all components and parts not sourced from the United States. The significant devaluation of the Mexican peso in 1994 only reinforced the focus on low-cost labour. The TV industry is the *maquila* sector that is most reliant on components and parts imported from Asia.

The entry into force of NAFTA improved the incentives for using United States, Canadian and Mexican-based suppliers, because its rules of origin require a certain minimum level of NAFTA content and it is more expensive to use dutiable components and parts from other sources. For example, a 15 per cent *ad valorem* import duty is now applied to cathode ray tubes produced outside NAFTA. These rules are leading to increased production of components within NAFTA.

Who are the new suppliers? There are three categories: (1) suppliers owned by the TNCs themselves; (2) independent foreign suppliers or joint ventures between the TNCs and other foreign companies; and (3) local Mexican suppliers. As far as the first category is concerned, there has been significant new investment within the NAFTA area, but some of the new facilities have been established in the United States rather than in Mexico. This is especially the case for relatively complex operations that require a highly skilled labour force and expertise in R&D. Different TNCs follow different strategies in this respect. Japanese firms such as Sony, Matsushita and JVC that have developed an engineering and support base in southern California over the past 10-15 years prefer to establish new component production in the United States. For example, Sony and LG Electronics now produce cathode ray tubes there, and export these to their assembly operations in Mexico. United States exports of such tubes to Mexico rose from $539 million in 1993 to $2 billion in 1996 (USITC, 1997b, pp. 6-184). However, there are also examples of major projects being started within Mexico. Some firms plan to increase the number of their "satellite" supplier firms (see below) within the next five years to concentrate the manufacturing process locally and achieve near-full vertical integration. For example, the new TNCs from the Republic of Korea, Samsung and Daewoo, are setting up plants to manufacture cathode ray tubes locally.

Most components and parts purchased from outside the TNCs' own network come from suppliers across the border in the United States. In the second category, a new tendency is for other (mainly Asian) foreign suppliers to set up close to the Tijuana or Ciudad Juarez clusters in Mexico itself. Here again, the two TNCs from the Republic of Korea are taking the lead. In contrast with Japanese operations, they are stand-alone facilities that incorporate resident foreign suppliers. For example, Samsung is implementing an important project for the production of glass together with Asahi and Corning.

In contrast, there has been very little progress with regard to the third category (local suppliers). The Mexican content of colour TV receivers only increased from 0.6 per cent in 1990 to 3.7 per cent in 1995. Local companies' share in the supply of inputs remains minute compared to locally based Asian-owned suppliers. According to the TNCs, the main reason is the inadequate technological level of the local companies. An official of Philips Consumer Electronics suggested that Mexican suppliers lacked the technological infrastructure necessary to support the high-volume requirements for leading electronics products such as televisions and computer monitor tubes (USITC, 1997b). All five TNCs complained about the lack of quality control and on-time delivery and the high prices charged by local suppliers. The high prices are partly a result of their small size, which prevents them from reaping economies of scale. TNCs believe that local suppliers had far less impact on their competitiveness than the favourable trade and investment regulations and the abundance of low-wage labour.

On the whole, therefore, NAFTA triggered a major relocation of component production away from Asian countries towards the North American area. It is unclear, however, whether this is going to translate into an expanded role for Mexican companies. The recent experience of the Tijuana cluster led the Government of Mexico in 1996 to actively promote national suppliers to *maquiladora* operations. A variety of incentives was introduced, including matchmaking at trade shows, tax cuts for those firms located outside major cities, special custom and financing preferences for newly defined categories of "sub-*maquiladora*" and "indirect exporter" suppliers, and tax exemptions for foreign companies that use national suppliers. The official goal is modest: to raise national content from 2 per cent to 4 per cent of the value of production. However, it is too early to assess whether these policies will have a significant impact.

3.4.2 *Malaysia*

3.4.2.1 *Setting and competitive performance of the industry*

In 1995-1996, Malaysia was the third-largest supplier to OECD countries (table 3.2). Its principal markets were Japan, where it occupies first place with a 30 per cent share of the import market, and North America, where it supplies 12 per cent of colour television imports (table 3.3).[37] Production for the domestic market was a mere 500,000 units in 1994. Out of a

---

[37] Its importance in the Western European TV receiver market is less; it is not among the top 10 suppliers in terms of import market share.

total production of 7.7 million units in that year, the bulk (7.2 million), was destined for export markets.

TV production has been one of the most dynamic subsectors of the electrical machinery and electronics industry. In the early 1980s, the industry was heavily dominated by semiconductor production, which accounted for about three-quarters of total production value (Department of Statistics of Malaysia, various years). Electrical components dominated exports of the industry, and suffered large cyclical fluctuations in the international market. By 1994, however, gross exports of electronic components (mainly semiconductors) had fallen to 33 per cent of total exports of the industry. The rest is accounted for mainly by "other electrical appliances" (59 per cent in 1994), in which TV sets are a major item.[38] While the production of semiconductor units almost doubled from 1981 to 1994, the number of television units produced grew about fifty-fold over this period.[39] This surge can be traced in large part to the burgeoning Japanese imports of TV receivers between 1980 and 1995. While the OECD import market expanded by about half during that period, Japanese demand grew by almost 6,000 per cent. Malaysia was well placed to take advantage of this rapid growth in demand, as well as growth of other markets in developing Asia.

Interviews with five big consumer electronics TNCs operating in Malaysia also demonstrate the extent to which the country's TV receiver sector has developed into an internationally competitive industry, and the leading role of TNCs in that development. The interviews included Sony and Matsushita, two of the three big Japanese-owned world-class operations, which produce about 90 per cent for export. They also covered the mainly domestic operations of the third big Japanese producer, Sharp's Roxy plant. Other interviews were conducted with two more recent entrants into the industry, LG Electronics and Samsung, both from the Republic of Korea.[40] Together, these firms accounted for over two-thirds of colour TV receivers exports from Malaysia and 87 per cent of domestic production. Therefore, the interview results are representative of the TV sector in the country.

The three Japanese companies, which define "best practice" in Malaysia and which are jointly responsible for over two-thirds of total output, operate differently from the two Korean companies. The Japanese firms are locally established production plants. Although they are sometimes referred to as "assemblers", a substantial number of parts and components are made by them or by (mostly foreign) supplier companies in Malaysia (see also subsection 3.4.2.4). They are far removed from simple "screwdriver" plants where imported CKD sets are assembled locally. In fact, a substantial share of their exports consists of Malaysian-manufactured CKD kits and components for assembly in other countries, especially Spain and the United Kingdom. Malaysia's leading TV producers have thus become indirect suppliers to Europe.

---

[38] At its peak in 1981, electrical components accounted for 78 per cent of gross exports of electrical machinery, appliances and parts. In 1985 its share was still 68 per cent. In 1990, it had come down to 44 per cent and in 1994 to 33 per cent (Bank Negara Malaysia, various years).

[39] Production of semiconductors grew from 1,775 million units in 1981 to 3,355 million units in 1994, whereas the number of TV sets produced increased from 158,813 units in 1981 to 7,702 million in 1994 (Department of Statistics of Malaysia, various years).

[40] These two are not listed in table 3.8 because they operate through local assemblers.

In contrast, the Korean firms have a much lighter local presence and they have a different objective: they use Malaysian firms to assemble imported CKD kits under contract for sale in the domestic market. There are several other small and medium-sized Malaysian assemblers operating under similar contract arrangements for TNCs, putting together units for well-known foreign brands such as Mitsubishi, JVC, Philips, Sanyo and Goldstar (see table 3.8). The existence of such arrangements can be traced to the domestic expertise in TV production built up in Malaysia in the import-substitution period. This has allowed foreign companies to "test the water" by entering the sector in top-down fashion without having to make heavy investments. The result of this is a dual industrial structure. It is very different from the case of Mexico, which lies somewhere between a regional assembly centre and a regional manufacturing centre. The Malaysian case is harder to classify. At the top end, it is well ahead of what has been achieved in Mexico: its TV industry can be classed as a regional manufacturing centre, and in some respects it can claim to be operating at the global manufacturing level. In contrast, at the lower end, the industry comprises small assembly operations aimed at the domestic market.

The assessment of the international competitiveness of the industry is based on interviews with three firms.[41] These three firms have raised their export market share since 1990.[42] They have been expanding aggressively in recent years, competing heavily against each other. Their competitive advantages are similar: low production costs, competitive prices, and product quality (in that order). In addition, they enjoy competitive advantages that derive from the conducive climate of their host country: good physical infrastructure, FDI-friendly policies (tax incentives, easy fund transfers and the absence of major restrictions on ownership and control) and the availability of trained human resources were mentioned as the most important factors. The availability of trained workers probably refers to the broad basic education level of the labour force, rather than the availability of highly educated specialists. Malaysia has considerable shortages of the latter, and TNCs tend to recruit expatriate specialist staff.[43] Though its investments in education have been considerable, much of it has been spent on tertiary education, especially abroad, with little emphasis on skill development at intermediate levels (Jomo, 1996).

In addition, the TNCs cited domestic economic strength and the stability of the Government as important positive factors. Some disincentives to further expansion were also mentioned, mainly problems relating to overvaluation of the ringgit, restrictions on employment of (presumably foreign) specialist manpower, high transport costs to overseas markets and high real wages. On the whole, however, the climate for FDI in Malaysia was considered to be excellent.

---

[41] Interviews with LG Electronics and Samsung are not pertinent because their contract producers in Malaysia do not export.

[42] Their domestic market share has also improved.

[43] The estimated number of scientists and engineers in R&D in the period 1981-1995 was only 87 per million people in Malaysia; Thailand had 173 and Mexico 95 (World Bank, 1999, pp. 226-227). Further evidence of Malaysia's modest skill base can be found in Lall (1998), which compares the technological capabilities of 10 Asian countries across a wide range of indicators.

Low-cost labour and trade preferences, still very important for Mexico's *maquiladora* industries, do not feature as sources of competitiveness for the big three TNCs in Malaysia. The "cheap labour" phase is clearly over. Malaysia's real wage level is higher than in neighbouring countries such as Thailand and Indonesia, and much higher than in China and Viet Nam. The companies interviewed indicated that the industry's continued appeal to foreign investors would increasingly depend on other factors, such as the further development of a high-quality and reliable supplier base and Malaysia's continued heavy investments in upgrading infrastructure systems (roads, sea ports, airports and electricity supply).

The role of trade preferences in Malaysia is quite limited, mainly because these arrangements are not common in this industry in Asian markets, which are the main target regions for the output of the three subsidiaries.[44] Only one of the firms interviewed, which exported part of its production to Western Europe and North America, enjoyed coverage under the Generalized System of Preferences on 40 per cent of its export value. This reveals the extent to which the international competitiveness of the Malaysian TV receiver industry is based on its real strengths at the national and firm levels. Although the Mexican clusters are more impressive than the Malaysian plants from the point of view of sheer production and export volumes, the actual competitive advantages of the export-oriented Malaysian production facilities appear to outdo those of the Mexican producers.

The three export-oriented TNC affiliates occupy a pivotal position within their parent company networks. The two subsidiaries that volunteered quantitative information contributed 20 to 30 per cent of total sales of their respective TNCs. One firm's regional responsibility covered the whole of Asia, while the other firm's sales region encompassed all regions except North America and Western Europe. One of the TNCs had transferred its Asian regional headquarters from Singapore to Malaysia. The role of the third company was to be a supplier base for its TNC's international operations, including Western Europe and North America.[45]

In contrast, the position of the two companies from the Republic of Korea in the sample is more modest. Their importance in their respective TNC networks derives solely from their presence on the Malaysian market. However, they need to be quite competitive in order to do well, since the "big three" export-oriented affiliates – Sony, Matsushita and Sharp – sell part of their output on the Malaysian market as well.

3.4.2.2 Human capital formation

The strategic objectives of the five companies in the sample differ. One emphasized the expansion of current operations, another the development of world-class technology, another the development of new markets, and another quality. In spite of these differences, the firms are similar in terms of the activities they undertake to reach their goals. The improvement of human resources is considered to be of central importance, second only to

---

[44] The situation of the recent entrants from the Republic of Korea may be a bit different, however. One of them stated that the prospect of an ASEAN free trade area had been a factor in its decision to enter the Malaysian market.

[45] One of the companies even produced a modern wide-screen model for the Japanese market.

technology. The three big exporters employed large numbers of production workers (about 8,000 in total), of whom approximately 20 per cent were skilled. Thus, the majority of the labour force still constitutes unskilled labour. In this respect there is very little difference between the Mexican companies in the Tijuana cluster and the large Malaysian exporters. Like the Mexican subsidiaries, the Malaysian exporters are devoting about 2 to 3 per cent of their payroll to worker training. They have considerable internal resources to conduct in-house training. They also carry out a considerable amount of training of personnel from other subsidiaries and affiliates of their TNC network, which is further evidence of their central role in their networks. They constitute an appropriate learning environment for staff from plants in the entire region, which suggests that they are at the leading edge in terms of technology and production methods used. Formal training by outside institutions was much less common.

3.4.2.3 Technology development

All five firms in the sample attach great importance to the improvement of productive efficiency, but differ in how they achieve it. While the big three exporters stressed technology improvement, the two Korean firms were more concerned with cost reduction. This suggests that competition in world markets is more demanding in terms of quality and design than the host-country market. This is reflected in technological differences between the two groups of firms. The exporters use world-class technology: in all three cases the production process is fully automated (including the receipt of inputs, assembly into final products or components, and the handling of inventories and shipping), using numerically-controlled machine tools, robots, computer-aided design stations and programmable transportation units. All three are ISO 9001 certified. In contrast, the two firms assembling CKD kits for the two companies from the Republic of Korea use considerably less sophisticated technology and do not have ISO certification.

Even in the three big exporters, the core technology came principally from the parent companies. Two firms received mainly process / production technology from their parent firms, while the third obtained primarily management technology. However, these companies had also developed considerable internal capabilities for generating technological improvements. One firm had begun to assume importance as a technology provider to other affiliates within its TNC network. All three companies had significant R&D facilities in Malaysia, employing a large number of professionals (about 70 per firm) and with a budget of about 1 per cent of the subsidiary's sales. Product design was an important activity, and prototypes were being made locally by two firms. One firm had a pilot plant.

However, the main focus of local R&D lies in applied incremental technological and organizational improvements rather than major innovations. This may help to explain the absence of linkages with local science and technology institutions. Improvements were mainly aimed at adapting equipment and components, saving on labour costs and achieving a higher level of commitment among workers who have a high tendency to "job-hop" (facilitated by the tight labour market conditions in Malaysia in the first half of the 1990s). The organizational improvements comprise the reorganization of production lines, the introduction of quality circles, the application of statistical control processes and the introduction of just-in-time inventory control systems. These changes had led to increased productivity and improvements in quality, delivery, sales and customer satisfaction.

The two firms from the Republic of Korea have no R&D facilities in Malaysia at all. This is related to the limited technological requirements of the assembly activities, but also to the fact that they are recent arrivals. They do, however, provide a technological input to their contract manufacturers in the sense that the assembly activities are undertaken under supervision of their own engineers and technicians.

3.4.2.4 Building local supplier networks

The local supplier base of Malaysia's electrical equipment and electronics industry is more developed than those of Mexico and Thailand. By 1994, imports of parts as a percentage of exports of finished electronics products were only about 38 per cent (compared to over 60 per cent in the case of Thailand).[46] However, the most critical and complex local parts and components were manufactured mainly by foreign-owned supplier companies rather than by national firms. The latter tended to supply simple items like metals, plastics and packaging materials (Rasiah, 1996, p. 186; Sieh and Yew, forthcoming). In contrast with Taiwan Province of China and Singapore, local firms were not involved in the production of parts and components with a significant technological content. The efforts of the TNCs interviewed to increase local content took the form of augmenting in-house production and inducing Japanese and other overseas suppliers to set up local facilities, rather than upgrading local producers. Other studies have reported similar findings.[47] Thus, the long presence of the consumer electronics TNCs has not led to significant backward linkages with the local economy, in the form of technology diffusion or transfer of modern management practices.

The Government of Malaysia did not do much to promote the development of local linkages until recently. It did stipulate minimum local sourcing requirements in 1989, but these were quite modest.[48] However, a growing awareness of the problem led to several new policy initiatives. The Second Industrial Master Plan of 1996 emphasized a cluster approach towards industrial development (Ariff and Yew, 1996, p. 4), based on four key elements: the value chain, local value added, key suppliers and the requisite economic foundation. One of the eight clusters highlighted in the Master Plan is the electronics and electrical equipment industry. A key objective is to capture a larger share of the value-added generated in the value chain locally. This requires encouraging localization of a variety of activities, including R&D, product design, subsequent product improvement, prototyping, process design, procurement of parts and materials, sub-assembly and final assembly, quality control, distribution and marketing. The strengthening of key local suppliers in partnership with large firms and government support institutions is a critical element in the cluster-based approach (Pyke, 1998).

---

[46] The comparable figure for Singapore was 32.7 per cent, which is not much lower than the Malaysian percentage (Rasiah, 1996, p. 176).

[47] ESCAP (1998, p. 109), refers to several relevant studies. See also Rasiah (1990) and Ariff and Yew (1996, pp. 24-25, 54 and 56).

[48] In order to be eligible for certain incentives associated with FDI, new entrants were required to reach 50 per cent local sourcing, later changed to 20 per cent local value-added and 30 per cent local sourcing (Ariff and Yew, 1996).

A second important policy initiative is the support provided to indigenous Malay-owned small and medium-sized businesses. Under the initiative, support is provided for product development and design, market promotion, quality and productivity improvement and the preparation of feasibility studies, with financial incentives to link smaller businesses with larger companies.

Judging from the responses of the three big exporters, it is evident that they need to put more emphasis on the localization of R&D. The promotion of technology transfer and diffusion through the building of backward linkages with national companies is well understood, but remedying the problem of limited local linkages will take considerable time and effort. The companies are required to deal with the problem just as they are in the process of moving into more sophisticated models with increasingly high-technology components, the manufacture of which requires advanced technological capabilities that domestic small and medium-sized suppliers may not readily possess. A significant amount of technical assistance will have to be provided by the TNCs as well as by the public sector to upgrade national suppliers to the level required.

3.4.3 Thailand

3.4.3.1 Setting and competitive performance of the industry

By 1995-1996, the TV industry in Thailand accounted for 5 per cent of total imports by OECD countries of television sets, making it the seventh-largest supplier in those countries (table 3.2). Like its counterpart in Malaysia, its main destination markets are Japan, where it holds 20 per cent of the market, and North America, where it holds 5 per cent (table 3.3). As with Malaysia, the industry's growth was driven predominantly by the booming demand for TV sets in Japan. Yet the Thai case is not as spectacular as those of Mexico or Malaysia. With a total production volume of 6.1 million sets, it is the smallest of the three centres. With 1.5 million units (almost 25 per cent of the total) destined for the local market, it is also the least export-oriented of the three. More importantly, however, the Thai TV industry mainly competes at the price-sensitive lower end of the international market. Its main competitive advantages derive from low-cost labour and government financial incentives, rather than from an advanced science and technology system, human capabilities, modern physical infrastructure and a strong local supply network. This is so even in the three leading exporters (Thomson, World Electric and JVC) that produce about two-thirds of total output.

This is reflected in interviews with five companies (marked with an asterisk in table 3.10). The most advanced of these companies is JVC, one of the three "first division" companies producing predominantly for export markets. Then there is a medium-sized joint venture exporting Sharp models, and three relatively small firms (Hitachi, Samsung and Philips) producing mainly for the domestic market. Hitachi and Samsung are joint ventures, while Philips is a full foreign subsidiary. The sample is a good cross-section of the industry, reflecting its diversity in terms of ownership structure, degree of export orientation and level of technological advancement. Together, the five assemblers account for about a quarter of the total productive capacity in Thailand.

The diversity of the industry is reflected in differences in the competitive situations of the five companies. The two large and medium-sized exporters, operating in the most competitive segment of the industry in international terms, have experienced an increase in export market share in recent years. One of the three smaller domestically oriented firms also increased its exports from 20 to 40 per cent of total sales, as a result of a deliberate policy change involving heavy restructuring of the relatively old plant. The fourth company, on the other hand, saw its exports decline, while the fifth did not export at all.[49]

The main markets of the Thai producers are in Asia. Only the biggest of the four exporters (JVC) sold a significant proportion of its production outside the region. Japan was also an important market for this company, as well as for the Sharp joint venture. About half of their output is sold there. On the other hand, the markets of the two smaller exporters were concentrated in less developed countries in Asia. All faced severe competition. The producers of the common 14-inch colour televisions found it difficult to compete with the Republic of Korea's Goldstar model, while the assemblers of larger models faced the toughest competition from Matsushita's Panasonic brand.

The three firms with growing export markets exhibited expansive strategies. The other two firms behaved defensively, aiming to contain the situation. The strategic objectives and activities of the three exporters were closely aligned with those of their parent companies, which suggests that the most successful affiliates in the sample constitute important elements in their TNC networks. The largest exporter was considered a principal production site within its parent network; the other companies did not occupy such a prominent position. The small domestic producer had a more modest role of catering to the domestic market. The other three companies were somewhere between these poles.

In spite of the diversity of competitive performance in the sample, all the companies' assessments of the Thai policy environment and the international market environment for FDI point to the importance of traditional competitive advantages. They were appreciative of the Government's labour policy, tax incentives, export duty drawback scheme and trade liberalization, and the financial incentives for FDI offered by BOI were considered to be good. With regard to international markets, the companies interviewed brought up the issue of trade preferences. Even though GSP does not apply in their main markets, trade preferences were considered to be potentially important in the context of the ASEAN Free Trade Area (AFTA). In this region, regional norms of origin will have a heavy impact on sourcing and heighten competition between Thailand and Malaysia.

However, the companies interviewed were critical of the main elements in Thailand's competitiveness, including weaknesses in physical infrastructure, skilled human resources, local supplier networks, and technology policies to promote supplier development and localization of R&D. In addition, they considered the 49 per cent foreign ownership limit on affiliates selling domestically as detrimental to the advancement of the industry.

---

[49] The fortunes of the companies on the domestic market were also mixed. Only two of the four increased their domestic market share (JVC did not sell in Thailand).

The following discussion illustrates that the TNCs have achieved little so far with respect to human resource development, technology upgrading, transfer and diffusion, and local backward linkages.

3.4.3.2 Human resources

As in the case of the Mexican and Malaysian firms, the parents of the Thai assemblers exerted most influence on their affiliates in the areas of technology selection, acquisition of equipment, implementation of organizational and managerial improvements, and selection of export markets (in that order). However, the Thai-based firms interviewed differed from the affiliates interviewed in Mexico and Malaysia in their assessment of the internal factors that had contributed most to their competitive performance. While the Mexican and Malaysian subsidiaries ranked technology-related aspects highest, followed by human resource-related elements, for the Thai assemblers, human resources came first, and technology second.

This may reflect the fact that reliance on low-paid labour had contributed more to their competitiveness than technological prowess. The average affiliate had 370 workers, of whom 77 per cent were production workers. Only about 12 per cent of the labour force was classified as skilled.[50] The scarcity of skilled workers in the labour market was considered to be the most important constraint in the human resources area. High salaries, high turnover (also a sign of tight labour markets) and low productivity (related to lack of skill and education) were also mentioned. Firms did try to remedy these problems to some extent through training. The average expenditure on training was 1.2 per cent of sales, but there were large differences between the individual firms.

Changes in work organization were considered more important tools for improving labour productivity than training. The principal measures introduced were quality control circles, just-in-time inventory control and work teams (in that order). They had resulted in improved quality, higher productivity and improved labour relations. The importance of these efforts suggests that Thailand is losing its low-wage advantage in the field of TV receiver assembly, but it does not yet possess a sufficiently skilled labour base to sustain the requirements for moving up-market.

3.4.3.3 Technology development

Technology-related factors were also important in increasing efficiency and competitiveness. The main pattern is similar to that observed in Malaysia and Mexico: the parent firms exercise a high degree of control in this sphere. Four of the five companies used fully automated state-of-the-art technology; the fifth used semi-automated equipment. Four out of five firms are ISO 9002 certified, while the fifth is in the process of obtaining certification.

---

[50] The question is whether labour is really not skilled, or whether it is categorized as unskilled so as to justify low wages.

But there are also some differences between these firms and those in the other two countries. In the Thai subsidiaries there is no product design or R&D whatsoever. Only minor innovations are applied in response to local demand and the nature of raw materials. There is nevertheless some diversity within the Thai sample between the top-end producers and those at the lower end. The expanding exporters (especially JVC) gave more emphasis to factors relating to technology, product quality, specialization and work organization, while the less successful companies mentioned low wages and competitive prices more often.

3.4.3.4 Building local supplier networks

Thailand displays less local sourcing of parts and components than countries such as Singapore and Malaysia, but far more than Mexico. For the electronics industry as a whole, imports of parts as a percentage of exports of finished products reached over 60 per cent in the early 1990s, down from 90 per cent in 1984 (UNCTAD, 1996, pp. 120-121). While this is an advance, locally-owned Thai companies were not involved. The pattern is similar to that in Malaysia and Mexico, but the magnitudes differ. There has been a tendency for existing foreign TV assemblers to extend backwards into major components assembly, and for new foreign companies to come in and start assembling components from imported parts. For example, National Thai (a Japanese-Thai joint venture) assembles tuners and speakers, for sale to TV assemblers producing for the domestic market. National Thai, JVC and Sanyo also assemble flyback transformers. JVC and Sanyo make transformers and capacitors and JVC and Tatung (a subsidiary from Taiwan Province of China) make printed circuit boards (PCBs). Even so, most of the critical components, for example the main PCB chassis, are still imported (Nipon and Pawadee, 1998, pp. 157-210).

The only significant step forward has been the establishment of a local cathode ray tube plant, which is a government-sponsored joint venture between a local cement company, Mitsubishi (Japan) and several local-based TV assemblers. It became viable to establish this plant in 1990 when import duties were raised from 10 to 30 per cent (until 1995). Production rose from 600,000 units initially to about 3 million in 1997. The plant operates with state-of-the-art technology. While the original product contained a very high degree (80 per cent) of imported components and parts, the more recent sourcing of the glass screen and other parts such as the electron gun have raised national content (Board of Investment, 1993, p. 8). Quality is reportedly good, as indicated by the fact that one-half of the output is incorporated into TV sets for export. This success has not, however, been followed in other major components (Supapol, 1996).

The Government of Thailand is aware of the problem and has been emphasizing the development of backward linkages since 1993. It offers a five-year exemption (including tariff-free imports of raw materials and capital goods) for component makers. However, this seems to have benefited mainly foreign-owned companies. As in Malaysia and Mexico, the integration of Thai-owned companies as suppliers of parts and components is problematic. A BOI study reported on the low quality of many existing would-be suppliers, the lack of local marketing facilities due to low national demand, and a preference to cater for export markets among those suppliers that do exist as a result of the tax structure. The reduction of import duties to 1 per cent in 1994 made it even more difficult for local suppliers to compete. For reasons of quality and delivery reliability, the TNC assemblers prefer to either produce in-house or to rely on established supplier networks abroad or on local-based foreign companies. These networks are difficult to penetrate by small Thai companies. In some cases, foreign assemblers also need headquarter authorization to try out Thai suppliers (Board of Investment, 1993, p. 42). For the situation to improve, more is needed than general incentives that do not discriminate between locally owned and foreign firms. This is a major challenge for the BOI Unit for Industrial Linkage Development (BUILD) in the years to come.

If the Thai TV industry is to progress towards regional assembly status and eventually become a regional manufacturing centre, it will have to promote a much stronger local supplier base, overcome the scarcity of skilled labour and remedy the weak science and technology infrastructure. These factors are beginning to emerge as serious obstacles now that the Thai TV industry is getting out of the first, low-wage assembly phase. While the country's industrial policy focusing on financial incentives for FDI was successful for the first stage, that does not seem to be the case for the consolidation of the second phase, and even less so for the stages that lie beyond.

3.5. Conclusions

The internationalization strategies of electronics TNCs are having a profound impact on the worldwide restructuring of activity in the TV industry. The scene is dominated by a limited number of world-class players who are currently shaping regional (and even global) systems of integrated production. Some developing countries are being incorporated into global production and distribution networks, while others are left behind. For countries that aspire to belong to TNC systems, it is vital to be familiar with the different corporate strategies pursued by these leading players. Policy makers must understand the factors motivating TNC investment location decisions, and the likely effects of their activities on industrial restructuring and the building up of industrial competitiveness of the developing countries in which they invest. Insight into these issues can help them to reap the potential benefits of TNC investments through well-designed and targeted policies.

The interviews conducted with leading TNCs in the TV receiver industry in Mexico, Malaysia and Thailand shed some light on these matters. They make it possible to assess the contribution made by these companies to production, exports, human capital formation, technological development and the building of local supplier linkages. Important inter-country differences and similarities emerge in terms of these variables, and in terms of strategic and policy factors. The impact is summed up in table 3.11.

Malaysia is the most advanced of the three countries with regard to these criteria. The operations of the leading three producers qualify it as an established regional manufacturing centre, on its way towards establishing a global presence. The industry makes a sizeable contribution to the country's industrial output and export earnings. It also holds a dominant share in the demanding Japanese market, employs modern production technology and organizational techniques, and has reached high levels of local value-added. The skill levels of its workforce are rising, and there is an emphasis on training for local as well as overseas employees. It has excellent quality standards and has an emerging independent R&D function

Table 3.11. Impact of TNCs on industrialization in Malaysia, Mexico and Thailand

Classification	Malaysia Ranging from **national assembly centre** to **manufacturing centre**	Mexico **Regional assembly centre**, moving towards **regional manufacturing centre**	Thailand Ranging from **national assembly centre** to **regional assembly centre**
Impact on:			
- Production and exports	Significant	Highly significant	Moderate
- Human capital formation	Modest until mid-1990s but rising. Specialized staff still mainly foreign, but significant training by leading firms, also for partners in their regional TNC networks. Rising skill levels and increasing numbers of specialized technical and managerial staff.	Very limited until early 1990s; first signs of upgrading apparent. Significant training efforts and linking with local education institutions, rising labour skill levels and increasing numbers of specialized technical and managerial staff.	Very limited until mid-1990s. First modest signs of improvement. Low but rising skill levels of labour force and emphasis on labour training; not much evidence of increasing involvement of more highly educated specialized staff.
- Technology development	Significant progress in automation, quality improvement, and localization of R&D and design is under way.	Significant progress in automation and quality improvement, but technology efforts limited to minor adaptive work. No independent R&D/design functions.	Top-end of industry uses world-class technology and quality standards, but rest of industry is less developed. No local R&D and design capabilities.
- Local supplier upgrading	Limited involvement of domestic suppliers in less complex areas. Considerable sourcing by foreign component suppliers.	Involvement of domestic suppliers is almost zero. Some links with foreign suppliers beginning to occur.	Limited involvement of domestic suppliers in less complex areas. Considerable sourcing by foreign component suppliers.

Source : UNCTAD.

that includes product design and prototyping. There is a considerable network of parts and components suppliers in the Asian region and within the country, although not much headway has been made with the integration of local Malaysian companies. Backward linkages occur predominantly through expansion of the assemblers into component production, and the local establishment of foreign-owned supplier companies. The lack of involvement of locally owned companies in the production of technologically demanding parts and components that would help diffuse new technological knowledge is the most critical weakness of the Malaysian TV production network.

The top three producers in Malaysia no longer exploit the traditional comparative advantages of low-cost labour, financial incentives and trade preferences. Importantly, upgrading was not achieved by trade privileges provided by other countries or exchange rate devaluations that drove up the cost of imported parts and components. Although the increasing strength of the yen played some part in the relocation of parts and components production from Japan to other countries in the region, FDI policy also played an important role in Malaysia. This encouraged TNCs to develop their Malaysian operations into an integral element of their global production operations. This was achieved in the first instance through various financial incentives and the absence of restrictions on FDI activities, but also through heavy investments in advanced physical infrastructure. The need to promote Malaysian companies as suppliers has been recognized and is receiving attention through various programmes and policy measures. Nevertheless, the scarcity of specialized technical staff is still a major weakness. Companies have filled the gap by relying on expatriates, but this will constitute a significant barrier to further upgrading the industry.

Foreign companies in Malaysia also benefited from "first mover advantages" and the existence of TV manufacturing expertise built up by local firms during the import-substitution period. The existence of these local capabilities enabled foreign TNCs to import their CKD kits into the country and have them assembled by domestic firms under contract, destined for the Malaysian market. Although contract activities cannot be expected to have spectacular spin-offs in terms of human capital formation or technological diffusion in the short term, they do contribute to employment generation and have enabled local companies to continue their participation in this important sector. They have to operate in a market environment in which the three top-end producers (which also operate on the domestic market) set the standards. It remains to be seen whether some of these contract arrangements will lead to more substantial manufacturing activity and higher value-added generation over time.

In Mexico, the Tijuana TV receiver cluster, involving the operations of Matsushita, Sony, Hitachi, Sanyo, Samsung and JVC, qualifies it as a regional assembly centre serving the North American market. In terms of quantitative impact on the economy, Mexico is the most impressive of the three cases. The industry has a significant share in Mexico's industrial output, employment and foreign exchange earnings. Moreover, since the entry into force of NAFTA and the peso crisis in 1994, there have been signs that the industry may be transforming into a regional manufacturing centre. In particular, the cluster is beginning to move beyond being an employer of large numbers of unskilled low-wage workers. Employment of technically and managerially qualified staff is rising, and relationships are emerging with local colleges and universities to cater for the skill requirements of the TV companies. This constitutes an important link with the national economy.

However, the Mexican case is less impressive in qualitative terms. In comparison with Malaysia, the emphasis in the Mexican cluster is still mainly on assembly, as evidenced by the extremely high import content. There is also less of an independent R&D function in the companies. This may be partly due to the recent establishment of the industry. Mexico's technical skill base is larger than that of Malaysia, which gives it good potential for upgrading in the years to come. However, limited promotion through national policy has also played a role. In contrast with Malaysia and Thailand, the location factor has been crucial, in combination with the trade preferences enjoyed in the United States market due to the existence of HTS 9802, and later the NAFTA rules of origin. The major contribution of the Government of Mexico was the establishment of the *maquiladora* free trade zone. The combination of these factors resulted in a very high degree of component sourcing from the United States, which resulted in very low value added in Mexico for long periods of time. Although the situation is now improving, these factors remain influential. For example, many of the major TV receiver TNCs continue to maintain their regional R&D facilities across the border in the United States. Only recently has Mexico begun to formulate a more proactive stance aimed at deepening the industrial activities in the cluster, but it will take considerable time and effort before any results can be expected, especially in the area of integrating Mexican supplier companies into the TV production networks. Their current level of involvement is virtually zero.

In terms of impact on the national economy, the achievements of the TV industry in Thailand have been the most modest of the three. Although the top end of the industry can be classified as a regional assembly centre, it is not in the same league as Mexico. The three largest assemblers are certainly competitive in Asian markets, in terms of technology and management practices. Yet the TNCs to which they belong are in the "second division" of the world's big producers, and they compete predominantly on the basis of the traditional advantages of low-cost labour and financial incentives. Employment of skilled workers is quite limited and independent R&D in the TNC affiliates is virtually non-existent. There are also infrastructure bottlenecks, and the local supplier base is weak. Most of the critical and technologically advanced components are imported. The involvement of Thai suppliers is very limited.

The medium and bottom segments of the Thai TV receiver industry do not even measure up to this level. There are quite a few medium-sized producers that produce for minor (not leading) Asian markets, as well as several smaller and older joint-venture companies producing for the domestic market. The latter remind us of the old national assembler type operations observed during the import-substitution period.

Government policy has played an important role in shaping the Thai TV industry, but not all of the policies have had the anticipated results. The companies interviewed welcomed the financial incentives, but felt that a lot more needed to be done in the area of infrastructure creation, education, and support for the localization of science and technology-related activities. The policy aimed at promoting Thai involvement in the industry through minimum local participation in ventures producing for the domestic market has not contributed much to the creation of a competitive industry. Recently, however, that policy has been redefined and some restructuring in the domestic market may take place. The current economic crisis will also contribute to fierce competition among the producers, which the weaker ones are unlikely to survive. The Government is now also giving attention to upgrading local suppliers through the BOI Unit for Industrial Linkage Development, which is a positive development, but it is too early to judge its outcome.

The analysis offers policy lessons. The Governments of developing countries cannot affect directly the location decisions of TNCs that are responding to technical and market dynamics. However, they can influence their own attractiveness as sites for TNC production. In the foreseeable future TNCs will continue to look for sites that are advantageous for simple assembly, both for domestic and regional markets. In such sites the main attractions are low-wage unskilled labour, liberal investment rules, tax incentives for equipment investment and basic physical infrastructure. With regard to qualifying as regional assembly platforms, export incentives and perhaps trade preferences in leading markets in economically advanced countries may be important inducements. In the longer term, TNCs will be increasingly interested in sites that allow the efficient production of complex products, and high-skill design and development functions. Upgrading into regional or even global manufacturing centres requires a proactive national policy aimed at transforming traditional sources of competitive advantage into more substantive forms.

The Malaysian case showed that it is possible for some developing countries to cater effectively to such interests. Important elements in Malaysia's support package were well attuned to what the TNCs concerned were looking for at each particular moment, and were flexible enough to evolve in line with the evolution of the internationalization process that the companies were going through. Over time, increasing attention was given to a local support structure for science and technology and advanced physical infrastructure. The Malaysian example shows that, under a conducive policy regime, TNCs gradually upgraded their activities. However, it also shows that more proactive policies are needed on education and local supplier development if the process is to be accelerated.

The discussion and interviews suggest that the effective advancement of host country sites can be extremely difficult, even if Governments are aware of their importance. Even in the relatively successful Malaysian case there was a notable lack of progress in the area of incorporation of local (as opposed to foreign) suppliers of parts and components. This is a significant shortcoming because the development of a local supplier base is crucial if advanced technological and managerial knowledge and skills are to be diffused throughout the country's industrial sector. Without the development of such backward linkages, TNCs are not functioning as "engines" of local industrial development. While all three Governments realize this and have policies and programmes aimed at upgrading the local supplier base, it remains to be seen how well these will succeed in bringing domestic suppliers up to the required standards. In this regard, there may be some tension between welcoming foreign investors and meeting long-term national development objectives. A constructive dialogue and cooperation between policy makers in the developing country and leading TNCs might be one element in ensuring success. This is all the more vital since various WTO and regional agreements are reshaping the rules on the use of policy instruments that were until recently widely used to encourage "rooting" of foreign investors in developing host countries, in particular as regards local content, industrial promotion through selective incentives such as credit, and ability to screen FDI.

Chapter 4

The garments industry

4.1. Introduction

Garment manufacturing, as an organized industrial activity, was essentially concentrated in the leading western countries and Japan in the 1950s. It began to spread to the four "Asian tigers" in the 1960s and 1970s, and then moved across the globe in the 1980s and 1990s. It is found in the poorest countries such as Eritrea and Viet Nam, and in island economies such as the Maldives (Gereffi, 1994a, p. 221). This geographical dispersal signals a sustained shift away from high-wage industrialized economies to low-wage developing ones. The share of developing countries in world clothing output has steadily increased since the 1980s.

Apparel manufacture is attractive for countries launching export-oriented industrialization. Labour-intensive techniques have remained economically viable, at least in important stages of production that are intrinsically difficult to mechanize (notably sewing). Improvements in communication technologies and falling transport and communication costs have reduced the disadvantages of being located far from destination markets and have shortened delivery times. This has allowed the geographical separation of the labour-intensive parts of the manufacturing process from the more skill- and capital-intensive parts. The location of production in the developing world was heavily influenced by the allocation of export quotas under the Multi-Fibre Arrangement (MFA). Latecomers with unfilled quotas were able to attract significant investment from countries with higher wages or filled quotas. Barriers to entry were low because of simple skill and technological needs. Governments responded by establishing export processing zones and providing incentives to assemblers. Together, these factors allowed account for the industry to take-off in developing countries.

This chapter examines the role played by TNCs in the development of the garment industry in developing countries, and assesses the extent to which this allowed host countries to use the sector as a launch pad for export-oriented industrial development and international competitiveness. We look at the industry in three countries that have recently developed into major garment exporters: Costa Rica, the Dominican Republic and Morocco.

4.2. Overview and setting

4.2.1 Global patterns of production and trade

The major garment-producing countries are a remarkably mixed lot. In terms of employment, the largest by far is China, which employs an estimated 1.6 million people in the industry. The second position is taken by the United States, with 770,000 workers. The Russian Federation comes third with 630,000 and Japan fourth with 450,000. There are also several big clothing producers in South Asia and the ASEAN countries. Advanced countries in Western Europe are also well represented. Four large countries – the United Kingdom, France, Germany and Italy – each employed between 115,000 and 170,000 people in the early 1990s. In addition, there are sizeable apparel manufacturers in Eastern Europe, and many smaller participants among the developing countries of North Africa and the Caribbean Basin.

The 50 largest clothing exporters to OECD countries together accounted for 90 per cent of all OECD garment imports in 1996. The two biggest source regions for the international trade in clothing are Asia and Europe. North America is a sizeable producing area, but its role as an exporter is very modest. Four out of the top 10 suppliers to the OECD market in 1996 were Asian: China, Hong Kong (China), India and the Republic of Korea. Turkey has the largest developing country share, after China and Hong Kong (China). Europe (especially Italy, Germany, France and Portugal) remains the second biggest source of garment imports to OECD countries (table 4.1).

This static picture does not show the dynamics of the industry. In the 1960s, the industry was the domain of North America and Europe. Things began to change with the rise of Japan, followed by the ascent of the four East Asian NIEs (Hong Kong (China), the Republic of Korea, Taiwan Province of China and, to a lesser extent, Singapore) in the 1960s and 1970s. In the 1980s, other Asian economies, especially ASEAN members and China, began to initiate large-scale export production (Oman, 1989). Japan and the four NIEs began to lose out to these new Asian arrivals, and also to other developing countries in North Africa (especially Morocco), and the Central Caribbean Basin (notably Costa Rica, the Dominican Republic and Honduras). Clothing output also expanded to some extent in Eastern Europe, especially in Bulgaria and Romania (Dicken, 1998, p. 291).

The comparison of countries' market shares in 1980 and 1996 in table 4.1 reveals these dynamic patterns. In broad terms, the developed countries and the four East Asian NIEs have been losing market share, while developing countries have been making significant inroads during the past 15 years.

- Europe is on a path of secular decline. Italy, a traditional stronghold of the garment industry, is still the number two supplier of OECD countries, but its share has been declining since 1980. The same holds for Belgium/Luxembourg, France, Germany, Greece, the Netherlands and the United Kingdom. The exception is Portugal, the country with the lowest wages in Europe, which has improved its position in the league table. However, taken together, the importance of European producers has been on the wane. In 1996 their joint share was under 30 per cent of total OECD countries' imports, down from 63 per cent in 1963, and 45 per cent in 1980.

- The initial challenge to Europe was posed by Japan and the East Asian NIEs (mainly Hong Kong (China), the Republic of Korea and Taiwan Province of China), but these countries are increasingly displaced by lower-income countries. Japan, the earliest Asian competitor, has now practically withdrawn from clothing production for export altogether. The three East Asian NIEs, which were major players in 1980, remain important suppliers, but they have suffered big reductions in OECD market share in the period 1980-1996. A dramatic decline occurred in the case of Hong Kong (China), which was the biggest OECD supplier in 1980, and is now in third place. The Republic of Korea was in third position in 1980, and by 1996 had slid to seventh place.

Table 4.1. Fifty largest garment exporters to OECD countries, 1980 and 1996

	Economy	Import market share in OECD [a]			Garments as per cent of country's total		
		1980	1996	Annual change Per cent	1980	1996	Annual change Per cent
1	China	2.74	17.70	12.4	10.52	19.11	3.8
2	Italy	12.89	8.05	-2.9	8.17	7.15	-0.8
3	Hong-Kong, China	13.72	6.72	-4.4	37.53	33.20	-0.8
4	Turkey	0.36	3.87	16.0	5.97	37.29	12.1
5	Germany	6.93	3.78	-3.7	1.78	1.44	-1.3
6	India	2.09	3.23	2.8	13.60	21.57	2.9
7	Rep of Korea	9.13	2.95	-6.8	25.82	6.96	-7.9
8	France	5.37	2.70	-4.2	2.45	1.81	-1.9
9	Portugal	1.72	2.51	2.4	16.25	17.64	0.5
10	Mexico	0.77	2.42	7.4	1.59	4.42	6.6
11	Indonesia	0.21	2.39	16.4	0.35	10.19	23.5
12	United Kingdom	4.12	2.34	-3.5	1.98	1.80	-0.6
13	Taiwan Prov. of China	6.62	2.18	-6.7	15.44	4.61	-7.3
14	Thailand	0.66	1.95	7.0	5.66	8.33	2.4
15	United States	2.04	1.78	-0.8	0.50	0.70	2.1
16	Tunisia	1.00	1.75	3.6	20.05	52.52	6.2
17	Malaysia	0.48	1.64	8.0	1.86	5.33	6.8
18	Philippines	1.41	1.62	0.9	9.17	14.45	2.9
19	Poland	0.80	1.60	4.4	5.75	13.43	5.4
20	**Morocco**	**0.37**	**1.60**	9.6	**6.30**	**36.72**	11.6
21	Netherlands	1.79	1.42	-1.4	1.05	1.42	1.9
22	**Dominican Republic**	**0.28**	**1.28**	10.0	**9.17**	**45.45**	10.5
23	Belgium/Luxembourg	2.30	1.18	-4.1	1.63	1.43	-0.8
24	Pakistan	0.24	1.16	10.3	7.41	33.09	9.8
25	Romania	1.01	1.06	0.3	10.50	28.13	6.4
26	Greece	2.73	0.99	-6.1	24.25	20.20	-1.1
27	Honduras	0.04	0.79	20.5	1.66	49.09	23.6
28	Hungary	0.98	0.79	-1.3	12.65	9.59	-1.7
29	Canada	0.45	0.77	3.4	0.26	0.61	5.5
30	Spain	0.77	0.69	-0.7	1.83	1.34	-1.9
31	Denmark	0.95	0.61	-2.7	2.43	2.52	0.2
32	Austria	1.60	0.60	-5.9	4.59	2.27	-4.3
33	Guatemala	0.01	0.55	28.5	0.47	33.26	30.5
34	**Costa Rica**	**0.12**	**0.54**	9.9	**4.65**	**23.22**	10.6
35	El Salvador	0.06	0.47	13.7	2.33	49.30	21.0
36	Israel	0.71	0.47	-2.5	6.20	4.53	-1.9
37	Singapore	1.01	0.41	-5.5	5.12	1.34	-8.0
38	Jamaica	0.04	0.41	15.7	1.71	33.07	20.3
39	Ireland	0.61	0.39	-2.8	2.81	1.48	-3.9
40	Switzerland	0.82	0.36	-5.0	1.05	0.75	-2.1
41	Egypt	0.04	0.33	14.1	0.34	10.56	24.0
42	Bulgaria	0.17	0.30	3.6	6.96	14.50	4.7
43	Colombia	0.10	0.27	6.4	1.05	4.91	10.1
44	Japan	1.11	0.17	-11.1	0.59	0.11	-10.0
45	South Africa	0.13	0.17	1.7	0.36	1.51	9.4
46	Peru	0.03	0.16	11.0	0.42	7.02	19.2
47	Sweden	0.61	0.16	-8.0	0.86	0.36	-5.3
48	Brazil	0.25	0.14	-3.6	0.63	0.68	0.5
49	Australia	0.04	0.10	5.9	0.10	0.53	11.0
50	Finland	1.63	0.10	-16.0	5.53	0.54	-13.5
	All countries	94.05	89.62				

Source: ECLAC, CANPLUS.

[a] Export values for 1980 are three-year averages, those for 1996 are two-year averages. The ECLAC CANPLUS database does not include some large garment exporters such as Bangladesh, Mauritius and Sri Lanka, each of which exports garments with around $1.5 - 2 billion per year (about the same level as Morocco). Case study countries in bold.

- The European and advanced Asian producers are being displaced by a number of less developed countries. The largest slices of the market are taken by large developing countries in Asia, especially China; some big ASEAN countries and India have also moved to high positions in the league table. Elsewhere, there has been strong growth in the Caribbean/Latin American area. Mexico is the largest supplier in this region. Other OECD suppliers from this region include the Dominican Republic, Honduras, Costa Rica, Guatemala, Jamaica, El Salvador, Colombia and Peru. Since garment imports in these countries grew from a very small base, their growth rates have been spectacular. Growth in North Africa is visible in the rising shares of Tunisia, Morocco and Egypt, resulting in an import market share increase for Africa from 1.5 to 3.8 per cent.

Garments are now the main export item for many developing countries and economies. They constitute one-fifth or more of total exports for Hong Kong (China), Turkey, India, Tunisia, Morocco, the Dominican Republic, Pakistan, Romania, Greece, Honduras, Guatemala, Costa Rica, El Salvador and Jamaica. The three countries examined in this paper are all in this group.

There are important regional factors that affect the importance of different developing regions as suppliers to the main markets.

The *North American region* has been a rapidly growing destination of garment exports from developing countries. Its clothing imports expanded from an annual average of $7.9 billion in 1979-1981 to $42.8 billion in 1994-1995. There were also important changes in the composition of the trade flows. Caribbean and Latin American suppliers (especially Mexico), China and ASEAN grew at the expense of Japan, several European suppliers and East Asian NIEs. African suppliers were absent. The retreat of the four NIEs was dramatic. They together supplied almost 65 per cent of total imports in 1980, and saw their market share decline to 23 per cent in 1995. This chapter will examine the case of two Caribbean Basin countries – Costa Rica and the Dominican Republic – that have emerged as important suppliers of garments to this market.

In the larger but less dynamic *Western European market*, garment imports rose from an annual average of $23.1 billion in 1979-1981 to $75.7 billion in 1994-1995. There was a shift to Turkey and countries in Eastern Europe and North Africa. China and developing countries in South and South-East Asia also gained market share at the expense of the East Asian NIEs and European suppliers. Italy is the only exception: it strengthened its position to become the region's principal supplier. Latin American suppliers were absent. The third case study in this chapter looks at the case of one of the leading "Mediterranean Rim" suppliers ‑ Morocco.

In the *Japanese market*, imports rose from an annual average of $1.7 billion in 1979-1981 to $17.1 in 1994-1995. Japan's supply chain became increasingly centred on Asia. China made a huge advance, accounting for over half of Japan's total garment imports in 1995. Thailand and Indonesia also made notable advances. The three East Asian NIEs, which had held major shares of the Japanese market, were the hardest-hit by this shift in regional supply. Their joint share declined from 58 to 15 per cent. Some European suppliers,

---

notably France and the United Kingdom, also lost ground; suppliers from other regions were absent.

The emergence of a steadily increasing number of developing countries as competitive garment suppliers coincides with intensifying competition in the industry worldwide, especially from 1990 onwards. There are increasing pressures to step up restructuring and rationalization in the established producing countries. Two major factors are responsible for this development. Firstly, the trade barriers imposed by the MFA are to be phased out by the end of 2004 under WTO rules. The responses of firms include technological modernization, increased outsourcing and relocation to lower-cost sites. These efforts will have positive as well as negative implications for developing countries as suppliers of garments on the world market (see section 4.2.3).

Secondly, although there are regional variations, the growth of demand in the major markets has been decelerating in the 1990s. Table 4.2 shows that over the period 1980-1995, garment exports grew by 10 per cent per annum, which was 1.4 percentage points faster than all manufactures. However, much of that growth was in the 1980s, when garment exports rose at 3 percentage points faster than world trade in manufactures. In the 1990s, growth decelerated. Demand for clothing is not highly income-elastic in rich economies, and there is only so much that firms can do to mitigate this trend by introducing quality and design improvements.

Table 4.2. World garment exports, 1980-1995

Product category	Values (Thousands of dollars)			Growth rates		
	1980	1990	1995	1980-1990	1990-1995	1980-1995
Men's outerwear, non-knitted	7 107 861.8	16 513 130.5	24 903 546.8	8.8	8.6	8.7
Women's outerwear, non-knitted	7 533 279.0	25 173 053.9	35 279 442.6	12.8	7.0	10.8
Undergarments, non-knitted	2 218 981.4	6 861 475.8	11 344 282.1	12.0	10.6	11.5
Outerwear, knitted, non-elastic	8 521 236.2	24 957 203.8	30 838 789.4	11.3	4.3	9.0
Undergarments, knitted	3 402 276.9	11 841 892.7	21 254 218.9	13.3	12.4	13.0
Textile clothing accessories, n.e.s.	1 607 521.8	4 763 952.4	6 584 617.6	11.5	6.7	9.9
Headgear, non-textile clothing	3 121 077.2	9 595 275.8	11 466 241.0	11.9	3.6	9.1
Garments, total	33 512 234.3	99 705 984.9	141 671 138.4	11.5	7.3	10.1

Source: Calculated from United Nations COMTRADE database.

Only two garment categories continued to grow at (lower) double-digit rates in the 1990s. Both are mainly mass-produced items, namely knitted and non-knitted undergarments. This suggests that room for expansion is concentrated in low-quality product segments, where lower wages are important for competitiveness and where competitive positions are least secure. Typically, these are market segments in which low-income countries do well. However, it is becoming increasingly difficult for new entrants to advance into higher value-added market segments. The boom that the garment industry as a whole experienced in earlier decades has come to an end, although specific high-growth niches are likely to continue to exist. We come back to this issue in section 4.2.3.

4.2.2 *Organizing the supply chain: FDI and inter-firm networks*

What are the major factors driving the rise and fall of countries in the trade league? Here, we look at the leading actors, how production and distribution is organized by them and why. We give special attention to the role played by TNCs.

During the past three decades, the garment industry has moved away from a system in which the entire chain from fibres to clothing was largely contained within national boundaries to a buyer-driven commodity chain (Doeringer et al., 1998a; Gereffi, 1996). This form of organization of production and distribution is characteristic of industries in which "large retailers, brand-name merchandisers, and trading companies play the pivotal role in setting up decentralized production networks in a variety of exporting countries, typically located in the Third World" (Elson, 1994, p. 194).

In contrast to more capital- and skill-intensive industries (such as the TV industry), the main players in buyer-driven chains are often not producers. Many leading actors do not own any production facilities; even if they do, their influence in the industry does not emanate from this fact. It comes from their capacity to set up and coordinate vast and complex (increasingly international) production networks with many actors, and to ensure that all the inputs supplied come together as an integrated whole. This ability to act as strategic brokers between factories, trading companies and consumers puts the big buying groups in a strategic position in the commodity chain, and gives them considerable leverage over their production networks.

There are two main reasons why a buyer-driven commodity chain has become the dominant organizational form in the garment industry:

- *The characteristics of the production process.* Sewing, the core phase of the production process, has remained labour-intensive and uses simple technology. The other three stages are more skill- and technology-intensive: design and engineering; pre-assembly, including pattern grading, marking and fabric cutting; and inspection and packaging. These functions have been growing increasingly sophisticated over time (see section 4.2.4), and can be retained in developed economies. Buyers who are not involved in production can play a leading role because advanced technical information about the production process is not required. The technology is largely embodied in equipment and can be quite easily transferred through training. The production of garments tends to be highly decentralized and fragmented, with numerous medium and small-scale garment manufacturing enterprises under local ownership. The process is suited to small-scale labour-intensive forms of production because of its modest skill requirements and because inputs other than labour (including raw materials, designs, inspection, quality control and sometimes even the equipment) can be readily provided by contractors.

- *The increasing complexity of the commercial function.* Demand growth is slackening in the high-income markets, and markets have become increasingly fragmented and differentiated. In the 1960s and 1970s, general retailers catered to mass markets with slow-changing fashions. In the 1980s and 1990s successful retailing has come to depend on the ability to create and cater to specific niches, and to initiate constant change in styles, models, colours and fabrics. This is especially so at the high end of the market. Only firms that are able to play the role of strategic brokers are able to do well; they need to be close to leading markets to collect the necessary information, and they need to mobilize and coordinate a variety of specialized services. They have to supply an array of functions, including product design, marketing, distribution, sales and provision of financial services.

The United States market shows many of the features of the buyer-driven network (Gereffi, 1996). The three principal types of participants are:

(1) large retailers, which may be department stores (e.g. J.C. Penney), mass merchandisers (e.g. Sears or Woolworth) or discounters (e.g. K-Mart or Wal-Mart);

(2) brand-name producers/merchandisers of fashion garments (e.g. The Gap, Liz Claiborne or Polo/Ralph Lauren);

(3) brand-name vertically integrated producers of standardized garments (e.g. Levi Strauss in jeans, or Fruit of the Loom in underwear).

In the United States and elsewhere, the importance of these big buying groups has been growing over time, whereas the proportion of clothing trade that finds its way to the market through independent traders and small independent retailers has been declining. For example, the 10 largest publicly-owned retailers in the United States are expected to have increased their share of the retail market from 34 per cent to 60 per cent between 1991 and 2000 (Gereffi, 1996). The increasing concentration in distribution and marketing activity has made the large buying groups increasingly powerful. There are high barriers to entry at the merchandising and retail levels. Companies' investments in product development, advertising and computerized inventory systems are huge (Gereffi, 1994a, p. 219). Typically, organizational arrangements are complex and may involve many other actors in specialized roles. Big retailers and brand-name merchandisers may rely on complex tiered networks of overseas production contractors that perform almost all their specialized tasks for them, including pre-assembly, assembly, inspection and packaging and shipping. Sometimes even the design and engineering function is partly or completely contracted out to specialist designer consulting companies.

The main pattern is that leading actors do not assume direct ownership of production, and a multitude of specialized firms is tied together under contractual relationships.[1] In the East Asian NIEs, for example, the garment industry has developed predominantly through such inter-firm networks (section 4.2.3). The garment industry is generally less FDI-driven than other major industries such as automobiles or electronics – there is less sheer "technology" involved. Outward FDI by the OECD countries in textiles, clothing and leather

---

[1] Buyer-driven chains have also developed in other labour-intensive consumer industries with similar market characteristics, such as footwear, toys and various household goods.

(TCL) together represents less than 2 per cent of the total, except for Japan and Italy (Audet, 1996, p. 345). The East Asian NIEs have become important sources of FDI to developing countries as their domestic garment industries have declined in the face of rising wage costs. They have established assembly facilities off-shore, not only in neighbouring countries (China) but also as far away as Latin America.

While there is some FDI in the industry, its role has varied by country depending on domestic industrial and entrepreneurial capabilities. Thus, in the East Asian NIEs, local firms were strong and FDI was never important; by contrast, newer entrants with weaker industrial traditions, serving the United States and Europe, have depended more on inward FDI. The countries considered below fall into this second category.

The main advantages provided by FDI in the garments industry are easy access to technical, management and organizational skills, modern production systems and labour training. There are also potential disadvantages, however. Affiliates in developing countries may be confined to the lower rungs of the quality ladder for long periods, without the option to develop independent design capabilities, different ranges, higher-value products or new markets. Independent producers may be able to upgrade and diversify more easily, provided they are supported in terms of technical and design skill development, export marketing assistance and access to finance (section 4.2.3).

The biggest outward investors in the TCL industries are Japan, with $4,615 million and the United States, with $1,954 million (at the end of 1991).[2] The other sizeable investors are France ($844 million) and Italy ($823 million). Other OECD countries are of minor importance. About 65 per cent of Japanese garment investments abroad have been in the Asian region, predominantly in the form of joint ventures. There is also much indirect involvement in the form of contractual assembly arrangements, under which Japanese partners provide the technology, pre-assembly inputs and textiles, while assembly is done by other Asian partners – increasingly in China. Most of the garments are exported to Japan itself (Audet, 1996, p. 346).

A major proportion of outward FDI from the United States has concentrated on assembly operations in the Caribbean Basin, Colombia and Mexico. It has come primarily in the form of assembly operations, taking advantage of provision 9802 of the United States Harmonized Tariff Schedule (HTS 9802), which provides duty concessions for goods made up of components made in the United States but assembled abroad, levying import tariffs only on value added abroad. FDI by European countries has been similar in character. The main aim has been to use low-wage sites on the Mediterranean Rim, primarily Morocco, Tunisia and Turkey for exports to the European Union. As in the United States, a combination of preferential market access and geographical proximity is the main driving force. In this case, they take the form of outward processing arrangements by the European

---

[2] Even though Japan is the biggest overseas OECD investor in garments, textiles and leather combined, its garment industry is far less internationalized than its textile industry; the opposite is true for the United States (see Dicken, 1998, p. 306).

Union and preferential trade agreements with Mediterranean countries. African countries can also benefit from lower tariffs and fewer restrictions on volume of exports to the European Union under the Lomé Convention (Audet, 1996, p. 331 and p. 346).

4.2.3   Possibilities for developing countries: past, present and future

The effects of garment production on the economies of exporting countries have been uneven. While the East Asian NIEs have used the industry as a vehicle for diversification and technological upgrading, others have made much less headway. Their principal involvement is still mainly in the nature of labour-intensive assembly operations that generate few benefits for their local economies except low-wage employment. This section sheds light on this divergence, and the implications for new entrants in the industry. To this end, we examine the main factors that drive the location decisions for garment manufacturing and that determine the nature of foreign involvement. These factors are:

- the specific sourcing strategies adopted by the leading actors, in interaction with
- important economic, technological and international trade-policy variables, and
- industrialization policies adopted by host Governments.

4.2.3.1   The East Asian NIEs: from export processing zones to original brand-name manufacture

The first players to obtain garments in low-wage countries were large United States retailers and brand-name merchandisers, who established buying houses in Japan and the East Asian NIEs, attracted by the entrepreneurial capabilities of these countries. The attractiveness of these NIEs was enhanced by their transition to export-orientation at a time when other developing countries were pursuing heavily inward-looking strategies. Clothing was made by local enterprises rather than foreign-owned plants. The buyers tended not to have manufacturing facilities at home. In the Republic of Korea, Taiwan Province of China and Japan, there were also pervasive restrictions on FDI. After a brief phase based on simple assembly, mainly in export processing zones (EPZs) near major ports, the industry moved to a system of brand-name subcontracting, also known as "specification contracting".[3] Under this arrangement, the supplying firm made products according to the design specified by the buyer (a separate firm). The product was distributed by the buyer under the buyer's brand name.

Brand-name subcontracting suited the retailers and brand-name merchandisers as well as the local suppliers. The former needed suppliers with manufacturing capability (which they did not possess) and with the logistical know-how to organize the supply of all parts that needed to go into production. The latter benefited by learning buyer preferences and international standards for price, quality and delivery, without bearing the costs of marketing and distribution. They also learnt to organize their own subcontracting networks, generating substantial domestic backward linkages in the process.

---

[3] The system is also commonly known as "original equipment manufacturing" (OEM), but this term is avoided in this chapter because no equipment is produced in the garment industry.

Over time, the learning generated by subcontracting enabled many local firms to proceed to original brand-name manufacturing (OBM). They established forward linkages to developed-country markets, creating their own design function and distributing their products under their own brands (Gereffi, 1997a). At the same time it enabled them to build extensive backward linkages overseas as they began to lose their competitiveness as manufacturing sites. Several factors pushed them in this direction. Rising wages and appreciating currencies began to erode their attractiveness. Trade regulations in destination market became increasingly restrictive. The voluntary export restraints negotiated by the United States and the United Kingdom in the 1950s formally became part of the General Agreement on Tariffs and Trade (GATT) in 1962. Under its Long-Term Arrangement, international trade in cotton textiles became subject to quotas. In 1973, the Long-Term Arrangement was replaced by the Multi-Fibre Arrangement (MFA), which was more restrictive in that it included all European countries and artificial fibre-based textiles (Dicken, 1998, pp. 299-302).

As quotas and rising costs began to constrain the industry in the NIEs, industrialists began to establish off-shore factories in lower-wage countries. These grew into extensive international networks. For example, Hong Kong (China) and Taiwan Province of China source extensively from China and South-East Asian countries; the Republic of Korea sources from Indonesia, the Democratic People's Republic of Korea and countries in the Caribbean region; while Singapore is present in Malaysia and Indonesia.[4] The East Asian newly-industrializing economies export directly to United States buyers from these assembly sites, taking advantage of the source countries' import quotas in the United States market.

The phenomenon has become known as "triangle manufacturing". It has changed newly-industrializing economy manufacturers from suppliers to United States retailers and merchandisers to important middlemen in the international commodity chain. Their networks encompass as many as 50 or 60 exporting countries, and are fiercely competitive in the industry. This development highlights the success of the strategy followed by the Asian newly-industrializing economies, built around continuous learning, from EPZs to brand-name subcontracting and original brand-name manufacturing (OBM). Their learning was supported by domestic policies to encourage export-oriented manufacturing and (in some of the countries) domestic entrepreneurship by placing restrictions on foreign ownership (Lall, 1996).

4.2.3.2 *Recent entrants: competing through EPZs, low wages and special access*

The East Asian strategy contrasts sharply with that of countries entering garment manufacturing in the 1980s, especially in Latin America, the Caribbean Basin and the Mediterranean Rim.[5] Their participation continues to hinge on the combined advantages of low wages and trade preferences. Their integration into international supply networks is driven primarily by the need of brand-name manufacturers in the developed economies to cope with stiff competition from Asia. Special market access, as granted by the HTS 9802

---

[4] For a case study of Taiwan Province of China, see Gereffi (1994b).

[5] There are several other major developing-country suppliers whose experience lies somewhere in between these two extremes, especially in the ASEAN region and in South Asia.

and the Lomé agreements, has also been very important. While there has been some licensing or subcontracting of garment assembly to local producers in these countries, there has been substantial FDI in assembly facilities.[6] This has afforded fewer opportunities for entrants to learn through brand-name subcontracting. FDI has been facilitated by economic liberalization in the 1980s and 1990s. Few countries currently impose substantial restrictions on foreign ownership, and over the past decade Governments have tried to attract export-oriented investments by building EPZs and offering tax and financial incentives.

Changes in market conditions have also limited opportunities for developing countries to use the industry as a platform for broader-based industrialization. Markets have become increasingly differentiated and fragmented, each segment having its own specific product characteristics. This has strongly influenced the sourcing strategies of all leading players. Essentially, the locations from which they decide to source depend on which client base they serve, since different regions or countries cater to different requirements. Five broad market segments with their specific product characteristics and the main corresponding sourcing areas have been distinguished in table 4.3.

Table 4.3. Main market segments and sourcing areas

Leading actors in commodity chain	Main product characteristics	Main sourcing areas
1. Fashion-oriented retailers	High-fashion designer products, expensive national brands	Italy, France, United Kingdom, Japan
2. Department stores, speciality chains, brand-name companies	Private label or store-brand products as well as national brands	East Asian NIEs and well-established producers in a few developing countries (Brazil, India, Mexico)
3. Mass merchandisers and manufacturers (e.g. of underwear)	Lower-price store brands	Medium- to low-cost mid-quality exporters (ASEAN countries in South-East Asia, lower-quality producers in the East Asian NIEs, India, Brazil, Mexico, China), **Dominican Republic, Costa Rica**
4. Large-volume discount stores	Inexpensive low-quality products	Low-cost suppliers of standardized goods (China, Indonesia, Bangladesh, Sri Lanka, Mauritius, **Dominican Republic, Costa Rica, Morocco** and many others)
5. Smaller 'scout' importers	Very cheap and low-quality goods	Countries or areas on the fringes of the international production frontier (Viet Nam, Myanmar, Saipan, and several others)

Source: Gereffi, 1997a, table 11 and pp. 220-223. Case-study countries in bold.

The highest value-added products (of fashion-oriented retailers – segment 1 in table 4.3) remain almost exclusively the domain of producers in Western Europe. Import protection enjoyed by these countries under successive MFA agreements is partly responsible for this pattern, but competitive factors play an important role. These high-priced, high-fashion items require advanced design skills. They also call for high-quality production capabilities that most developing countries cannot provide. Production is in small batches. The order-to-delivery time has to be very short, and turnover of styles is rapid, requiring flexible and quick

---

[6] Germany, especially, is noted for the use of subcontracting. The United States is noted for FDI in wholly-owned subsidiaries (see Piatti and Spinanger, 1995; Spinanger, 1994, p. 127).

response in the development of new models. Brand names are crucial in this segment. Designer labels are instant indicators of quality.

As one moves down the table, the cost of production, product sophistication and the need for high turnover (fashion) gradually decreases, while delivery time increases. Only a minority of non-Western suppliers (mainly in the Asian NIEs and to a lesser extent in South-East Asia) that entered export-oriented garment production relatively early, can supply the products marketed by leading department stores and speciality stores.

The majority of low-income economies supply the mass-market, cheap products in segments 4 and 5, and to a lesser extent segment 3, of table 4.3, where price-conscious mass merchandisers, discount stores and manufacturers operate. In these parts of the commodity chain, low wages, unfilled production quotas and preferential market access play a dominant role. For example, underwear manufacturers have established large assembly facilities in the Caribbean Basin (in particular in Costa Rica and the Dominican Republic and in Mexico). In the higher value-added segments, these factors do not play a role, which explains why many countries have been able to remain dominant producers (and even exporters) of apparel despite their high labour costs. Table 4.4 illustrates the large variation in unit labour cost among countries.

The great majority of developing-country garment producers, serving segments 4 and 5, may not be able to move into higher value-added activities in the way that the Asian NIEs did earlier. In the 1960s and 1970s, the markets that absorbed large and fast-growing standardized products provided an ideal learning environment in which exporters could acquire production, design, organization and marketing capabilities. By the time market requirements became more demanding and export quotas tighter, their capabilities had grown enough to enable them to tap into fashion-driven higher-income markets with higher value-added products. Meanwhile they hived off low-value activities to new producers in lower-cost areas through "triangle manufacturing".

This learning cycle is now more constricted and difficult. Markets are demanding, quota restrictions have tightened, and competition in the higher-value market segments is more intense, while market growth has slowed down. Trade-incentive structures militate against production facilities managed by local companies, and instead promote FDI in simple assembly. Most developing countries may have become locked into mass export processing based on low-cost labour and market access.

In sum, using garments as a launch pad for export-oriented industrialization is becoming increasingly difficult for new entrants. Recently established export platforms are notoriously footloose. Since sunk costs are low, they can be moved easily when labour costs, market access or other variables affecting profitability affect competitive advantage. In this respect the garment industry differs from other industries.

Table 4.4. Labour costs in the apparel industry, 1990-1995

Rank	Economy	Hourly costs (Dollars)		Annual growth rate 1990-1995
		1990	1995	Per cent
1	Switzerland	14.19	22.42	9.6
2	Japan	6.34	20.95	27.0
3	Germany	7.23	20.35	23.0
4	Italy	12.50	13.68	1.8
5	United States	6.56	9.62	8.0
6	Spain	7.08	7.78	1.9
7	Greece	4.33	7.19	10.7
8	Taiwan Province of China	3.41	5.18	8.7
9	Hong Kong (China)	3.05	4.32	7.2
10	Singapore	2.43	4.01	10.5
11	Portugal	2.30	3.85	10.9
12	Republic of Korea	2.46	3.29	6.0
13	**Costa Rica**	**1.09**	**2.23**	**15.4**
14	Hungary	0.92	1.68	12.8
15	Mexico	0.92	1.61	11.8
16	Malaysia	0.56	1.59	23.2
17	South Africa	1.07	1.58	8.1
18	Czech Republic	2.79	1.55	-11.1
19	Jamaica	0.91	1.55	11.2
20	Turkey	1.35	1.52	2.4
21	**Dominican Republic**	**0.67**	**1.52**	**17.8**
22	El Salvador	0.69	1.43	15.7
23	Poland	0.50	1.42	23.2
24	Guatemala	0.45	1.3	23.6
25	Mauritius	NA	1.28	NA
26	**Morocco**	**0.92**	**1.22**	**5.8**
27	Thailand	0.63	1.11	12.0
28	Philippines	0.46	0.72	9.4
29	Egypt	0.34	0.51	8.4
30	Zimbabwe	NA	0.45	NA
31	Sri Lanka	0.24	0.41	11.3
32	Kenya	0.47	0.34	-6.3
33	Indonesia	0.16	0.33	15.6
34	India	0.33	0.29	-2.6
35	Pakistan	0.24	0.29	3.9
36	Viet Nam	NA	0.29	NA
37	China	0.26	0.25	-0.8
38	Nigeria	0.2	0.24	3.7
39	Bangladesh	NA	0.20	NA
40	United Republic of Tanzania	NA	NA	NA

Source: Werner International, Inc. (1996).

Note: Costs include social and fringe benefits. Case study countries indicated in bold.

4.2.3.3 The outlook

The phasing out of the MFA and technological change heavily influence the outlook for developing countries. Since the first MFA was adopted in 1973, trade regulations affecting the garment industry have become increasingly complex, opaque and discriminatory. Historically, the textile and clothing industry has been one of the most and longest protected (Shepherd, 1981). Tariffs are higher than for other goods, and they rise with the degree of

93

processing. The use of quotas has given importing countries considerable bargaining power over suppliers and allowed high-cost producers to postpone restructuring. Special tariff regimes such as HTS 9802 and outward processing trade agreements promote the assembly in developing countries of garments from cloth manufactured by the home country. All these features have served to counter home-market penetration, on the basis of comparative advantage, by the competitive textile and clothing industries in developing countries. In particular, it has hindered the advancement of integrated industries (from textile fibres through to final products) in those countries.

The restrictions existing at the end of 1994 are being phased out in four stages: 16 per cent of the total (by volume) were phased out in 1995 and 17 per cent in 1998; 18 per cent will be phased out in 2002 and the rest in 2005. Although most industrialized countries have postponed market access for items of most interest to developing countries until the last phase, the Marrakesh Agreement establishing the WTO imposes a calendar for dismantling the impediments. A major innovation is that market access conditions are to be notified to the WTO Textiles Monitoring Body and are no longer subject to the unilateral impositions of importing countries. Thus, factors such as price, quality and rapid and reliable delivery, rather than market access regulations, will increasingly define countries' international competitiveness and market share.[7] This means that countries whose competitive advantage rests on preferential market access and low wages will be particularly vulnerable. These countries do not have much experience either in managing and promoting the industry at the governmental or at the private level. Moreover, the current trade-incentive structures militate against the local establishment of backward linkages and higher value-added operations in these countries. It is to be expected that these countries will see their market prospects collapse in the face of stiff competition from Asian producers.

The new technologies and organizational practices being developed in the economically advanced countries will affect the competitiveness of developing countries. There are three major restructuring strategies in developed-country manufacturers: technological upgrading,[8] cost reduction through offshore assembly, and specialization in high-fashion segments.[9] The main impact of these technological developments is that "they reduce the effect of differences in labour rates between the emerging nations and the developed countries of the world. They provide a way to substitute capital intensity for labour intensity, increase productivity and make the competitive playing field more level" (Hunter, 1990, p. 148). While the assembly of garments has remained difficult to mechanize, there has been considerable technical progress in the other stages of manufacturing. Therefore, while wage advantages remain important in the assembly process, they are no longer sufficient to maintain a competitive edge in the other stages of production. The impact of these new

---

[7] This does not mean that access will always be easy. For some of the complex aspects related to quality, for example, see International Trade Centre, UNCTAD/GATT (1994).

[8] Japanese and United States producers in particular are emphasizing this strategy: see Spinanger (1994, pp. 114-115), for the Japanese case; for developments in the United States, see Doeringer et al. (1998).

[9] Italy is a good example of the high fashion specialization strategy. see Barba Navaretti and Perosino (1995); Formengo Pent (1994).

technologies is especially pronounced where design, quality, the production of small batches and rapid turnover are important.

In general, while the garment industry is not technology-intensive, it is not static in technological and market terms. Its skill and marketing needs are constantly evolving. Closer integration with designers, access to new production technologies and the availability of an efficient supply base of textiles, accessories and capital goods are important to quality upgrading, lowering of production and inventory costs, and responding rapidly and flexibly to fast-moving markets. Needless to say, world-class infrastructure is also necessary for exporters to meet tighter and more stringent delivery schedules. Only a few developing countries will be able to muster these requirements: these will thrive in the industry in the long term, achieving high export growth driven by upgrading and adaptation to change. There will be many other countries that will find this "high-road" strategy too demanding, especially those countries which have recently entered the industry as FDI-based platforms, whose competitive advantages are based on low wages, special market access and EPZ facilities. It is likely that these countries will settle for more limited upgrading within the assembly stage, centred on high quality standards, reliable supply and high worker productivity. This is unlikely to lead to long-term competitiveness in the industry, but it can be a source of competitive advantage in the short to medium term.

4.3. TNC involvement in the case-study countries

The three case-study countries – Costa Rica, the Dominican Republic and Morocco – are small players in the international garments industry. They are nevertheless important newcomers in their respective principal destination markets. Moreover, they are representative cases since we want to analyse the effects of TNC activity in the industry on industrial restructuring and the international competitiveness of countries that have followed the EPZ – low-wage – special access route.

4.3.1 Costa Rica

Costa Rica's industrialization started in 1940, when it formulated the Law of New Industries that provided tax benefits to new manufacturing activities. This initiative did not produce many results, however, because the country was enjoying a boom in traditional exports, particularly coffee. More serious efforts relying on import substitution, began in the late 1950s. The Law for Protection and Industrial Development of 1959 produced a significant boost to national industrial development through protective tariffs and a favourable tax regime for domestic investors. However, a policy to promote exports was also implemented by means of the Export Promotion Law of 1973, aiming to reduce the country's dependence on traditional natural resource-based exports. The country also joined the Central American Common Market (CACM) in 1963, which aimed to lessen dependence on extra-regional trade through greater regional integration. Through a customs union and a common external tariff, it sought to overcome the problem of small markets and thereby reap the advantages of economies of scale and specialization.

Unfortunately, the import-substitution strategy led over time to increasing structural rigidities and inefficiencies. The export promotion policy did not produce good results, while the CACM initiative did not live up to its promises. The industries established under the regional integration scheme did not develop into strategic components of countries' industrial development. Costa Rica remained highly dependent on natural resource exports, especially bananas, coffee, meat and sugar, all slow-growing items in world trade, subject to cycles with large price fluctuations and low price elasticity of demand. The debt crisis of the 1980s added to the country's economic malaise and forced a rethink of development strategy. The result was a mixed policy starting in 1984, in which liberalization and structural adjustment ran in parallel with policies of active promotion of exports, including an emphasis on new, non-traditional activities. The main elements were:

- A shift in trade policy, with tariff reductions to reduce effective protection of industrial activities, aiming for a maximum of 20 per cent for consumer goods and 5 - 10 per cent for intermediate and capital goods.

- Financial support for manufactured exports. Subsidies were granted in the form of income tax and tariff exemptions, and, in the case of export contracts, granting of tax credit certificates based on the free-on-board values of exports (for those outside the Central American subregion). An export promotion fund was established in the Central Bank.

- The establishment of institutions for foreign investment promotion in export-oriented activities. The Export and Investment Programme of the Office of the President of the Republic, established in 1983, gave political priority to this endeavour. The Coalition for Developmental Initiatives of the Private Sector was created with the assistance of the United States Agency for International Development (USAID), with the aim of attracting FDI for production and export of new products. In 1986, the Ministry of Foreign Trade was assigned to coordinate all initiatives of the various executing agencies, such as the Centre for the Promotion of Exports and Investments and the Corporation for Export Free Zones.

- The liberalization of capital movements. Costa Rica's FDI regulation is liberal, and does not discriminate between foreign and domestic investors. There are some restrictions on private (domestic as well as foreign) investment in certain important service sectors, but not in manufacturing (WTO, 1995a, p. 33).

- Institution of two important export-promotion mechanisms. The regime of *temporary admission* suspends all taxes and import duties on goods that enter Costa Rica to be assembled, processed, repaired and so on, in order to be re-exported within a definite period (ranging from three to six months depending on the items concerned). Further, companies operating in *export free zones* benefit from good infrastructure, fiscal incentives and a preferential foreign trade regime. The free zones are the mainstay of the country's current export and investment strategy (Mortimore and Peres, 1998,

p. 38). *Export contracts*, a third mechanism, were in force until 1996 (with minor exceptions).[10]

These efforts made Costa Rica an attractive destination for foreign investors. In addition, several structural features have worked to its advantage. These include high literacy rates (93 per cent), with a large number of skilled professionals, technicians and supervisors; modern infrastructure (seaports and airports, road and telecommunications networks, reliable and widely available hydro power); high living standards and social and medical facilities; and a stable democratic regime.

International competitiveness was enhanced greatly after the mid-1980s by a steep devaluation of the national currency. This greatly reduced the cost of local wages in dollar terms. Even so, Costa Rica's wages have risen considerably during the first half of the 1990s, and they are now high in relation to that of other major garment exporters. With an hourly rate of $2.23 in 1995, it ranked just below Portugal and the Republic of Korea, and well above Mexico (a major competitor in its own region) and leading suppliers in Eastern Europe, the countries of ASEAN and China (table 4.4). It has joined the league of middle-income countries in which an educated and skilled labour force and the availability of a good physical infrastructure are replacing low-cost unskilled labour as the chief ingredients of their competitive advantage, although wage-based competition remains a factor of considerable importance within this group.

The favourable incentive climate helps to explain why Costa Rica has been one of three main destinations of FDI in the Caribbean Basin in the 1990s (the other two are the Dominican Republic and Jamaica), in spite of the fact that its wage levels are the highest in the region.[11] FDI inflows, predominantly from the United States, increased significantly and consistently since the change in macro-economic policy in the mid-1980s, from an annual average of $100 million during 1985-1990 to an estimated $500 million in 1997 (UNCTAD, 1998, p 363). Manufacturing received a sizeable share of FDI, although until recently the biggest chunk went into natural resource-based projects (table 4.5). FDI in manufacturing went into a variety of assembly activities, largely located in the free zones.

Table 4.5. Costa Rica: net inflows of FDI, by sector, 1970-1993

Period	Agriculture and mining (Per cent)	Manufacturing (Per cent)	Services (Per cent)	Others (Per cent)	Total (Per cent)	Total (Million dollars)[a]
1970-1974	54	35	1	10	100	34.7
1975-1979	28	59	7	6	100	60.8
1980-1984	69	12	12	7	100	57.4
1985-1989	46	36	12	6	100	94.7
1990-1993	48	28	20	4	100	203.4
1975-1993	48	33	14	6	100	82.6

Source: ECLAC, 1993.
[a] Annual averages by period in current values.

[10] The export contract mechanism was designed primarily for national companies to take advantage of the Generalized System of Preferences, which requires a minimum Costa Rican value of 35 per cent of the value of the product exported to the United States. Under the mechanism, companies had access to tax credit certificates.
[11] Excluding off-shore financial centres (Mortimore and Peres, 1998, p. 19).

The garment industry received a major boost from the changes in the incentive climate in the mid-1980s. The industry leads the country's integration with the international economy, especially that of North America. Costa Rica, along with the Dominican Republic and Mexico, became the chief off-shore assembly site for United States producers making use of special tariff arrangements.[12] In 1993, two-thirds of the total value of the imports of clothing into the United States under HTS 9802 came from these three countries (Mexico, 31 per cent; the Dominican Republic, 26 per cent; and Costa Rica, 11 per cent) (United States International Trade Commission, 1995a, pp. 2-22). In addition to the HTS 9802 provisions, special regimes exist for certain countries or groups of countries that offer additional benefits in the form of guaranteed access levels of imports into the United States. The Caribbean Basin countries have benefited from guaranteed access levels since June 1986.[13]

Many United States firms established affiliates in Costa Rica,[14] but many others also established licensing or subcontracting relations with local producers. In 1994, there were 700 companies operating in the Costa Rican textile and apparel industry (15 per cent of all manufacturing companies). Of these, 138 were registered as exporters. Sixty-one of those were operating under the temporary admission scheme, and another 30 were operating from export processing zones: thus, nearly two-thirds of the exporters operated under regimes benefiting from preferential access to the United States market via HTS 9802. In 1993, 80 per cent of United States apparel imports from the Caribbean Basin countries took place under HTS 9802. For Costa Rica, the figure was 84 per cent.

Value added by apparel exports jumped from $10 million in 1985 to $160 million in 1995. The garment industry now employs about 40,000 persons, equivalent to a third of manufacturing employment,[15] and accounts for 5 per cent of total industrial production. By creating a climate conducive to foreign investment, Costa Rican policy facilitated this process, but the principal driver of its recent boom was preferential access to the United States market. How secure then is its competitive position? This question will be dealt with in section 4.4.

4.3.2 The Dominican Republic

The economic background of the Dominican Republic is very similar to that of Costa Rica. Commodity exports such as sugar, coffee, cocoa and tobacco were the backbone of its economy for many years. It began import-substitution policies from the mid-1940s onwards and strengthened the regime in 1968 with high protective tariffs, non-tariff barriers, subsidized credit and foreign exchange, and an overvalued Dominican peso. At the same

---

[12] Although Costa Rica's wages were not the lowest in the region at that time, its hourly labour costs in the garment sector were still close to those in major competitors in the region, especially Mexico. Since then, the situation has changed substantially as wages in Costa Rica have been rising much faster than those in other countries in the region countries (see table 4.4).

[13] Mexico's guaranteed access level dates back to January 1989, and Andean countries have had one since July 1992.

[14] Unfortunately, no data are available on FDI in Costa Rica's garment industry specifically, so that it is not possible to determine the real extent of direct foreign involvement in the industry. The lack of data is explained by the lack of any registration or compulsory administrative requirements other than those relating to the incentive regimes (WTO, 1995,p. 35).

[15] If indirect employment is also included, the figure is about 80,000.

time, it also began to actively promote exports, adopting an extensive industrial free zone (IFZ) programme. Over time, this IFZ programme grew into a major focal point for improved competitiveness in the Caribbean region. The success of this programme is the main reason for including the Dominican Republic in this study.

Initially, both the inward and the outward components of the strategy had good results; the average real GDP growth rate was 12 per cent between 1968-1974 (World Bank, 1992). However, from the mid-1970s onwards the import-substituting sector of the economy showed increasing inefficiencies. It also suffered the effects of the oil crisis and declining commodity prices (especially for sugar). This gave rise to increasingly uneven development, with a dynamic and competitive IFZ sector and a stagnant, uncompetitive, inward-looking domestic sector. This pattern continued through the 1980s. A first adjustment programme was introduced under the auspices of the International Monetary Fund (IMF) in 1984-1985, partially reversing the anti-export bias of the domestic economy. However, the country continued to suffer from a number of domestic problems, including a high degree of discretion and distortion in its trade regime. The problems culminated in a serious economic crisis in 1989-1990.

Meanwhile, the IFZ-based export sector, with a separate policy regime, remained remarkably unaffected by these developments. It experienced high rates of growth in export earnings and job creation, especially after the devaluations of the local currency in the mid-1980s (which reduced the monthly wage rate in dollar terms from $125 to $67). Other factors were the market-access privileges described above. IFZ exports grew from 11 per cent of total exports to 53 per cent in 1990 – in value, from $117 million to $839 million. During the same period non-IFZ export earnings declined from $962 million to $744 million.[16]

By 1990, continued insulation of the IFZ sector proved impossible, as it began to suffer from electricity and petrol shortages, inflation and currency overvaluation. The Government was forced to embark on an adjustment and reform programme. This focused on fiscal and monetary restraint, the liberalization of the financial markets, and reforms to the trade regime (including tariff reduction to between 5 and 35 per cent *ad valorem* for most products) and the tax system. It unified the exchange rate, eliminated substantial debt arrears and accumulated international reserves. New rules and regulations on foreign investment were implemented. A new law governing free zone investment was enacted in 1990 (see below). The macroeconomic situation improved greatly, and between 1992 and 1995, the economy registered an average growth of 5 per cent. The IFZ sector continued to be the principal source of growth, benefiting from privileged access to the United States market and the European Union market (under the Lomé IV Convention, which the country joined in 1990).

From 1984 to 1994, the IFZ programme contributed an average of 15,000 new jobs each year and a total of 356 new firms. The number of IFZ parks grew from three in 1980 to 34 in 1995; another 10 are under construction (Mortimore and Peres, 1998, p. 40). Total employment generated by the IFZs increased from 20,000 in 1980 to 176,312 at the end of

---

[16] Data from the Centro Dominicano de Promociones de Exportaciones (CEDOPEX).

1994, from 1.3 per cent of total employment in 1980 to 6.7 per cent in 1994 (International Labour Organization, 1984; Consejo Nacional de Zonas Francas, 1994). IFZs now account for more than half of all manufacturing jobs in the country.[17] Exports from the IFZ sector have grown continuously in the 1990s, to a total of $1,392 million in 1995, 69 per cent of total Dominican exports. Growth of IFZ exports between 1970 and 1993 averaged 25 per cent annually. Non-IFZ exports, in contrast, stagnated. In 1995, they were worth just $626 million, down from $744 million in 1990.[18] The United States market remains the dominant market for IFZ exports, accounting for around 90 per cent of the total (compared to 48 per cent for non-IFZ exports).[19] In the mid-1990s, 76 per cent of the companies located in the IFZs were foreign-owned, with a total stock of FDI worth approximately $1,230 million in 1996,[20] out of a total (non-IFZ) stock of FDI of $1,550 million. United States firms were the largest group of investors, accounting for nearly 48 per cent of companies operating in IFZs.

The most rapid growth in IFZs has been in unskilled labour-intensive manufactured exports, especially garment assembly. Net export earnings from garments were approximately $300 million in 1995.[21] About 63 per cent of the total number of firms located in the IFZs are garment producers, and they employ 64 per cent of the IFZ labour force, i.e. approximately 100,000 people. There are only a handful of apparel producers outside the IFZ programme; foreign clothing producers are almost all operating from IFZs. In addition, subcontracting and licensing by large foreign companies to local contractors and manufacturers to perform "cut-make-trim" operations has been growing in importance. Table 4.6 shows the origin of the exporting firms.

Table 4.6. Origins of the garment firms in Dominican export processing zones

Country of origin	Number of firms	Percentage of firms
United States	118	40.0
Dominican Republic	111	37.6
Republic of Korea	31	10.5
Other	35	11.8
Total	295	100.0

Source: Compiled from statistics of the National Council of Industrial Free Zones, Dominican Republic.

In the early 1990s, the Dominican Republic became the largest exporter of garments in the Caribbean Basin (WTO, 1996a, p. 78). With the success of this programme, together with rising revenue from tourism, the country began to overcome its dependence on the export of agricultural commodities. Natural resource exports remain very important (nickel

---

[17] Estimates of the indirect employment effect of IFZ firms range from 0.6 to 1.5 jobs per direct job (Fundación Economía y Desarrollo, 1989).

[18] Over the period 1970-1993 as a whole, non-IFZ exports declined by 0.4 per cent on average per year.

[19] Based on 1993 figures; does not include exports to Puerto Rico and other United States territories.

[20] Data from the Statistical Department of the National Council of the Industrial Free Zones, Dominican Republic.

[21] Its total export value was $1,773 million in 1996, but the value-added figures give a better indication of the contribution of the industry to the economy in view of the high import content of the goods.

accounted for 25 per cent of non-IFZ export earnings, and sugar for 28 per cent), but they are no longer the backbone of the country's foreign exchange earnings. In 1995, export earnings from garments were about twice as large as the total gross export value of sugar and its by-products.

The Dominican Republic is thus a classic case of the export processing zone − low wage − special access route, very similar to the pattern observed in other successful countries in the international garment industry in their early years. The implications of this situation will be considered in section 4.4.

4.3.3 Morocco

Morocco's economic development is another case of dependence on natural resources combined with import-substitution industrialization, followed by attempts at diversification into export-oriented manufacturing and tourism. For two decades, after independence in 1956, foreign-owned agricultural land and industrial activities were transferred to locals (Moroccanization). The main exports were phosphates and phosphate-based products. The country failed to adjust its public expenditures when the world market price for phosphate, rising in the 1970s, fell towards the end of the decade. The situation was aggravated by the second oil shock of 1979 and interest-rate increases in the industrialized countries. A series of structural adjustment programmes were undertaken from 1983, with measures to liberalize imports, encourage exports, promote foreign (as well as domestic) investment, and privatize State-owned enterprises. Economic performance improved, helped by external financial assistance and debt rescheduling. The budget deficit was brought down from around 12 per cent in the early 1980s to below 3 per cent since 1992, and the current account deficit was lowered to less than 2 per cent. The main economic problem is high unemployment (about 16 per cent) (WTO, 1996b, p. 1).

One reason for improved performance was the new incentive regime, favouring investment (local and foreign) in export-oriented manufacturing activities. The main ingredients of the regime were:

- *Trade policy.* Goods for export were exempt from VAT, and granted duty and tax relief on the inputs used in their production. Temporary admission was granted duty- and tax-free for intermediate goods to be re-exported after processing or manufacturing. Free industrial warehousing and duty- and tax-free importation of equipment, spares and intermediates was available for exporting firms. There was exemption from export duties and taxes on products of Moroccan origin, or imported with duties, or imported under the temporary admission procedure, if sent abroad for further processing or manufacturing. Duties, taxes, etc. imposed on inputs consumed in manufacturing export products were refunded.

- *Investment policy.* The Government ended the policy of transferring land and industrial activities to locals, and allows foreigners to invest and remit earnings freely. In 1996, it passed a new investment code, eliminating sector-specific incentives, streamlining approval procedures, and exempting equipment from VAT.

Free trade zones have been comparatively unimportant; in 1995 there was only one such zone (in the port of Tangier). The regional trade agreement with, and proximity to, the European Union has been the most important factor in attracting labour-intensive export-oriented investment. This has been helped by its low wages (below other major countries in the Mediterranean Rim – see table 4.4). Moroccan industrial goods can enter the European Union duty-free if they meet rule-of-origin regulations (goods that do not originate in Morocco must have sufficient local value added). Since 1991, there has been only one voluntary export restraint, on trousers, but it is not strictly enforced and exports have exceeded agreed limits by a wide margin in some years (WTO, 1996b, p. 73). Not surprisingly, the European Union is Morocco's dominant trading partner, supplying about 54 per cent of merchandise imports, and taking 63 per cent of exports. France, Spain, Italy and Germany have the largest shares. Trade with the United States and Japan is on the increase, but still accounts for a minor share of the total.

FDI has increased almost threefold, from an annual average of $132 million in 1986-1991 to $417 million in 1992-1997.[22] This makes Morocco the third largest FDI recipient in Africa (UNCTAD, 1998, p. 361). The share of the textile and garment sector in total industrial FDI fell from an average of 10 per cent in 1985-1989, to 5 per cent during the 1990s.[23] The extent of foreign involvement in the industry is larger than the FDI data indicate, however, because agreements in the form of subcontracting and licensing to local companies are also very important. About 90 per cent of the country's garment exports are destined for the European Union.

By the early 1990s, the textile and garments industry accounted for 42 per cent of manufactured, and 20 per cent of total, exports, making it the largest export earner. The value of garment exports tripled between 1980-1984 and 1985-1989, and further doubled between 1985-1989 and 1990-1994. Within the industrial sector, the industry comes second in sales value (15 per cent, after the agro-industry, at 25 per cent); it has 1,800 firms (30 per cent of all industrial firms in the country) and employs 183,000 workers (of whom 56 per cent are women) (WTO, 1996b, p. 71). Out of Morocco's 10 principal OECD export categories in 1995, four were garment items. Morocco is clearly a rising star on the international garment scene. As in the case of the Dominican Republic, its performance is based on incentives, low wages and special access, as well as geographical proximity to, a large developed-country market – in this case, Europe.

---

[22] An increasing share has been going to the services sector, from just 14 per cent in the early 1980s to 38 per cent in the early 1990s. The manufacturing sector saw its share decline from 58 to 40 per cent over the same period. However, the dominance of service activities, such as banks, consumer credit firms and hotels, has less to do with the incentive climate than with the predominance of service-related activities in Morocco's privatization programme (Office des Changes, Morocco).

[23] The share of construction in total industrial FDI inflows was 15 per cent, and the share of oil was 24 per cent in 1995-1997. The share of the latter has been rising fast since the early 1990s due to privatization. Other industries that have attracted significant FDI after 1980 include pharmaceuticals, electricals, metals and chemicals (Office des Changes, Morocco).

4.4. FDI, restructuring and competitiveness

4.4.1 Costa Rica

4.4.1.1 Setting and industry performance

The rise of the TNC-driven export-oriented garment industry in Costa Rica has led to rapid diversification in its export structure. From 1980 to 1995, the share of natural resources in total exports dropped from 91 to 60 per cent, while that of manufactures rose from 8 to 39 per cent. Garments are an important category of manufactured exports. Costa Rica's share in OECD imports of clothing grew from 0.1 to 0.5 per cent in this period, which is considerable, given the size of the economy. The 10 main clothing export items accounted for 21 per cent of its total exports to the OECD. These data suggest that Costa Rica is, unlike many other countries in the region, a case of successful industrial restructuring.

However, Costa Rica's garment export growth began to stagnate in 1995. Its share of clothing in its total exports to the United States, which had risen from 9 per cent in 1980 to a high of 42 per cent in 1993, began to decline, reaching 36 per cent in 1996. During 1996, it lost United States market share in 8 out of its 10 principal clothing export items. There were two important reasons for this. The first was NAFTA, which provided a significant boost to Mexico, pushing it into first position as a garment supplier to the United States and Canada. The principal benefit for Mexico was tariff- and quota-free entry for these exports (Bannister and Low, 1992, p. 14). In contrast, Costa Rica and other Caribbean Basin countries face tariffs of approximately 6 per cent (United States International Trade Commission, 1995a, pp. 3-8 to 3-13) in addition to quotas and calls.[24] Mexico also benefits from privileged market access for clothing produced by in-bond assemblers using cloth made in third countries but cut in the United States (up to 25 million square metres). It also has market access for certain cotton, synthetic fibre and woollen clothing of non-North American origin (Lande and Crigler, 1993, p. 22). A recent initiative in the United States Congress to grant NAFTA parity to Caribbean Basin countries was unsuccessful.

The United States imposed quotas in 1995 on many of Costa Rica's most important clothing export items, a serious threat to the expansion of important lines of the industry. Costa Rica took the case to the WTO, where a dispute settlement panel advised in Costa Rica's favour. Even though Costa Rica won its case, the skirmish created uncertainties among investors and may contribute to a diversion of FDI from the Caribbean Basin countries to Mexico (United States International Trade Commission, 1995b, pp. 41-46; ECLAC, 1994, p. 73). Some of the principal apparel assemblers operating in Costa Rica, such as Warnaco and Sara Lee, chose Mexico as a site for their new plants.[25]

The second reason for the stagnation in Costa Rica's apparel exports is increasing competition from lower-wage countries in the region. By 1994, hourly wages in Costa Rica

---

[24] In 1994, over half of Costa Rican apparel exports to the United States were subject to quotas and that figure rose to almost two-thirds in 1995 due to the calls applied to undergarments and pyjamas.

[25] "NAFTA and Caribbean textiles", *Latin American Economy and Business,* May 1995, p. 11.

were considerably higher than in the Dominican Republic, El Salvador, Guatemala and Mexico (table 4.4). Since wages account for about 30 per cent of total costs in garment assembly, such differentials are crucial determinants of competitiveness, assuming similar levels of productivity.[26]

Our assessment of industrial upgrading in the garment industry is based on information collected from 12 foreign-owned and 4 domestic garment exporters catering to the United States market. These 16 firms together export goods worth about $120 million annually (about 20 per cent of Costa Rica's clothing exports) and employ about 13,000 workers, about one-third of the labour force in the industry. The sample provides a range in terms of products, size, establishment year, ownership, use of export regime, principal export market, export market restrictions faced and competitive situation in 1990-1995 (see table 4.7). There are three subgroups:

- Five large United States-owned companies that assemble undergarments, exporting via HTS 9802 (group I). These are leading firms in Costa Rica, not just in terms of size but also in terms of competitive performance. They are subsidiaries of large international companies with branches in many other countries in the region. All five managed to improve their market position between 1990 and 1995. Their employment doubled from 1985 to 1990, and again from 1990 to 1995.

- Seven medium-sized and small companies exporting a variety of products under HTS 9802 (three make men's/boys' outerwear, four make "other products") (group II). Like the first subgroup, they are foreign-owned (five are United States-owned and two are Asian-owned), but they belong to smaller international networks and are in the second division as far as competitive performance is concerned. Their employment grew by one-third from 1985 to 1990, and by 40 per cent from 1990 to 1995, but four companies in this group did not improve their market position between 1990 and 1995.

- Four relatively small nationally owned firms which access the United States market through non-HTS means (group III). Two of these make undergarments, and two make other types of garments. The international links of these companies are indirect, through export contracts with foreign buyers. They had some success in improving their international market shares in the period 1985-1990, but the period 1990-1995 has been difficult for them. While their employment doubled from 1985 to 1990, subsequently it fell by one-third.

---

[26] Labour productivity may well be higher in Costa Rica than in the surrounding countries, because of its well educated labour force and excellent infrastructure. However, it is unlikely that this advantage in terms of unit labour costs would be sufficient to offset the labour-cost advantages enjoyed by the other countries.

Table 4.7. Costa Rica: characteristics of sample firms

Item	Number of companies	Share of total exports by sample firms (Per cent)	Share of total no. of workers in sample (Per cent)
1. Principal activity: all firms	**16**	**100**	**100**
SITC 846 (undergarments)	5	62	63
SITC 842 (men's and boys' outer garments)	5	14	20
Other SITC 84 categories	6	24	17
2. Firm size (exports & employees):	**16**	**100**	**100**
Large	5	62	63
Medium	5	27	20
Small	6	11	18
3. Year established: all firms	**16**	**100**	**100**
Before 1983 ("old firms")	8	43	62
1983 or after ("new firms")	8	57	38
4. Ownership: all firms	**16**	**100**	**100**
Foreign firms	12	93	91
National firms	4	7	9
5. Source of FDI: all firms	**16**	**100**	**100**
North America	10	79	81
Asia	2	14	11
No FDI	4	7	9
6. Export regime: all firms	**16**	**100**	**100**
Temporary admission	7	41	51
Export processing zone	6	55	44
Export contract	3	4	5
7. Principal export market:	**16**	**100**	**100**
United States	15	99	99
Other	1	1	1
8. United States market access instrument:	**16**	**100**	**100**
HTS 9802	13	96	95
Other	3	4	5
9. United States market access restrictions:	**16**	**100**	**100**
Quotas	6	21	22
"Calls" in 1995	5	62	63
None	5	17	15
10. Competitive situation, 1990-1995:	**16**	**100**	**100**
Improved	11	81	81
Not improved	5	19	19

Source: UNCTAD, based on company interviews.

4.4.1.2 *Human capital formation*

Although there were some differences among the sample companies, they agreed that improvements in human resources were the most important input into increased competitiveness. However, the evidence about their training and other skill development efforts is disappointing. Incentives are used to increase labour productivity and to reduce high turnover rates (especially by large employers in group I). High turnover may be one reason why training has received comparatively limited attention. Only 5 of the 16 companies invested over 1 per cent of total sales in training, and almost all the training took the form of in-house instruction for new arrivals. There was no culture of sending workers to educational institutions. There was no perceptible change in the structure of employment of these firms over time. Eighty-five per cent of the workforce continues to be shopfloor workers, and there was no change in the ratio of unskilled to skilled workers in the 1990s compared to the second half of the 1980s.

4.4.1.3 Technological and organizational development

According to the sample companies, improvement of technology and organizational practices was the second important strategic factor in competitiveness. Thirteen firms felt it contributed to improvement in the designs and quality of their products. Foreign affiliates obtained new product and process technology primarily from their headquarters and simply applied them. Only four firms made significant adaptations themselves. The big firms in group I in particular were inactive in terms of technological adaptation. The technologies they received from their international networks were world-class, and not much scope existed for further local improvements. Competition through quality and service overrode cost/efficiency considerations in these companies. The situation was different for companies in group II and (even more so) in group III. Access to best-practice technology was less easy, especially for the group III companies, and efforts to improve technological performance were considered very important.

Automation did not play a major role: only three firms had automated their operations to a significant degree, and mainly in receivables and shipping rather than in production. The major technological innovations in production were limited to the use of programmable sewing machines. Their introduction had positively affected competitiveness through reduced production cost and increased production capacity. New organizational practices were observed more frequently, with 15 of the 16 firms implementing these in recent years. These changes involved (in order of importance) increasing the flexibility of the production line, forming work teams, installing statistical control processes and adopting just-in-time inventory controls. Some of these practices, such as multi-tasking, were also used as incentives for staff. The principal benefits of these efforts were improved product quality, reduced costs of production (or improved productivity), reduced non-production costs, and faster delivery (in that order). The big group I firms also reported improved labour relations.

4.4.1.4 Building local supplier networks

The companies were also invited to give their opinions regarding the importance of local procurement as a factor in promoting competitiveness. However, this aspect was considered to be quite unimportant. In 1990-1995, only 5 of the 16 companies increased the degree of local sourcing. This included one firm in group I, one in group II and two in group III. The extent of local sourcing in the companies in groups I and II was particularly limited – over 95 per cent of their physical inputs are supplied "in house" through their respective TNC networks. They also felt that they could not improve their competitiveness by means of increased local sourcing. Local sourcing is somewhat more important among the national firms (30 per cent of inputs).

Local sourcing comprised relatively low-technology inputs such as packaging materials, thread, buttons and other accessories. There was very little subcontracting by foreign affiliates, but two national firms had appreciable subcontracting that helped them reduce costs through increased specialization. The low level of subcontracting by affiliates was attributed to poor quality control, lack of price competitiveness, unreliable delivery and (in some cases) lack of the required technology in potential supplier firms.

4.4.1.5 Concluding remarks

The evidence suggests limited upward diversification and backward integration from labour-based assembly in Costa Rica. There was some effort to improve product quality and process technology, but there was no growth of local design activities or significant innovativeness. Efforts to improve human resources and backward linkages remained limited. Export growth based on assembly has not led to the establishment of a local textile industry. Preferential access to export markets remains the most important competitive factor. This is a risky base, as privileged market access is likely to be phased out by 2005.

Moreover, Costa Rica's competitive position has been eroding due to rising labour costs. While a sign of economic success, in the absence of technological upgrading, this puts acute pressure on exporting companies. When the managers were asked to rank the country as a host for FDI in terms of the categories used in UNCTAD's *World Investment Report*, their verdict was that it had deteriorated from good to average. This is in spite of its favourable FDI regime, fiscal incentives and EPZ schemes. Costa Rica initially possessed many advantages over other Caribbean Basin countries because of its relative social and political stability and labour skills and discipline. By the mid-1990s, however, rising wages and social security contributions began to price Costa Rica out of the low-end garment market, just as the sociopolitical climate in competitor countries with lower wages began to improve. In these conditions, the main strategic response of firms (especially foreign-owned firms) is likely to be to relocate or expand assembly activities in other countries in the region. The nature of the trade privileges militates against the establishment of an integrated textile industry in Costa Rica.

The main contributions of the garment industry to Costa Rica's development have been (possibly temporary) export earnings and employment rather than technology and skill development. Such earnings and employment could nevertheless provide a base for entering other, more skill- and technology-intensive industrial activities, building upon its infrastructure, experience with FDI and educated labour force. Indeed, Costa Rica has already achieved notable success: in 1995 it attracted Intel's first major semiconductor plant in Latin America, a $500 million assembly and testing facility for microprocessors (Spar, 1998).

4.4.2   The Dominican Republic

4.4.2.1 Setting and industry performance[27]

The experience of the Dominican Republic is similar to that of Costa Rica. The annual average export growth of the country's seven largest garment categories was 24 per cent in 1980-1990, and 17 per cent in 1990-1995 (annex table 4.1). In absolute terms, its garment exports increased from $92 million in 1980 to close to $1.7 billion in 1995 (compared to $765 million for Costa Rica in the same year).[28] As a result, its OECD import market share for garments grew by 10 per cent on average in 1980-1996, from 0.28 to 1.28 per cent (see table 4.1), taking it to second position in Latin American and the Caribbean region, behind Mexico. Four of its top 10 export earners are clothing items, which constituted 42 per cent of total export earnings in 1995. As with Costa Rica, the structure of its exports was transformed. The proportion of natural resources in overall exports to the OECD fell from 62 to 15 per cent from 1980 to 1995, while that of manufactures rose from 29 to 82 per cent. Garments increased their share from 15 to 70 per cent.

Over 95 per cent of Dominican garment exports are destined for North America. Excluding Mexico, the country is the largest exporter of apparel to the United States in the region, accounting for nearly one-third of total United States regional imports. It also ranks fifth worldwide in exports of apparel to the United States market. Six of its 10 principal exports to the North American market are apparel items, which together accounted for almost half of its total export value to that region.

The Dominican Republic is clearly a successful example of adaptation to the recent trade and investment challenges in the Caribbean Basin. It has been one of the main beneficiaries of the shift in United States corporate strategies to counter competitive pressures from Asia. The question is the extent to which this expansion is sustainable in the longer term.

In 1995, Dominican market share in the United States began to drop (to 6.4 per cent, down from 6.8 per cent the previous year). Its success in penetrating the United States market created strong pressures for protection. By 1994, the United States had imposed quotas on 20 major apparel categories, notified under the Uruguay Agreement on Textiles and Clothing. Competition from Mexico increased. Fierce competition is emerging from lower-wage countries in the region, mainly Honduras and El Salvador. The abundance and productivity[29] of the Dominican labour force, its chief competitive advantage, are beginning to erode. The basic monthly minimum wage $70-87 during the 1980s and early 1990s, rose to $125 in 1995. In 1992 the country's fringe-benefit ratio was raised from 32 per cent to 40 per cent,

---

[27] This sub-section is based on data from the ECLAC CANPLUS computer software.

[28] It is estimated that about one third of total export value represents net foreign exchange income for the Dominican Republic.

[29] Productivity measures in the garment industry (as reported by, e.g. *Bobbin* magazine) often claim an average of 80 to 85 per cent of United States standards. Turnover rates and absenteeism are also considered reasonable according to regional standards; one 1990 survey found an average of 14.5 per cent in 1990, compared with 25 per cent in Mexico's *maquila* industry.

taking the monthly wage rate, including fringe benefits, from $114.50 in 1989 to $174.22 in 1995, a 40 per cent increase. This wage level is higher than in surrounding countries (with the exception of Costa Rica).

Although the effect of these developments has not been as severe as in Costa Rica, the need for upgrading and diversification into higher value-added activities is manifest. The mainstay of the country's garment industry is simple activities by foreign investors taking advantage of the HTS 9802 programme. These activities are characterized by a high degree of standardization, involving long production runs for a small number of items.[30] The share of these items in total exports, increased from 51 per cent in 1986 to 64 per cent in 1992. The first signs of a move towards production of apparel requiring higher levels of production flexibility and management and sewing skills in the Dominican Republic are only just becoming visible.

A survey was conducted of 16 clothing manufacturers in the Dominican IFZ. Twelve of these were TNCs, six of United States origin, two from the Republic of Korea, and four joint ventures with 25 per cent foreign ownership. The remaining four were entirely domestically owned. The main exports were men's, women's, boys' and girls' trousers, women's underwear and children's wear; the United States was the largest market. The sample firms together employed over 16,000 workers.

4.4.2.2 Human capital formation

Five of the 12 TNCs interviewed did not respond to the question on expenditure on training. However, the responses of the other seven TNCs suggest that investments in human resource development had increased significantly in recent years. Expenditure on training varied between 0.3 and 3.0 per cent of sales in 1995. In contrast, in 1990, only two companies had spent between 1 and 2 per cent, while the rest spent much less. The results for the four domestic companies are similar. The majority of firms (both TNC and domestic) adopted a formal training programme, mainly directed at skilled production workers, production supervisors, professionals, mid-level technical personnel and administrators. Eight of the companies offered training to between 90 and 100 per cent of their skilled production workers and formal technical training to production supervisors, professionals, mid-level technical personnel and administrators. Five had formal technical training for at least 40 per cent of their managerial staff.

This suggests that Dominican firms are more active in human-resource upgrading than their Costa Rican counterparts, despite their high personnel turnover, which is their most important labour problem. There may be two reasons for this. First, the lack of skilled workers, technicians, supervisors and middle-level management staff [31] is a more acute problem than in Costa Rica, making it crucial to provide training. Second, the Government facilitates training. Firms are obliged to pay 1 per cent of their payroll as a levy to a training institute (the Institute of Professional Technical Training), and have a say in how these funds

---

[30] The principal items are trousers of cotton and artificial fibres (both for men and women), knitted and non-knitted shirts, blouses, foundation garments (mainly bras), cotton underwear, and coats and jackets.

[31] Highly capable senior managerial staff are more readily available than middle-level managers.

are utilized. There is an agreement between the Dominican Free Zone Association and the training institute, which allows companies to decide how some of the Institute's resources are used. This programme has helped both local and foreign firms in the IFZs; many have been able to provide basic as well as more advanced training to their workers.

Over the years, domestic firms have played an increasing role in the industry through wholly local as well as joint ventures, suggesting learning and capability development by local entrepreneurs. This offers advantages to foreign investors, especially in their dealings with local administration and labour, and in facilitating access to local support services. However, the activities undertaken by joint ventures and the wholly domestic firms do not differ substantially from TNC subsidiaries. Both remain heavily concentrated in simple assembly operations.

4.4.2.3 *Technological and organizational development*

The Government of the Dominican Republic has no policy to regulate or promote technology transfer and improve production standards. In 1990-1995, the TNCs in the sample (as well as the local companies) aimed mainly at increasing the efficiency of production (i.e. cost reduction), raising international market share and improving the quality of production. There was no concern with increasing local involvement in design or marketing, or with backward integration into the more capital-intensive stages of production. Firms undertook efforts to increase labour productivity through incentives, training the workforce and acquiring new equipment. The number of TNCs using programmable machines, for example, increased from two in 1985-1989, to nine in 1990-1995. One firm was also installing numerically-controlled machine tools. The number of personal computers increased from 10 units in just three firms in 1985-1989 to 50 units in five firms in 1990-1995. Local innovations or adaptations of technology and the adoption of new foreign organizational management practices were also mentioned, but assigned lower priority.

The responses of the four local companies were slightly different. They also stressed increased flexibility of production processes and the use of new organizational and management practices. In one firm, in particular, the sources of competitive advantage had changed dramatically, from low wages, reduced defect ratios and low prices to high product quality, flexibility and fast delivery. The other three domestic firms also emphasized just-in-time delivery and flexibility in their strategies in the 1990s. None mentioned low wages as a source of competitive advantage.

These strategic concerns of local firms are reflected in their activities. As in the TNCs, their efforts included productivity-enhancing activities such as improved staff incentives and training and the use of more advanced equipment (especially programmable sewing machines). One company also acquired eight numerically controlled machines and 20 robots (arms). The average number of personal computers in production (just one) was still low. However, the application of new organizational and management practices such as modular manufacturing, quick response, just-in-time management, computerized control of production and inventory and multi-tasking assumed importance. In fact, the new incentive structures and training were introduced in the context of these changes.

The main barrier to the successful introduction of technological and organizational improvements was inadequate training of personnel and the production-oriented (as opposed to customer/market-driven) culture, for both domestic and foreign-owned firms. This may be one reason why so far only one TNC has been planning to apply for ISO 9000 certification. The other firms did not show any interest, or were not even aware of it.

4.4.2.4 Building local supplier networks

The Dominican garment industry has made less progress than the industry in either Costa Rica or Morocco in terms of developing local linkages. There remains a significant bias towards importing raw materials, components and parts, as a result of both the trade regime and the incentives created by the United States production-sharing arrangement. Analysts identify weak local capabilities as a major problem (Willmore, 1996), but this may reflect an incentive structure that does not give local suppliers a real chance to develop these capabilities.[32] As in Costa Rica, weak supplier capabilities are likely to become a major problem as the country competes with countries with a long tradition of local production of fabrics. The Government has sought to strengthen the support of IFZ linkages with the local economy, but its policies have not been well implemented.[33]

In recent years, a small number of suppliers to the apparel industry have appeared within several free zone parks, supplying inputs like sewing thread, sewing machines and replacement parts. However, efforts to create larger supplier chains in items requiring higher capital investment, such as fabric, have been largely absent.[34] Local design and marketing functions have not taken root.

The local content of production in the firms interviewed was very low and had not increased since the period 1985-1989 for 14 of the 16 firms (the other two had marginal increases of 0.1 per cent and 4 per cent). None of the companies reported any subcontracting linkages with local firms. However, four firms subcontracted between 5 and 20 per cent of their production to firms operating within the IFZs to implement just-in-time practices and increase flexibility. Local subcontracting reportedly suffered from the usual problems of poor delivery, quality control and technological capacity.

4.4.2.5 Concluding remarks

The industry remains heavily geared to exploiting the traditional advantages of market access and low labour costs. As in Costa Rica, the leading TNCs aim to prolong the exploitation of these advantages rather than develop new ones. However, the limits of this strategy are in sight, as manifest in rising wages, increased competition and growing United States protection (through calls). In the medium term, the country's privileged access to the

---

[32] As discussed in more detail below.

[33] A USAID programme designed to improve local linkages was set up in the late 1980s. The programme was to run for five years, but funding was withdrawn after its first few months, following a decision in the United States Congress to put a brake on the use of funds that might move jobs from the United States to beneficiary countries.

[34] One exception is the establishment of one fully-integrated knitting firm from the Republic of Korea, Kunja Knitting Mills, which operates 10 plants with over 3,000 workers. It performs fabric knitting, dyeing, sewing and cutting as well as regular finishing operations. However, this does not involve local companies.

United States market will disappear as global garment trade is deregulated. Will the Dominican Republic go the way of Costa Rica, where no major efforts are being mounted to upgrade the garment industry?

Our survey suggests some positive response in the Dominican case. There is increased emphasis on flexible production systems and a move away from standardized production runs, especially among local firms. Both foreign and local firms are stepping up efforts to develop skills at all levels. However, the regional, multilateral and local trade regimes militate against the upstream industries that would be needed if the country is to achieve new sources of skill- and technology-based competitiveness in the apparel industry. Nor is the Dominican Government helping to develop the skills and capabilities needed for high-quality clothing production.

As far as the local trade laws are concerned, local suppliers have faced administrative obstacles in establishing links with export-oriented companies in IFZs. In theory, Law 69 allows companies in both sectors to use preferential customs treatment to their advantage, but in practice the mechanism imposed by CEDOPEX and customs have worked as impediments. Because of customs restrictions, IFZ firms also find it cumbersome to link up with plants located in different IFZ parks for specialized operations such as washing. It is important that such regulations are changed to facilitate local sourcing, and that assistance is provided to local companies to pull themselves up to the level required by the international market.

4.4.3 Morocco

4.4.3.1 Setting and industry performance

Morocco's growth performance in garment exports resembles that of the two Caribbean cases. Its seven most important categories of garment exports to OECD markets grew by 27 per cent per annum between 1980 and 1990, and 10 per cent between 1990 and 1995. This growth transformed Morocco's export structure. The share of natural resources in the total value of exports to Western Europe fell from 78 per cent to just 32 per cent, while the share of manufactures rose from 22 per cent to 68 per cent. Four of the country's top 10 exports to Western Europe in 1995 were garment items, mainly non-knitted and knitted outerwear of various types. Together these four product categories accounted for well over one-third (37 per cent) of total exports, up from just 6 per cent in 1980.

These changes were driven by rapid expansion during the 1980s, but Moroccan growth slowed down thereafter (similar to the other countries studies). It specialized in low-value items that China and large producers in South Asia can also supply at a fraction of the labour cost. Geographical proximity, privileged access and incentives cannot fully compensate for these cost differences over the longer term. Thus, in order to retain a niche in the garment trade, Morocco will need to develop new sources of competitive advantage, involving the upgrading of the industry in terms of product segments, design activity and localization.

involving the upgrading of the industry in terms of product segments, design activity and localization.

The following discussion is based on a survey among 11 garment firms and four textile producers in 1995. With one exception, the firms were established in the export-oriented period of the1980s or 1990s. Five firms are almost fully foreign-owned subsidiaries, three have a foreign involvement of 50 per cent or higher, and the remaining seven are companies with a minority foreign stake. With the exception of two textile firms that have United States partners, the investors come from different countries in the European Union. The firms were selected for their high involvement in export markets, they export on average 94 per cent of their sales and account for 21 per cent of the industry's total exports, 7 per cent of sales, and 5 per cent of the workforce. The workforce ranges from more than 1,000 employees to fewer than 400.

4.4.3.2 Human capital formation

Morocco faces serious problems in human resources. The main complaint of the sample firms was the low skill level of production labour, which forced them to undertake a lot of training. Training is widespread, but it is informal and on the job. There is little or no formal external training. A second labour-related problem is cumbersome legislation, which makes it difficult to lay off workers. Low productivity and resistance to change were also mentioned, but as secondary factors.

The lack of middle-level managers and technically qualified staff was a pressing concern, reflecting a general tendency of educational institutions to emphasize social sciences rather than technical subjects. Morocco has just 11 engineering students per 100000 people, which is very low compared to other regional countries at a similar development level; Tunisia, for example, has 77 per 100 000. Since 1989, public vocational training schools and some universities have begun to establish links with private firms through internships and adult training sessions. However, the results of these efforts to respond to industry needs are weak and mismatch in the labour market continues to be severe. Ironically, large numbers of university graduates are unemployed while firms complain about the shortage of middle-level managers and supervisors. In the sample companies, these types of employees constituted only 1 per cent of the total labour force.

4.4.3.3 Technological and organizational development

The sample firms used relatively simple technologies: each had only non-programmable sewing machines. New technology, whether from parent firms (in 47 per cent of cases) or from unrelated foreign companies, tended to be product-related and did not include plant design, management or marketing. There was no technology licensing or technical assistance. Only two firms in the sample carried out some limited R&D activity. Fourteen of the 15 respondents reported that there was no need to modify the technology to local conditions, suggesting weak capabilities.

There have been some changes in the functional activities carried out in the firms since 1990, but the changes are disparate and no clear picture of technological upgrading introduction of work teams, was considered of some importance. The use of quality control circles, multi-tasking and reorganization of production lines was reportedly less frequent.

4.4.3.4 Building local supplier networks

The local content of the garment industry's principal exports is estimated at about 10 per cent. This is higher than in the two Caribbean countries, and can be explained by the existence of a largely State-owned textile industry producing primarily for the domestic economy. This industry came into being before the advent of the export-oriented clothing industry, and the linkages have diminished since the early 1980s (in 1983, local content was 62 per cent). Inputs for exporting plants are increasingly provided by the foreign parent companies or unrelated foreign suppliers, and enter the country duty-free. Moreover, the local textile companies cannot generally meet the quality, delivery and design needs of garment producers.

A similar trend is manifest in local subcontracting linkages. The proportion of subcontracting in production came down from 11 per cent in 1985 to 8 per cent in 1990 and 6 per cent in 1995. Local value-added in the garment industry is estimated to be just 24 per cent. Along with adverse trade and financial incentives, the firms interviewed also blamed the lack of competitiveness of subcontractors. They complained in particular about inadequate quality control. Technological and delivery-related problems were mentioned as lesser problems.

Such inadequacies are difficult to overcome. The local textile industry is unlikely to reach international levels of competence as long as the incentive climate penalizes local sourcing. Domestic suppliers have not attracted FDI, which could have boosted their efficiency and modernization. The sample companies pointed out that problems with the legal framework, physical infrastructure and bureaucracy have also hindered FDI in upstream industries. Unlike investment in garment assembly, which can be moved quite easily when conditions deteriorate, investments in textile manufacturing entail a longer-term commitment as well as substantial financial outlays. Thus, such problems in the FDI climate are likely to exert more influence in investment decisions in this industry.

4.4.3.5 Concluding remarks

As in the case of the two Caribbean countries, the main competitive advantages of Morocco have been its geographical proximity and privileged market access to a large market in combination with low wages. Its political and economic links with France have also played an important role. Without the special market access, however, it is unclear whether those historical ties and locational advantages on their own would have provided the country with a competitive position in the lower end of the garment market. Clearly, this will spell trouble in the years to come. There is increasing competition from large Asian suppliers (particularly China) who offer similar products at a much lower cost and who are investing heavily in upgrading their quality. Unless Morocco can upgrade its supply and design capabilities and enter higher-quality segments at a faster rate, its exports will be strangled when the European Mediterranean partnership comes to end in the early years of the next century.[35]

The outlook is not rosy. Of the three countries, Morocco is the worst placed to upgrade its industry. Its skill shortages, bureaucratic problems and inadequate physical infrastructure deter foreign (and local) investors. While there have been improvements in quality, reliability and productivity within the given product range over the past 15 years, there has been comparatively little upgrading to higher value-added product segments.

4.5   The competitiveness challenge in the garment industry: conclusions and policy needs

TNCs in the apparel industry have played a crucial role in launching export-oriented industrialization in many developing countries. However, the implications of TNC involvement differ from country to country. Early participants have benefited a great deal more than have recent entrants. In the 1960s and 1970s, when the industry first reached East Asia, foreign buyers primarily used local developing-country suppliers. Many inputs for these garments – the fabric and trim – were also sourced from Asia. Such arrangements reflected local industrial capabilities, and in turn fed into local technological and commercial learning. They allowed local firms to advance across the entire supply chain, from the production of fibres to the manufacturing and marketing of final products. Early entrants also benefited from "first-mover advantages". Markets were growing fast and were not very demanding. Technologies were simpler and fashions changed less rapidly. Thus, the first developing-country entrants were able to transform their low-wage advantage into advantages based on technological, organizational, design and commercial capabilities. They used the apparel industry as a stepping stone towards the development of higher value-added, complex and design-driven activities.

Later entrants, hampered by a combination of lower industrial capabilities, face very different conditions in world markets and technology. The recent development of export-oriented clothing industries in developing countries has been driven mainly by distortionary trading arrangements. Host countries are trying to entice foreign companies to assemble in their countries with low-wage semi-skilled labour and incentives, but offer little by way of coherent industrial strategy to upgrade local capabilities (Lall, 1996). This is not to say that garment exports have not offered substantial benefits for host countries. The three case studies show how the garment industry has contributed to a dramatic transformation of export structures, increased industrial production and generated employment. The activity has boosted economic growth, and helped these countries to learn about industrial exports. Perhaps more importantly, it has spawned local entrepreneurship.

However, this rapid growth has resulted from a specific phase of relocation in the garment industry. In its present form, it is clearly not sustainable. Relatively simple, standardized products are put together with largely unskilled labour, with specifications

---

[35] However, it is conceivable that the Mediterranean Rim countries may become part of an enlarged European Union by 2010.

provided by importers. Highly skilled workers and advanced technologies are not needed. The trade regimes in importing countries discourage value addition in the sourcing sites. The primary interest of TNCs is to use host sites as cost centres. They can quickly scale down or relocate when other sites become more attractive. The TNCs surveyed for this study showed few signs of upgrading human resources, and there was no evidence of efforts to enter design and marketing. Linkage development with local suppliers was also rare. In Morocco, where a textile industry already existed, traditional linkages were in fact diminishing.

Export success in the sample countries has depended heavily on a source of competitive advantage – special access to major markets and the distribution of imports by quotas – that is highly evanescent. Only a few countries have used the temporary rent provided by this advantage to build up more sustainable sources of competitiveness and to diversify into other activities. Most will not sustain competitiveness once market distortions are removed. Time is thus running out fast for those producers that remain in mass-produced price-sensitive garments with low skill requirements. Asian producers might swamp this market after 2005, unless regional trade groupings continue to protect this vulnerable set of economies or they can upgrade faster than Asian producers.

Long-term competitiveness in garment exports inevitably requires a move away from low-end assembly to higher-quality and design-intensive products. This requires much higher levels of technical, development, management and organizational skills, a better developed local supply network, more subcontracting and "cluster" networking, faster response times and more advanced technological capabilities. This calls for advanced training facilities, local vertically integrated production facilities, strong small and medium-sized suppliers of specialized services and inputs, and advanced infrastructure of transport and communications. In broad terms, it calls for more coherent and coordinated industrial policy.

TNCs could play a larger role in upgrading the industry than they do at present – but only if the skills, training facilities, supplier and support industries and the infrastructure available are improved. Host Governments have much to do to overcome the market failures that hold back industrial deepening. They also have much to do to improve the incentive climate, so that biases against localization are removed, and to mount proactive FDI strategies. Policies to upgrade factor inputs and improve trade and financial incentives will also benefit local firms. These firms have greater freedom to diversify and upgrade products than foreign affiliates have – as the East Asian experience shows, with strong capabilities, local firms can go a long way towards establishing independent competitive positions. Assuming that macroeconomic and FDI policies are well-managed, future competitiveness in garments will be determined crucially by policies to upgrade factors markets, rather than by attracting FDI inflows. Simply having a passive but attractive FDI regime will not count for much unless these structural determinants of competitiveness rise in line with growing competition and wages, once market distortions are removed.

Chapter 5

TNCs, industrial restructuring and competitiveness in the automotive industry in NAFTA, MERCOSUR and ASEAN

5.1. Introduction

The manufacture of automobiles and components is the world's largest industrial activity. It employs 3 to 4 million workers directly and another 9 to 10 million in the manufacture of inputs; total employment, adding those involved in distribution, servicing and repairs, comes to around 20 million (Dicken, 1998, p. 316). The industry is also highly linkage-intensive, with significant spillovers to other sectors. It plays a large role in world trade. Automotive products accounted for 11 per cent of imports by OECD countries in 1995 (up from 7 per cent in 1980); automotive exports were $299 billion in 1994, up from $97 billion in 1980. Trade in complete vehicles went up from $58.6 to $181.7 billion, and trade in components from $38.4 to $117.1 billion.[1]

As a highly scale-intensive industry, automotive production and trade is increasingly dominated by a few large (increasingly global) companies, and is a prime example of a producer-driven production chain (Gereffi, 1994). Of the world's 50 largest manufacturing companies, 13 are automobile firms.[2] These companies manufacture critical components and assemble large numbers of parts and components made by others. Their activities have become more internationalized over time, through trade and FDI. Initially FDI flowed across the developed economies, but it later spread to many developing countries. Most recently, a few middle-income countries have been becoming tightly integrated into TNC global production systems, with the industry undergoing significant relocation as a result.

5.2. Overview

5.2.1 Production and consumption patterns

The developed market economies accounted for four-fifths of world automobile production in 1995 (table 5.1). In that year, 94 per cent of the world automobile trade was between the three major producing regions: East Asia, North America and Western Europe (table 5.2). The rise of Japan as a producer is the most striking development of the 1970s and 1980s: Japan's share of world output increased from 1 to 26 per cent between 1960 and 1989; it fell to 21 per cent in 1995, reflecting the relocation of Japanese production. Its export market share in the OECD countries rose from under 1 per cent at the beginning of the 1960s to almost 20 per cent by 1980. The subsequent slowdown is again due to increased production by overseas Japanese affiliates.

---

[1] However, employment in the industry fell from 4.5 to 4.3 million between 1979 and 1994 (Vickery, 1996, p. 163).

[2] "Global pile-up", *The Economist*, 10 May 1997, pp.19-23.

Table 5.1. Automobile production by major countries, 1960-1995

Country/region/territory	1960 Production (000 vehicles)	1960 World share (Per cent)	1989 Production (000 vehicles)	1989 World share (Per cent)	1995 Production (000 vehicles)	1995 World share (Per cent)
1. Japan	165	1.3	9 052	25.5	7 611	20.6
2. N. America	6 998	53.9	7 807	22.0	7 689	20.7
United States	6 675	51.4	6 823	19.2	6 350	17.1
Canada	323	2.5	984	2.8	1 339	3.6
3. W. Europe	5 092	39.1	13 267	37.5	12 712	34.3
Germany	1 817	14.0	4 564	12.9	4 360	11.8
France	1 175	9.0	3 409	9.6	3 050	8.2
Spain	43	0.3	1 639	4.6	1 959	5.3
United Kingdom	1 353	10.4	1 299	3.7	1 532	4.1
Italy	596	4.6	1 972	5.6	1 423	3.8
Sweden	108	0.8	384	1.1	388	1.1
4. Others		0.7	3 078	8.7	5 621	15.2
Republic of Korea	-	-	872	2.5	2 003	5.4
Brazil	38	0.3	731	2.1	1 303	3.5
Mexico	28	0.2	439	1.2	699	1.9
Poland	-	-	289	0.8	392	1.1
Australia	-	-	357	1.0	292	0.8
Taiwan Province of China	-	-	-	-	282	0.8
Czech Republic	-	-	184	0.5	228	0.6
Argentina	30	0.2	112	0.3	227	0.6
Malaysia	-	-	94	0.3	195	0.5
World	12 999	100.0	35 455	100.0	37 045	100.0

Source: Dicken (1998), p. 319.

Table 5.2. OECD market shares in automotive products, 1963-1995 [a]

	1963	1971	1980	1990	1995
1. Japan	0.6	7.8	19.3	21.9	18.6
2. North America	23.0	37.5	23.3	19.7	21.6
United States	21.4	19.0	14.9	10.0	10.9
Canada	1.6	18.5	8.4	9.7	10.7
3. Western Europe	74.6	53.1	51.5	51.8	51.2
Germany	32.3	22.1	22.9	22.2	18.2
France	9.6	8.9	10.3	8.3	8.2
Belgium/Luxembourg	3.9	6.1	5.7	5.1	5.7
Spain	0.1	0.4	1.5	3.8	5.5
United Kingdom	18.4	7.0	3.2	3.8	5.3
Italy	6.1	5.0	4.4	3.8	3.4
Sweden	3.0	2.6	1.8	2.6	2.5
Austria	0.2	0.2	0.8	0.8	1.3
Netherlands	1.0	0.8	0.9	1.4	1.1
4. Others	1.8	1.6	5.9	6.6	8.6
Mexico	0.0	0.2	0.4	2.3	3.6
Republic of Korea	0.0	0.0	...	0.9	1.3
Brazil	...	...	0.6	0.6	0.4
All others [b]	1.8	1.4	4.9	2.8	3.3
Total	100	100	100	100	100

Source: Mortimore (1997), p. 69, based on ECLAC CAN and CANPLUS databases.

[a] Defined as SITC 713, 781 and 784: engines, passenger vehicles and auto parts.
[b] Countries which possessed less than 1 per cent each of the OECD market in 1995.

Table 5.3 shows the market shares of national and foreign enterprises in the biggest consumer markets in 1993. The data suggest that the three markets have distinct characteristics. In the United States market the "Big Three" national companies – General Motors, Ford and Chrysler – account for about two-thirds of new passenger car registrations, with Japanese companies controlling most of the remainder and European companies having only about 3 per cent. In contrast, in Japan, national companies dominate new registrations, accounting for 96 per cent of the total. The situation in Europe is more varied. The share of national firms varies from zero in the United Kingdom, to over a quarter in Sweden, to 42 per cent in Germany, 45 per cent in Italy and 60 per cent in France. In Europe, United States companies have appreciably higher market shares than the Japanese companies.

Table 5.3. Competition in principal automobile markets, 1993 [a]
(Percentage of new registrations)

Car manufacturer	United States	Western Europe					Japan
		Germany	France	Italy	United Kingdom	Sweden	
National	66.4	42.0	60.3	44.9	0	26.6	96.0
Foreign	33.6	58.0	39.7	55.1	100	73.4	4.0
- United States	X	25.6	14.5	16.8	39.4	27.5	1.1
- Japan	29.3	13.7	4.4	4.2	12.7	20.3	X
- Europe	3.2	14.0	20.1	32.8	46.0	24.7	2.8

Source : Based on Vickery (1996), p. 189.
[a] New registrations of passenger cars by country of ultimate ownership of producing unit.

Considerable growth in exports (although from a small base) has also occurred for some developing countries, mainly the Republic of Korea, Mexico and Brazil.[3] The destination of Brazil's and Mexico's exports is strongly concentrated: most of Brazil's exports go to other Latin American countries, and 88 per cent of Mexican exports are focused on North America. In contrast, the Republic of Korea's export pattern resembles that of Japan: exports are primarily directed to Europe and the United States. Exports from the Republic of Korea have grown from virtually nothing to a share of 5 per cent in world production in 1995, contributing to the "Asian challenge".

Total global automobile production capacity is 68 million cars (including pick-ups and sport utility cars). However, total demand and production was only 50 million (73 per cent of capacity) in 1996. In Western Europe, production was 33 per cent (6 million cars) below capacity, in Japan 50 per cent (4 million) and in North America 25 per cent (3.8 million). This excess capacity has led to declining profit rates for more than 10 years.[4] The slow growth of demand in the mature European and North American markets is due to structural factors: the balance between new and replacement demand is shifting in favour of the latter. Car manufacturers have adapted to this situation by frequently introducing new models and promoting them in massive advertising campaigns (Dicken, 1998, p. 324).

---

[3] However, only in the Republic of Korea are exports undertaken by national companies.
[4] "Global pile-up", *The Economist*, 10 May 1997, pp.19-23.

The fastest growth in demand in recent years has occurred in some of the East and South-East Asian countries, but production capacity in the region has grown even faster. Expectations of fast growth in demand in Latin America have attracted large investments in capacity. Both of these factors contribute to global over-capacity. Eastern Europe may also turn into a rapidly growing automobile market, depending strongly on the rate of economic reconstruction there. Thus it appears that over-capacity will remain an important feature in all the major regions during the coming years.

5.2.2 Leading players and their strategies

A small group of firms dominate the automobile industry (table 5.4). Just 17 firms from Japan (6), Europe (6), the United States (3) and the Republic of Korea (2) accounted for nearly 90 per cent of world production in 1994. These TNCs fall into three groups.

Table 5.4. Major automobile TNCs and degree of internationalization, 1993-1994

Rank 1994	Rank 1981	TNC (home country)	1994 production (millions of units) [a]	Domestic sales	(of which: exports)	Per cent outside home country
		First group	**19.7**			
1	1	General Motors (United States)	8.0	52.4	..	47.6
2	2	Ford (United States)	6.5	41.2	..	58.9
3	3	Toyota (Japan)	5.2	85.2	(33.3)	14.8
		Second group	**18.6**			
4	5	Volkswagen (Germany)	3.2	57.2	(21.8)	42.8
5	4	Nissan (Japan)	2.8	68.8	(30.8)	31.2
6	12	Chrysler (United States)	2.8	54.3	..	45.7
7	7	Fiat (Italy)	2.4	74.9	(36.4)	25.1
8	8	PSA (France)	2.0	81.1	(55.9)	18.9
9	6	Renault (France)	1.9	77.0	(44.6)	23.0
10	10	Mitsubishi (Japan)	1.8	83.3	(37.3)	16.7
11	11	Honda (Japan)	1.7	67.0	(34.3)	33.1
		Third group	**6.1**			
12	9	Mazda (Japan)	1.2	79.8	(53.7)	20.2
13	-	Hyundai (Rep. of Korea)	1.2	98.2	(42.7)	1.9
14	21	BMW/Rover (Germany)	1.1	100	(61.2)	-
15	15	Suzuki (Japan)	1.0	99.4	(43.3)	0.6
16	14	Daimler Benz (Germany)	0.9	100	(56.4)	-
17	-	Kia (Rep. of Korea)	0.7	100	..	-
Total		**Major players**	**44.4**			
Total		**All firms**	**49.7**			

Note: 1993 production [b] — Per cent in home country (Domestic sales, of which: exports).

Source: Based on Vickery (1996), pp. 160 and 171.
[a] Passenger cars and commercial vehicles.
[b] Passenger cars only.

The first consists of three giants – General Motors, Ford and Toyota – that accounted for about forty per cent of world production. These TNCs have been the pioneers in terms of design, production technology and organizational practices. While the two United States firms in this group have extensive facilities outside the United States (about one-half of their global production), the Japanese firm has minor production outside Japan (about 15 per cent of its global production), and competes mainly by exports from its home country.

The second group consists of eight mid-sized companies from Europe (4), Japan (3) and the United States (1), accounting for over 37 per cent of world production in 1994, which compete internationally in different ways. International production systems are more important than exports from their home country for Volkswagen and Chrysler, about the same for the Japanese companies, Nissan and Honda, and less important for the other, mainly European corporations. The third group consists of six smaller producers from Japan (2), the Republic of Korea (2) and Germany (2). These compete mainly via exports from their home country, and accounted for 12 per cent of world production in 1994. The two Korean car-makers were the only notable newcomers during the last decade or so.

The international production systems of these firms in respect of passenger vehicle production are shown in table 5.5.

Table 5.5. International production systems of automobile TNCs, 1993
(Per cent of TNC's worldwide production of passenger cars outside TNC's home country)

Auto TNCs	Per cent international	Industrial countries							Developing economies		
		United States	Canada	United Kingdom	Germany	Spain	Australia	Others	Mexico	South America	Taiwan Province of China
First group											
General Motors	47.6	X	9.4	4.8	16.7	7.2	1.7		2.9	4.9	
Ford	58.9	X	9.3	7.5	12.1	5.9	2.8	9.6	4.7	4.6	2.4
Toyota	14.8	10.5	2.2				2.1				
Second group											
Volkswagen	42.8				X	18.0			8.6	16.2	
Nissan	31.2	13.2		11.1			0.7		6.2		
Chrysler	45.7	X	28.2						17.5		
Fiat	25.1									25.1	
PSA	18.9			3.8		15.1					
Renault	23.0					17.9				5.1	
Mitsub.	16.7	12.0					4.7				
Honda	33.1	26.5	6.6								
Third group											
Mazda	20.2	20.2									
Hyundai	1.9		1.9								
BMW	-				X						
Suzuki	0.6		0.6								
D. Benz	-				X						
Kia	-										

Source: Based on Vickery (1996), p. 160.

The TNCs with the most internationalized production systems, responsible for over 40 per cent of total production, are Ford, General Motors, Chrysler and Volkswagen. Those with moderately internationalized ones, with more than one-fifth of total vehicle production located outside the home country, are Honda, Nissan, Fiat, Renault and Mazda. Roughly half of this group, including Toyota, have production systems which are not very internationalized (less than 20 per cent foreign-based). The older firms, from the United States and Europe, tend to be more internationalized. The United States firms are more prone to service world markets through international production systems while the Europeans use exports from their national production systems. Relatively newer European firms often license local companies to undertake production in overseas markets rather than establish affiliates. During the last two decades, the Japanese car-makers have been catching up with United States companies by investing in international production operations.

The most internationalized companies focus on a few markets. Ford and General Motors supply the European market from plants in Germany, Spain and the United Kingdom, the North American market from plants in Canada and Mexico, and South American markets from local production facilities. Volkswagen has a similar structure in Brazil/Argentina, Mexico and Spain. Chrysler focuses exclusively on the North American market. Japanese TNCs concentrated on the North American market until 1993, serving it from production facilities in the United States (Toyota, Nissan, Mitsubishi, Honda and Mazda), Canada (Toyota, Honda and Suzuki) and Mexico (Nissan). Only Nissan invested in core facilities in Europe. European auto TNCs had a few core production facilities in other European countries, mainly Spain and the United Kingdom, and South America (primarily Brazil and Argentina).

Two major advances in the manufacturing process are worth noting. The first, observed during the early twentieth century, was the introduction of mass production systems developed by Ford, to exploit scale economies from long production runs of a few standardized products. Production took place in massive plants using rigid methods in which each assembly worker performed a highly specialized and narrow task, very quickly and repetitively. "Fordist" production methods yielded enormous cost savings, and other United States automobile makers followed Ford. United States firms gained international market shares through exports, later consolidating their advantages in Europe and Latin America through FDI. Components and parts needed in assembly lines were sourced from low-cost suppliers all over the world, necessitating huge inventories at the assembly plants. The major drawback of the production system was its rigidity: assembly lines were designed specifically for one model, and changing models was costly and time-consuming.

The second major change was the lean production system pioneered by Toyota in the 1970s, and later adopted by nearly all automobile companies in one way or another. The principal elements of the Toyota Production System that distinguish it from the Fordist system are:[5]

- Just-in time (JIT) production of small batches, with minimal inventories of components, parts and work-in-progress. Production is pulled by customer demand, not pushed to suit machine loading. *Kanban* controls (tags to monitor and control the flow of parts) are used extensively. JIT requires close coordination of the whole supply chain from raw material to finished product, through partnerships with suppliers and dealers.

---

[5] See: Womack, Jones and Roos (1990); "Motoring lessons", *The Economist*, 20 June 1998; and Kaplinsky and Posthuma (1994), section 1.3.2.

- Zero defect ratios, rather than tolerable defect rates. This is done through defect prevention rather than rectification. When something goes wrong, a worker can pull a cord and the fault is identified and corrected immediately.
- Team-based work organization, with flexible multi-skilled operators and few indirect staff.
- *Kaizen*: the process of continuously seeking small improvements to gain greater efficiency, better ergonomics and higher quality. Defect prevention and teamwork are major ways to promote this.

This does not mean that scale economies are no longer important. The optimal size of an assembly plant is still around 250,000 units per year, although the model-specific optimum may be lower.[6] In order to implement lean production, however, a different relationship with suppliers is needed: preferably long-term and very tight in functional terms, with design and production of components being carried out in very close consultation. More responsibility and risk is shifted onto the supplier firms, with the most important trend being "modular manufacturing", that is, suppliers who manufacture entire "sub-assemblies" or "modules" rather than individual components.

The competitive advantages obtained by Toyota, and later by other Japanese auto makers, allowed them to make large inroads in world markets. In the first instance, they exported from Japan. This produced a strong reaction on the part of the United States Government, which eventually succeeded in imposing voluntary export restraints on Japanese automobile producers. In response, Japanese automobile producers began to invest in assembly plants in the United States. While the total production of passenger vehicles in the United States remained in the order of 6 million vehicles during the period 1987-1993, there was a significant change in producers. The foreign-owned production of automobiles in the United States rose from about 0.5 million units in 1987 (9 per cent of total production) to over 1.5 million in 1993 (26 per cent). Once Volkswagen moved its United States plant to Mexico, Japanese companies formed the only foreign presence in the United States automobile industry, operating alone or through joint ventures with United States producers. By 1993, Japanese automobile producers controlled almost 30 per cent of the United States passenger car market via local production combined with imports from Japan (Vickery, 1996, p. 189).

In Western Europe, a similar development is taking place. Many European countries (France, Italy, Portugal, Spain and the United Kingdom) reacted to the Japanese challenge with trade restrictions. The institution of the European Single Market led to bilateral negotiations between the European Commission and Japan, beginning in 1991, to eliminate national restrictions during a transition period. The initial idea was to allow Japan to export 1.23 million units annually (later reduced) to Europe until 1999, when the European Communities' commitments to WTO would require such trade restrictions to be eliminated. As earlier in the United States, Japanese companies began to invest in local plants, particularly in the United Kingdom, in order to supply Europe from within. By 1993, Japanese automobile companies had captured significant market shares in many European countries through imports and/or local

---

[6] This number relates to the minimum efficient scale in production. R&D outlays in the automobile industry tend to be very large, making it unlikely that R&D-related economies of scale are exhausted at the volume mentioned. In addition, economies in distribution and servicing increase the minimum efficient scale (Kathuria, 1996, pp.57-58).

production: its share of the market in Sweden reached 20 per cent, in Germany 14 per cent, in the United Kingdom 13 per cent, in France 4 per cent, and in Italy (4 per cent) (Vickery, 1996, p. 189).

The advance of Japanese car manufacturers is also explained by their productivity (table 5.6). In 1989, the Japanese producers in their home country were substantially more productive than firms in the United States, with fewer defects, a smaller repair area, lower stocks, more teamwork, fewer job classifications and more multi-tasking. They provided more training to new workers, had much lower absenteeism, and were much more automated in welding, painting and assembly. By 1993-1995, United States and European auto firms had caught up a bit, but Japanese firms (both in Japan and their affiliates in North America) continued to set the pace. All these advantages translated into lower prices, better quality and faster delivery. European auto TNCs were even less productive than United States firms. Moreover, the Japanese plants in the United States were more competitive than United States-owned auto plants there, even though they were somewhat less efficient than the Japanese plants in Japan.

Table 5.6. Manufacturing indicators of leading automobile producers, 1989 [a]

Item	Japanese firms in Japan	Japanese firms in North America	US firms in North America	European firms in Europe
Productivity (hours per vehicle)	16.8	21.2	25.1	36.2
Assembly defects per 100 vehicles	60.0	65.0	82.0	97.0
Repair area (per cent of assembly space)	4.1	4.9	12.9	14.4
Stock (days) [b]	0.2	1.6	2.9	2.0
Workforce in teams (per cent)	69.3	71.3	17.3	0.6
Number of job classifications	12	9	67	15
Training of new workers (hours)	380	370	46	173
Absenteeism (per cent)	5.0	4.8	11.7	12.1
Share of process automated (per cent):				
- Welding	86.2	85.0	76.2	76.6
- Painting	54.6	40.7	33.6	38.2
- Assembly	1.7	1.1	1.2	3.1

Source : Womack et al., 1990, figure 4.7.

[a] Averages for plants in each region, 1989.
[b] For eight sample parts.

A similar situation holds for parts and components makers, although it is a more complex and diverse industry. One study found that the link between performance and the lean production system was unequivocal (Andersen Consulting, 1992). Another found that the productivity performance of Japanese component manufacturers had improved by 38 per cent between 1992 and 1994 (Andersen Consulting, 1994). This study was based on a sample of 71 automotive component plants (seats, exhausts and brakes) in nine countries (Canada, France, Germany, Italy, Japan, Mexico, Spain United Kingdom and the United States). Of the 71 automotive component plants in the study, only 13 were categorized as world-class: the gap between them and the other 58 plants was very large in terms of productivity (2:1), quality (9:1 for seats, 170:1 for exhausts and 16:1 for brakes) and management.

The Asian advance, intensified competition, saturation of leading consumer markets and the emergence of global overcapacity are all changing the nature of the industry. An industry that was organized on national, regional and exporting lines is becoming global.[7] All companies are aggressively trying to cut costs and seeking new markets in an effort to maintain market share. The important trends are:

- *Increasing FDI* in new facilities and modernization of old plants in countries with high growth potential, or where costs of production are lower than in established sites. South-East Asia and Latin America are the two main destinations for FDI in the developing world; Spain, the United Kingdom and parts of Eastern Europe are popular destinations in the advanced countries. In emerging markets, investment has been encouraged by trade barriers that create protected regional markets, as in the case of MERCOSUR and ASEAN. First-mover advantages have also motivated TNCs to invest overseas: it is vital to establish one's presence before others do in order to capture sufficient market share and thus be able to realize economies of scale. However, although such strategies may be optimal for individual TNCs, they are sub-optimal for the industry because they lead to over-investment, aggravating existing overcapacity.[8]

- *Reorganization of TNC supply chains* in order to support lean production. There is a clear trend towards reducing the number of "first-tier" suppliers (with whom the assemblers have direct dealings). At the same time, more vertically organized structures have emerged, in which many second- and third-tier suppliers of parts are coordinated by a core of first-tier suppliers. This leads to the emergence of modular manufacturing systems. Assemblers also put pressure on suppliers throughout the supply chain to cut costs. First-tier suppliers also have to share the cost of design and development. The use of JIT methods and increased joint design and development between the assemblers and first-tier suppliers has created the need for geographical proximity of suppliers (although, for some components, proximity may only mean the same broad region, such as Europe). Assemblers are persuading core suppliers to set up facilities near their own plants. Such "follow sourcing" gives rise to parallel global networks of component producers (Humphrey, 1998; Pyke, 1998, p. 4).

- *Development of vehicles tailored to different markets*. TNCs are building "world cars", on global platforms (chassis, gearboxes, engines, etc.) compatible with a variety of car bodies. The aim is create generic production capacity through increased standardization to make assemblers less vulnerable to overcapacity, in contrast to the days when investments tended to be highly model-specific (Humphrey, 1998, p. 10; Oliber, 1998, p. 19; UNCTAD, 1995, pp. 150-153).

- *Centralization of design and R&D in parent companies*, which facilitates the development of common products and processes and exploits economies in R&D. TNCs are getting away from the earlier pattern in which subsidiaries conducted R&D and were relatively

---

[7] "Global pile-up", *The Economist*, 10 May 1997, pp. 19-23.

[8] *Ibid.* The situation is akin to a game of musical chairs. No one wants to be left out when the music stops. Just as TNCs do not want to forego investments in new promising markets, they also try to avoid being the first to close down a factory and lose market share.

autonomous in this regard. Considerable efforts were made in these plants to adapt models to local conditions and demand characteristics and to conduct process engineering. Design is more standardized and conducted increasingly together with the core suppliers, who are also centralizing this task in their headquarters. The subsidiaries of assemblers and core suppliers receive their designs from headquarters and play a more limited role in R&D than earlier (Humphrey, 1998, p.11; Oliber, 1998, pp. 19-20).

- *A wave of mergers and acquisitions.* The number of global players continues to decrease. Recent examples of consolidation include the merger between Daimler-Benz and Chrysler in May 1998, the acquisition of Volvo by Ford in January 1999, the absorption of Ssangyong and Samsung by Daewoo, and that of Kia by Hyundai in 1998.

5.2.3 Opportunities for developing countries

The leading auto TNCs increasingly consider that activities in developing countries as integrated parts of their global production strategies, for three main reasons. First, developing countries can now be incorporated into their production networks as sites for less advanced and labour-intensive activities, rather than as points of entry to protected domestic markets. TNCs used to focus on securing market share in developing host countries and, faced with import-substitution policies that stipulated high levels of national content and strict balance-of-payments obligations, they assembled poor-quality and technologically obsolete vehicles for the local market at high cost. The plants operated quite separately from their main production base in their home countries. This pattern changed with liberalization. Along with rapid improvements in transport and communication technologies world-wide, policy liberalization created significant opportunities for TNCs to pursue a truly global division of labour. Second, some developing countries have developed their infrastructure and their industrial base, making them attractive as production sites for more advanced operations, particularly as regional production platforms. Third, several developing countries provide prospective high-growth markets. Along with the trend towards regional integration in important markets, there is a strong incentive for TNCs to serve these markets with integrated systems of production. Regional integration schemes provide firms with local production facilities that afford privileged access to larger markets coupled with regional preferences through rules of origin. So far the efforts of TNCs to build integrated production networks have centred on a few developing countries; it would clearly be inefficient to build advanced plants in a large number of countries.

Table 5.7 shows TNC auto firms in developing countries in the early 1990s (many more new plants have been set up in developing countries since this information was collected). Japanese firms tended to focus on countries or territories in Asia (15 of their 17 plants are located there), especially in countries belonging to ASEAN (5 plants in Indonesia, 5 in Thailand, and 2 in Malaysia). United States and European firms tended to concentrate on countries in Latin America; 16 of their 26 plants are located there (5 in Argentina, 4 in Brazil, 4 in Mexico and 3 in Venezuela). Japanese TNCs in Asia are more amenable to joint ventures with local companies than United States or European TNCs in Latin America, which operate almost exclusively by way of wholly-owned subsidiaries (Mortimore, 1993, pp. 29-32).

There are four distinct patterns of development in the auto industry in developing countries. The first is that of the Republic of Korea, which followed Japan in establishing a competitive auto industry with national companies. TNCs were allowed to participate primarily through minority shareholding or licensing. The plants of auto manufacturers from the Republic of Korea are still largely located in the home country, although several affiliates have been set up abroad.

Table 5.7. Auto TNC vehicle plants located in developing countries, early 1990s

Plant sites (total number)	Japanese (17 plants)						United States (15 plants)			European (11 plants)			
	Toyota	Nissan	Honda	Mazda	Mitsubishi	Suzuki	General Motors	Ford	Chrysler	Volkswagen	Fiat	Renault	Peugeot
Indonesia (5)	X		X	X	X	X							
Malaysia (2)	X				X								
Thailand (5)	X	X	X	X	X								
Republic of Korea (4)				X	X		X	X					
Taiwan Province of China (2)		X						X					
China (4)							X		X	X			X
Mexico (5)		X					X	X	X	X			
Brazil (4)							X	X		X	X		
Argentina (5)								X		X	X	X	X
Venezuela (3)							X	X			X		
Turkey (4)	X						X	X				X	
Total (43)	4	3	2	3	4	1	6	7	2	4	3	2	2

Source: Calculated from O'Brien and Karmokolias, 1994, chart 2, p. 14.

There are two patterns in Latin America. One is the integration of the Mexican automobile industry into North American production, under NAFTA. The United States "Big Three" car-makers have extended their production systems into Mexico to supply the North American market, which will be fully integrated by 2008. The other is undergoing vigorous restructuring and modernization of the auto industry in MERCOSUR (Brazil, Argentina, Paraguay and Uruguay). European firms such as Volkswagen and Fiat are placing considerable emphasis on expanding regional production systems in this market.

The final pattern is observed in the ASEAN region, which is pursuing the consolidation of a regional automobile industry in the context of the ASEAN Free Trade Agreement due to be implemented by 2008. There are several automobile producers in this region, ranging from the national car-maker Proton in Malaysia to majority-owned affiliates in Thailand and the Philippines. Japanese auto TNCs have been very active in launching regional production systems here.

5.3 FDI and determinants: NAFTA, MERCOSUR and ASEAN

5.3.1 The automotive industry in Latin America

The automobile industry has played a critical role in Latin American industrialization, especially in the larger countries – Argentina, Brazil and Mexico.[9] TNCs have been the leading players in this industry. Table 5.8 shows that 14 of the 50 largest firms in Latin America are subsidiaries of auto TNCs, occupying 10 of the top 25 spots of all TNCs in Latin America and 6 of the top 25 spots of all firms. While United States and European auto TNCs were present in force, Japanese and other Asian auto companies were initially absent (with a few exceptions, notably Nissan's operation in Mexico).

Table 5.8. Principal automobile firms in Latin America, by sales, 1996
(Millions of dollars)

Rank[a]		Company				
All firms	TNCs	(Location of affiliate)	Country of Origin	Sales	Exports	Imports
5	1	Volkswagen (Brazil)	Germany	7 003.3	555.6	1 000.5
7	2	Chrysler (Mexico)	United States	6 455.4	2 936.0	2 695.1
8	3	General Motors (Mexico)	United States	6 345.6	4 532.5	4 410.0
10	4	General Motors (Brazil)	United States	5 432.9	611.6	4 675.4
12	5	Fiat (Brazil)	Italy	4 742.9	329.9	2 670.2
18	8	Ford (Mexico)	United States	3 879.1	2 387.1	1 940.8
19	9	Ford (Brazil)	United States	3 830.1	849.2	425.0
49	19	Mercedes Benz (Brazil)	Germany	2 130.9	249.0	956.8
63	20	Nissan (Mexico)	Japan	1 800.0	1 050.9	2 229.8
85	28	Ford (Argentina)	United States	1 464.6	338.7 [b]	805.1
89	30	Volkswagen (Mexico)	Germany	1 450.0	1 160.7	1 034.1
109	37	Volkswagen (Argentina)	Germany	1 229.7	237.1 [b]	544.6
120	..	SEVEL (Argentina) [c]	Argentina	1 169.1	-	156.8
125	45	CIADEA (Argentina)[d]	France	1 121.3	133.3	293.5

Source : Mortimore, 1998b.
[a] Among the 500 largest firms in Latin America, according to sales volume.
[b] 1997.
[c] Locally-owned producer of Fiat and Peugeot vehicles until 1997.
[d] Joint venture with Renault.

The industry was established in the 1950s to serve protected domestic markets, with high local content requirements (usually in the 60-90 per cent range) and a battery of government controls. Vehicle producers were required to submit investment programmes for authorization, and sectoral restrictions applied to foreign investors. The production of auto parts was often reserved for national firms or joint ventures. Performance requirements, such as minimum export volumes or compensation with exports for imported components and parts, abounded. Sometimes vehicle producers were required to export parts produced by national firms. Price controls were often placed on the industry. The main result was that the industry lagged behind

---

[9] Within MERCOSUR, Brazil and Argentina together account for 99 per cent of vehicle and component production (Kolodziejski, 1998).

international efficiency and productivity standards and turned out old-fashioned, overpriced and poor-quality vehicles. Assemblers faced a tense bargaining relationship with sectoral authorities preoccupied with the balance of payments. Since their cars could not compete in export markets, the industry was responsible for considerable balance-of-payments deficits generated by the high level of component imports. Local sales were extremely sensitive to changes in national income and credit policies. This import substitution strategy made automobile industries in Latin America suffer great volatility in the period of macroeconomic instability in the 1980s.

In 1980, the Brazilian auto industry was more than double the size of that of Mexico, which in turn was approximately double the size of that of Argentina (table 5.9). Exports were only 14 per cent of Brazilian production, 4 per cent of Mexican production and 1 per cent of Argentine production. As a consequence of the Latin American debt crisis, the national automobile industries went into a severe skid. They recovered their 1980 production levels only a decade or so later (in 1993 in the case of Brazil and Argentina, 1988 in the case of Mexico). In the interim, it was only in Mexico that the industry developed a significant export orientation. The 1990s brought a revolution to the industry. By 1996, vehicle production volumes had well surpassed 1980 levels, with Mexico's 2.5 times higher, Brazil's 1.6 times, and Argentina's 1.1 times. Export values in 1996 exceeded those in 1980 in Mexico by a factor of 54 and in Argentina by a factor of 29, and were twice the 1980 level for Brazil. At the same time, vehicle imports expanded considerably, corresponding to 48 per cent of production for the domestic market in Argentina (1996), 23 per cent in Brazil (1995), and between 3 and 5 per cent in Mexico (1994-1996).

Table 5.9. Mexico, Brazil and Argentina: vehicle production, exports and imports, 1980-1996
(Thousands of units)

	Mexico			Brazil			Argentina		
Year	Total production	Export production	Imports	Total production	Export production	Imports	Total production	Export production	Imports
1980	490.0	18.2	*	1 165.1	157.0	*	281.8	3.6	*
1981	597.1	14.4	*	780.8	212.6	*	172.4	0.3	*
1982	472.6	15.8	*	859.3	173.3	*	132.1	3.2	*
1983	285.5	22.4	*	896.4	168.6	*	159.8	5.2	*
1984	358.0	33.6	*	864.6	196.5	*	167.3	4.2	*
1985	458.7	58.4	*	966.7	207.6	*	137.6	0.8	*
1986	341.0	72.4	*	1 056.3	183.2	*	170.5	0.4	*
1987	395.2	163.0	*	920.0	345.5	*	193.3	0.5	*
1988	512.8	173.1	*	1 068.7	320.4	*	164.1	1.7	*
1989	641.2	196.0	*	1 013.2	253.7	*	127.8	1.8	*
1990	820.5	276.8	*	914.4	187.3	2.7	99.6	1.1	*
1991	989.3	350.6	*	960.0	193.1	27.8	138.9	5.2	17.2
1992	1 080.9	382.5	6.1	1 073.7	341.9	45.1	262.0	16.4	105.9
1993	1 080.1	471.9	3.4	1 391.4	331.5	97.4	342.3	30.0	109.6
1994	1 097.4	575.0	56.4	1 581.4	377.6	218.2	408.8	38.7	174.3
1995	931.2	778.7	17.0	1 629.0	263.0	369.0	285.4	52.7	101.1
1996	1 211.3	970.9	30.2	1 813.9	305.7	223.7	313.3	109.0	151.7

Source: Mortimore, 1998a, based on data from the following national automobile producers' associations: AMIA (Mexico), ANFAVEA (Brazil) and ADEFA (Argentina).

* Practically zero.

The restructuring of the global automobile industry stimulated significant changes in the Latin American operations of auto TNCs. There were major investments to modernize and expand capacity, aiming not just at the national market but also at regional markets. NAFTA and MERCOSUR both had special provisions for the automobile industry, designed to facilitate the expansion of TNCs. The two schemes produced similar results. Both facilitated the rejuvenation of established manufacturers, and attracted new entrants and substantial FDI inflows. They resulted in large increases in exports and rises in productivity and competitiveness. However, there are important differences between the two schemes in terms of their objectives, rules and regulations, and impact (see below).

5.3.1.1 Mexico

The automobile industry has been the largest destination for manufacturing FDI in Mexico. During the 1980s, approximately $10 billion FDI flowed into the industry, and inflows were even larger in the 1990s. The Mexican Ministry of Commerce and Industrial Development (SECOFI, 1994) put the total of registered foreign investments in 1994 at $2.5 billion. According to the United States International Trade Commission, the United States "Big Three" car-makers alone invested about $3 billion in Mexico between 1993 and 1996, about one-tenth of their investments in the United States.[10] FDI in the industry ranged from 9 to 12 per cent of total inflows into Mexican industry between 1994 and 1997.[11] General Motors has become the largest private employer in Mexico.[12]

During the import-substitution phase (1978-1982), built-up vehicles could not be imported. This prompted investment in local assembly plants, mainly by Ford, Chrysler and General Motors. Production for the domestic market reached an average of 300,000 units per year. Due to low exports and large imports of components, the industry contributed much to the balance-of-payments deficit between 1977 and 1982. The Government put pressure on producers to raise local content and to export more parts and accessories. This, combined with growing competitive pressure from emerging Japanese producers in the United States market, heralded a new phase (1983-1987), when General Motors, Ford and Chrysler began to use Mexico as a sourcing site for the United States market. They made major investments, starting with engine plant, and following these with small front-wheel drive cars, also primarily for export to the United States market. The engine projects came on stream in the early 1980s, just as the Mexican domestic market collapsed, and the car projects followed soon after (around 1987).

The restructuring was helped by significant changes in Government policy towards the auto industry. The changes were greatest in the auto parts industry, where the Government had been most interventionist. In the import-substitution era it had attempted to limit the assemblers' supplier options to in-house parts (mainly engines) and sourcing from national Mexican companies, rather than from affiliates of auto parts TNCs. The foreign share of auto parts firms

---

[10]   Recent investors include Volkswagen, with its restyled Beetle Model. Of a total expected production of about 100,000, half are destined for the American market (see "Return of the Beetle", *The Economist*, 10 January 1998, p. 52.

[11]   Based on data from SECOFI, as cited in UNCTAD (1998b), p. 77.

[12]   "Setback for Mexico's expanding workforce", *Financial Times*, 16 July 1998, p. 6.

could not exceed 40 per cent. Liberalization lowered national content requirements to just 30 per cent for export models, which severely damaged the Mexican companies that had been established under the previous policy.

Vehicle exports boomed after 1988. The industry reached a trade surplus of $1.3 billion in 1990. Even before the 1994 foreign exchange crisis and devaluation of the peso, the three United States TNCs exported two-thirds or more of their passenger vehicle production from Mexico. There were also large investments by Volkswagen and Nissan in this period, in anticipation of NAFTA. New entrants (BMW, Mercedes Benz and Honda) appeared for the same reason. Thus, substantial investments in export-oriented production were made in the years leading up to the entry into force of NAFTA in January 1994. NAFTA provisions for the automobile industry include:

- Tariff barriers on Mexico-North America trade in automobiles and parts are to be phased out over 10 years (1994-2004). United States tariffs on automotive exporters in Mexico have already dropped from 2.7 to 0.6 per cent for vehicles, and from 1.7 to 0.4 per cent for auto parts.

- The trade must meet the NAFTA norms of origin at the end of the transition period, that is, at least 62.5 per cent of the value-added must come from NAFTA sources. The net-cost formula ensures that imports from non-NAFTA sources will be traced through the production chain.

- During the transition period, Mexican value-added is reduced by counting in-bond assembly (*maquiladora*) as United States national content; national value-added rules will be eliminated after 2004.

- "NAFTA investors" (from Canada and the United States) are allowed to convert national suppliers into subsidiaries (non-NAFTA investors face a 49 per cent capital shareholding limit). NAFTA investment rules take precedence over Mexican national ones.

- Until 2004, the existing limitations on passenger car imports into Mexico specified by the country's Automotive Decree of 1989 remain in force. Only the five foreign producers that have production facilities in Mexico are allowed to import. Their volume of permitted imports is linked to the volume of their local production.[13]

- The "trade-balancing" requirement of Mexican automotive policy has been amended and is to be phased out.

5.3.1.2 Brazil

The development of Brazil's automotive industry falls into two phases: the import-substitution period (until about 1990), and the subsequent phase of economic liberalization and

---

[13] In 1996, the producers with the largest market share in Mexico were Volkswagen with 32.5 per cent, General Motors with 25.8 per cent and Nissan with 19.6 per cent.

regional integration.[14] Foreign investors have dominated the assembly industry since its early years, while Brazilian companies have played a large role in the supply of parts and components. In the course of the 1970s, however, foreign companies also began to enter the components industry, both with joint ventures and fully owned subsidiaries. This trend has continued in the 1990s.

The main characteristics of the industry in 1990 (before the economic liberalization of the Brazilian economy and before MERCOSUR came into existence) are shown in table 5.10. There were four main assemblers, all leading TNCs: Fiat, General Motors, Ford and Volkswagen. Although the industry was primarily geared towards meeting domestic demand, component exports had grown under the Fiscal Benefits for Special Export Programme (BEFIEX) in the 1970s and the slump in domestic vehicle sales in the 1980s. Half of Brazil's exports went to the United States in the 1980s, inducing major efforts by producers to upgrade quality.

Table 5.10. Brazil's automobile industry: basic statistics, 1990

Mean annual output of cars, 1986-1990	735,000
Number of big auto assemblers	3 [a]
Ownership, component companies	Mixed, with TNCs important among largest firms
Output of components, 1990	$12,244 million [b]
Component exports, 1990	$2,127 million
Component imports, 1990	$945 million

Sources: Carvalho et al. (1997) and Sindipeças (1994), as cited in Humphrey (1998), table 5, p. 39.

[a] Ford and Volkswagen had merged their operations.
[b] Production figures translated into $ at prevailing exchange rates.

In the 1990s a big wave of new investments took place. Fiat, General Motors, Ford and Volkswagen had begun to expand heavily by 1994-1995 and there were also several new entrants (table 5.11). The automobile industry was the largest recipient of FDI in the manufacturing sector.[15] By March 1995, the stock of foreign investment in the industry reached $4,468 million, 15 per cent of the total FDI stock (including portfolio investment) in the manufacturing industry (WTO, 1997, p. 16). Between 1995 and the devaluation of Brazil's *real* in January 1999, the industry received an additional $11 to 12 billion of FDI.

The four major players – Volkswagen, Fiat, General Motors and Ford – account for the lion's share of new investments announced since 1995, with investments aimed at the modernization of existing plants as well as expansion of capacity. Among the modernization investments should be mentioned Fiat's Palio model, launched in 1996 from its Brazilian factory, a small car with which it plans to break into emerging markets, not just in Latin America but also in Asia and Eastern Europe. Another noteworthy effort is Ford's re-equipment of its Sao Bernardo plant, to make small cars to European specifications.

---

[14] The discussion of the first phase is based on Humphrey (1998).
[15] The automobile industry accounted for 8 per cent of Brazil's total foreign investment stock in 1995 (WTO, 1997, p. 16).

Table 5.11. Announced investment projects in the Brazilian automobile industry, as of August 1997

TNC	Value (Million dollars)	Capacity (Thousands)	Stated purpose	State
I. Existing producers:	12 330			
Volkswagen	2 000	n.d.	Various	São Paulo
	500	n.d.	Passenger car (Golf)	Paraná
	300	n.d.	Engines	São Paulo
	250	n.d.	Trucks/buses	Rio de Janeiro
Fiat	950	n.d.	Various	Minas Gerais
	600	n.d.	Passenger cars (Palio/Tipo)	Minas Gerais
	500	n.d.	Engines	Minas Gerais
	250	n.d.	Trucks (Iveco)	Minas Gerais
	200	n.d.	Utility vehicles	Minas Gerais
General Motors	2 000	n.d.	Passenger cars (Corsa)	São Paulo
	600	n.d.	Passenger cars	R. Grande do Sul
	500	n.d.	Components	Sta. Catarina
	150	n.d.	Components	São Paulo
Ford	1 400	n.d.	Various	São Paulo
	450	n.d.	Passenger cars (Fiesta)	São Paulo
	350	n.d.	Engines	São Paulo
	300	n.d.	Trucks	São Paulo
Mercedes Benz	580	n.d.	Buses	São Paulo
Scania	300	n.d.	Trucks	São Paulo
Volvo	150	n.d.	Trucks/buses	Paraná
II. New entrants:	4 914			
Renault	1 000	100	Passenger cars (Megane)	Paraná
Asia Motors	719	60	Utility vehicles	Bahia [a]
PSA	600	70	Passenger cars	Rio de Janeiro
Toyota	600	80	Passenger car (Corolla)	São Paulo
Mercedes Benz	400	70	Passenger cars	Minas Gerais
Honda	400	15	Passenger cars	São Paulo
Chrysler	315	12	Utility vehicles	Paraná
	250	400	Engines	Paraná
Hyundai	286	20	Passenger cars	Bahia a/
Audi (Volkswagen)	250	30	Passenger cars	Paraná
BMW	250	400	Engines	Paraná
Suzuki	160	60	Utility vehicles	Nordeste [a]
Subaru	150	25	Passenger cars	Ceará [a]
Mitsubishi	135	4	Utility vehicles	Goiás [a]
Skoda (Volkswagen)	100	2.2	Trucks	Bahia [a]
	100	1.0	Trucks	Sta. Catarina
All others [b]	1 213	-	Motorcycles, tractors	Various [a]

Source: Kiyoshi Tonooka (1997), p. 2.

[a] Northern and Northeastern states defined by incentive programme.

[b] Mainly Asian companies.

The new entrants include seven Asian companies setting up new operations in Brazil, often taking advantage of the incentives offered by the northern and north-eastern states at small scales of production. Also highly significant are the investments by Renault and PSA (Peugeot/Citroen), which are much larger than the Asian investments and which are aimed at integrating their new operations in Brazil with existing ones in Argentina. Toyota seems to be the only major Asian TNC able to rival the established European and American auto TNCs. Its new plant for its Corolla model is estimated to have an annual capacity of 80,000 vehicles. Compared to their position in the NAFTA and ASEAN regions, however, the position of Japanese TNCs in the industry is very modest.

In addition to huge investments in vehicle production, there have been large inflows in the parts and components industry. Foreign companies are on a takeover spree, acquiring domestic medium-sized manufacturers who cannot survive independently in Brazil's liberalized market.

MERCOSUR has been a major factor driving these new investments. The sectoral provisions of the MERCOSUR agreement for the automotive industry will be (as of 1 January 2000):

- a subregional automobile industry based on tariff-free internal trade;
- a common external tariff;
- rules of origin defining required levels of MERCOSUR content (67.5 per cent in 1999);[16]
- prohibition of trade-distorting incentives for the sector.

MERCOSUR differs from NAFTA in that it is essentially a policy-led integration scheme, whereas in the case of NAFTA, policy followed investment, driven by the wish to consolidate the position of incumbent players. Mexico's automobile industry underwent major restructuring in the 1980s, well before NAFTA started. In contrast, the establishment of a competitive automobile industry in Brazil (and Argentina) began only in the 1990s after the establishment of MERCOSUR, and the process is still far from completed. At the outset of the 1990s, Brazil's industry possessed very serious deficiencies.[17]

The restructuring of the industry in Brazil and Argentina does not yet rival that of Mexico. MERCOSUR's car regime is "a monument to managed rather than free trade".[18] For firms with no local production, import tariffs were still a stiff 62 per cent in 1997, whereas firms that produce locally are allowed to import models with 35 per cent duty. Although tariffs are due to be lowered under WTO rules to 20 per cent by 2000, it remains to be seen whether this will actually happen. Nevertheless, MERCOSUR has stimulated large investments. In fact, aggregate capacity in Brazil and Argentina is expected to be about double that needed for expected demand for vehicles in the region in the coming years. Emerging regional overcapacity has become a concern, and was becoming evident before the recent slump: overcapacity could reach 750,000 cars annually in the coming years.[19] Some investors have scaled back or

---

[16] The Argentine auto parts suppliers are currently asking for the new regime to be postponed as they fear that they will be disadvantaged *vis-à-vis* Brazilian suppliers.

[17] For example, according to a 1991 study by the Massachusetts Institute of Technology, the Brazilian automobile industry had the lowest level of productivity, the second-worst quality rating, and the oldest product mix in the world.

[18] "Making cars in Latin America. trouble in Eldorado", *The Economist*, 13 December 1997, pp. 71-72.

[19] See, for example, "Buy, buy, buy", *The Economist*, 6 December 1997, pp. 15-16, and "Making cars in Latin America: trouble in Eldorado", *The Economist*, 13 December 1997, pp. 71-72. It is argued that over-investment has been stimulated by government policies to protect the industry.

postponed investments after the crisis, but several are going ahead because the long-term outlook is still considered to be good. If recent trends continue, Brazil will have 17 vehicle manufacturers (compared with 13 in the United States and 11 in the European Union) by 2003, and production capacity is set to rise to 2.5 million in 2001 and 3.5 million in 2003.

The second major factor behind the auto FDI boom in Brazil was government policy towards the automobile industry. In 1990 the Government tried to revitalize the sector via international integration by liberalization (Ferro, 1995, p. 3). Tariffs on vehicles were reduced from 85 per cent in 1990 to 20 per cent in 1994, producing an increase in imports from 27,800 vehicles in 1990 to about 97,400 in 1993, to 329,000 in 1995, equivalent to 19 per cent of domestic sales. Import competition eventually began to have a major impact on the automobile industry in Brazil. The Government also negotiated a pact with Argentina, with tariff-free automobile trade based on reciprocal quotas for vehicles. The quotas were to rise progressively from 1989 to 1994. Auto parts had common lists and trade was to be compensated for at the company level.

In 1993, the Government changed its strategy to promote a self-sufficient industry with reduced exposure to international competition (Ferro, 1995, p. 2). It raised tariff protection and promoted a cheap and economical car. Beginning in February 1995, tariffs jumped to 70 per cent, accompanied by emergency import quotas for auto TNCs that did not have local production facilities. This halted mushrooming imports (36 per cent of all units sold in the domestic market in January of 1995). Export growth suffered as a result.

In 1995 the strategy was changed again, with the emphasis on industrial policy and the need for greater international competitiveness. The Government re-installed programmed tariff reductions (from 35 per cent in 1995 to 20 per cent in 2000) and offered benefits for investors in the form of lower tariffs on imported capital goods, price stability, accelerated depreciation for capital equipment, tax reductions for budding auto parts exporters, etc. A distinction was made between importers with production facilities in Brazil and others: the former were charged a 35 per cent tariff while the latter faced 70 per cent. An import quota of 50,000 units was established for firms without local production facilities. The new agreement elicited a response from TNCs. They announced investments of $15 billion between 1995 and 2000, which would raise production to 2.5-3 million units.

Another important policy initiative was a new agreement with Argentina in January 1996. This agreement extended special treatment of the industry until the end of 1999, when bilateral free trade was to be established. Until then, both vehicles and parts could be imported duty-free, as long as the importer balanced foreign purchases with exports (except for replacement parts). It provides for an average local content of at least 50 per cent calculated over a three-year period.

Initiatives on the part of state governments in Brazil to influence the siting of new TNC plants constitute a new factor. "After depending for decades on Brasilia for money and direction, states and municipalities are taking the initiative in spearheading their own development and luring foreign capital".[20] An incentive war broke out between Rio de Janeiro

[20] "Brazil: road to Rio", *Business Latin America*, 7 August 1995, p. 2.

and São Paulo over the Volkswagen project for trucks and buses (FIAS, 1995, p. 5).[21] Later, an incentive plan for automotive companies to set up plants in the northern and north-eastern states before 1 January 2000 was approved by the Brazilian Congress. The incentives included tax reductions or exemptions on industrial products and drastically reduced import tariff payments.

The incentives provoked complaints from Argentina that FDI in new automotive plants was being diverted from Argentina to Brazil. There have been many such disagreements in the past. Argentina, the smaller of the two, is more dependent on the success of the subregional scheme, which gives it more clout in trade negotiations. Moreover, in both countries, national priorities have often overshadowed subregional ones. The relationship has often been tense, and the road towards subregional free trade has proven to be a rough one. Although the tensions do not appear to have discouraged investors, they have left their mark on the industry in both countries.

5.3.1.3 Argentina

Argentina's automobile industry started in the 1950s under an import-substitution regime. FDI was actively encouraged and several TNCs set up operations. Many national auto parts firms were also established. By 1974, the industry employed more than 55,000 people (Oliber, 1998, pp 9-14). In 1976, the new Government started to emphasize liberalization, efficiency and price reductions. There was a rapid rise in imported vehicles, leading to a fall in domestic production from 280,000 units in 1980 to fewer than 180,000 in 1981. By 1990, production reached only 99,000 units, the same as in 1960 when the industry was being established crisis (Oliber, 1998, pp. 15-18).

Some TNCs (General Motors, Citroen and Chrysler) left the country in this period, while others formed mergers (e.g. Volkswagen with Ford) to cope with the crisis. Yet others sold out to local companies (assembly of Fiat and Peugeot models was licensed to Sevel). In contrast to the situation in Brazil, local firms with licensed models held the largest domestic market shares in Argentina until the early 1990s. However, after 1991 auto TNCs returned in force. The automobile industry accounted for 15 per cent of the more than $2 billion FDI inflows to Argentina in the period 1994-1996 and 16 per cent of projected inflows for the period 1997-2000.[22] Between 1991 and 1998, production increased by 220 per cent.[23]

Three factors explain the revival of the industry in Argentina: macroeconomic policy, a special regime for auto producers implemented in 1991, and the bilateral trade agreement with Brazil. With stabilization, incomes rose and led to a rapid increase in the demand for automobiles. This resulted in an investment boom in the sector. Production rose rapidly, from 140,000 units in 1991 to 446,000 in 1997 (with a short dip in 1995 due to a recession).[24] The special regime offered significant incentives to automobile firms to invest in rationalization and

---

[21] For examples in developed countries, see Mytelka (1998).

[22] Data and survey results from Fundación Invertir Argentina (1997). A similar figure for the period 1992-1995, (14.5 per cent) is found in Chudnovsky and Lopez (1997, table 7).

[23] "Foreign makers give sector a push", *Financial Times*, 27 July 1998, p. 5 of Survey.

[24] Data from the Asociación de Fabricantes de Automotores, as quoted in Oliber (1998, table 1). The numbers quoted include both passenger and commercial vehicles.

modernization and to develop export markets. Since 1991, local production of vehicles has been protected through quotas, with established producers allowed to import (with a 2 per cent tariff) within the quota. In exchange for imports, auto producers had to generate exports[25] and undertake investments to modernize facilities and reduce the range of vehicles produced (Chudnovsky, Lopez and Potra, 1997, p. 177). The level of mandatory national content was reduced from 80 to 60 per cent.

During the period 1991-1995 the new automotive regime gave Argentina significant advantages over Brazil as a site for automobile plants, and offered Argentine firms tariff-free access to the much larger Brazilian market. A further attraction was the country's liberal foreign investment regime, with virtually no restrictions on inflows or repatriation, no approvals or formalities of any kind and unrestricted access to foreign exchange markets (OECD, 1995, p. 4). About $2.2 billion of FDI entered Argentina for restructuring old plants and building new ones between 1991 and 1995. This meant that TNCs possessed new or renovated plants while local companies with the largest domestic market shares (Sevel and Ciadea) were left with old ones.

The Brazilian market became Argentina's principal export outlet. The bilateral trade pact for the industry gave tariff benefits to firms with plants in both countries. This resulted in cumulative investment commitments in Argentina of $5.6 billion until the year 2000.[26] It also ensured that nearly half of the 446,000 cars produced in the country in 1997 were exported to Brazil, up from 5,000 units in 1989 and 35,000 in 1994. Thus, administrated trade has played a fundamental role in the renewal of Argentina's automobile industry.

If the devaluation of Brazil's real in January 1999 does not have a lasting unfavourable effect on Argentina's economy, the period 1995-2000 might be one of even stronger investment, reaching an estimated $4 to 5 billion. This would raise the vehicle production capacity of Argentina to about 800,000 units, outpacing domestic consumption, which is expected to remain at about 400,000 in the coming years. In the longer run there is potential for growth. Cars in Argentina are generally old, and with 5.7 inhabitants per car there are relatively few of them around (although Brazil's car density of 9 people per passenger vehicle is still lower than Argentina's). However, Brazil's economic problems may slow down investment. The devaluation of the real has affected Argentina's exports badly, while cheap imports from Brazil are flooding in. Since its own peso is tied to the dollar, it cannot devalue to restore competitiveness.

5.3.2 The automobile industry in South-East Asia

The four major ASEAN members (Indonesia, Malaysia, the Philippines and Thailand) began assembling automobiles in the late 1950s and early 1960s, under import-substitution policies with high tariffs, quota restrictions and local content requirements. However, local part suppliers lacked technological capabilities, and assemblers were allowed to import CKD kits at lower tariff rates than those imposed on imported parts and components. Effective rates of

---

[25] Vehicle and parts exports were valued at 20 per cent more than registered trade. Capital goods and 40 per cent of investment in new production could also be used to offset imports. Companies that did not fulfil the trade compensation obligations were fined.

[26] "Foreign makers give sector a push", *Financial Times*, 27 July 1998, p. 5 of Survey.

protection in assembly were extremely high (over 200 per cent). There were many sub-optimal scale assemblers, with considerable inefficiency and fragmentation. Every country had worsening trade deficits in auto parts.

The industry entered a new phase after the mid-1980s because of rapid economic growth, the appreciation of the yen (which put pressure on Japanese firms to establish local suppliers), and the conclusion of regional trade agreements. Significant investments were made, especially in Thailand after 1992, the country with the most favourable regime for foreign investors in the auto industry. The industry continued to enjoy protection, allowing investors to become established before liberalization took full effect. The effective rate of protection for the car assembly industry in Thailand, which had the lowest tariff rates on completely built-up units (CBU), was estimated at 757 per cent in 1995 (Thailand Development Research Institute, 1996). The effective rate of protection in Indonesia was 919 per cent. CBU tariff rates were particularly high in Malaysia and Indonesia, the countries that promoted national cars while trying to reduce the importance of foreign assemblers and imports. CBU rates in Thailand and the Philippines were lower, but certainly not negligible. However, the situation is changing as a result of the financial crisis of 1997-1999, which has forced some of the Governments to deregulate.

Rapid increases in incomes were a powerful stimulus for investments in the expansion of local production capacity. Regional car sales surged from 787,300 units in 1990 to 1.46 million in 1996.[27] By the mid-1990s, Thailand accounted for 1 per cent of global vehicle demand (Brooker Group, 1997a), and industry sources predicted that total car production capacity in ASEAN member countries would reach 2.2 to 2.8 million units by 2000. Of this, 41 to 43 per cent would be located in Thailand, which became known as the "Detroit of the East". However, even before the financial crisis, it was argued that there would be overcapacity of between 0.5 and 1.1 million units.

Japanese assemblers led the growth of the industry, although over time significant competition from the American Big Three and new firms from the Republic of Korea emerged. The strategies of the Japanese companies had some common elements. First, all Japanese firms expanded production capacity significantly, or had plans to do so. In some countries this entailed a move away from contract production towards joint ventures and wholly-owned subsidiaries (Takayasu, 1996a). Many planned countries for the export of commercial vehicles. In the passenger car segment, Japanese assemblers (especially Toyota and Honda) concentrated on developing affordable Asian cars by establishing large, modern production facilities and sourcing strategies aimed at cost reduction. They also persuaded Japanese suppliers to set up plants in ASEAN countries (a strategy known as "follow sourcing") and expanded regional networks of suppliers. They formed strategic tie-ups to establish reciprocal supply systems among assemblers, and sourced from non-affiliated parts manufacturers locally.

Second, Japanese firms influenced policies in the region to further their strategic objectives. From the late 1980s, when imports of Japanese parts and components became expensive as a result of the rising yen, they mobilized the Japanese Ministry of International Trade and Industry to assist with schemes to promote the parts and components industry in

---

[27] "The downpour in Asia", *The Economist*, 1 November 1997, pp. 71-72.

ASEAN countries.[28] Through local partners and the ASEAN Committee of Commerce and Industry, Japanese TNCs also influenced ASEAN Governments to establish two schemes to develop a regional network of parts suppliers. The first was the 1988 Brand to Brand Complementation (BBC) scheme, under which a producer of a particular brand could import parts from another ASEAN country and pay the duty at half the normal rate. The imported parts had to be used to produce a specific model of car (or electronics product).

The BBC scheme was replaced by the more comprehensive ASEAN Industrial Cooperation Scheme (AICO) in 1996. Under this scheme, companies operating in an ASEAN member country and with a minimum of 30 per cent national equity (with some exceptions) are eligible for privileges, the most important being a preferential tariff of 0-5 per cent.[29] AICO was designed to help establish a more efficient regional division of labour and strengthen competitiveness of the automobile industry. It would also help Japanese manufacturers to strengthen their position in 2000 when the Asean Free Trade Association (AFTA) is to be implemented. They will have first-mover advantages over their competitors from Latin America and the Republic of Korea, which have not yet established regional part supply systems.[30]

The financial crisis marked the next phase.[31] Regional car sales plunged by 37 per cent and output by 30 per cent, leading to considerable downscaling, postponement and cancellation of investment projects. However, it did not provoke a massive exodus of auto TNCs from the region. Investors believed in the long-term outlook for the region; in any case, many found it difficult to withdraw once they had committed their investments. The crisis also improved investment opportunities in Indonesia and Malaysia, which had favoured national automobile projects but had to liberalize under IMF pressure.[32] As a result, all regional governments intensified their efforts to attract FDI, both individually and at the regional level.

Two different approaches to the development of the automobile industry have evolved in ASEAN countries. The first approach is represented by Thailand; its strategy involves attracting FDI, developing regional markets and increasing local supplier capabilities. Until the recent economic problems, Thailand hosted nine large auto TNCs and was the biggest automotive producer in ASEAN. By 1997, approximately $2.5 billion of FDI had entered the industry, [33] about half of total automotive FDI in ASEAN countries (and 11 per cent of Thailand's FDI

---

[28] The Government of Japan has actively used its aid programme to influence industrial development in the region since the mid-1980s, through technical aid programmes, market research and support for Japanese companies relocating abroad (Jomo, 1996, p. 10).

[29] In contrast to the brand-to-brand complementation scheme, producers do not have to use imported parts for any specific model of cars under the AICO.

[30] However, the implementation of AICO has not yet lived up to its objectives. Lack of clear planning provisions for AICO benefits, burdensome approval requirements, onerous product eligibility requirements and high equity requirements which have discouraged new investment have been noted (American Chamber of Commerce in Thailand, n.d.).

[31] "Fledgling vehicle makers 'facing bleak future' ", *Financial Times*, 10 September 1998, p. 7. Indonesian producers were the worst hit. In 1998, car sales in Indonesia fell to a mere 2,000 per month, 5 per cent of the 1997 level. Even though the drop in the rupiah made Indonesian cars the cheapest in the world, most plants had to stop production ("After the storm, a sales trickle", *Financial Times*, 3 September 1998, p.VII of Survey).

[32] "Will East Asia slam the door?", *The Economist*, 12 September 1998, p. 88.

[33] "The downpour in Asia", *The Economist*, 1 November 1997, pp. 71-72.

stock) (UNCTAD, 1998a, p. 376). Vehicle sales reached 589,126 units in 1996 (although they fell to 363,156 during 1997).[34] The Philippine approach was similar, but its car market is significantly smaller and its parts producers less developed. The second approach, represented by Malaysia, centres on a national car strategy (see below), and has enjoyed some success.

5.3.2.1 Thailand

Most early producers in Thailand were Japanese-Thai joint ventures. Local firms also began to produce replacement parts. In the early 1970s, the Government of Thailand launched a plan to rationalize the industry. It prescribed the expansion of local content and implemented such measures as limits on vehicle types, models and engine sizes, and minimum plant capacity and investment. Japanese assemblers supported the model-reduction measure since it favoured small cars, in which they had a marked advantage over European and American firms. However, by 1971 political support for these measures had weakened. Limitations of vehicle type, model and engine size were dropped. Only the 25 per cent local content requirement was kept. This provided substantial business for large, independent ancillary firms who were able to take advantage of rising auto sales in the period 1971-1977. The range of components produced in Thailand became increasingly comprehensive (the number of parts firms had increased to 180 by 1997). After five years of inaction, the Government adopted several new measures between 1978 and 1980. These included a partial ban on CBU imports, tariff increases, a gradual increase and change in the method of local content, a ban on new assembly plants and vehicle models, and a diesel engine manufacturing project. Local content was mandated to increase from 25 per cent to 50 per cent between 1978 and 1986 for passenger vehicles, and from 15 per cent to 50 per cent for commercial vehicles.

These rules on local content were determined through negotiation between assemblers and the parts producers, with government officials playing an intermediary role. Local parts suppliers were permitted to form an association to represent the interests of local entrepreneurs. This gave Thailand's policy on local content a high degree of flexibility, and created a climate in which local suppliers could master the technology of successively complex parts over time. In contrast, Malaysian policy on the auto industry was highly top-down and interventionist.

By the end of the 1980s it was clear that the industry was suffering from large inefficiencies arising from fragmentation and lack of scale economies. No less than 14 plants were making a total of 24,000 automobiles with 54 to 80 per cent local content (Pasuk and Baker, 1998, p. 36). The yen appreciation and the increase in import duty on CKD kits in 1987 pushed up prices further. The Government sought to liberalize the auto industry in 1991. Import duties on small passenger cars were lowered to 42 per cent and on CKD kits to 20 per cent. All restrictions on the number of models and bans on the establishment of new assembly plants were also removed, and CBU import bans were lifted (Brooker Group, 1997b, p. 2). The Thai Ministry of Industry and the Board of Investment (BOI) adopted policies to promote exports of cars and auto parts. Nine foreign investors entered in response to fast-rising domestic demand and the prospect of regional sales growth (Pasuk and Baker, 1998, p. 37). The incumbent Japanese assemblers were joined by United States and Korean companies. In 1999, the

---

[34] "Capacity rises, demand slides", *Financial Times*, 3 September 1998, p. VI of Survey.

Government decided to phase out local content requirements, and raised tariffs on finished automobiles to 80 per cent to compensate. Thus, to date the industry remains highly protected.

The economic crisis led to diverse responses among the TNCs. Some have pushed ahead with their investment plans in the hope that recovery in Thailand will start in 1999 and that long-term growth will be strong. Thus, companies like Toyota and Honda have injected funds into their affiliates and subcontractors and used the collapse in sales to carry out restructuring, including relocation of parts production, boosting exports, increasing domestic sourcing and staff training. Other TNCs, however, have put investment plans on hold or cancelled them.[35]

Four Japanese assemblers – Toyota, Honda, Mitsubishi and Nissan – dominate the Thai market with close to 80 per cent of sales of passenger cars and virtually 100 per cent of sales of light pick-ups in 1996.[36] They have concentrated on developing Thailand's home market by providing affordable vehicles to suit local tastes, as well as developing their facilities in the country into a base for regional exports. Most of Toyota's Soluna sedan production is meant for the local market. It exports a modest number of Hilux cars to 22 countries (mostly in Asia) and is planning to gradually step up exports. Honda operates on a much smaller scale than Toyota, since it is a newcomer in Thailand (its first factory was built in 1992). It has successfully penetrated the Thai market in a short period because of its extensive after-sale services network. Like Toyota, Honda promotes an "Asian car". It uses Bangkok as the headquarters for the ASEAN market (Toyota has its headquarters in Singapore). Thailand is the only production and export base for Mitsubushi's one-ton diesel trucks. Mitsubishi and Mazda plan to terminate their production of one-ton pick-up trucks in Japan and will export these models from Thailand. Since Isuzu is also expanding its production capacity of one-ton trucks in Thailand, the country is likely to become the second-largest production base of pick-up trucks in the world, after the United States.

The American Big Three re-entered the Thai market in the mid-1990s (they had left in the early 1980s during a recession in the United States). Ford teamed up with Mazda to make pick-up trucks for export and Chrysler unveiled plans to make 100,000 cars, also predominantly for export. General Motors launched an ambitious project to use Thailand as an export base for Opels with engines less than 1,800 cc. Finally, two car makers from the Republic of Korea, Hyundai and Daewoo, set up assembly plants.

Thailand thus seems well placed to grow into ASEAN's main parts supplier. The supplier base has received significant assistance from Japan. In 1991, a team of technical experts from the Japan International Cooperation Agency (JICA) and the Japanese Ministry of International Trade and Industry (MITI) prepared the first detailed study of the Thai supporting industry. Following this, BOI announced the BUILD (BOI Unit for Industrial Linkage Development) programme for promoting supporting industry by matching the Japanese parts producers with Thai counterparts. A second JICA team carried out a comprehensive competitiveness study of the Thai supporting industry in 1995. Moreover, JICA provided financial and technical assistance to the Government of Thailand to set up the Machinery Industry

---

[35] *Ibid.*, for details about the strategic responses of individual TNCs to the crisis in Thailand; see also UNCTAD (1998b), pp. 19-21 and pp. 24-25.

[36] See Brooker Group (1997b, p. 3) and "The downpour in Asia", *The Economist*, 1 November 1997, pp. 71-72.

Development Institute in 1998, which is meant to provide training and technical services to small and medium-sized enterprises in the machinery industry.

5.3.2.2 Malaysia

Problems of fragmentation and proliferation were also much in evidence in Malaysia in the first two decades of its automobile industry (from the late 1960s to the early 1980s). This in turn prevented the establishment of a viable parts and components industry. In response, the Malaysian Ministry of Trade and Industry (MTI), with a strong lobby from the Malaysian Automotive Component Parts Manufacturers Association (MACPMA), adopted a mandatory deletion programme in 1979. This required foreign assemblers to "delete" – omit – certain components from imported CKD packs and procure them locally. The Government was concerned that Malaysia, as the country with the least developed auto sector, would be excluded from the ASEAN automotive complementation programme. It also hoped that the initiative would boost the position of ethnic Malays (or bumiputras) *vis-à-vis* the Chinese business community.[37]

However, established (mainly ethnic Chinese) assemblers obstructed these efforts (Doner 1991). By 1982, local content was still only 18 per cent. Although the number of parts firms had grown to roughly 200, the bumiputra policy had not delivered significant results. In 1980, the Ministry of Trade and Industry launched a feasibility study for a national car project to rationalize the industry.[38] After eight months of negotiation, a contract was signed with Mitsubishi in May 1983. It led to the establishment of Proton, a joint venture with HICOM, Malaysia's new State-owned Heavy Industry Corporation. By August 1985, the first car came off the production line. To avoid potential obstruction from parties with vested interests in the industry, the negotiations conducted between the Government and Mitsubishi were clouded in secrecy, and disregarded the interests of existing entrepreneurs.

The project was viewed as economic folly by most auto TNCs (Doner, 1991), in part because they were threatened in the local market. The negotiations were successfully concluded quickly not only because they were conducted under strict secrecy and tight time constraints imposed by the Ministry of Trade and Industry, but also because Mitsubishi was able to secure quite favourable terms.[39] Several important contractual aspects were left vague and provided Mitsubishi with considerable power to pursue its own objectives. These included future local content levels, CKD prices, royalty payments, the use of non-Japanese technology and parts, technology transfer and exports (Doner, 1991, p. 104). Some of these affected the technological impact of the project on the national economy (see section 5.4.5).

Initially the Government provided extensive support to the national car project, in terms of extensive tariff exemptions and formal and informal mechanisms to squeeze competing

---

[37] Ethnic division has always been a major concern of the Government of Malaysia. While the ethnic Malays dominate in terms of numbers of people, the ethnic Chinese minority dominates manufacturing and domestic trade. In the early 1970s the Government had already adopted a preferential programme under the New Economic Policy to provide business opportunities for Malays, but its results were disappointing.

[38] The then Minister of Trade and Industry, Mohamed Mahathir, was the driving force behind the negotiations. He later became Prime Minister of Malaysia.

[39] "The Proton in a nuclear automobile family", *Far Eastern Economic Review*, 14 February 1985.

assemblers. It froze the number of car import permits, restricted the range of foreign makes and forced assemblers to reduce the number of models offered. Moreover, assemblers were told unofficially that price competition with Proton would be seen as undermining national interests. Assemblers were also given options to adjust, by diverting to higher-income market segments that did not compete with the Proton, or by converting to the manufacture of parts and components.

The performance of the first national car has been creditable. Production rose from 8,600 units in 1985 to 153,898 units in 1995; domestic market share rose to 60 per cent for passenger cars with engine capacities of 1,300 and 1,600 cc. There were several model upgrades, and the firm expanded into the 2,000 cc range with the launch of a new car, the Saga, which began to be exported in 1987, reaching 19,741 units in 1995 (Abidin, 1996). After the Saga's success, the Government launched a second national car project, Perodua, in 1992, in the small car segment. Its Kancil model, with an engine capacity of 660 cc, came on stream in 1994. One important achievement of Proton was to develop the base of domestic supplier firms, something foreign assemblers had been unable to do. However, Malaysia's performance in the automobile sector does not match that of Thailand in depth or range of production as opposed to their respective performance in the electronics industry.

Even before the financial crisis, the Government of Malaysia began to move from protection towards boosting international competitiveness, realizing that its car projects would be endangered if they continued to rely on public support. WTO rules restrict the use of protective tariffs on imported vehicles as a tool to promote national cars; their use will also be restricted under the ASEAN Free Trade Agreement. The tariff reduction to 5 per cent by 2003, agreed under the latter, presents the first serious challenge to Malaysia's car industry. Trade liberalization in ASEAN could reinforce Thailand's dominant position in this industry. Moreover, the Agreement on WTO's Trade-related Investment Measures does not allow the use of local content policies to encourage the local components industry. Therefore, Proton has come under pressure to increase its competitiveness; it has been partially privatized and subjected to normal market forces. When Perodua was established, tariff exemption to Proton was discontinued. It now has to pay a 13 per cent tariff on CKDs, while Perodua is still exempted from this tariff for the time being.

5. 4.   FDI, restructuring and competitiveness

5.4.1 Mexico

5.4.1.1 Industrial restructuring and competitive performance[40]

By 1992, three of the five largest Mexican manufactured exports were automotive: passenger cars, automobile parts and internal combustion engines and their parts. Table 5.12 gives basic information on these products.

By 1997, Mexico was producing 1.3 million vehicles, 63 per cent more than in 1990 and three times more than in 1980. It exported over 70 per cent of its production, compared to 5 per

---

[40] See also Mortimore (1998a and 1999).

cent between 1980 and 1984 (ECLAC, 1998). Between 1990 and 1997, Mexican exports of automotive products rose 4.7 times, from $4.5 billion to $20.8 billion. Although imports also increased, exports grew faster, and an initial trade deficit ($1.7 billion in 1990) turned into a substantial surplus ($7.8 billion in 1997). NAFTA partners, especially the United States, are the most important destinations. The automobile industry accounted for 22 per cent of the total value of Mexico's exports to North America and for 16 per cent of its total exports to OECD countries in 1996.

Table 5.12. Performance of the automobile industry in Mexico
(vehicles, components and engines), 1990-1997

Item	1990	1994	1997
Production (thousands of vehicles)	820.5	1 097.4	1 338.0
-domestic market	543.7	522.4	353.8
-exports	276.8	575.0	984.4
Exports ($ billion)	4.5	10.4	20.8
-Per cent to North America [a]	91.2	90.3	...
-Per cent market: North American auto imports	3.82	7.91	10.9 [b]
-as per cent of all exports to North America	15.6	20.8.0	21.8
Imports ($ billions)	5.8	11.5	13.0
Trade balance	-1.7	-1.1	7.8
Employees (thousands of persons)	57.7	49.7	44.8

Source: Mortimore (1998a), based on AMIA (national automobile producers' association of Mexico) and ECLAC CANPLUS and PADI databases.

[a] United States and Canada.
[b] 1996.

The changes in exports reflect FDI patterns. Auto parts first dominated exports, followed by an export boom in engines as new engine plants were established in the early 1980s. The explosion in passenger cars exports occurred after new assembly plants were built in the late 1980s. TNCs were almost entirely responsible for the surge in vehicle exports. In 1993 the five Mexican subsidiaries of auto TNCs operating in Mexico (General Motors, Ford, Chrysler, Volkswagen and Nissan) were among the principal exporters from all of Latin America, ranking third, fifth, sixth, tenth and twenty-sixth respectively.[41] The in-bond assembly industry for auto parts has been the most dynamic maquiladora sector. Employment in this industry grew at 22 per cent annually (as compared to 12 per cent for all in-bond activities) and its value-added grew at 23 per cent between the early 1980s and 1995. The auto parts sector accounted for 26 per cent of value-added in the in-bond industry in 1994. Between 1979 and 1986 40 auto part in-bond plants operated by TNCs were established in northern Mexican border towns.

The success of the Mexican automobile industry can also be measured by the responses of the industry to foreign exchange crises. At the beginning of the 1980s, domestic demand for vehicles nosedived (production fell from 597,000 units in 1981 to 286,000 in 1983) and with it so did the fortunes of the industry, since vehicles could not be exported because they were not

---

[41] *América Economia*, 1994 edition.

internationally competitive. In 1995, as a consequence of the foreign exchange crisis of December 1994, domestic demand again collapsed; however, this time exports grew dramatically (from 575,000 units in 1994 to 971,000 in 1996) and production only fell marginally and temporarily. By 1996, the industry was producing more vehicles than before the crisis.

The survey conducted for this project covers 12 automobile parts producers in the border region of northern Mexico. Three firms are Mexican and nine are foreign-owned (more than 75 per cent foreign capital ownership), of which eight are from the United States and one is Asian. Four of the firms were TNC subsidiaries producing final products, six were subcontractors and two were independent operations. Nine of the 12 operated via the in-bond assembly scheme. In the case of foreign affiliates, the parent company had on average six plants in Mexico. The average age of the plants in the survey was 14 years. All sample firms succeeded in increasing or at least maintaining their international market share during the period 1985-1990 and 1990-1995.

5.4.1.2 Development of human capital

The sample firms experienced large changes in skill needs and process and product technology. According to these firms, the three most important measures to improve efficiency during the period 1990-1995 were: purchasing better technology embodied in modern capital equipment (21 per cent); further training of the company workforce (20 per cent); and increasing the productivity of labour through incentives (14 per cent). This suggests that the firms were engaged in increasingly skill- and capital-intensive operations, and that they attached increasing significance to human resource development.[42]

Although vehicle assemblers are the most important exporters in the industry, followed by engine manufacturers, the auto parts sector is the most important in terms of employment. In 1992, it accounted for 40 per cent of the 455,800 employees in the industry; it also paid the highest wages in the industry (Carrillo, 1998). The largest employers are the in-bond assemblers (28 per cent), followed by distributors (18 per cent) and vehicle assemblers (14 per cent). Mexican-owned companies generally specialize in the more labour-intensive auto parts, illustrated by the large share of production workers in employment: 84 per cent in the survey sample and 81 per cent sector-wide in 1995. In the in-bond auto parts sector as a whole, 10 per cent of employees were technicians and engineers (4 per cent in the sample), and 9 per cent were in the administrative category. The number of technicians has been rising and the ratio of production workers to technical personnel fell from 9 in 1980 to 8 in 1995.

In 1990, one-fifth of the employees in in-bond assembly were technicians or professionals trained in local secondary or higher education centres. In the sample firms, managers considered 37 per cent of the production workers to be "skilled". On-the-job training was the most important type of training given to employees. Annual expenditures on training by the firms in the survey sample were quite high: around 3 to 4 per cent of annual sales, with the American firms having a higher score than Mexican and Asian ones. On average, employees received 40 hours of training per year (37 hours sector-wide in 1995). A high proportion of

---

[42] "The Tijuana triangle", *The Economist*, 20 June 1998, Manufacturing survey, p. 15.

personnel (around 80 per cent) received training. Foreign-owned firms in the sample gave more training than national firms to professional, administrative and supervisory personnel. TNCs provided more formal training (on average 66 hours in 1994) than subcontractors (45 hours), who in turn give significantly more than independent firms (8 hours). Firms were strengthening their relations with local training institutions to redefine curricula so as to ensure the industry had a supply of engineers and technicians corresponding to their needs.

5.4.1.3 Development of technology and organization

The automobile industry is becoming more sophisticated and technology-intensive over time, and productivity is rising. In Mexico's vehicle industry as a whole, real value added per person employed rose by 150 per cent between 1987 and 1996. The number of vehicles produced per employee rose from 12.2 a year to 18.8 between 1970 and 1993 (ECLAC, 1998, p. 249). In this context, the following points emerge from the survey.

First, product complexity is rising significantly. This gives rise to increased production requirements and, even in assembling, sophisticated processes. The increasing diversity of car models further raises the complexity of production processes (for example, of wire harnesses).[43] The technology required to deal with increasing complexity comes in most cases from parent companies. Technology was the most important input obtained from that source, with 58 per cent of the firms obtaining their technology directly from their parent company and 17 per cent from other firms in the corporate network. Only a quarter of the firms obtained it outside the parent company network. Since only three firms in the sample were Mexican, this implies that most of the technology is imported, with the highest proportions for product (100 per cent) and process technology (82 per cent), and somewhat less for quality control, management and marketing technologies (60-70 per cent). Only plant design was developed fully by local firms in Mexico.

Secondly, most firms made only minor adaptations of imported technology to local conditions. Most adaptations are to production processes rather than products. Just one of the firms had acquired or developed a patent. Nevertheless, 6 of the 12 sample firms engaged in R&D: two in design, and the other four in activities like component research or prototype design. On average, 4 per cent of expenditures were dedicated to these activities, with 12 engineers per firm working on them. This is a surprisingly high figure considering the low significance attached by the managers interviewed to affiliate technological activity. R&D was undertaken without any support from universities or technological institutes, except for the Mexican firms that were supported by the Tecnológico de Monterrey, a leading private institute in technological education.

Even though most technology came from parent companies, local technologies were gradually incorporated into product design and equipment adaptation. Flexible production practices were widely used in the auto parts industry, adopting elements of the Japanese model

---

[43] Even though wire harnesses are generally assumed to be low-skill, low-technology items of mass production, each car requires wires of different size, thickness and finishes for specific automobile systems. One firm in the sample produces all the different sets of wires needed for 250,000 Chrysler cars, including a wide range of car models.

(Abo, 1994) in each firm. All firms deployed more than one flexible organizational technique, each making a selection among techniques. However, none systematically applied the whole model.

The introduction of these practices started in 1986. First came statistical process control, and quality control circles were introduced a year later. New techniques were added virtually every year. Recent introductions include flexible line reorganization, work teams, and decentralization of decisions to the shop-floor. The local firms, not the parent companies, were responsible for the introduction of organizational techniques. The techniques were considered very important for developing competitiveness, especially the use of statistical process control, cell manufacturing and business units. JIT, quality circles, teamwork and real-time process control were considered less important. A commonly acknowledged obstacle to the introduction of these techniques was quoted as worker resistance to change. Finally, most firms in the sample tried to comply with ISO 9000 quality control standards. Foreign affiliates had already applied for certification, while the firms outside transnational networks were not applying or just had plans to apply. In terms of origin, there are also interesting differences: the Asian firms already have obtained certification, the Mexican ones have applied for it, whole the North American firms are still in the process of planning for application.

A mixed picture emerges on the automobile industry's impact on human capital formation and technology development. Although Mexican firms and employees increasingly acquire technological and other skills and capabilities, this occurs mainly in the easy parts of the production process. Technology for the more complex processes is largely obtained from parent companies abroad, but significant amounts of money are spent on local R&D as well. Roughly two-thirds of the production workers, who account for over 80 per cent of total employment in the auto parts in-bond assembly sector, are unskilled, although many receive some training. As Carrillo (1998, p. 3) describes it, the development of R&D facilities, based on highly skilled jobs, is still embryonic.

Box 5.1. The Delphi design centre

One illustration of human capital formation and the acquisition of technology and organizational capacity is General Motors' Delphi research, design and development centre in Ciudad Juarez. Delphi – now a spin-off of General Motors – is the most important global player in the auto part industry. In 1978 Delphi was one of the first United States companies to take advantage of the maquiladora trade regime. It now employs 72,000 Mexicans, including 20,000 in its 15 plants in Ciudad Juarez. In 1995 it shifted one of its United States R&D facilities to Juarez. The centre's record in terms of technical capacity is good, with six United States patents awarded for products developed at the centre. It reduced its global costs by 60 per cent and its delivery times by 20 per cent just one year after starting operations. Almost half of the 1,400, mainly Mexican, staff have first degrees, and six per cent further degrees.

Source: Carrillo (1998).

5.4.1.4 Development of local suppliers

Liberalization had two effects on the auto parts sector, one favourable and the other not. On the one hand, it led to denationalization[44] (i.e. takeover by foreigners of national partners) and decimation of many Mexican-owned auto parts firms.[45] On the other hand, the national companies that did survive became much more competitive. Between 1997 and 2000, $6 billion is to be invested in the modernization and expansion of the auto parts sector. Most will come from auto parts TNCs but some will also come from local conglomerates like the Desc group.[46]

The United States "Big Three" invested $2.9 billion between 1993 and 1996 to take advantage of the new policy both in order to supply their assembly facilities in Mexico and further integrate their North American production capacity, mainly by way of in-bond production. As a consequence, new or widened supplier networks with auto TNCs and some competitive national firms are emerging. Recently, Nissan and Volkswagen have established a host of new suppliers. This suggests that, after the initial shock, liberalization is leading to deepening of the industry.

Subcontracting, which had been very low because of long delivery times, poor quality, lack of appropriate technology and high prices, rose sharply over time. In contrast to the in-bond auto assembly industry, which had low and stagnant levels of local content, the auto parts industry had average local content (from Mexican suppliers and subcontractors) of 30 per cent between 1990 and 1995, a large gain from the 8.5 per cent recorded in 1985. TNCs played a significant role in supplier upgrading. Half the firms in the survey trained their main Mexican subcontractor in quality control (all six), worker training (five out of six), and product design, technical norms and specifications (three out of six).

Box 5.2. TNC restructuring in Mexico: Ford Motor Company

Ford has gone further in integrating its operations in Mexico into its continental production system. Like other American producers of passenger cars, Ford was losing competitiveness in the United States market. Internationally, its strategy relies on strategic alliances with or minority equity participation in rivals with superior technology or organizational practices. This was the case with Mazda: Ford held 25 per cent (today, 34 per cent) of Mazda (Japan) and 50 per cent of Mazda (United States). Mazda was important in Ford's attempt to put together a "world car" based on the Tracer/Escort model. Developing new models at reasonable cost had been described as "Ford's biggest headache".

/...

---

[44] Between 1992 and 1995, the number of foreign-owned auto parts companies jumped from 6 to 33 per cent of the total. Mexican-owned suppliers declined from 52 to 33 per cent of the total. The rest is made up by in-bond assembly firms, that dropped from 42 to 34 per cent of the total number (United States International Trade Commission, 1997, p. 6-6).

[45] See, for example, Zapata, Hoshino and Hanono (1994).

[46] This group controls the Spicer auto parts production (engines and parts, transmissions, etc.) in Mexico. It will purchase the United States transmission operations (in Tenessee, Arizona and Ohio) of the auto part TNC Dana Corporation, and transfer them to Querétaro, Mexico (*América Economía,* September, 1997, p. 102).

5.4.2 Brazil

5.4.2.1 Industrial restructuring and competitive performance

The creation of MERCOSUR strongly stimulated the growth of Brazil's auto industry, with the number of units produced rising by 73 per cent between 1990 and 1994. In the process, labour productivity also increased significantly: fewer employees produced 1,581,400 vehicles in 1994 than it had taken to produce 914,500 cars in 1990. So did exports. While the number of units produced for the domestic market rose by 69 per cent, production for export increased by 102 per cent. The value of exports increased from $1.9 billion in 1990 to $2.7 billion in 1994. The agreement with Argentina led to a rise in exports of automobiles to that country from 37,197 to 274,815 units. Between 1990 and 1994, the proportion of automotive exports (including auto parts) going to Argentina grew from 3 per cent to 30 per cent of Brazil's total

---

(Box 5.2, concluded)

Ford's investments in Mexico, almost $3 billion in the period 1982-1992, were aimed at improving its position in the American market for smaller cars. Ford's original production facilities, based in Cuautitlan, close to Mexico City, were established in the 1960s to assemble cars and trucks for the domestic market. They have been described as "horribly inefficient", with an annual capacity of only 60,000 units. In 1983, however, Ford launched a new strategy. It established an engine plant in Chihuahua with an annual capacity of 200,000 units for export to the United States. This was "a high-volume, export-oriented facility meant to compete with the most successful engine plants anywhere in the world" which demonstrated that "advanced production processes can successfully be transferred to newly industrialising countries" (Shaiken and Herzenberg, 1987, pp. 2 and 119). From 1992 to 1993, the plant was expanded to an annual capacity of 500,000 units, and the engine was upgraded in design and sophistication.

The next major investment in Mexico was the Hermosillo vehicle assembly plant, established in 1986 and expanded in 1990 to 160,000 units. This plant, designed by Ford's partner Mazda, introduced Japanese production techniques to Mexico. The result was world-class quality and productivity. The plant makes the highest quality Ford car in North America and received the fifth-highest quality rating of 46 car assembly plants. Its defects per vehicle score was 0.276, close to the world optimum, as compared to a weighted average for all Mexican auto producers of 0.665 (Shaiken, 1995; Olea, 1993). Ford's success with flexible production techniques in Mexico has, however been uneven, varying considerably from plant to plant (Carrillo, 1995).

Ford's corporate strategy during the 1980s had a significant impact on the Mexican automobile industry. The centrepiece of the new strategy was to specialize in one engine (the modern Zeta) and two passenger vehicles (the Mercury Tracer and later the Ford Escort), all for export. In 1996, Ford exported 186,249 passenger vehicles and, by the first half of 1997, it accounted for 33 per cent of all passenger vehicle exports from Mexico. By 1996, Ford's car production for the domestic market fell to 14,780 units, and it became a car importer, with imports reaching 23,300 units in 1994, falling to 16,651 units in 1996. Ford did not initially modernize and upgrade the original Cuautitlan plant, whose production was destined for the domestic market. Instead, it set up new and high-technology engine and vehicle assembly facilities for the highly competitive North American market, integrating its Mexican facilities into its North American system.

Source: Mortimore (1997 and 1998b).

---

auto exports. By 1994, over one-fifth of Brazil's total exports to its MERCOSUR partners emanated from the automotive industry, up from 14 per cent in 1990 (even though its import market share in the MERCOSUR market for automotive products fell from 18 per cent to 16 per cent).

Table 5.13. Performance of the Brazilian automobile industry, 1990-1997

Item	1990	1994	1997
Production (thousands of vehicles)	914.5	1581.4	2067.0
-domestic market	712.6	1203.8	1655.0
-exports	187.3	377.6	412.0
Auto industry exports (billions of dollars)	1.9	2.7	4.6
-Per cent to Argentina	2.4	35.1	42.3[a]
-Per cent market: MERCOSUR auto imports	17.5	15.63	14.6[a]
-as per cent of all exports to MERCOSUR	14.3	21.5	20.5[a]
Auto industry imports (billions of dollars)	0.7	2.6	5.4
Auto industry trade balance	1.2	0.1	-0.8
Employees (thousands)	117.4	107.1	106.1

Source: Mortimore (1998a), based on data from ANFAVEA and ECLAC CANPLUS and PADI databases.
[a] 1996.

The 1993 strategy coincided with a downturn in the exports of passenger vehicles, more as a result of the exchange rate crisis in Argentina in early 1995 than of a more inward-looking automotive policy. The exports of Brazilian vehicles to that market collapsed from 274,815 units in 1994 to 189,721 units in 1995, bringing down overall exports from 377,600 units in 1994 to just 263,000 units in 1995. Strong domestic demand compensated for the loss in export revenue. The Real Plan of 1995, which stabilized Brazil's prices, played an important contextual role in re-igniting domestic automobile demand. Overall production increased by 30 per cent, while that destined for the domestic market increased by 42 per cent, between 1993 and 1995. The level of imported vehicles rocketed, peaking at 369,000 units in 1995.

There were also internal changes. Fiat saw its share grow spectacularly during the 1990s, while the other major auto TNCs operating in Brazil, especially Ford, lost ground. Fiat's "economic car" strategy was at the centre of these changes (see box 5.3). The MERCOSUR market played a secondary role at this time. The 1995 sectoral strategy elicited a strong response from the auto TNCs which, as mentioned above, announced major investments (see p. 135). Automobile exports recovered from the large fall in 1995, reaching 305,700 units in 1996 and growing further to 412,000 units in 1997.

While Brazil's automotive industry has undergone significant upgrading and modernization since 1990, there are symptoms of weak systemic competitiveness. Its recent expansion has been driven primarily by a protected domestic market, trade relations with Argentina, the promotion of popular cars and stimulation of demand. Trade liberalization was reversed, and import tariffs are still high. The trade surplus of $1.2 billion in 1990 turned into a deficit of $0.8 billion by 1997. Exports of vehicles still accounted for less than 20 per cent of production in 1997, contrasting with Mexico, where close to three-quarters of production was exported. Competitive weaknesses became more evident in the aftermath of the Asian crisis.

The initial determination of the Government of Brazil to protect the *real* threw the automotiveindustry into deep recession. Car sales dropped by 21 per cent in 1998, but the brunt was borne by locally made cars (down 38 per cent) while sales of imported cars went up by 14 per cent.[47]

This was partly due to the overvaluation of the real; however, it also showed inefficiencies in local auto manufacturing. High trade barriers had fostered high-cost production. Average productivity in Brazil is still only about a quarter of levels in the United States, although the newest plants (such as Fiat's) approach world standards. One reason for high costs may be that the automotive supply chain is still in the middle of its own reorganization and upgrading effort. Another may be that production runs are still sub-optimal, except for the four leading models (Fiat's Uno and Palio, General Motors' Corsa and Volkswagen's Gol). Production volumes are hard to expand because trade within MERCOSUR has to be kept in balance, and significant expansion of exports to other parts of the world is difficult because of high production costs.[48] The low presence of Japanese TNCs may be an additional factor: Japanese firms tend to be strong and aggressive international competitors.

Thus, only by further restructuring to reduce fragmentation and increase efficiency can Brazil's car industry hope to become a real force in world competition. It remains to be seen what the effects of the 1998-1999 economic crisis will be. There are signs that it will slow down modernization efforts, as several auto TNCs are reviewing their investment plans. But it may also induce rationalization by forcing the weaker plants to exit, leaving more space for the stronger players in the future.

5.4.2.2 Development of human capital and technology

The modernization drive in the auto industry led to considerable emphasis on education and training in the assemblers as well as in the first-tier suppliers (many now also owned by TNCs). However, this was not the case in the small parts producers; many had very limited resources and faced serious competitive pressure (Humphrey, 1998, p. 31). Leading companies invest in basic education, including numeracy and literacy, reflecting the inadequate provision of basic skills from the general educational system. They also provide considerable training. Production workers receive 50 to 80 hours training per year; in some firms, training has been linked to job restructuring and promotion (Humphrey, 1998, p. 30).

However, there has been some erosion of engineering and technical skills, caused by the increased centralization of R&D in TNC headquarters. In contrast to the situation in the import-substitution period, new models and major variants of existing models are no longer designed specifically for the Brazilian market. A similar trend exists among component companies, which increasingly buy their designs from the TNC networks to which they belong. The one major exception is Fiat's Palio car project. The car was designed in Turin in 1993-1994 by a 300-

---

[47] ANFAVEA, *Carta de ANFAVEA*, no. 153, February 1999. Estimates about the extent of the slump vary somewhat. The *Financial Times* quotes a 21 per cent drop below the 1997 level, with a 26 per cent decline in domestically-produced cars to 707,570 units in the first eight months of 1998. Imported cars went up by 14 per cent to 136,373 units in the same period. See "Out comes the melting pot", *Financial Times*, 3 December 1998, p. IV of Survey.

[48] "Making cars in Latin America: trouble in Eldorado", *The Economist*, 13 December 1997.

person team which included 120 Brazilians, ranging from engineers to shopfloor workers. Fiat then chose its Betim plant as the manufacturing site for the Palio, where local staff had considerable experience with adapting European models to Brazilian road conditions and tastes.[49] Judging from the car's initial success, this strategy has paid off (see box 5.3).

In general, skill development and technological modernization reflect efforts to increase efficiency and quality. They are directed to using new production technologies and methods from the headquarters of the leading TNCs. There is a move away from local design – only minor adaptation and testing continue locally.

5.4.2.3 Development of local suppliers

By 1990, Brazil had achieved high levels of local content (around 85 per cent) and had an extensive auto parts industry. In the 1980s, when the assembly sector was stagnating, the auto parts industry expanded significantly. Its sales increased from $5,287 million in 1980 to $12,244 million in 1990, and its exports grew from $773 million to $2,127 million (17 per cent of sales). After 1990, there was a severe shakeout in this part of the industry, following rapid import liberalization (Posthuma, 1995, p. 19). Import penetration for components rose from 8 to 24 per cent of production between during 1990 and 1996, compared to a much lower share of 11 per cent for complete vehicles (albeit a significant increase from only 0.2 per cent in 1990). The effects on the smaller and less competitive national companies were traumatic (Mesquita Moreira, 1997). The number of auto parts firms dropped from 2,000 in 1990 to 750 in 1993. Concentration rose rapidly, with just 15 producers – among which were 10 TNCs – accounting for three-quarters of the value of exports by 1993. Employment in the components sector declined by 7 per cent between 1992 and 1995 (Bedê, 1997, p. 373).

Although productivity rose, a crisis enveloped the industry. A major factor was the implementation of strategies by the assemblers to make "world cars" in Brazil. This led auto firms to "standardize component designs and benchmark prices internationally, giving them the option of importing when local prices do not meet international standards" (Posthuma, 1995, p. 11). After 1990, when the components market was opened to imports, assemblers moved increasingly towards global sourcing for their new models.[50] However, there was also significant restructuring of Brazilian suppliers, with major new investments as well as buyouts of older local companies. The established vehicle makers are playing a major role in this. Significant engine and component investments were announced by Volkswagen ($300 million), Fiat ($500 million), General Motors ($650 million), and Ford ($350 million), as well as by newcomers (the Chrysler/BMW engine plant). There is also extensive "follow sourcing" by foreign auto TNCs. For example, Chrysler's new factory relies heavily on Dana, an American producer of rolling chassis, which has set up shop nearby. Chrysler has a similar arrangement for seating made by Lear Corporation, a car seat manufacturer from Missouri.[51] The result was rapid denationalization of the components sector. By the end of 1997, four of the biggest nine local companies had been sold to TNCs (Humphrey, 1998, p. 27).

---

[49] "A car is born", *The Economist*, 13 September 1997, pp. 74-75.
[50] "Buy, buy, buy", *The Economist*, 6 December 1997, pp.15-16 of Survey "Business in Latin America".
[51] "Car making: the modular T", *The Economist*, 5 September 1998, p. 62.

In addition, assemblers have tended to reduce the number of first-tier suppliers, inducing a more vertical supply structure. A good example is Chrysler, where a few key suppliers deliver complete sub-assemblies. The chassis manufacturer, for example, delivers its products with wires and hoses already in place, and with tyres mounted and balanced. A more revolutionary form of such modular manufacturing is the "Lopez system", started in 1996 in Volkswagen's Resende truck plant. Seven key component suppliers operate relatively independently within the plant, and even fit their complete sub-assemblies on the assembly lines. Other TNCs in Brazil plan to experiment with modular manufacturing as well, such as Ford's new Amazon and Blue Macaw plants. Brazil is a test ground for TNCs for innovations that may be used in the industry worldwide.[52]

5.4.3 Argentina

5.4.3.1 Industrial restructuring and competitive performance

The new automotive regime and improved economic situation in Argentina gave it significant advantages over Brazil as an investment site for automobile plants between 1991 and 1995. At the same time, the creation of MERCOSUR promised automobile producers in Argentina tariff-free access to the much larger Brazilian market. The result was $2.2 billion of new investment. Vehicle production jumped from about 100,000 units in 1990 to 408,800 units in 1994. Employment rose from 17,430 to 25,734 people in the same period. After a temporary slump in domestic demand in 1995-1996 caused by the foreign exchange crisis, growth resumed to reach nearly 445,900 units in 1997 (see table 5.14). The impact of the devaluation of the *real* in January 1999 was severe, but probably temporary.

While several producers reached economic levels of scale (Sevel/Citroen, Ciadea, Fiat and Ford), others still operate at very low volumes. The high levels of investment entailed considerable modernization. According to the Argentine Automobile Manufacturers

Table 5.14. Data on the automobile industry in Argentina, 1990-1997

Item	1990	1994	1997
Production (thousands of vehicles) [a]	99.6	408.8	445.9
- for the domestic market	98.5	370.1	232.7
- for export	1.1	38.7	208.2
Exports (billions of dollars)	0.3	1.0	2.8
- exports to Brazil (per cent)	35.0	75.4	...
Automotive exports as % of total national exports to MERCOSUR	6.0	18.3	...
Imports (billions of dollars)	0.4	3.4	4.9
Trade balance (billions of dollars)	-0.1	-2.4	-2.1
Employees (thousands)	17.4	25.7	25.0

Source: ECLAC (1998) based on information from ECLAC CAN PLUS and PADI databases and data from the Argentine Automobile Manufacturers Association (ADEFA).
[a] Commercial vehicles, passenger cars and others.

---

[52] *Ibid.*

Association, the number of vehicles produced per employee rose from 4.79 a year in 1990 to 8.49 in 1994. However, the industry is still far behind the international frontier (Oliber, 1998, p. 21). For example, Ford (Chile) imports Escorts from Spain, because this is more economical than importing from neighbouring Argentina.[53]

The industry has become highly internationally oriented, with increasing specialization in both Brazil and Argentina in the production of vehicles and parts and components.[54] The advent of MERCOSUR removed the scale constraint that had earlier been a major cause of low productivity. Between 1990 and 1997, automotive exports rose from $100 million to $2.8 billion (table 5.14), comprising some 47 per cent of vehicle production in 1997 (between Brazil's 19 per cent and Mexico's 75 per cent). Most exports went to Brazil (86 per cent by value in 1996). By 1995, over 18 per cent of Argentina's exports to its MERCOSUR partners emanated from the automobile industry.[55] Imports also jumped in this period, from virtually nothing in 1990 to around half of national production in 1996. This led to a widening trade deficit (from $100 million in 1990 to $2.1 billion in 1997).

Growing exports could not prevent the emergence of overcapacity, which stimulated significant restructuring and rationalization. Local assemblers of Fiats, Peugeots and Renaults saw their market shares collapse. Sevel's Fiat market share dropped from over 30 per cent in 1993 to less than 20 per cent in 1996, and its Peugeot share from about 14 to almost 8 per cent. Ciadea's Renault domestic market share declined from 28 to 23 per cent. Volkswagen, Ford, General Motors and an independent new Fiat operation (making the Palio and Siena models) gained market shares. PSA (Peugeot-Citroen) purchased 15 per cent of Sevel in 1997, with an option to purchase a controlling share before July 1999. Sevel will assemble Citroen for the MERCOSUR market from 1997 onwards.[56] Fiat stated its intention to buy a local representative (Iveco trucks), in addition to setting up new production facilities. General Motors came to an agreement with Ciadea in which the latter would operate a General Motors truck plant transferred from Brazil (25,000 units per year).

Exports are necessary to accommodate new capacities – Argentina has to export about half its production. In an attempt to reduce dependence on Brazil, new markets are being explored. Ford, for instance, began exporting its Ranger and Escort models to the Middle East at the end of 1997 (as Brazilian demand fell by 40 per cent in the wake of financial crises). The following year, the company was planning to enter Bolivia, Chile, Nicaragua and Peru.

5.4.3.2 Development of human capital and technology

As firms in Argentina are increasingly integrated into international production systems, they tend to specialize in activities in which they have cost advantages – manufacturing rather than R&D, product and process design and marketing. The larger market created by MERCOSUR has led companies to create generic production capacity in the region: production

---

[53] "Ford Sale del Bache", *América Economía*, August, 1997, pp. 25-26.

[54] Argentina specializes in medium-sized to large automobiles, with engines in the 1,500-3,000cc range.

[55] Argentina significantly improved its import market share of the MERCOSUR automobile industry, from 8.9 per cent to 16.1 per cent in the period 1990-1996.

[56] *América Economía,* August 1997, p. 92; and *Business Latin America*, 14 July 1997.

platforms with standardized processes and components that can be adapted to local needs through minor variations. As a consequence, local subsidiaries no longer play a role in design and adaptation, in contrast to the situation before 1990, when local affiliates had sizeable engineering departments and R&D budgets. Most TNC subsidiaries have practically closed down their engineering departments and R&D centres. Only a limited number of engineers and technicians remain to interpret designs from headquarters (Oliber, 1998, pp. 23-24).

For example, Fiat Sevel employed around 30 people in product engineering to make adaptations to local conditions – Fiat has now discontinued all design and engineering in Argentina. Fiat Argentina receives the blueprints, as well as the process designs and production organization directly from Fiat Italy. The instructions for the Palio model come from Fiat Brazil (Oliber, 1998, p. 31). However, there are also some positive effects. By overcoming scale problems, it becomes possible to use world-class technologies and manufacturing techniques, leading to increased productivity, improved quality and ultimately increased competitiveness. These new technologies require a more skilled labour force. The setting up of Fiat's new facility for the Palio and Siena involved worker training at a cost of an additional $40 million.

5.4.3.3 Development of local suppliers

As in other countries, the restructuring of the automotive industry has decimated the domestic auto parts industry in Argentina (Moori-Koenig and Yoguel, 1992). There is a trend for auto TNCs to reduce the number of first-tier suppliers, while strengthening relationships with those that remain. There are several examples of TNCs taking direct control of important auto parts production, through takeovers and new investments. General Motors and Renault made separate deals with Ciadea for auto parts production and vehicle assembly. Ford purchased a majority share of Sistemaire. By buying the Brazilian auto parts producer, COFAP, Fiat obtained a number of subsidiaries and associates (including Indufren) in Argentina, while Volkswagen enlarged its transmission plant in Cordoba (see also boxes 5.3 and 5.4).

Local suppliers are being replaced by subsidiaries of auto parts TNCs in a process of "follow sourcing". Examples of recent activity by auto parts TNCs in the country include ZF (Germany), which set up a $90 million transmission plant; Delphi Packard (United States) established paint and electric circuit facilities; Magneti-Marelli (Italy) bought local silencer and air-conditioning manufacturers; and Valeo-Neiman (France) bought majority shares in a local radiator producer. A number of Brazilian auto parts firms set up local plants, but only the Degussa Bradesco plants for catalytic converters seems to represent a major commitment. These foreign suppliers are generally technologically highly advanced, with considerable design and engineering capabilities. Their entry means that several Argentinan suppliers have gone out of business, while others have gone from first- to second- or third-tier status, manufacturing relatively simple parts (Oliber, 1998, p. 24).

Box 5.3. Restructuring in MERCOSUR's auto industry: Fiat

Fiat is the seventh-largest auto TNC and ranks fifth in its principal market, Western Europe. Its international production system for passenger cars is concentrated in Europe and South America. In South America, the main production base has been Brazil after the company withdrew from direct involvement in car production in Argentina and Colombia. After the setting up of MERCOSUR, Fiat has been strengthening its operations in Brazil and re-establishing itself in Argentina.

Fiat is one of the largest foreign enterprises in Brazil, with sales of $4.7 billion in 1996. It produces mainly for the domestic market; exports were just 7 per cent of sales in 1996 and go mainly to Argentina. Its production totalled 463,669 vehicles in 1995, of which 396,517 were passenger cars. The Uno model accounted for 253,259 units and was Brazil's second best-selling car. Fiat also imported 89,870 passenger cars in 1995, making it the country's largest vehicle importer; the main import was the Tipo model (92.1 per cent of total imports).

Encouraged by the "economic car programme", Fiat announced a $1 billion investment programme for 1995-2000. All its Uno production was to be transferred from Italy to Brazil, giving Brazil an export platform function in its global production network. For this purpose Fiat restructured and modernized its old Betim plant. It also set up a new plant for the new Palio model (500,000 units) for local sale and export. This model was specifically designed for developing countries.

Fiat re-established itself in Argentina as a producer from 1995 onwards, after an absence of almost 20 years. It bought out its local representative and set up new production facilities. As a result, its market share jumped from 0 in 1994 to 28 per cent in 1997. It produced 22,654 units locally in 1996; its former licensee Sevel still assembled some models but in sharply declining numbers. The Fiat Duna was the second best-selling model in Argentina. The economical Mille model will apparently be assembled in Argentina for export to Brazil. Fiat also stated its intention to re-purchase the shares of its Iveco truck-making facility in Argentina and to increase its production of light trucks (the Daily).

The biggest new addition to the Fiat line in Argentina is a $600 million plant in Cordoba to produce an estate version of the modern Palio/Siena lines, mainly for export to MERCOSUR. This plant will have an annual capacity of 200,000 vehicles and associated investment in auto parts should reach $130 million. It is located beside a new Fiat engine plant. In the first year after its launch in April 1996, nearly 250,000 Palios were sold in Argentina and Fiat is now trying to launch the Palio in other markets. Assembly plants are being set up in Poland and Venezuela, and similar facilities in India, Morocco, South Africa and Turkey have been mentioned.

Its main objective in the region is to improve its competitive situation in the large MERCOSUR market in a few models, giving it large scales and exploiting the regional export scheme. The production of its Brazilian plants will be fully coordinated with its Argentine plants. The combined facilities will make 3,100 Palio vehicles, 2,400 engines, and about the same number of transmissions per day. Three-quarters of the vehicles and one-half of the engines will be sold in Brazil.

Fiat's strategy is a major shift for a company which has had limited experience of integrated production internationally. It is reducing the number of suppliers and consolidating its supplier networks in the region. Its auto parts company purchased 70 per cent of the Brazilian company, COFAP, for about $130 million, providing it with a base to meet MERCOSUR rules of origin. The purchase also provided it

/...

(Box 5.3, concluded)

with subsidiaries and associates in Argentina. It has put significant pressure on its suppliers in Europe to invest in Latin America, resulting in the establishment of 70 new facilities within 120 km of its Betim plant. This supplier network now meets 60 per cent of the plants needs. Fiat hopes to produce 750,000 vehicles a year in the region, which would make it the biggest car maker in Latin America.

Sources: Mortimore (1997 and 1998a).

Box 5.4. Restructuring in MERCOSUR's auto industry: Volkswagen

Volkswagen, unlike Fiat, has long been a major international player, with production systems encompassing Europe, Latin America and, to a certain extent, Asia. It is the largest producer in Western Europe, with a market share of over 17 per cent. Under strong competitive pressures, it has been reorganizing its international production system for some time. During the 1980s it transferred its passenger vehicle plant from the United States to Mexico to improve its competitiveness in the North American market. To cope with severe difficulties in Brazil, in 1986 it merged its subsidiary with Ford's to form Autolatina. The joint venture had an Argentine sister, which could have given it a head start in MERCOSUR. However, Autolatina broke up when the market started to recover.

By 1995, Volkswagen was the largest foreign company and auto producer in Brazil, with $7.2 billion in sales and a market share of over 30 per cent in the vehicle market. It made nearly 600,000 vehicles (427,000 thousand passenger cars). Its orientation was primarily the domestic market; exports were less than 8 per cent of sales. It was also a major importer of vehicles, bringing in 63,984 units.

By the mid-1990s, Volkswagen Brazil had a mixture of old and new production facilities. In response to the "economic car" policy it set up a new plant to make the Gol model, which became the top seller in 1996. It continued with existing models (Beetle, Santana, Parati, Kombi, etc.), as well as engines, transmissions, components, parts and a foundry operation in older plants elsewhere in Brazil. It has started on a massive modernization and expansion programme and plans. The major part is aimed at raising its "economic car" capacity to 500,000 units. Another significant investment would go into new capacity for the Golf ($500 million) and the Audi A3 ($250 million). It is to invest about $250 million in a new truck and bus facility. Volkswagen is bringing in its Skoda subsidiary to produce trucks in Bahia and Santa Catarina. A new engine plant is being constructed in Sao Paulo. Exports of vehicles and parts to Argentina reportedly reached $320 million in 1996.

In Argentina, Volkswagen's subsidiary had sales of $1.2 billion in 1996, and accounted for about $237 million of exports. The company plans to invest $500 million in 1995-2000 to improve production systems and integrate them better with its Brazilian operations. It is enlarging its transmission plant, and is transferring some Brazilian operations to Argentina to take advantage of the trade agreement. The Gol continues to be the centrepiece of Argentine production (58,000 units in 1996). A new line of trucks is to be established. Its domestic market share has increased from about 14 per cent in 1985, before the Autolatina venture, to over 19 per cent in 1996, raising it to second place in that market. Volkswagen (Argentina) exported about 43,000 units to Brazil in 1996 and will also export significant volumes of parts and components from Argentina.

Sources: Mortimore (1997 and 1998a).

5.4.4   *Thailand*

5.4.4.1 *Industrial restructuring and competitive performance*

Attracted by rapid growth and economic liberalization in the early 1990s, many auto TNCs set up or expanded capacity in Thailand. Reductions in import tariffs on completely built-up units (CBU) led to rising imports (car imports rose by 113 per cent in 1992-1993) and increased pressures for modernization. However, the industry still lacks full international competitiveness. Only Toyota's Hi-Lux pick-up truck and Isuzu's pick-up facilities reach scales of 100,000 units per annum; this is just economic, but is well below world-class plants that make 250,000 to 400,000 units. Labour productivity is low: factories in developed economies produce between 40 and 45 vehicles per employee per year, compared to 4 or 5 in Thailand. It takes 16-18 hours to build a car in Japan, but 30-92 hours in Thailand (Brooker Group, 1997a).

Automotive exports from Thailand are mainly in parts and components rather than CBUs. Component exports reached almost $1 billion (i.e. about half of total automotive exports) in 1996. Mitsubishi has been the only exporter of cars from Thailand since 1988. It is expected, however, that exports of CBU cars by General Motors, Honda, Ford-Mazda and Toyota from new plants in Thailand will increase in the future.

5.4.4.2 *Development of human capital*

A survey of the industry in 1997 by the Thailand Development Research Institute (TDRI) shows that workers with primary-level certificates accounted for 79 per cent of employees in the period 1990-1996, declining to 72 per cent in 1997 (table 5.15). Over this period, the employment of technical workers, graduates and engineers increased. Between 1990-1996, technical and vocational graduates and graduates with bachelor degrees accounted for 12 per cent and 5 per cent of the total workforce respectively. In 1997, the former had risen to 19 per cent and the latter to 6 per cent. Engineers accounted for 3 per cent of employment in the industry.

The data suggest that the industry predominantly employs poorly educated workers.[57] This may account for the fact that an assembly line in Thailand needs about 1.5 times more labour than in Japan (Brooker Group, 1997a). It is, however, difficult to create more employment for technicians and engineers. The Thai education system produces too few engineers, and the secondary school base is narrow, making it difficult to increase enrolments in engineering. The shortage of engineers has lowered the quality of technical inputs, since firms have had to employ technical or vocational graduates in engineering positions. The lack of higher-level skills hampers technological upgrading and productivity increases in the automobile industry.

---

[57] Production workers in small auto-parts firms are mostly educated up to primary school level, whereas in the large-scale automotive firms the lowest education qualification is the lower secondary certificate.

**Table 5.15. Distribution of employment by educational attainment in the
Thai automobile industry**

(Per cent of employees)

Educational level	Average 1990-1996		1997
Primary to higher secondary	79		72
Technical or vocational training	12		19
Bachelor degree	5		6
Engineering degree	NA		3
	Survey by the Thai National Statistics Office		
Educational level	1986-1987	1991-1992	1996-1997
Primary level or lower	71.7	67.9	61.7
Lower secondary	11.1	14.9	18.7
Upper secondary	4.1	4.2	5.5
Technical or vocational training	6.9	7.3	7.4
University/ teacher college	5.0	5.5	6.5
Others	1.1	0.0	0.0
Total (per cent)	100.0	100.0	100.0
Total (thousands of people)[a]	195	314.4	441.2

Sources: Thailand Development Research Institute (1998), National Statistics Office, Bangkok, Third Survey.

[a] Total number of workers in auto assembly and the auto parts industries.

Training programmes in the automobile industry range from basic on-the-job training to formal seminars or advanced training programmes abroad for employees. Most firms provide training at all levels, depending on the skills required. All new production workers are required to attend basic training on fundamental production processes and skills. A common approach, used by the Japanese affiliates, is job rotation or on-the-job training; these approaches enable employees to understand the job responsibilities of various functions. At the middle or supervisory level, employees attend training programmes at local affiliates as well as at foreign headquarters. In the affiliates, training programmes are conducted by senior engineers or engineers from headquarters. In addition to local training programmes, some employees are sent for training to headquarters, and in turn arrange courses for other employees locally.

In large companies such as Honda, Toyota and General Motors, training programmes are more intensive than elsewhere in the industry. For instance, General Motors has begun to institutionalize its training programme in the form of its "General Motors University" project to provide training for workers or technicians in the automotive or auto part industry as a whole. The Government of Thailand has pledged financial support for this initiative to the tune of $16 million (Brooker Group, 1997b, p. 3).

However, the employment of local executives faces several constraints. First and foremost, the organizational structure of foreign affiliates, especially in Japanese affiliates, favours the employment of expatriates. In most Japanese affiliates, approximately 90 per cent of executives are Japanese expatriates. Weaknesses in the Thai educational system, which emphasizes theoretical rather than practical perspectives and puts insufficient emphasis on science and mathematics, are another problem.

5.4.4.3 Development of technology

While the affiliates of leading auto TNCs employ advanced production technologies and organizational systems, key strategic decisions on designs, marketing and technology remain centralized in the parent companies. The size of the local market and skill constraints in Thailand make it difficult to shift these functions to affiliates. Technological development is thus heavily dependent on imported technologies and organizational techniques (the Toyota affiliate implements the same kanban system as the parent). As for local suppliers, auto TNCs transfer quality systems, technical specifications and the various skills needed to ensure reliable delivery.

Local R&D is limited to minor process adaptation or incremental product improvement. However, Toyota has recently taken a significant step, with the local R&D team developing the design for its economy Soluna model with the team in Japan. Moreover, the Thai Rung Union Car research department has helped design the body of their multi-purpose vehicles, and the research unit of Sammit Motor, one of the leading auto part and truck manufacturers, conducts product innovation as well as product improvement. However, such developments are still limited and confined to a few large firms. The small and medium-sized firms that dominate parts manufacture are labour-intensive and technologically backward; they carry out practically no R&D.

Some TNCs are introducing advanced systems to promote international integration. For example, Japanese firms have introduced electronic information systems to facilitate regional sourcing in ASEAN. Because of the small size of individual national markets, parts manufacturers in Asia supply several assemblers; this makes it difficult to respond smoothly to each customer's designs and specifications. By linking these manufacturers into an electronic network, manufacturers can obtain information about parts and orders, and can respond more rapidly to specification changes. Toyota and the Japanese Ministry of International Trade and Industry (MITI) have jointly established a "Commerce at Light Speed" network linking part producers in various countries in Asia (Takayasu, 1996b). This integrated information system will shorten lead times, lower costs and facilitate the regional division of labour. To ensure the smooth operation of the network, Toyota has established a regional headquarters in Singapore, and Honda and Mazda have done the same in Thailand.

5.4.4.5 Development of local suppliers

Past policies in the ASEAN countries were not very successful in promoting efficient local parts production. Firms could not achieve economies of scale in small, protected and fragmented markets. Although most assemblers were able to satisfy the local content requirements, local suppliers developed largely for simple parts and components and concentrated on the local replacement market. Within this setting, however, Thai component firms are more advanced than in the other ASEAN countries – at least as far as numbers of firms are concerned (Doner, 1991). This was a major factor in attracting auto TNCs to Thailand in the 1990s.

Thailand has more than 725 components producers, with roughly 225 supplying the OEM market and the rest catering to the after-market (Brooker Group, 1997b). Even so, the level of localization is relatively modest. Official local content figures (45-60 per cent, depending on the model) appear to be overestimates; the actual local content rates of passenger and heavy commercial vehicles are around 19 per cent, and for pick-up trucks 25 per cent (Brooker Group, 1997a).

The local content policy was the critical factor behind the development of Thailand's components and parts industry. It created a captive market for components and parts producers, and the Thai market was open only to automakers willing to procure locally. Although the measure imposed costs on the assemblers, most of the burden was shifted to consumers through higher prices backed by tariffs on imported cars and lower tariffs on CKD products. However, the local-content programme was relatively flexible and gradual. It began with simple labour-intensive products in which Thailand had comparative advantage, and moved to complex parts over time.

Although the policy created the conditions for the growth of component and parts firms, it was the Japanese assemblers who played the leading role in their promotion. To improve the quality of suppliers, they introduced "cooperation clubs" of the sort that are widespread in Japan. These clubs not only held social gatherings to create deeper relationship between assemblers and component firms, but also arranged for quality control presentations, meetings at which case studies on quality improvement, value analysis and cost reduction activities were presented, and workshops on technical guidance and training in Japan. These activities have led to significant improvements in quality and delivery times and led to cost reductions by suppliers.

Political and institutional factors also promoted the development of the parts and components industry. The local-content policies of 1978 would have been unlikely without the organization, initiatives and political influence of the local components and parts firms. The 201 registered parts manufacturers had strong connections and put considerable pressure on the Government. Dissatisfied with the resistance to higher local content by the Automotive Parts Industry Club, the large supplier established a separate association solely for parts firms, the Thai Automotive Parts Manufacturers' Association. The new association also attracted small parts makers. This group was able to lobby to overcome the resistance of the foreign assemblers, who then designed the local-content formula in response to pressures from the parts firms (Doner, 1991, p. 200).

After 1985, Japanese TNCs started to convince their domestic parts suppliers to invest in ASEAN countries. This resulted in two large movements of Japanese component manufacturers to Asia, in particular to Thailand (table 5.16). Between 1986 and 1992, the proportion of FDI by small and medium-sized Japanese companies rose from 43 to 65 per cent of the total. The number of auto parts companies moving to Thailand jumped from 4 in 1981-1985 to 32 in 1986-1990. The number of Japanese investment applications, mostly from small and medium-sized firms, reached 400 in 1988, then dropped to 71 in 1992 and again increased to 171 in 1993. Most of these investments took the form of joint ventures. In the mid-1990s, 59 per cent of suppliers to the assemblers (excluding suppliers to the after-market) were joint ventures with Japanese companies, up from 25 per cent five years earlier (Brooker Group, 1997a).

Table 5.16. Movement of Japanese component manufacturers to Thailand

Year	No. of companies established in each period
Up to 1965	5
1966-1970	5
1971-1975	11
1976-1980	5
1981-1985	4
1986-1990	32
1991 and after	5
Total	67

Source: based on Yukawa, as quoted in Higashi (1995), figures 2 and 3.

As a result of the rapid increase in car production, cost pressures and the movement of Japanese parts suppliers, the Government of Thailand was able to increase local-content requirements. They rose from 50 per cent in 1984 to 54 per cent in 1987 for passenger cars, and from 40 per cent in 1984 to 61 per cent in 1988 for commercial vehicles. A further impetus to the parts industry came with the initiative of car assemblers to introduce a regional network of part suppliers in ASEAN countries.

The idea behind the scheme was for assemblers to source from common suppliers to allow the latter to reach economic production scales. This kind of "cross *keiretsu* system" has grown well in Thailand (table 5.17) (Higashi, 1995). Toyota, Nissan and Isuzu, for example, formed a reciprocal parts supply system in 1996 for cast engine cylinder blocks, a very capital-intensive item (Fujita and Hill, 1997). Such a cross-*keiretsu* system also has beneficial spillover effects. For example, Honda is able to produce cheaply the stamping parts of its City model because it can rely upon the three experienced producers of dies from the Toyota cooperation club.[58]

The target of the *keiretsu* and cross-*keiretsu* supplier network is to increase local content to 70 per cent. Toyota was the first company to start such a network, followed by other major Japanese auto TNCs. Although Toyota does not export cars from its ASEAN base, it is actively

Table 5.17. Regional network of trade of parts under the brand-to-brand complementation scheme

Source country of auto parts	Toyota	Nissan	Honda	Mitsubishi
Thailand	Diesel engine floor panel	Large panel interior-trim	Press-parts	Bumper intake-manifold
Philippines	Transmission	Medium panel	Intake-manifold	Transmission
Malaysia	Steering-gear shock-absorber filter	Medium panel steering-gear	Bumper & plastic parts	Door steering-gear
Indonesia	SK engine	NA	Engine block	NA

Sources: UNCTAD, based on company reports from TMSS, T&K Autoparts, Toyota-Astra Motor, Siam Toyota and company interviews.

---

[58] Toyota can source parts and raw material in Thailand since there are more than 700 suppliers of parts and raw materials. The Toyota cooperation club is seen as a means to create deeper relationships with its component firms (Higashi, 1995, p. 21).

promoting the regional network. This is why Siam Toyota Manufacturing[59] is exporting diesel engines and camshafts to Malaysia, New Zealand, Portugal and Singapore. The cross-*keiretsu* supply networks extend beyond national boundaries (Fujita and Hill, 1997). Nissan and Isuzu buy Thai-made Toyota cylinder blocks for their production sites in Malaysia. Nissan purchases steering gears from Toyota in Malaysia for all its sites in ASEAN countries. In their choice of production sites in ASEAN, Japanese TNCs try to assign production on the basis of comparative advantage.[60] They have convinced the Governments of the ASEAN countries to set up a BBC scheme (discussed earlier) which gives tariff preferences to the parts and components exchanged. In 1995, the trade value of parts under Toyota's BBC scheme was $100 million.

The record of technological upgrading among parts suppliers is mixed, however. Strong competition in the local market is a stimulating force,[61] but protection of auto assembly and high tariffs on imported components have been detrimental. The suppliers who manufacture products to clients' specifications and under OEM arrangements do not invest in product development capabilities. On the other hand, parts manufacturers that sell on world markets have initiated the development of product technologies.

There are two main channels of technology transfer to auto part manufacturers: joint ventures with foreign companies and technological assistance from their customers. The first has played an important role since the early 1980s, when the progressive localization scheme induced TNCs to invite their domestic suppliers to invest in Thailand. The second has become significant as local suppliers have had to upgrade their production processes to keep abreast of TNC needs. Kato (1992) concludes that the transfer of production capabilities has been moderately successful, whereas that of more advanced capabilities such as design has been relatively limited. Foreign assemblers have also provided technical assistance and training to their local suppliers.[62]

On the whole, however, technology deepening in parts suppliers remains relatively limited. The centralization of decision making and R&D activities in auto-maker headquarters reduces the need to develop these capabilities locally. The trade regime continues to protect the parts industry and reduces incentives to invest in more advanced capabilities. As local affiliates of TNCs undertake little R&D, they have very little to offer suppliers in collaboration in this field. Thus, the country's parts and components industry needs considerable upgrading in order to reach world standards.

---

[59] Toyota has four companies in Thailand: Toyota Motor Thailand, assembling cars; Thai Himo Industry, assembling Dyna trucks; Siam Toyota Manufacturing, producing diesel engines; and Toyota Auto Body Thailand, producing stamped parts (UBS Global Research, 1997).

[60] For example, since Malaysia has a large number of plastic parts suppliers in the electronics industry, it is the prime source of bumpers. Thailand is to export diesel engines because it has the largest market in the ASEAN region.

[61] In general, Japanese auto assemblers in Thailand have 40 to 50 suppliers, influencing their suppliers to continually upgrade technological capabilities.

[62] For instance, Thai Rung Union, the Thai manufacturers of adapted, multi-purpose Isuzu pick-ups, contends that Isuzu has influenced its technology transfer and know-how.

5.4.5 Malaysia

5.4.5.1 Industrial restructuring and competitive performance

Malaysia's national car project drove the rationalization of its automotive industry, both in the assembly and component segments. As far as assembly is concerned, before the advent of Proton in 1983, there were 36 models of passenger vehicles and 41 models of commercial vehicles from 16 different assemblers, each operating at low scales of production (Abidin, 1996). Capacity utilization rates averaged 64 per cent. There was general unwillingness to standardize design, material and dimensions (Doner, 1991, p. 51). Local content was low.

By the mid-1990s, the number of foreign assemblers had fallen to eight, with a joint domestic market share of about 20 per cent, focused on the upper income market. Proton's Saga alone had a domestic market share of about 60 per cent, and its exports were growing. Ireland and the United Kingdom were the main overseas markets (85 per cent); other export destinations included Australia, Germany and Singapore. Altogether, Proton exports to 28 countries, including a number of developing ones.[63] In addition, it has joint-venture assembly plants in the Philippines and Viet Nam (Abidin, 1996). By ASEAN standards, Proton performs very well in terms of productivity. In comparison to Thailand, where an average of 4-5 vehicles per employee are produced annually, Malaysia makes an estimated average of 15-18 vehicles (Brooker Group, 1997b). However, Proton relies heavily on State support. The Government helps it by fixing prices and protects it from imports. Its exports have also benefited from preferential treatment (through the Generalized System of Preferences) and are implicitly subsidized through protection at home.

Proton has grown in 12 years to become the biggest car manufacturer in the ASEAN region, with an annual output of more than 155,000 units and installed capacity of 180,000. However, this is low by industry standards: a capacity of 500,000 is considered the threshold for a viable global manufacturing presence in the mass market and over 1 million for significant design and development. Proton plans to expand production to 500,000 units by 2000. Since the Malaysian market can absorb 240,000 units at the most, it will have to expand exports significantly if this output is to be absorbed by the market. This will entail investment in distribution and after-sale service networks abroad, as well as product development to incorporate new safety features and environmental standards. It will also need to give priority to multiple input sourcing, to increase competition and achieve cost reductions in the components industry.

5.4.5.2 Development of human capital, technology and local suppliers

The Malaysian component industry too has undergone considerable reorganization. The emergence of one dominant car company significantly reduced fragmentation. Rationalization was encouraged by Proton's single-sourcing strategy, aimed specifically at encouraging scale economies in component production. Foreign auto companies set up component production when their assembly operations came under pressure, using their capabilities developed by

---

[63] For example, Brunei, Bangladesh, Malawi and Zimbabwe (Abidin, 1996).

previous in-house component manufacturing. Some even established themselves as Proton component suppliers. Others became international OEM suppliers. Exports of parts and components from Malaysia grew from 64.8 million ringgit in 1992 to 196.5 million ringgit in 1995 (Abidin, 1996).

Nevertheless, the start was not auspicious. Although the Government of Malaysia intended its national car policy to be something more than simply a Mitsubishi vehicle with body parts stamped in Malaysia, the contract between the Heavy Industry Corporation (HICOM) and Mitsubishi merely mentioned both parties' commitment to increased localization. Since it did not spell out the practical implications of this commitment, it provided Mitsubishi with the opportunity to pursue its own interests, which at times impeded local sourcing of inputs and technology transfer. While it did not protest over the use of local components that had already been deleted prior to its start-up, it strongly opposed plans to increase further localization, claiming that the quality of local parts was too poor. When the mandatory deletion programme was expanded, Mitsubishi insisted that it alone had the testing facilities and capabilities needed to determine whether samples submitted by local parts producers were up to standard. The Government was handicapped by a lack of expertise in the auto industry, and it also suffered from a lack of unity among different agencies over the status of the national car project. In the early years of its existence, increased use of supposedly local inputs appeared to come predominantly from Japanese transplants owned by Mitsubishi itself, or from companies having a close affiliation to the company. Concerns were expressed that the Proton project would lead to serious erosion of the domestic car parts industry (Doner, 1991).

However, over the years Proton gradually came to accept increased localization. Local suppliers played a vital role in this, through the component manufacturers' association (MACPMA) that lobbied actively for increased localization. These suppliers constituted the technologically most advanced segment of the components industry and could most readily meet Mitsubishi's quality requirements. However, the Government, in its desire to increase the role of bumiputra entrepreneurship, had initially bypassed them as they were predominantly of ethnic Chinese origin. MACPMA's role was strengthened after the Government established a Joint Technical Committee for Local Content (JTC), in recognition of its limited technical expertise and weak bargaining position *vis-à-vis* Mitsubishi. Four parties participated in the JTC: MACPMA, the assemblers association, the dealers' association and the State. JTC became the State-backed arena for bargaining over local content, but its operations had broader consequences. It generated expertise in localization policy and strategy among officials. It strengthened the component firms as participants in the bargaining process and in terms of production capacity. Its role was boosted when the Government mandated Proton to participate in the JTC in the determination of local content. MACPMA also persuaded the Government to merge two Proton departments responsible for local procurement. The merger and Proton's participation in JTC resulted in Proton's acceptance of more locally produced parts. Local components constituted about 60 per cent of the total value of its cars by 1996, which was a considerable achievement. Moreover, local content for the foreign assemblers is much lower (about 30-40 per cent). It should be pointed out that the programme has achieved little by way of the intended ethnic restructuring in the components industry.

Proton initiated a vendor development programme to promote the development of small and medium-sized enterprises through close support and (in the first instance) a system of single sourcing. Under this programme, Proton provides market and technical assistance, and the Government and financial institutions offer financial aid to the vendors. Technical support helped the local vendors to meet required quality standards. In some instances, Proton initially manufactured parts in-house, with a subsequent transfer to independent companies. The single-sourcing system was important in assuring a market for the vendors' products, enabling them to reach a minimum efficient scale of production (Abidin, 1996).

The vendor development programme has therefore had positive consequences for the local parts industry. Proton has recognized 134 vendors, producing 3,000 components. Many of these producers, in turn, have procured inputs from other subcontractors, generating widespread linkages with supporting small and medium-sized firms. However, the tight control of the foreign partner over design and technical development has had clear disadvantages. Most of Proton's vendors are required to maintain technical assistance arrangements with parts suppliers or directly with Mitsubishi in Japan. These agreements typically involve high fees and specify the entire production process, including the sources of raw materials. This leaves little room for autonomous learning and discourages initiatives by local firms. In the absence of local design and development capabilities in Malaysia, product development may take longer and costs may be higher.

Such high dependence on the foreign partner will have to be reduced if Proton is to transform itself from a domestic manufacturer into an internationally competitive company. This transformation will require significant human resource upgrading and the development of technological capabilities in advanced functions. The training levels of Malaysia's workforce are not yet sufficient to move into the production – and ultimately design and development – of cars incorporating modern safety and environmental technologies that can hold their own in a competitive world market.

5.5 Conclusions and policy implications

The comparison of TNCs in the automobile industries of Mexico, Brazil, Argentina, Thailand and Malaysia yields interesting similarities as well as some minor differences. All five countries encouraged the automobile industry as part of their import-substitution industrialization drive in the 1960s and 1970s. TNCs played an important role, especially in assembly, in launching the industry. However, the activity was largely inefficient, selling to small markets, with sub-optimal-sized plants making a diversity of models with little import competition. Modernization and expansion began in the late 1980s or the early 1990s as a result of policy liberalization and intensifying competition among a limited (and decreasing) number of TNCs. It has proceeded significantly, but at a different pace in each economy according to the market stimulus and the firms involved. On the whole, the industry provides a classic example of restructuring by TNCs.

The activity is highly skill-, technology- and scale- intensive. While not as R&D-driven as electronics, automobile production requires a great deal of capability-building in production, design and supply-chain management. Thus, technological capabilities and modern organizational techniques, applied to very large volumes of production, are critical to efficiency and competitiveness. The current battle for global markets, with the accompanying mergers and alliances, are manifestations of the search to optimize these factors in an integrated way across national economies. Production facilities are increasingly aimed at large national, regional or global markets. Not surprisingly, automotive FDI in the developing world is highly concentrated – most developing countries do not have the wherewithal to attract TNCs for establishing globalized production facilities. Given the scale, skills and linkages involved, only a few (those with large and diverse industrial bases) have done well.

Long-established automobile TNCs wield considerable political and economic power in host economies because of their contribution to employment, exports and FDI inflows, and their linkages to other companies. The position of incumbent firms in the new regional groupings is especially favourable. Regional rules of origin benefit firms with established supplier networks, and those with local production facilities enjoy a preferential import regime. In the ASEAN countries, Japanese firms are in this position, while in Latin America it is the United States and European TNCs. In all three cases, the ability of established firms to influence automotive policy has helped keep newcomers at bay to some extent.

Mexico is primarily an example of efficiency-seeking FDI. Policy changes, combined with the proximity of the world's largest car market, have given United States TNCs the opportunity to reduce their costs. In Brazil and Argentina, the main attraction has been the large regional market. The ASEAN case has been largely driven by rapidly growing domestic markets, but elements of efficiency-seeking FDI are appearing. The financial crises in Asia in 1997-1998 and Brazil in 1998-1999 do not appear to have had much effect on the long-term strategies of TNCs.

The restructuring and upgrading process in each of the regions has taken different forms, but there have been common elements, however, reflecting technological and global competitive trends.

- The realization of *scale economies* is perhaps the most important factor – despite the greater flexibility offered by new process technologies, large production runs remain vital in the industry. Realizing scale economies has been facilitated in enlarged regional markets such as those offered by NAFTA, MERCOSUR or ASEAN.

- Greater locational *specialization and standardization among affiliates* in terms of model and component ranges have accompanied the pressure to raise scales. Such standardization in design, development and production hassled to *growing centralization of R&D* in the developed countries and to a corresponding reduction in adaptive work in developing-country affiliates.

- Technological upgrading has necessitated the introduction into affiliates of *modern plant and equipment* and *modern organizational practices*. Both have required *human resource development*, especially by the leading assemblers.

- Finally, modernization has involved a *reorganization of supplier networks*. Assemblers are developing intense collaborative relationships with a limited number of core suppliers who assume responsibility for entire sub-assemblies (modular manufacturing). These suppliers are often technologically advanced companies that have followed their customers abroad. Assemblers themselves have also made big investments in components production.

As a result of these developments, affiliates in all five case-study countries have made impressive advances in productivity and efficiency. However, the nature and pace of advance differ among them. Mexico has taken the process furthest – at least in the export-oriented segment. The automobile industries in MERCOSUR and the ASEAN countries have smaller segments of competitive activity, and large parts of them still rely on protection. Supplier chains are less technologically advanced and are not benefitting from economies of scale. The difference with Mexico is partly a matter of timing: Mexican restructuring started in the mid-1980s, well before the investment wave in MERCOSUR and the ASEAN region. But there are other factors too. Proximity to the United States market enabled Mexican facilities to be integrated into the TNCs' core operations in a manner not feasible for the other countries studied. Policies pursued by the Governments of the United States and Mexico, in particular the setting up of NAFTA, facilitated the process greatly. Since integration with United States operations required reaching world-class levels of competitiveness, the regional factor fostered greater upgrading in Mexico than in other countries.

Restructuring in Brazil and Argentina has been driven by regional integration in a different fashion, strongly shaped by the nature of the agreements. Free market forces had less to do with the process than the specific sectoral interventions mounted by the two Governments. In general, the industry – particularly in Brazil – remains more inward-looking than in Mexico. While there has been significant modernization and new-world class facilities have been set up, competitive lags remain. There has been massive over-investment in relation to the size and likely growth of MERCOSUR markets, perpetuating market fragmentation and lack of scale economies. The industry suffers from low productivity, and will not be able to export enough to compensate for low domestic sales. While NAFTA also has overcapacity problems, they are leading old high-cost production facilities in the United States to relocate to Mexico.

The automobile industry in ASEAN has developed under a mixture of policy-led and market-led incentives. There are larger differences between countries, particularly between the relatively TNC-dependent regime in Thailand and the State-led programmes in Malaysia; the investment climate in the Philippines resembles that of Thailand, and that of Indonesia resembles that of Malaysia. Both the Thai and the Malaysian economies protect their automobile industries and offer strong support for local content. Thailand has built up a well-performing supplier base, sustainable largely because of its larger domestic market. Malaysia has developed considerable manufacturing and design capabilities. However, the industry as a whole suffers from lack of economies of scale, low efficiency and growing overcapacity. It has some export capabilities but these are relatively limited. Table 5.18 summarizes the findings of the case studies.

Against this background, what has been the impact of TNCs on restructuring? The answer is mixed. Given the national and policy context, TNCs have invested heavily in raising the capacities and capabilities of their affiliates. The introduction of new equipment, organizational techniques and large plants has taken the host-country industries nearer to world-class standards. Where exports have taken off, as in Latin America, they have transformed the

Table 5.18. Restructuring and competitiveness of the automotive industry in the case study countries

Country	Competitiveness in export markets	Technology upgrading / development of R&D Capacity	Human resource development	Local suppliers
Mexico	Very good (in North American market)	Up-to-date equipment and modern work practices in leading assemblers and component plants. R&D mainly limited to adaptive work in such plants.	Beginning trend away from low wage-based simple assembly operations; increasing emphasis on training.	Severe shake-out among Mexican firms completed. Leading foreign firms have moved in and are strengthening their position. Significant follow- sourcing (in-bond parts production).
Brazil	Very limited	As in Mexico for new plants; little modernization of hardware in some old plants. Erosion of broad-based local R&D base, but significant design work continues in leading assemblers and foreign component firms (e.g. Fiat Palio).	Significant efforts to upgrade skills among assemblers and leading first-tier firms, but not further up the supply chain.	Similar to situation in Mexico, but restructuring still in shake-out phase. Severe shake-out and marginalization among Brazilian manufacturers; increasing internationalization / foreign investment-driven modernization. Significant experimentation with new forms of supplier relations (modular manufacturing).
Argentina	Very limited	Similar to situation in Brazil. Local licensees were more important in assembly, and are now losing ground to foreign modern plants. Very significant erosion of local R&D base, even worse than in Brazil.	Similar to situation in Brazil.	Similar to situation in Brazil.
Thailand	Emerging in regional markets	Same pattern as Brazil. Some instances of local involvement in design activity in leading TNCs.	Clear trend towards increasing skill levels / more training, but general level still low.	Significant local / joint-venture Involvement due to strong local-content policies and continued protection. Increasing TNC Involvement alongside this (follow-sourcing).
Malaysia	Limited (state-supported)	Similar to above, but protection of national car joint venture has muted competition and drive for efficiency. Limited local R&D capacity because the project is heavily dependent on Mitsubishi Japan, also for supplier development.	Inconclusive. Lack of technically qualified manpower in the country in general is a serious constraint towards further upgrading.	Significant local involvement alongside foreign TNCs due to. strong local-content policies and protection.

Source: UNCTAD.

competitive structure of the host economies. TNCs have helped local suppliers upgrade their scale, skills and technologies. There are examples of assemblers and component affiliates that play a major role in design and development in their global networks, using their base of capabilities developed in the import-substitution period. In Brazil, some firms are experimenting with novel modular manufacturing methods that may, if successful, be adopted in the auto industry worldwide.

On the other hand, closer integration into global production systems has adversely affected the deepening of certain capabilities in affiliates. Design capabilities have been transferred only in rare cases – though the fact that such transfers have taken place means that it is at least possible that more will take place in the future. Large numbers of domestic suppliers have suffered from the impact of globalization, particularly in Latin America. By contrast, the Malaysian national car firm Proton has managed to deepen its capabilities and develop the local supplier base.

The experience of the studies suggests that a careful mixture of market forces and policy intervention is the best approach in efforts to develop a competitive auto industry. Given the lengthy learning processes involved, an initial period of sheltered development is probably essential; it is difficult to imagine a world-class automobile industry emerging in a country that cannot build on domestic manufacturing experience and the relevant engineering skills. However, given the scale and supply chains needed for full competitiveness, gradual liberalization and a strong involvement of TNCs – as a means to access globally integrated production resources – is essential over time. The liberalization process needs to be carefully managed. The countries studied have managed to maintain a high involvement of domestic firms and joint ventures through active localization and supplier upgrading policies. Policy makers have withstood the short-term interests of the TNCs by forming powerful alliances with local supplier groups. Mexico's hands-off approach, in contrast, has adversely affected its domestic supplier base, and Brazil and Argentina are rapidly sliding down the same slope.

The experience of the countries reviewed here suggests that there is not much room for newcomers in this industry. The overcapacity problem is immense. Moreover, it is difficult to envisage how newcomer countries could successfully develop the industry to the same degree of sophistication as the incumbents have done. Many of the Government interventions used to support the creation of local capabilities are no longer permissible under WTO rules or subject to notification. It is likely that only those countries and regions with already developed technology, skill structures and a dense network of suppliers will attract technologically dynamic companies (Mytelka, 1998).

Chapter 6

FDI, restructuring and competitiveness
in two resource-rich economies:
Chile and Zimbabwe

6.1 Introduction

Chile and Zimbabwe share similar histories of inward-looking industrialization, followed by a phase of liberalization and outward-orientation. Both are rich in natural resources and have long traditions of manufacturing activity. They are roughly comparable in terms of population, Chile having 15 million people and Zimbabwe 11 million. Despite their similarities, they of course differ greatly in terms of history and geography, political setting, institutions, and in economic variables such as GDP, income levels and the FDI flows they have attracted. With an income per capita in 1997 of $12,080 (in purchasing power parity terms), Chile's standard of living is much higher than that of Zimbabwe, where income per capita is only $2,280 (World Bank, 1999).

These differences have affected their industrial restructuring processes. Chile's manufacturing industry was exposed to sweeping and drastic liberalization some two decades ago, and went into prolonged decline. Its subsequent industrial growth was driven by resource-based activities; other segments of manufacturing, in particular those in high-technology activities, still lag badly. Zimbabwe's industrial base is the most developed in sub-Saharan Africa (excluding South Africa), and it has strong competitive advantages in neighbouring countries in certain manufacturing activities. But these activities use simple technologies and most are still rooted in the import-substitution period – Zimbabwe began to liberalize relatively recently and the process is incomplete. Chile has attracted considerable FDI, and has become a significant exporter of direct investment; much of inward FDI has gone into export-oriented activities. Zimbabwe attracted relatively little new FDI until the mid-1990s, and the TNCs present are largely affiliates established in earlier decades.

This chapter analyzes these contrasting patterns of restructuring and industrial competitiveness, and the role played by foreign investors. Section 6.2 gives a brief historical overview of the industrial development process in Chile and Zimbabwe and of the environment for TNCs after the two countries adopted export-oriented strategies. Section 6.3 focuses on the role of TNCs in industrial restructuring, partly based on surveys of TNC subsidiaries. Section 6.4 concludes with policy lessons for other resource-rich developing countries.

The discussion is based on firm-level interviews. Most of the companies interviewed are among the leading companies in their respective sectors and they have all been operating for more than 20 years. Hence, they have operated under various market and policy settings – from earlier inward-looking policies to the open market approach under ESAP – and they have all been faced with pressures to adjust their strategies accordingly. The study analyses their responses to change and how it has affected their competitiveness. Basic operational data for each of the sample companies are given in annex 6.1 and annex tables 6.1, 6.2, 6.3 and 6.4.

6.2   Government policy and FDI trends

6.2.1   Chile

Chile's economy was closed and highly protected until the mid-1970s, when it adopted a liberal, export-oriented strategy. Price controls, high tariffs, subsidies and restrictions were eliminated and a stabilization programme was implemented to restore macroeconomic equilibrium. Public spending was reduced, taxes reformed, a single exchange rate introduced and interest rate controls eliminated. Many segments of Chilean industry suffered badly from the withdrawal of protection. Many firms died out; manufacturing employment fell to around half of its level in the pre-liberalization period. At the same time, the new incentive framework provided an impetus for export-oriented industries, especially in resource-based activities where there was "natural protection" and less need for prolonged technological learning (Pietrobelli, 1998). Chile has almost 20 per cent of world copper reserves and 23 per cent of world molybdenum reserves, its two most significant natural resources. It also has close to 100 per cent of natural nitrate, 15 per cent of iodine, and 40 per cent of lithium and rhenium reserves. Native forests cover more than 7 million hectares. Geographic and climatic conditions are favourable for the cultivation of a large variety of fruits and vegetables. It also has considerable marine resources.

Liberalization led to the fuller exploitation of these resources. Mining, forestry, the agribusiness and fishing have enjoyed sustained growth. Copper and copper-based products – the country's traditional resources – are still the largest revenue earners, but rapid progress has been made in the development of several non-traditional export sectors, including fresh fruit (especially grapes and apples), cellulose, timber, fish-meal and fresh fish (Pietrobelli, 1998).

FDI, attracted by a welcoming policy climate, favourable investment conditions and a stable regime, has played a significant role in this growth. The Government favoured private investment and aimed to reduce the role of the public sector through liberalization, deregulation and privatization. International trade was encouraged through a stable exchange rate. Import tariffs were reduced over time, reaching a uniform 11 per cent *ad valorem* rate in 1991; quantitative import restrictions were eliminated much earlier. Exports were encouraged through drawback schemes exempting inputs from VAT; exporters were offered deferred payment of import tariffs on and fiscal credit for imported capital goods, special storage facilities, export credits, as well as financial support for promotion and marketing activities abroad. Chile has signed several bilateral trade agreements with several countries in the region, and is actively pursuing integration in regional groupings. It is already an associate member of MERCOSUR, and is keen to join NAFTA and the Free Trade Area of the Americas (FTAA).[1]

Chilean foreign investment regulation is among the more liberal. Almost all restrictions imposed by the Andean Pact (to which Chile belonged earlier) were abolished in 1974. The regime is simple, transparent, non-discretionary and stable; foreign investors are

---

[1] 'Slow track to fast -track', *The Economist*, 13 September 1997, p. 67.

subject to the same rules as local investors. The only extra incentive for foreign investors is an 18 per cent VAT exemption on imported capital goods not produced in Chile. There are no limitations on foreign participation. Modest capital controls existed until September 1998, designed to protect the country against unpredictable short-term movements of hot money, with investors required to hold an interest-free deposit of 30 per cent of incoming capital for one year, after which free repatriation was possible.[2] Profit remittances are not subject to any restrictions. Mining concessions can be renewed indefinitely. Thus, even though the State continues to be the legal owner, exploitation rights are so liberal that foreign companies effectively own the resources they extract (Hellinger, 1997). Foreign investors have the option of choosing from two tax regimes. Under the regular scheme, a 15 per cent corporate tax is paid when profits remain in the country and 35 per cent when profits are remitted abroad. Under the invariable tax regime, the firm pays 42 per cent for a maximum period of 20 years.[3]

Direct government intervention in economic activity generally decreased after 1974, though some "non-traditional"[4] export activities continued to benefit from promotional measures. In forestry, the Government replaced its earlier regime of public investment by indirect support through subsidized credit to private investors. Thirty-year tax exemptions, in force since 1931, were renewed in 1974, with a direct subsidy of 75 per cent (90 per cent in

Table 6.1. Chile and Zimbabwe: inward FDI flows and inward stock, 1970-1998

Year	Chile			Zimbabwe		
	FDI flows (millions of dollars)	FDI inflows (per cent of gross fixed capital formation)	Inward stock/ GDP	FDI flows (millions of dollars)	FDI inflows (per cent of gross fixed capital formation	Inward stock / GDP
1970	-79	..	..	0	..	..
1980	123	..	3.2	2	..	
1988	141	..	..	-18	..	..
1989	1 289	..	..	-10	..	..
1990	590	21.5 [a]	33.1	-12	1.8 [a]	-0.9
1991	523	7.3	..	3	0.2	..
1992	699	7.4	..	15	1.3	..
1993	1 034	9.3	..	38	2.5	..
1994	2 583	21.8	..	41	2.7	..
1995	2 977	19.1	23.1	118	6.4	2.1
1996	4 724	27.5	27.3	81	4.3	7.7
1997	5 417	27.9	33.3	135	7.8	4.8
1998	4 792	..	..	444	..	..

Sources: World Bank (1997); UNCTAD (1995a) and (1999a).
[a] Annual average for 1985-1990.
Note: Fluctuations are, in part, due to breaks in the reporting database.

---

[2] Although the scheme was much praised, Chile found that it could not maintain it when capital started flowing out in a big way in 1997 after the onset of the Asian crisis. The interest-free deposit was cut to 10 per cent of incoming capital in July 1998, and finally completely abolished in September 1998. ("Battering down", *The Economist*, 29 September 1998, p. 54; *De Volkskrant*).

[3] Firms that have opted for the invariable tax scheme can change to the regular scheme, but not *vice versa*.

[4] The term 'non-traditional' is not strictly correct for some of these activities, especially fisheries and forestry, as they already existed in the decades prior to liberalization. However, at that time, exports were of minor importance.

1983-1984) for the cost of replanting. The fresh fruit sector was another beneficiary, primarily through subsidized credit. These incentives helped some of these activities to become significant export earners.

FDI inflows have grown steadily since the mid-1980s.[5] Inward stock was estimated at $16 billion in 1995, $30 billion in 1998 (UNCTAD, 1998a, p. 490). In the period 1985-1990, FDI inflows accounted for 22 per cent of total gross capital formation and the total FDI stock reached 33 per cent of GDP in 1990 and again in 1997. About 60 per cent of the total flowed into the mining sector. Other resource-based industries – forestry and wood products, fishing and food processing – together received about 9 per cent.[6] Fresh fruit is perhaps the best known success case among these. Investment in this sector increased substantially from the mid-1970s, with the planted area growing by 30 per cent and fruit production increasing by 51 per cent between 1973-1974 and 1980-1981. After a temporary lull as a result of a recession in the early 1980s, there was another investment boom during the mid-to-late 1980s. Chile became the southern hemisphere's main temperate fruit exporter and the world's leading exporter of table grapes (Jaffee and Gordon, 1993, p. 84).

6.2.2 Zimbabwe

Southern Rhodesia began to industrialize in the early part of this century with the exploitation of natural resources for export (Biggs, Shah and Srivastava, 1995). It became an exporter of ferrochrome, lithium and asbestos; it also produces chromate, gold, nickel and copper. Zimbabwe's agricultural resources are sizeable. The main crops – maize, cotton, sunflower and tobacco – form the base for its food processing industry, one of the country's leading manufacturing subsectors (Durevall et al., 1998, p. 49). Many are also significant direct exports.

Foreign firms have been traditionally very important in all these sectors. The mining industry attracted such companies as Anglo American Corporation (South Africa), Lonhro (United Kingdom), Rio Tinto Zinc (RTZ) (Australia and United Kingdom), Union Carbide (United States) and Turner Newall (United Kingdom). Together, these five conglomerates account for over half of Zimbabwe's mining production (Chachage, Ericsson and Gibbon, 1993). Foreign involvement in the food processing industry is also significant. Local firms also played a significant role in early industrialization, by servicing, repairing and later producing equipment for the mines and the railways (Watanabe, 1975). By the early 1940s the country had a relatively sophisticated manufacturing sector, accounting for 10 per cent of GDP and 8 per cent of exports, capable of producing a wide range of industrial goods (Latsch and Robinson, 1999).

International sanctions after the Unilateral Declaration of Independence (UDI) in 1965 gave a powerful impetus to the development and deepening of the industrial sector.

---

[5]   The Chilean Foreign Investment Committee publishes figures which include the loan portion of mining projects and other aspects (ADRs) and give higher figures for FDI inflows than those in table 6.1, namely, in millions: 1991: $981; 1992: $1,000; 1993: $1,728; 1994: $2,518; 1995: $3,041.

[6]   Of the remaining 30 per cent, about 25 per cent found its way into the services sector, which includes mainly financial services, public utilities, construction, retail, tourism, transportation and storage, communications and insurance. A mere 5 per cent flowed into manufacturing.

Impressive growth and diversification took place between 1967 and 1974, especially in the engineering industry where import restrictions induced firms to reproduce spare parts and recondition equipment (Watanabe, 1975). The contribution of manufacturing to GDP rose from 17 per cent in 1965 to 24 per cent in 1980. At the same time the share of foreign trade in GDP declined substantially, reaching 15 per cent in 1974. Manufacturing became heavily oriented towards the domestic market, creating extensive forward and backward linkages with other sectors.

FDI played an important role in the early years of import substitution. There were large inflows during the years following the creation of the Federation with Northern Rhodesia and Nyasaland (now Zambia and Malawi) in 1953. An estimated 68 per cent of gross domestic capital originated in foreign companies by 1963. While fresh inflows declined considerably after UDI, the large stock of foreign funds accumulated in earlier years continued to be a major resource for industrial expansion.[7] Since profits and dividends could not be repatriated, companies frequently decided to re-invest them to avoid having their assets frozen in so-called "locked funds". This led to considerable diversification as well as high degrees of vertical integration within firms.

Economic performance was disappointing in the decade following independence in 1980. Average annual GDP growth was 1.5 per cent and manufacturing growth 2.1 per cent in the period 1980-1990. Inward FDI was negative during this period. The only significant new foreign investment came when Heinz bought a 51 per cent share in a local company. The cumbersome negotiations associated with this deal, as well as the deteriorating security situation in Matabeleland, deterred further investors. The Government was unable to reassure the international investment community. It refused to sign the United States Overseas Private Investment Corporation (OPIC) agreement, which contains a guarantee not to nationalize without compensation (Jenkins, 1996).

Manufactured exports declined in the early 1980s, but revived after 1986 mainly due to the introduction of export incentive schemes and the lifting of sanctions by neighbouring countries. In the 1990s, export growth accelerated to double-digit rates. A fair share of these exports were to the region, as Zimbabwean firms exploited the considerable technological capabilities they had built up in simple engineering and consumer goods. However, the country's competitiveness in international markets was still very limited, and the main products exported to developed countries consisted of resource-based products (Lall, Robinson and Wignaraja, 1998). A large number of bureaucratic obstacles and excessive controls, erratic government policies, an ageing capital stock and inadequate skills held back the development of more broadly based export competitiveness (Lall, Robinson and Wignaraja, 1998; Latsch and Robinson, 1999).

An enhanced structural adjustment programme (ESAP) was implemented from 1991 to increase the openness of the country and reduce State controls. The impact of ESAP has been mixed. The macroeconomic situation is uncertain. The currency went through several devaluations, and full convertibility was adopted in early 1995. By the end of 1998 the

---

[7] FDI inflows to Zimbabwe picked up in the mid-1990s; in 1998, inflows of $440 million made Zimbabwe the third-largest host to FDI in sub-Saharan Africa (after South Africa and Nigeria).

currency had not stabilized *vis-à-vis* the United States dollar. Trade liberalization has been progressing haltingly. While import licences and foreign exchange allocations have been abolished and restrictions on profit repatriation lifted, tariffs remain high and variable. Effective rates of protection are elevated, and the tariff structure far from transparent.[8] Until 1997, when a new tariff structure was introduced, Zimbabwe had one of the higher effective tariff rates of developing countries. Tariffs were levied on basic inputs where many other countries apply zero duties which pushed up the cost of imported inputs and made it difficult for exporters to compete. Drawback schemes for exporters were complex and apparently did not work efficiently. Repayment of duties either took place with considerable delay, or did not occur at all, forcing enterprises to include an extra mark-up on their products to cover the risk of non-recovery (World Bank, 1996). In the new tariff structure, raw materials attract zero or low tariffs; intermediates and spares moderate ones; and consumer goods high tariffs to protect local producers. Capital goods, which previously had tariffs up to 25 per cent, are also zero-rated.

Substantial improvements have been made in FDI regulation since the onset of ESAP. In 1989 an investment code was issued which redefined companies as foreign if non-Zimbabweans owned 25 per cent (previously 15 per cent) or more of their shares. The Zimbabwe Investment Centre was established, with the authority for independent approval of up to Zimbabwean $10 million (about US$100,000) investment, although the Centre's promotion capabilities are still weak (see Lall, Robinson and Wignaraja, 1998). In addition, Zimbabwe recognized the international investment protocols of the Multilateral Investment Guarantee Agency (MIGA) and OPIC.

In January 1994, additional measures to encourage FDI were introduced. Foreign investors became exempt from sales tax, surtax and customs duty on imported machinery and equipment. Exporters are now entitled to keep 100 per cent of their revenue in foreign currency accounts, which could also be used for investment flows and capital transfers. Dividend remittances of up to 50 per cent became possible for pre-1979 investors; "blocked funds" were abolished. Dividend remittances of 100 per cent were permitted on investments placed after April 1993. Foreign investors can hold 100 per cent equity in most sectors; the exceptions are construction and specialized services, where foreign ownership is limited to 70 per cent, and "reserved sectors" (food and fish crops, forestry, transportation, retail and wholesale trade and grain mill products), where it is limited to 25 per cent.

In 1997, the Government designated two industrial areas as export processing zones, with tax incentives for firms exporting at least 80 per cent of their output. The main incentives include a five-year tax holiday and subsequently a corporate tax of 15 per cent. There are exemptions from customs duties, capital gains taxes and withholding taxes. However, the EPZs did not meet with immediate success: only circa 20 projects have been approved at end 1999, mostly by domestic firms seeking a more conducive tax and operating environment.

---

[8] The average nominal rate of protection for manufacturing as a whole was estimated to be around 40 per cent and the average effective rate of protection around 70 per cent in 1992-1995, with large variations in the latter (Latsch and Robinson, 1999). This is about the same as in South Asian countries.

Zimbabwe's export potential has improved as a result of these measures. The industrial – particularly engineering – capabilities developed during UDI are unique in the region (South Africa apart). It has a relatively well-educated and disciplined labour force, and low wage rates.[9] Its physical infrastructure is fairly good. All these advantages should lead to fuller exploitation of its natural and human resources. However, the realization of this potential faces formidable difficulties. The country's landlocked position poses problems. Technologies in use are generally obsolete, and the stock of capital and skills needs thorough upgrading. Management and organizational techniques are well behind best-practice levels, though there are exceptions (Kaplinsky, 1994). Many activities are too small scale to compete on world markets. Firms invest too little in worker training. There is practically no R&D in industry. The industrial structure is heavily dominated by low-technology activities.

FDI could play a critical role in upgrading Zimbabwean competitiveness. However, the frequent policy changes of the 1980s have left a perception of uncertainty. In addition, Zimbabwe suffers from regional spillovers – sub-Saharan Africa has a reputation of poor economic performance, crises and unfavourable FDI regimes and has been perceived as a risky destination for investment flows.[10] High interest rates and inflation are disincentives for foreign investors (Jenkins, 1996, p. 10). The FDI agency is lagging in terms of its promotion capabilities and efforts. Many prospective investors in dynamic parts of the developing world economy, such as Asia, are insufficiently aware of local potential (Lall, Robinson and Wignaraja, 1998; UNCTAD, 1999a, pp. 45-52; UNCTAD, 1999b).

FDI inflows have been accelerating since the mid-1990s. Inward FDI stock has been accumulating steadily, albeit from a low level, reaching an estimated $817 million in 1998 (UNCTAD, 1999a). Nevertheless, this is but 3 per cent of the scale of inflows observed in Chile. Inflows as a percentage of total gross fixed capital formation fluctuated between a mere 0.2 and 7.8 per cent over the 1990-1998 period (table 6.1). Most FDI went into services, tourism, finance and construction; mining received 26 per cent, and manufacturing 20 per cent. Some resource-based TNCs have been prospecting the country recently. Politics permitting, FDI may step up and, with it, restructuring and competitiveness in resource-based activities.

6.3 FDI, restructuring and competitiveness

6.3.1 Chile

This section documents the role of FDI in restructuring and upgrading competitiveness in the resource-based sector, based on interviews conducted with 27 leading companies. The fallout from the Asian crisis has exposed important structural weaknesses in the Chilean model, which had been concealed earlier when export market conditions favoured export growth for resource based products. In essence, the Chilean model led to insufficient industrial diversification and technological upgrading. Large segments of

[9] Wages in clothing were $0.30 per hour in the early 1990s, the same as in the northern provinces of China (Swinden, 1994, p. 9).
[10] For example, there have been several major strikes due to the fragile economic situation and political tensions among urban and rural populations. See, "Zimbabwe, poorer and angrier", *The Economist*, 15 August 1998, pp. 32-33 and "Zimbabwe, staying home", *The Economist*, 7 March 1998, pp. 77-78.

manufacturing, in particular those with scale economies and advanced technologies, failed to grow and become competitive. These activities tend to have long and costly learning processes if undertaken exclusively by local enterprises, and the lack of government support for these processes stifled their development (Pietrobelli, 1998). Without government support, they require the input of TNCs in the assembly of high-technology products (as in the South-East Asian model). Chile, however, does not display the low wages of many Asian countries, nor has it developed a strategic FDI targeting approach, enabling the country to attract the desired type of FDI.

Chile has one of the best education enrolment records in the developing world, particularly in technical subjects. Despite this strong base of skills, however, it has failed to deepen its industrial sector and its technological base. TNCs have stayed away from technology- and scale-intensive activities. The heavy reliance on slow-growing resource-based activities, with limited spillover benefits to other industries, constitutes a structural weakness of the Chilean model.

6.3.1.1 Setting and performance

Chile's industrial restructuring led to the replacement of existing manufacturing industries with new non-manufacturing activities.[11] After a short depression in 1980-1984 associated with instability of some policies and the external debt crisis, Chile's resource-based sectors expanded continuously and became increasingly integrated with global markets. At the same time, the importance of manufacturing fell steadily, from 22 per cent of GDP in 1975 to 17 per cent in 1995. Even the country's three principal manufacturing activities, which are resource-based, have not been a major source of export growth in the post-liberalization period.[12]

The shift towards resource-based industries during the 1980s and 1990s resulted in a major change in the country's export composition (table 6.2). The share of manufactures in total exports fell from 49 per cent in 1980 to 30 per cent in 1995, while that of non-manufactured exports rose from 49 per cent in 1980 to 68 per cent in 1995. Copper remains the largest export item, but other less traditional commodities, such as fruits, fruit-based products (such as wines), nuts and various forestry products, have been growing in importance. Salmon has become a major export product.

(a) Competitive performance

As a result of the rapid growth of resource-based exports, Chile increased its international market share (table 6.2).

---

[11]   The economic effects of such a pattern are not necessarily disadvantageous, provided that exports are sufficiently diversified, especially if they include a high number of high-value foods (see Jaffee and Gordon, 1993; UNCTAD, 1997b).

[12]   The three main areas of activity are food products (ISIC 311), non-ferrous metals (ISIC 372) and other chemical products (ISIC 352), which together account for about 40 per cent of manufacturing value added.

The growth of these exports was associated with good growth performance until 1997, when the copper price started to fall. Table 6.3 shows that GDP growth accelerated from 3 per cent per annum in the period 1975-1979 to almost 7 per cent in the period 1985-1995. Growth in gross fixed capital formation picked up, and trade grew rapidly, especially after 1985. Inflation came down from 27 per cent in 1990 to 8 per cent in 1995. New

Table 6.2. Chile's international competitiveness in the OECD market: selected indicators,1980-1995

Indicator		1980	1985	1990	1995
I. Import market share in OECD market		**0.23**	**0.21**	**0.27**	**0.28**
Natural resources 1/ + 2/ + 3/		0.26	0.34	0.60	0.87
Agriculture 1/		0.32	0.54	0.94	1.11
Energy 2/		0.00	0.00	0.00	0.01
Textile fibres, minerals, etc. 3/		1.85	1.55	1.49	2.95
Manufactures 4/+5/		0.21	0.14	0.15	0.11
Based on natural resources 4/		1.97	1.77	1.85	1.39
Not based on natural resources 5/		0.01	0.01	0.02	0.02
Others 6/		0.21	0.31	0.30	0.21
II. Export structure for OECD market, (per cent)					
Natural resources 1/ + 2/ + 3/		49.0	53.8	55.8	67.8
Agriculture 1/		19.9	32.9	42.3	47.4
Energy 2/		0.5	0.2	0.2	0.2
Textile fibres, minerals, etc. 3/		28.7	20.7	13.4	20.2
Manufactures 4/+5/		49.3	42.7	41.5	30.2
Based on natural resources 4/		46.9	39.2	36.0	24.3
Not based on natural resources 5/		2.4	3.5	5.5	5.9
Others 6/		1.7	3.5	2.7	2.0
III. 10 principal exports of Chile to OECD market (percentage of total exports) 7/		**75.4**	**75.4**	**78.2**	**78.0**
682 Copper	-	44.1	35.9	34.7	21.7
287 Ores and concentrates of base metals n.e.s.	+	14.9	11.9	8.3	15.7
057 Fruit and nuts (not oil nuts) fresh or dried	+	6.4	14.0	15.4	12.3
034 Fish, fresh (live or dead), chilled, dried or frozen	+	1.4	1.9	5.7	8.5
251 Pulp and waste paper	+	1.8	2.6	2.7	6.2
081 Feeding stuff for animals (excl. unmilled cereals)	+	4.2	6.5	4.6	3.8
246 Pulpwood (including chips and wood waste)	+	0.0	0.2	2.7	3.7
248 Wood, simply worked and railway sleepers	+	0.9	0.9	2.3	2.9
058 Fruit, preserved and fruit preparations	+	0.2	0.5	1.1	1.6
289 Ores and concentrates of precious metals, waste, scrap	+	1.4	1.0	0.6	1.6

Source: ECLAC CANPLUS database.

Note: 1/ Sections 0, 1 and 4; divisions 21, 22, 23, 24, 25 and 29 of the Standard International Trade Classification SITC Rev.2. 2/ Section 3. 3/ Divisions 26, 27 and 28. 4/ Divisions 61, 63 and 68; groups 661, 662, 663, 667 and 671. 5/ Sections 5, 6 (minus the divisions and groups mentioned in 4/), 7 and 8. 6/ Section 9. 7/ Groups in which the market share increased (+) or decreased (-) during 1980-1995.

employment creation at 3.3 per cent per year between 1987 and 1994 outpaced labour-force growth of 2.8 per cent. As a result, unemployment fell from 13 per cent in 1985 to 5 per cent in 1995. Real wages grew by 3.9 per cent between 1990 and 1995, while real productivity registered a growth rate of 4.1 per cent during the same period. External debt has been falling steadily as a percentage of GDP (32 per cent in 1996) and reserves have been growing.

Table 6.3. Principal macroeconomic indicators for Chile, 1975-1995

Period	Gross fixed capital formation	Exports	Imports	Gross fixed capital formation	Exports	Imports	GDP
	Percentage of GDP			Annual real rate of growth			
1975-1979	16.0	20.9	28.2	3.1	12.9	8.2	2.6
1980-1984	18.0	24.9	34.3	2.8	2.4	-1.1	0.7
1985-1989	19.8	29.7	29.1	15.4	11.4	10.9	6.6
1990-1995	24.7	35.7	39.5	9.5	9.6	12.4	6.7

Source: Central Bank of Chile.
Note: Export and import data refer to goods and services only.

(b)   The contribution of foreign investors

Foreign investment has been one of the driving forces behind these improvements. By 1995, 401 out of a total of 5,920 exporting companies were foreign affiliates. These affiliates accounted for 31 per cent of Chile's total exports in 1995, up from 24 per cent in 1991. Their exports grew by 19 per cent on average in the period 1991-1995, as compared with 11 per cent for total exports. The importance of foreign affiliates in exports was much greater in specific industries: their principal export products were copper and its concentrates, copper cathodes, semi-bleached chemical wood pulp from conifers, fishmeal, methanol, refined copper, gold, grapes, refined copper wire and wood boards. Exports of these products came to $2.9 billion in 1995, over 70 per cent of all exports by affiliates.

Interviews were carried out with a sample of 26 TNC affiliates and one local company (11 in mining, 9 in forestry, 6 in agribusiness and one in fishing).[13] These firms account for nearly 20 per cent of total Chilean exports (table 6.4), and represent a total cumulative investment of $3.9 billion, or over 25 per cent of investment by foreign companies in exports.

Table 6.4. Selected indicators of the group of Chilean firms surveyed, 1995
(Per cent)

Sales / GDP	6.0
Exports / GDP	4.7
Exports / Chile's total product exports	20.0
FDI / Chile's total inward FDI during 1974-1995 (in industry)	27.0
FDI / Chile's total inward FDI during 1974-1995 (in goods and services)	19.0
Employment / Chilean labour force	0.3

Source: UNCTAD.

---

[13] A methodological note on the selection of the sample can be found in annex 6.1.

Nearly all the firms in the sample were highly export-oriented. The average export share in total sales in the sample was 83 per cent; 14 firms in the sample did not operate on the Chilean market at all. They used state-of-the-art technologies, and their exports were distributed as follows: 37 per cent to the Asia and Pacific region, 28 per cent to Europe and 25 per cent to North America, all of which are open and highly competitive markets.[14] They increased their share in Chilean exports from 14 per cent in 1992 to 20 per cent in 1995. Twenty-one firms claimed that their export market share had improved; only one firm reported that its share had declined.

Chile's welcoming and non-discriminatory policies, combined with stable and sustained economic growth, helped these companies to achieve their favourable export performance. The most important element of the policy framework was the foreign investment regulation guaranteeing stability and legal security. According to 30 per cent of the sample firms, the FDI regulatory framework was conducive to their export competitiveness. The respondents especially appreciated non-discriminatory treatment. Other major advantages mentioned (in decreasing order of importance) were: favourable property rights legislation; the absence of restrictions on foreign participation; the transparency of the procedures; and tax exemptions. Only 13 of the 27 companies stressed a negative aspect relating to foreign investment regulation. Here, the restriction on external credit was the main issue. It especially affected mining companies that relied heavily on international financing. Some bureaucratic obstacles relating to authorization, information and transfer of funds were also mentioned. On the whole, however, Chile's FDI regime was considered attractive, and had induced these TNCs to invest there rather than in other developing countries with similar resource endowments.

Thirty-four per cent of firms cited liberalized trade and export promotion as the most important policy determinants of their international competitiveness. They mentioned that Chile's openness, low levels of protection and fiscal incentives (such as drawback schemes and tax exemptions on imported capital goods) had been important for their export expansion. Improving access to export markets, a favourable exchange rate, and unrestricted access to imported inputs and new technology were also underlined. Other policy-related factors considered positive, although of less importance, were flexible labour market policies that minimized conflicts, the availability of educated technical and managerial personpower, the quality of transportation and telecommunications facilities, and immigration policies.

The parents of the affiliates are mainly based in the United States, Canada, Australia, New Zealand and the United Kingdom. They are generally firms with considerable international experience and spread. Twenty-two affiliates rated their role in their parents' international networks as "important" or "very important". Their position in these networks is to a considerable extent reflected in the strategic behaviour displayed by the affiliates. Even though affiliates have considerable autonomy, especially in operational matters, parents exercise strong control in strategic matters relating to international expansion, such as export

---

[14] The ability to sell in demanding international markets is a good indicator of competitiveness of certain non-traditional exports where quality and price differentiation is important. On the other hand, it is not important for copper which is a standardized commodity; competitiveness in this sector largely depends on the cost, and hence margin against world market prices, of production.

sales, market development and foreign investment. Some parent firms also play a significant role in activities at the operational level. Seven firms reported that their parents were involved in sales activities, including determination of export markets, product marketing and export volumes. Headquarter involvement in finance was mentioned by six firms. Other areas of parent involvement were purchase of technology (four firms), coordination and management (three firms), production (three firms) and human resources (one firm).[15] In the sample firms' view, the most important sources of competitiveness are high productivity, process technologies, product quality and access to foreign markets (table 6.5). All these factors relate to internal resources and effort. Raw material supply is the only important determinant that relies primarily on the host-country environment rather than on firms' strategy and efforts.[16]

Although there are exceptions like processed fruits, efforts by affiliates to develop new areas of competitiveness have been limited. As noted, Chile's non-interventionist industrial policy led to the development of sectors with relatively easy learning processes. It largely failed to catalyze a broadening and deepening of the industrial base, or to induce complex technology-based activities. TNCs were interested in exploiting existing resource advantages in Chile and to upgrading them in relatively low-cost and low-risk ways. The lack of strategic interventions by the Government to promote local enterprises or to guide TNCs into advanced activities has led to a structure that is dominated by low-technology activities. This accounts for the relatively stagnant technological composition of Chile's competitiveness.

Table 6.5. Sources of competitiveness: assessment by sample firms

Item	1985-1989 (Percentage of sample)	1990-1995 (Percentage of sample)
Overall productivity	11.2	17.5
Process technology	13.3	16.2
Product quality	16.3	15.6
Access to foreign markets	19.4	14.9
Raw material supply	14.3	10.4
Organizational practices	2.0	7.8
Competitive pricing	9.2	3.9
Other	14.3	13.7
Total	100.0	100.0

Source: UNCTAD, based on company interviews.

(c) *Effects of the Asian crisis*

The limitations of Chile's high dependence on exports based on static comparative advantage became obvious during the Asian crisis. The main trigger was falling Asian

---

[15] While a high degree of involvement by TNC headquarters may have significant benefits for the subsidiaries in terms of cost levels, it may also limit the extent of skill transfer. However, no evidence of such drawbacks emerged from the survey.

[16] Note also that low wages, which are usually a very important source of competitiveness in developing countries, are quite insignificant in this sample. This factor received only 3.1 per cent and 0.6 per cent of responses for the periods 1985-1989 and 1990-1995, respectively.

demand for copper,[17] which led to a major slide in the world copper price from $1.19 per pound in June 1997 to $0.75 in March 1998. Since copper accounted for 42 per cent of Chile's total exports in 1997 and one third of this went to East Asia, the effects on the current account and the exchange rate were dramatic.[18] The current account deficit nearly reached 7 per cent of GDP in October 1998. Interest rates were raised to 14 per cent, and an austerity budget was proposed for 1999. For an economy accustomed to 7 per cent annual GDP growth during the previous decade, the prospects of close-to-zero growth are chilling indeed.[19]

Chile's fastest-growing exports are concentrated in low-technology activities. Exports from low-skill and low-R&D-intensity industries accounted for a larger share of manufactured exports in the 1990s than three decades before (Pietrobelli, 1998, pp. 63-64). Its world share of high-skill products has fallen over time. Thus, even though the companies interviewed for this study employed state-of-the-art technologies within their respective industries (see section 6.3.1.3), these technologies themselves are comparatively undemanding. International markets for most resource-based and low-skill products are growing relatively slowly compared to those for products with a high-technology content. More than four-fifths of Chile's exports consist of products whose importance in world trade is declining. Clearly, this export structure is not conducive to long-term competitiveness.

6.3.1.2 Human capital formation

In contrast to the East Asian economies, Chile's manufacturing sector developed slowly during the 1980s and 1990s, mainly in technologically simple activities. The existing level of human resources was relatively high, and allowed a degree of diversification and technological upgrading. However, because of the lack of support, learning processes remained restricted to resource-based industries (mainly biotechnology, which was supported through a number of government programmes). There was limited upgrading in more complex industrial activities which require non-negligible technological learning (Pietrobelli, 1998, p. 64). In sum, little effort was made to use the rich base of educated labour to produce the technological capabilities that require experience and learning to be used efficiently.

Sample firms invested significantly in employee training, spending on average 1.3 per cent of sales in 1995 and providing formal technical training to 54 per cent of workers. Training was more prevalent among specialized production workers (71 per cent), production supervisors (64 per cent) and production technicians (62 per cent). Incentives granted by the Government through the national training and employment service helped. The growing scarcity of certain types of skilled workers also led firms themselves to invest in training.

The sample firms are generally highly capital-intensive and do not create much employment. Their total employment was 13,400 in 1995 (496 persons per firm on average), only 0.3 per cent of the Chilean labour force. Of this total, about a quarter have higher technical and managerial qualifications.

---

[17] The effects of the Asian crisis on commodity prices are detailed in United Nations (1998).
[18] "All good things must slow down", *The Economist*, 7 March 1998, pp. 71-72.
[19] "Battering down", *The Economist*, 4 July 1998, p. 54; "The cold winds blow", *The Economist*, 3 October 1998, pp. 86-87.

6.3.1.3 *Technological and organizational development*

Chile's policy of unrestricted foreign access to the extraction and export of natural resources has done little to foster a technology-intensive industrial base. Domestic technological activity has received low priority, and industrial and technology policy has been neglected since the early 1980s. Chile's R&D effort (just below 1 per cent of GDP in 1996), with 364 R&D scientists and engineers per one million people, is comparable to that of countries such as Argentina or Tunisia. The bulk of Chilean R&D is conducted in the public sector; private enterprises account for only 14 per cent of national R&D spending. Given its strong base of technical graduates and its income level, Chile could be expected to be making considerably greater technological efforts.

Low R&D in Chile has a lot to do with its specialization in resource-based activities and its neglect of support for technological upgrading in manufacturing. Sample affiliates conducted practically no internal R&D. Half the firms undertook some technological adaptation to take into account local labour factors, raw material and climatic conditions, but these activities were usually on an ad hoc basis, in response to specific problems. They claimed to spend 1.2 per cent of total revenue on R&D, but this seems rather high in view of the nature of their activities and the number of R&D staff (four per firm); the firms may have counted non-R&D technical work in this figure.

The main technological contribution of sample affiliates to the economy lies in their provision of state-of-the-art capital goods and operating technologies, which have led to high productivity and enhanced competitiveness. In 40 per cent of cases, the technologies originated in the parent companies or suppliers related to the parent companies. There are several instances of technology transfer from parent companies to their affiliates, with benefits for affiliate productivity (table 6.6). Some of this new knowledge must spill over to the Chilean economy, through absorption of new knowledge by staff and increased pressure on competitors to keep up with best practice. However, it is not possible to assess this spillover with the evidence at hand.

Improved organization of work was also a significant source of increased productivity, better labour relations and improved product quality. As with technological improvements, the new practices came mostly from abroad. Improved supply chain management, mainly via increased subcontracting, led to increased flexibility, specialization and cost reduction. Major internal organizational changes included the introduction of work teams and just-in-time systems. Also important were multi-tasking through job rotation, reorganization of production lines and statistical process control and increased functional specialization. Twelve affiliates had enjoyed productivity increases as a result of these changes.

Table 6.6. Details of technologies transferred from parent companies to Chilean-based affiliates

Transferred technologies	Importance of the technologies to the affiliate companies	Reported benefits of the technologies
- Copper wire production	- Enable affiliate to reach international standards	- Reduction of production costs
- Copper treatment through bacteria lixiviation process of sulphur deposits	- Enable affiliate to improve the quality of the final product	- Increase in international competitiveness
- Determination of the degree of acidity and probable alcohol content of wine; optimal fermentation and maceration processes	- Enable affiliate to reduce costs	- Increase in productivity
- Lixiviation process through the use of ammonia; joint developments with parent company in order to produce highly pure copper cathode	- Enable affiliate to process low grade ore at a minimal cost	
- Adequate selection of equipment; productive process flexibility	- Quality and prestige	- Improved image and credibility in dealing with clients
- Construction of modern industrial plants	- Product flexibility and innovation - Process of continuous improvement of affiliate's know-how	

Source: UNCTAD, based on company interviews.

6.3.1.4 Building of local supplier networks

Backward linkages are an important spin-off from the activities of affiliates. However, the share of local component and parts production is low because production processes are continuous. Of the material inputs procured locally, 63 per cent come from unrelated local suppliers, 20 per cent from other local affiliates, and 7 per cent from local subcontractors. Service linkages are increasing in importance; the number of affiliates that subcontracted services rose from four in 1985 to 11 in 1995. Subcontracting was most common in forestry and mining, where it mostly involved support services such as detonation, equipment repair and food supply. As far as the use of local engineering services is concerned, sample affiliates involved local firms in the contracting and the engineering stages of projects. However, hardly any used local engineering firms for pre-feasibility studies and start-up. About half the sample said that the main constraint to greater utilization of local engineering firms was the integrated nature of the processes. They also noted problems with quality, prices and timely delivery by local firms.

6.3.2 Zimbabwe

TNC involvement in Zimbabwean industry is mostly in long-established industries that have traditionally served local markets. The industrial base is badly in need of modernization. Firms need modern technology, know-how and management practices, as well as more and better skills, to gear themselves for international competition. However, many firms have adopted a wait-and-see attitude because of considerable uncertainty about the macroeconomic situation and trade negotiations with South Africa and the Preferential Trade Area for Eastern and Southern African States (PTA). Regional markets are important destinations for Zimbabwe's exports – currently about 15 per cent goes to South Africa and another 15 per cent to PTA countries.[20]

6.3.2.1 Setting and performance

(a) Industrial restructuring

Table 6.7 presents selected data on Zimbabwe's exports to the OECD countries. It must be kept in mind, however, that well over half of Zimbabwe's total exports are not destined for OECD markets. The pattern of Zimbabwe's exports is quite different from Chile's. The latter shared a massive shift towards resource exports after import substitution was dismantled, while the former has remained more or less unchanged since 1985. The share of manufactures has remained at around 40 per cent; within manufacturing, resource-based products predominate, though some non-traditional products like garments have been gaining ground. However, Zimbabwe's competitiveness in these products is deteriorating in the face of severe Asian competition, and the privileges it has enjoyed because of the Lomé Convention may not last much longer (Lall, Robinson and Wignaraja, 1998).

This picture of limited economic restructuring is reflected in the results of interviews with 20 firms (10 foreign and 10 local).[21] Of the 10 foreign firms, eight are 100 per cent affiliates; the others have 45 and 51 per cent foreign ownership. Of the 10 local companies, five are wholly locally-owned and the others are joint ventures. In contrast to the Chilean sample, the joint ventures in Zimbabwe are quite old – as old as the local firms. The youngest foreign firm in the sample was established in 1980.[22] All the firms, regardless of ownership, developed in a sheltered environment and face the same competitiveness problems during the liberalization process.

The sample includes seven firms in the agro-business and seven in garments – two industries that should do relatively well in an open economic regime – and six in metalworking. Metal-working is a large industry in Zimbabwe, accounting for over 20 per cent of manufactured output, having grown particularly rapidly during UDI so as to provide equipment and spares to other industries. Although its share in manufacturing output has been declining after the opening-up, it remains the second largest sub-sector (after food processing) with many important linkages to other sectors. It produces a wide range of products, ranging from simple agricultural implements to relatively complex machinery. The six sample companies (three TNC affiliates and three locally-owned companies) produce trailers, trucks and truck bodies, mining equipment, heavy earth-moving equipment, lifting equipment, cables, diesel engines, agricultural implements, capstan lathes and discs.

---

[20]   Out of its total exports in 1996, 38.4 per cent went to other African countries, and 14.6 per cent went to other developing countries in Asia, the Middle East and Latin America (UNCTAD, 1998b, p. 205). In recent years, exports of engineering products to other countries in the region have been strong.

[21]   See annex 6.1 for more details about the sampling methodology.

[22]   More detailed information about this can be found in the annex 6.1.

Table 6.7. Zimbabwe's international competitiveness in the OECD market, 1980-1995

Item	1980	1985	1990	1995
I. Import market share in OECD markets	**0.03**	**0.05**	**0.04**	**0.03**
Natural resources 1/ + 2/ + 3/	0.04	0.08	0.09	0.08
Agriculture 1/	0.08	0.13	0.12	0.12
Energy 2/	0.00	0.00	0.01	0.00
Textile fibres, minerals, etc. 3/	0.17	0.31	0.24	0.13
Manufactures 4/ + 5/	0.03	0.03	0.03	0.02
Based on natural resources 4/	0.28	0.32	0.28	0.18
Not based on natural resources 5/	0.00	0.00	0.01	0.01
Others 6/	0.01	0.08	0.12	0.02
II. Export structure for OECD market (per cent)				
Natural resources 1/ + 2/ + 3/	52.4	56.8	49.9	56.8
Agriculture 1/	34.3	37.1	34.7	47.8
Energy 2/	0.0	0.0	1.5	1.1
Textile fibres, minerals, etc. 3/	18.1	19.7	13.7	7.9
Manufactures 4/ + 5/	47.1	38.9	43.1	41.3
Based on natural resources 4/	45.0	34.1	34.2	29.2
Not based on natural resources 5/	2.2	4.8	8.9	12.1
Others 6/	0.5	4.3	7.0	1.8
III. Ten principal exports of Zimbabwe to OECD market (per cent of total exports)	**89.2**	**74.3**	**70.6**	**75.1**
121 Tobacco, unmanufactured; tobacco refuse	16.2	21.0	21.4	24.8
671 Pig iron, sponge iron, ferro-alloys	33.3	20.4	17.0	15.3
683 Nickel	9.6	6.8	12.7	9.6
061 Sugar and honey	12.4	4.9	4.4	6.0
292 Crude vegetable materials, n.e.s.	0.1	0.2	1.2	4.4
011 Meat and edible meat offal, fresh, chilled or frozen	0.9	2.3	1.2	4.4
263 Cotton	7.6	11.5	7.0	3.4
278 Other crude minerals	9.1	6.2	3.9	2.5
971 Gold, non monetary	0.0	n.a.	n.a.	2.3
842 Outer garments, men's and boys' of textile fabrics	0.0	0.3	1.2	2.3

Source: ECLAC CANPLUS database.

1/ Sections 0, 1 and 4; divisions 21, 22, 23, 24, 25 and 29 of the Standard International Trade Classification, SITC Rev.2

2/ Section 3

3/ Divisions 26, 27 and 28

4/ Divisions 61, 63 and 68; groups 661, 662, 663, 667 and 671

5/ Sections 5, 6 (minus the divisions and groups mentioned in 4/), 7 and 8

6/ Section 9

(b)   Competitive performance

Zimbabwe's industrial restructuring since 1990 has been limited. Annual real GDP growth has been 1 per cent in the period 1991-1995. The volume of manufacturing declined by 21 per cent in this period, while the share of manufacturing in GDP fell from 23 to 19 per cent. New investment has been very low until recently. Gross fixed capital formation declined between 1990-1996 by 3 per cent per annum (IMF, 1997). Domestic demand was initially depressed due to high inflation and a severe drought in 1992-1993.[23]

The picture for exports is more encouraging (table 6.8). The fastest growth in 1990-1995 has come from resource-based activities, such as the production of processed foods, wood products (mainly furniture), beverages, and ferrochrome or cotton ginning. However, exports of printing, metal, machinery and art products have also grown significantly. The share of manufactures in total exports (26 per cent in 1992) is higher than in other African countries. Both local and foreign firms have developed considerable technological and managerial capabilities in comparison with those of neighbouring countries, and they are exploiting these capabilities in their export activity. Regional markets have been the main engine of recent export expansion; the share of total exports to other African countries rose from 30 per cent in 1988 to 38 per cent in 1996 (UNCTAD, 1998b, p. 205).

Table 6.8. Zimbabwe: selected macroeconomic performance indicators, 1990-1996

Item	1990	1991	1992	1993	1994	1995	1996	Growth rate 1990-1996 (Per cent)
GDP growth rate								(1991-1996)
Per cent	7.0	5.5	-9.0	1.3	6.8	0.1	0.1	2.0
Gross fixed capital formation								- 3.4
Exports (millions of dollars)	1 753	1 783	1 530	1 610	1 947	2 217	2 499	6.1
Imports (millions of dollars)	1 512	1 700	1 781	1 512	1 788	2 128	2 213	6.6

Source: IMF.

In contrast, Zimbabwe has not been able to increase its share in OECD markets. In the recent past, many firms exported only because of the slump at home, with no commitment to developing long-term markets overseas. Competitiveness in technologically complex products is largely limited to regional markets, and is declining over time (as in Chile). The share of such complex products in manufactured exports declined from 62 per cent in 1990 to 45 per cent in 1995 (Lall, Robinson and Wignaraja, 1998). While this share appears large, most exports are at the simple end of the technological scale (simple machinery) aimed at neighbouring countries: there are practically no sophisticated manufactured exports to OECD countries. It is unclear how much of the import-substitution industrial base will be able to upgrade successfully to competitive levels.

The sample companies illustrate the competitive problems of Zimbabwean industry. The percentage of export to sales is very low (zero to 20 per cent) for the six metal-working

---

[23] Inflation reached about 40-50 per cent towards the end of 1992, and fell to 30 per cent in 1993 and 25 per cent in 1994. During 1995 and 1996, it averaged 22 per cent with a slightly downward trend.

firms. Their exports go entirely to the southern African region, where they have transport cost advantages and are suited to local market needs. However, this also reflects their lack of competitiveness in more demanding markets. The three TNC affiliates in the sample are not significantly more export-oriented than the local companies. The record of the agro-processing sample firms is similar. Exports averaged 10-12 per cent between 1989 and 1995 for the seven firms, and the local firms' export profile was no different from that of the six foreign-owned firms in the sample.

The garment industry in Zimbabwe consisted, in 1992, of over 250 companies; it was the most highly export-oriented of the three industries in the survey. Exports grew particularly in the first half of the 1990s, but slackened as Asian competition intensified. The domestic market also faced increasing import penetration; sales are only 80 per cent of 1991 levels. The seven sample firms were all relatively large, with exports around 50 per cent of total output, mainly aimed at the OECD markets. However, TNC involvement in this sector is very limited, and there is just one TNC affiliate in the sample of companies in the garment industry. This affiliate is the most domestic-oriented company in the group, with an export share in total sales of only 5 per cent.

The main determinants of performance in Zimbabwe lie in external (i.e. extend to the firm) market and policy factors. This is not to say that the firms' strategies were unimportant, but their economic environment was exceptionally difficult. This restricted their scope for strategic action and frustrated their efforts to reorient and restructure their activities. As far as the metal-working industry is concerned, firms retain an advantage in the local market because of transport costs and adaptation to local needs. As a result, import penetration has been low so far, and firms seem able to survive by supplying specialized custom-made products and services, based on long-standing relations with customers (Latsch and Robinson, 1999). Nevertheless, sample firms feel that competition in export markets has intensified. They have traditionally performed well on price because of relatively low labour costs. Moreover, during the 1980s they benefited from a 9 per cent tariff rebate on intermediate inputs for exports. The withdrawal of this incentive hit them hard, especially since tariffs continued to be levied on raw material inputs until 1997. South Africa, which has generous export incentive schemes, is a fierce competitor, which protects its own markets. Firms increasingly find that they cannot focus on price competition only. They need to compete on a whole range of variables including quality, delivery and customer service. There is an urgent need to incorporate new technologies and organizational practices, including cost-effective production methods and improved quality standards.

The output of the agro-processing firms consists of mass-produced low-value items, which gives them a transport cost advantage over other exporters in the same bracket from outside the region. Again, South Africa is Zimbabwe's main competitor. Traditionally, Zimbabwean firms competed on the basis of abundant and cheap agricultural raw materials, relatively low wages and export incentives. However, periodical raw material price increases following the droughts of 1992 and 1995, the withdrawal of the export rebate and high tariffs on imported raw materials have created problems. On the other hand, some companies mentioned that they benefited from easier access to imported inputs after liberalization. [24]

The garment firms in the sample indicated that their exports were driven less by external incentives than by the limited size of the domestic market and by the need to earn the foreign currency required for the import of raw materials. One effect of ESAP measures has been considerable import competition in the domestic market from Asian and South African sources (which has been exacerbated by illegal imports of second-hand clothing). The outlook for export expansion is not very favourable. Zimbabwe's garment exports are only a fraction of those of other recent world market entrants such as Mauritius and Sri Lanka, and there are no signs that this will improve. Initially, the industry was able to compete because of cheap local cotton, low wages, the export rebate and good freight services. However, rising local cotton prices and the withdrawal of the rebate have affected price competitiveness, while the industry has not built up the capability to produce higher-quality items. The quality of the fabrics produced by local textile mills is low and is not suitable for export production (despite the high quality of local cotton), while the liberalization of imported inputs has proceeded slowly. In order to compete on quality, Zimbabwe's garment producers must import their textiles from abroad. However, in order to remain eligible for duty-free access to markets in the European Union under the Lomé Convention, Zimbabwe must import from other African, Caribbean and Pacific countries, which tend to be more expensive than Asian suppliers. Moreover, regional exports were badly hit in 1993 when South Africa raised import duties on clothing from 30 per cent to between 60 and 80 per cent (although this was later reduced).

6.3.2.2 *Development of human capital, technology and local supplier linkages*

Both TNC affiliates and local companies are restructuring in the face of the recent changes, though some are more active than others, and there is no clear relationship in the firms surveyed between ownership and the vigour with which restructuring is pursued. Firm size, product range, market structure, tradition, financial resilience and so on appear to be more important in explaining recent strategic behaviour.

Most metal producers (both local and foreign) are aiming to expand regional exports by setting up distribution agents and sister companies in neighbouring countries. They are modernizing their machinery, equipment and production methods to improve product quality and increase efficiency. Exports are necessary to justify heavy investments in new technologies, since the Zimbabwean market is not large enough to generate economies of scale. The most aggressive TNC affiliate in the group (BICC-CAFCA, a producer of power and construction cables, bare copper products and flexible cords and cables) is going further than the others in that it aims to become a world-class regional supplier. This affiliate has been given responsibility for launching export development within sub-Saharan Africa by its parent company which is based in the United Kingdom. It has entered into a technology

---

[24] However, the Zimbabwean food processing industry is more export-oriented. The firms are relatively large and there is a substantial TNC presence; in 1989, 47 per cent of investment in the food processing industry was foreign (Selassie, 1995, p. 101). The industry accounts for over 20 per cent of manufacturing output, a substantial share of which is exported, mainly to regional markets.

agreement with its parent: in return for a fee of 2 per cent of sales it can draw upon technical staff and the corporate R&D system. It is improving productivity levels, delivery and inventory management through a planned strategy. It emphasizes the development and recruitment of highly-educated individuals, and has introduced teamwork to improve customer service. Six per cent of its personnel costs are spent on training, which is only 2 per cent lower than the average proportion spent by the world's leading companies in this sector. Staff are sent to the United Kingdom for middle- and higher-management courses, and the parent company also often sends trainers to its Zimbabwean affiliate to conduct training courses on the spot. In this way the parent firm transfers new organizational and management practices to the affiliate.

The affiliate was the first Zimbabwean company to obtain ISO 9002 certification, which helped push its products in new export markets and put pressure on the firm's local suppliers to adopt the same quality standards. This has been beneficial in diffusing a new awareness about "doing things better". At the same time a local firm in the sample (Almin Metal Industries) obtained ISO 9001 certification (which is more comprehensive than ISO 9002) and played a similar role in upgrading local quality standards. Export-oriented restructuring in the two other TNC metal affiliates surveyed has been more limited than for BICC-CAFCA. Where the parent company owns other affiliates in the region, competition is discouraged by assigning a specific market territory for each. After the relaxation of restrictions on profit remittances, some affiliates are also remitting more to their parents than they receive in investment inflows. Commercial borrowing has become the main source of finance for new investment, and high interest rates are proving a major constraint to upgrading.

The agro-processing firms in the sample were also pushing regional exports, and to a limited extent sales to European niche markets. They were setting up sister companies and distribution agents to market their products. Some affiliates were eyeing the west African market, and one intended to become a regional headquarters for the region. As in the metal-working firms, restructuring emphasized product quality improvement and modernization of the production process, making use of access to the training facilities, technologies and expertise of the parent companies. One particularly dynamic case, the joint venture Olivine, is worth noting. The foreign parent helped with the business plan and shifted it from family to corporate management. Olivine was able to re-invest all its profits and improved its personnel policies, filling major positions with qualified professionals and offering training to personnel at all levels. The parent assisted with renovation of machinery, technical know-how and product development, helping the affiliate with cost reduction. During the early 1990s, marketing also began to receive more emphasis (Selassie, 1995).

The one garment affiliate in the sample did relatively little to boost exports. As noted, it reduced its export share over time, in contrast to the local firms; this had to do with its product range (rainwear and gloves), which were not competitive in European markets. It was, however, modernizing its equipment and planning to develop regional exports.

In sum, restructuring in Zimbabwe is proceeding, but rather fitfully and slowly. Foreign firms are not significantly more active than other firms. Most affiliates are not particularly advanced in terms of technology, management or marketing skills. However, these findings are based on a small sample, and some important industries and sectors – notably mining – were not included in the analysis. Hence, the conclusions must be seen as tentative, though they reflect the general performance of the manufacturing sector.

Another study of manufacturing firms in Zimbabwe did find that foreign affiliates performed marginally better than local firms, using a sample of 41 food, textile, woodworking and metal-working firms (Teitel and Thoumi, 1994). The proportion of professional personnel in the nine foreign-owned and joint venture companies in this sample was higher than in the sample as a whole (1.26 compared to 1.01 persons), as was the proportion of technical personnel (4.07 and 3.72 persons, respectively). The authors calculated an index of "total operating capability",[25] on which the foreign-owned firms and joint ventures scored 7 points compared to 5.7 for the sample as a whole. Affiliates and joint ventures were also more active in planning technological improvements, but the difference was not very large (table 6.9).

In general, the Zimbabwean experience illustrates the constraints imposed by the larger economic and policy environment. As Latsch and Robinson (1999) conclude from their analysis of 33 garment and engineering producers: "... the advantages of being foreign-owned are limited. For almost all firms these options have remained hypothetical, since uncertainties mean that investments are being postponed." It is difficult in such circumstances to generalize about the impact of the presence of TNCs.

Table 6.9. Existence of plans for technological improvement among Zimbabwean firms

Plans for technological development capacity	No. of firms (whole sample)	Percentage of firms	Foreign firms / Joint Ventures	Percentge of firms
No changes	13	31.7	3	33.3
Same capacity but upgrade technology	5	12.2	2	22.2
Same technology but increase capacity	1	2.4	0	0.0
Invest in technological upgrading and expansion	14	34.1	4	44.4
No definite plans	7	17.1	0	0.0
Other (relocation to other city)	1	2.4	0	0.0
Total	41	100.0	9	100.0

Source: Teitel and Thoumi (1994), table A7.

---

[25] Total operating capability (TOC) is the sum of in-house maintenance and repair capability (minimum score 1 point, maximum 4), the existence of technical documentation and formal technical offices (minimum 1, maximum 3), and the sophistication of the quality control system used (minimum 0, maximum 3) (Teitel and Thoumi, 1994, p 113). A study of Kenya, Tanzania and Zimbabwe (Lall, 1999) adopts a similar methodology to calculate a "technology capability index" for sample firms, and compares scores across these three countries. It finds that Zimbabwean firms have higher capabilities than similar firms in Kenya and Tanzania but these are well below international frontiers. Biggs et al. (1995) report similar findings in comparing Zimbabwe with Ghana and Kenya.

6.4. Conclusions and policy lessons

Chile and Zimbabwe have gone through very different liberalization experiences. Chile has had massive inflows of FDI in traditional and non-traditional resource-based sectors since it liberalized. The investors have developed considerable exports in mining, forestry, fishing and agribusiness. This has not happened in Zimbabwe. Foreign involvement in manufacturing and mining dates back to the UDI period; new FDI inflows after opening up have stepped up only recently, and are on a much smaller scale than in Chile.

There are many reasons for this divergence. There are differences in the two countries' resource endowments and access to dynamic regional and world markets, and in the ways they are affected by the "image" of their respective regions. The liberalization process was managed very differently. In Chile it was enforced by military rule, and embodied an extreme free-market ideology. Zimbabwe started with a strong legacy of import substitution (almost unmatched in other developing countries in Africa or elsewhere); and the need to appease non-African settlers influenced government policy for a long period after independence. Its liberalization process has been slow, hesitant and not always predictable. Macroeconomic management skills as well as the human capital base in general have been much weaker in Zimbabwe than in Chile.

The influence of these factors precludes a straightforward comparison between the two countries. Likewise, one has to exercise caution in drawing lessons about government policies across resource-rich developing countries. Nevertheless, it is clear that the policy environment is one major factor in explaining the different responses of TNCs in terms of restructuring. In Chile, the policy climate was conducive for foreign investors to make large commitments. The outlook of continued stability in an outward-oriented setting, the existence of non-discriminatory FDI regimes favourable to private enterprise and strong macroeconomic management provided an ideal climate for TNCs. In Zimbabwe, a combination of factors accounts for the low levels of FDI inflows, including uncertainty about the dynamics of regional markets (particularly the market in South Africa), sub-Saharan Africa's poor image among investors, as well as the less FDI-oriented policy environment.

From the perspective of attracting FDI, raising exports and improving general economic performance, Chile has clearly been much more successful than Zimbabwe. However, its strategy also raises important issues of industrial policy (Pietrobelli, 1998). Its neo-liberal approach has allowed the exploitation of its existing natural resources. It has not, however, been as successful in exploiting industrial advantages or in using fully its human resources. Chile remains highly dependent on exports of a narrow range of resource-based products, among which copper is still dominant; this leads to considerable vulnerability in a market which is growing slowly, and which is threatened by technological substitution (for instance a shift to fibre-optic cables). In addition, resource-based activities have limited spillover effects on other activities and do not lead to much technological learning. As a result, the industrial and export structure is weak in skill and technological terms, and has regressed at a time when the most dynamic developing countries have been advancing significantly.

Having exploited its static resource base, Chile needs to mount a coherent industrial and technological policy to diversify its productive base, by creating linkages from its resource-based activities and attracting new, more complex activities. As a first step, the promotion of forward linkages from resource-based industries into high value-added manufacturing is essential. Local firms and affiliates need to upgrade their R&D capabilities and advanced skills. A strong technology support policy has to complement an aggressive and targeted FDI attraction strategy, along the lines of the strategy pioneered by Singapore, and more recently replicated by countries such as Costa Rica.

From a global perspective, Zimbabwe does not appear to have much scope for export competitiveness in new manufacturing activities in the short run. However, it has a considerable edge over other African countries in terms of the technological capabilities it acquired during the previous import-substitution regime. It also has a stronger skill base and a reasonably good infrastructure to support its natural resources. It should be able to become a strong regional player in industries where market proximity is relevant, such as heavy engineering and construction materials. An assessment of export prospects for members of the Southern African Development Community in regional markets concluded that Zimbabwe had considerable potential in a variety of industries (von Kirchbach and Roelofsen, 1998). However, it needs to follow much more coherent and consistent policies than it has in the past. The manufacturing sector still suffers from structural weaknesses resulting from the prolonged period of import-substitution. There is a need for proactive policies in finance, technology acquisition and training. While FDI regulation has improved, promotion is still weak. Macroeconomic stability and policy credibility are vital to success. However, success will also depend significantly on regional markets and image, and here matters are largely outside the control of the Government of Zimbabwe.

Chapter 7

The competitiveness challenge: conclusions and policy recommendations

7.1 Introduction

The case studies illustrate clearly the massive changes taking place in the geographical organization of world manufacturing activity. Vast international networks of interdependent production and exchange are emerging, taking advantage of differences in human, natural and technological endowments across countries and regions. Their development is facilitated by revolutionary advances in information and telecommunications technologies and the increasing efficiency and speed of transport systems. They are fostered by liberal trade and FDI regimes and market-driven economic systems.

In contrast to earlier periods of openness in the world economy, the new context is characterized not just by fast growth in international trade but, under pressures of technical change, by a proliferation of other forms of cross-border linkages. These include FDI (driven to a large extent by cross-border mergers and acquisitions (M&As)), technology flows including licensing agreements and strategic alliances, franchising, and a variety of subcontracting links such as original equipment manufacturing. It is these linkages, rather than the expansion of trade *per se*, that are giving rise to globalized production systems. These systems involve closer and more complex international links than traditional arm's-length trade.

TNCs control, organize and coordinate these global production systems. They are increasingly developing a portfolio of locational assets across the globe to match their immobile assets. In the process, they are also shifting components of their economic activity – such as R&D, training and strategic management – within internationally integrated production and marketing systems. For developing countries, the ability to offer the necessary immobile assets has become a critical part of FDI – and competitiveness – strategies. While a large domestic market remains a powerful magnet for investors, TNCs serving global markets increasingly look for other attributes, in response to policy liberalization and technical change. The opening of markets creates new opportunities for TNCs and gives them a broader choice of modes with which to access those markets. It also makes them more selective in their choices of potential investment sites.

Apart from primary resources, the most attractive immobile assets for export-oriented TNCs are now skilled and productive labour, world-class infrastructure and an agglomeration of efficient suppliers, competitors, support institutions and services. Low-wage unskilled labour remains a source of competitive advantage, but its importance is diminishing. As noted in chapter 1, "raw" labour no longer provides a base for sustainable growth – rising incomes and wages erode its advantage. The same applies to natural resources. They provide a competitive basis for growth as long as they are plentiful in supply and face growing demand. However, most primary exports face slow-growing markets and are vulnerable to substitution. Sustained growth on the basis of natural resources requires the upgrading of the technologies used or the setting up of downstream industries. In both cases, to draw the most dynamic mobile assets of TNCs, host countries need to improve their immobile assets.

The trend towards the decomposition of production processes and the siting of specific activities (or particular sub-processes) in different countries means that significant opportunities may emerge for countries irrespective of their levels of development. Countries that find it difficult to meet the requirements for hosting a full production facility might be able to attract specific sub-processes that match their endowments and competitive advantages. However, this does not imply that all developing countries will automatically be drawn into global TNC networks. Even attracting a small sub-component of a global production network may require advanced production skills and capabilities that many less developed countries do not have. The highly uneven distribution of FDI flows across the developing world suggests that many countries risk being (and remaining) marginalized in the emerging, technology-based system of global production.

The critical issue for developing countries is how and under what conditions they can benefit from increased TNC involvement. However, FDI is not always beneficial; it may lead to a mixture of positive and negative effects. Moreover, the amount of FDI countries receive as well as these effects are subject to policy influence. In economic terms, the private interests of TNCs can diverge from the social interests of the host economy. Also, information flows are imperfect and there may be problems in coordinating host factor markets with the needs of foreign investors. It is only under strong assumptions of efficient markets that all FDI can be assumed to be economically beneficial and the investment process could be left entirely to markets.

These assumptions do not apply to real economies. In many developing countries, "under-development" is typified by an absence of efficient markets and institutions, and information markets are particularly prone to failure. The neo-classical theory of international investment posits that the existence of TNCs is a manifestation of market failure. Large oligopolistic firms operate over national boundaries precisely because they have specific ownership advantages over other firms, enjoy scale and scope economies, internalize deficient markets for information and skills and have privileged access to finance. All these violate the requirements of perfect competition, where each of their assets should be sold between independent firms. It is clear that the interaction between the efficient internalized markets of TNCs and the deficient ones of developing countries cannot automatically lead to mutual benefit.

Moreover, investors may not have the information to allocate resources efficiently across countries, even from their profit-maximizing perspective. There can be high transaction costs in a particular country and deficient knowledge on its economic potential that can prevent them from setting up in profitable locations. More importantly, local endowments are not static (in an absolute sense): a host Government can create new skills, facilities and infrastructure to meet the needs of investors it wants to attract, and improve the match between assets sought by TNCs and local immobile assets. Thus, host economies may be able to influence the amount of inward investment and improve its quality (by targeting specific kinds of investment) by improving their images and information provision, providing better services and gearing their assets to TNCs' needs. This is known as "marketing a country" effectively to investors. The countries that have succeeded most in using TNCs to restructure and upgrade their industries – Singapore and the Republic of Ireland, for example – have been professional and aggressive in such marketing.

In brief, therefore, FDI policies must address two sets of market failures. One arises when the private interests of investors diverge from the economic interests of the host country, leading FDI to have negative effects or positive but static effects. The other arises from information or coordination failures in the investment process, leading a country to attract insufficient FDI or the wrong type of FDI. The first calls for policies to remove the source of divergence or restrict undesirable forms of FDI. The second calls for strategic attraction and targeting of TNCs.

7.2 Case studies: review of the findings

The case studies presented in the preceding chapters illustrate the role of FDI and TNCs in international production. More specifically, they show how inward FDI can transform the export structures in developing host economies by integrating them into new international production networks. Consumer electronics manufacturing in Malaysia, Mexico and Thailand is dominated by TNCs, as is garment manufacturing in Costa Rica, the Dominican Republic and Morocco. FDI has created considerable automobile assembly capacity in the context of regional integration schemes, Mexico in NAFTA, Brazil and Argentina in MERCOSUR, and Thailand and Malaysia in the ASEAN. Chile (less so Zimbabwe) illustrates how large-scale FDI has gone into natural resource-based industries.

This FDI has had a substantial impact on the economic performance of the host countries. The nature of that impact varies considerably, depending on the motivations and strategies of the investors and the environment of the host countries. Export-oriented investments, based on the exploitation of existing advantages like low-cost labour or natural resources, have often boosted export performance in garments, food processing, mining and the TV industries. The FDI-based transformation of an established import substituting industry has resulted in integration with a much larger market, as with the automotive industry in Mexico. In these cases, there has also been a significant effect on local employment. Capital-intensive resource-based FDI, using local physical inputs, has contributed more to *net* foreign exchange earnings than export-oriented assembly activities based predominantly on imported components, but has contributed less to generating employment.

Where the investments have been placed in protected local or regional markets, their effects on exports and efficiency have been different. The automobile industries in the MERCOSUR and ASEAN, groupings with fast growing and relatively protected regional markets, have seen large increases in productive capacity and productivity. However, the impact of FDI on exports has been relatively small (though rising). Liberalization has led to rapid increases in imported inputs, particularly in MERCOSUR, with negative effects on the trade balance and on local suppliers.

The impact of the FDI inflows on countries' industrial upgrading, diversification and competitiveness is more difficult to summarize. There are many differences among the examined industries and countries. These differences are important because they offer policy lessons for other developing countries that wish to boost local TNC involvement. Broadly speaking, FDI in the two engineering industries, TV and automobiles, has provided more opportunity for industrial upgrading than low-technology garments and natural resource-based investments. The results in the four industries are examined separately below.

7.2.1 TV receivers

The international TV industry is organized in a producer-driven chain controlled by a small (and steadily decreasing) number of players competing fiercely for market share. The emergence of powerful Japanese TNCs (later followed by TNCs from the Republic of Korea) has shaped the competition, along with a few European firms that have survived the rigours of intense competition. On the technological front, the drivers have been enormous economies of scale in the production of key components, along with rapid product development, continuous improvements in efficiency and quality, and new organizational practices. The industry is very linkage intensive, and the supply chain – notably the higher technology and scale-intensive components – has also internationalized, with suppliers following the lead companies.

Production in the developing world has gone through various stages. In the days of import substitution, it started with relatively small-scale assembly for domestic markets, with some deepening into component manufacturing in a few larger developing countries. This evolved into simple assembly of imported component for exports, mainly in South-East Asia, where low-cost labour, strong export-oriented trade policies and liberal FDI regimes were the main competitive factors. A few sites graduated into larger scale manufacturing for export of finished TVs and assembly kits within a region; even fewer are in the process of becoming exporters for global markets. The capabilities required here are more advanced. Regional manufacturing calls for technical and organizational skills, along with excellent logistics and locational advantages. Global manufacturing calls for more advanced technological capabilities, with independent research and design capabilities. As the development of capabilities in this industry is an evolutionary process, TNCs are not highly mobile: other things being equal, they tend to base themselves in specific sites that meet their initial requirements. There are thus strong first, mover advantages to host countries, displaced only by strong shifts in locational parameters.

These factors have been clearly at play in the countries studied here, which account for the bulk of FDI in the industry. Malaysia was the first major TV assembly site for export markets, and over time grew to become a regional and partly global manufacturer, with massive scales of production. The depth and sophistication of operations rose over time, and several foreign component suppliers invested there to support the assemblers. There was also an increase in sourcing from local firms, but primarily in the low technology end of the components spectrum. The Government is concerned about this and is trying to help raise their capabilities. In response, TNCs are building local design and development capabilities, transferring the responsibility for smaller sets to their Malaysian affiliates and introducing leading-edge technologies and state-of-the-art work practices.

While skill levels in Malaysia are low relative to industrial or the more advanced newly industrializing countries, they have been rising over time. The base of technical education in Malaysia is particularly small. While TNCs have devoted considerable resources to worker training and upgrading the skills of higher level employees, this can not substitute for university education. Future progress up the technological ladder will therefore depend crucially on Malaysia's ability to enlarge tertiary level technical skills. Further deepening of the supply base will also depend on the technological capabilities of domestic suppliers. On the whole, Malaysia is secure as a regional centre. However, whether or not it can develop into a full-fledged global supply base remains to be seen.

The TV industry in Thailand has not evolved to the Malaysian level, though it shares similar characteristics. TNCs transfer modern technologies and work practices, and export significant amounts. However, the scales of production are smaller, as are the levels of sophistication of processes and products. Thailand does not yet function as a regional centre; there are no product design activities. Thai affiliates still rely predominantly on low-cost labour and incentives as their main sources of competitive advantage for exports, and specialize in the lower (price-sensitive) range of the market. Backward linkages to local companies are weak, and despite government efforts (through local content rules) progress has been slow.

Mexico is rather different. Its main competitive edge (as one low-wage country among many others) lies in its proximity and privileged access (via United States tariff provisions and NAFTA) to the world's largest national market. In the absence of this access, TNCs earlier showed a clear preference for export-oriented operations in South-East Asia. With it, however, the locational parameters have changed significantly, in particular because local content is eligible for preferential market access under NAFTA. Changes in the trade and FDI regimes in Mexico triggered massive FDI inflows by Asian electronic TNCs. Two major TV production clusters have been formed, with assembly and growing production of components by the major firms, and recently their international suppliers also have established affiliates in the country.

As a result, Mexico has become by far the largest supplier of TVs to the developed world. As with Malaysia, there has been considerable training to use state-of-the-art equipment and work practices. A process of technological deepening is starting, with R&D activities in product and component design. The main weakness, however, of the Mexican TV industry is its linkages with local suppliers: these are very low, the lowest of the three cases examined. The industry, dynamic and efficient as it is, remains largely an enclave operation. Policies and institutions to upgrade local suppliers' capabilities are weak. The heavy dependence on the United States market means that Mexico will remain a regional centre for the foreseeable future, though if its technological capabilities deepen (Mexico has a much stronger human capital base than Malaysia). TNCs may develop their facilities there to serve also the Latin American market.

What are the implications for other developing countries? The three countries in the study have now established strong competitive bases. Given the evolutionary development of these advantages, it is unlikely that the TNCs will relocate to other countries. They may set up facilities elsewhere to assemble kits and components manufactured in these centres, but the scale-, technology- and skill-intensive parts of TV production will continue in the first movers, in particular in Malaysia and Mexico. Less sophisticated operations, in which threshold scales of viable production are lower and labour costs are important competitive factors, might be established in other regions or large markets. Large and protected markets (e.g. India) will continue to attract the whole range of TV manufacturing FDI as long as they do not liberalize fully, but they are unlikely to become direct competitors to the export-oriented centres. With the progress of trade liberalization, however, it is not clear how many manufacturing (as opposed to sales and servicing) bases TNCs will need in developing countries. Given the pace of technical change, it is not clear also how many countries will be able to furnish the skills and supplier bases that efficient production will require.

To the extent that there is scope for simple assembly operations in the future, new entrants in the developing world will be able to attract FDI into the industry. To do so, they will have to offer stable trade and FDI regimes, good infrastructure, and low-cost skilled labour. However, the prospects of major regional manufacturing operations emerging in the developing world seem confined to countries that have already established a significant presence. Few countries, for instance China (assuming considerable upgrading of skills and infrastructure), stand a chance of competing directly with Malaysia. If sub-Saharan Africa provides a more stable and promising market, a regional base may be established in South Africa.

7.2.2   *Garments*

The garment industry was the first engine of export growth in manufactures in the developing world, and still provides substantial revenue and employment to a large number of countries. Of all export-oriented activities, it has spread the widest, relocating first from the developed countries to the East Asian newly industrializing economies, then spreading to other countries in Asia and to Latin America, North Africa and, to some extent, parts of sub-Saharan Africa. TNCs from developing countries have become dynamic players in diffusing the industry, driven largely by the allocation of quotas under the Multi-Fibre Agreement (MFA). The relocation process has probably peaked but international buyers and investors are still searching for new, low cost production sites. This makes it a "buyer-driven" production system, unlike the other two industries in the study (and most others in manufacturing), in that the internationalization process includes not just manufacturers but also retailers, wholesalers, designers and traders.

There are technological reasons for the rapid spread of garment manufacture throughout the developing world. At the entry level, it has low skill needs. It can function efficiently on a small scale, and massive plants with thousands of workers can coexist with small ones, and with subcontracting to cottage industries. Most of its technology is embodied in the equipment, and workers can be trained in a few weeks. The product is light and easy to transport. Buyers are constantly and actively searching for new suppliers. They are able to provide the designs, specifications and materials needed for assembly. Local firms can acquire the capabilities needed to compete with TNCs in world markets as far as production is concerned. However, there are sharp differences in the quality and fashion-orientation of the product. The manufacture of mass-produced, standardized garments is best suited for relocation to low wage sites with semi-skilled labour and relatively slow response times. However, this activity has very limited technological learning potential and few spillover benefits to other activities.

The production of higher quality garments where rapid delivery, advanced skills and logistics are required needs more developed supply and training bases. Most offshore assembly of garments in developing countries concentrates on the low- to medium-quality segment. Very few producers, mainly in the mature newly industrializing economies, have moved into the higher segments; none has reached the design and quality levels of the leaders like Italy or France. Upgrading is certainly possible for all garment producers, but after a certain level it becomes extremely difficult. It calls for a constellation of design and technical skills, equipment manufacturing capabilities and backward linkages to efficient textile and accessory production that few countries can muster.

Ease of entry in simple products and the continuous search for suppliers by a large range of buyers make garment FDI perhaps the best means for developing countries to launch export-oriented manufacturing. As long as wages remain competitive, it offers new entrants not only valuable foreign exchange and employment, but also an opportunity to learn exporting and entrepreneurial skills. If the country uses the period of "rent" yielded by the exploitation of low-cost labour to upgrade the industry and diversify into other export activities, the activity can provide a base for long-term competitiveness. Some countries, particularly in East Asia, have used it in just this way, moving into electronics assembly and other export activities as they lost competitiveness in garments.

Many other countries have not restructured. They have stayed in clothing, despite its limited learning and technical spillovers to other industries. Often, this was because they were not able to develop textile industries to provide fabrics of the range and quality required by exporter industries. They found upgrading beyond a certain level very difficult. Many foreign assemblers move from locations where wages are rising to cheaper ones. The original locations can retain competitive advantages with rising wages only if they can develop the capabilities to compete in higher quality segments. Some upgrading comes from learning and training within exporting firms, but much depends on the ability of the country to develop deeper skills and capabilities. While this applies to other industries also, the "crunch" seems to come earlier in garments – and its low technology nature means that other benefits (in particular technological learning and diffusion, or the potential to attract FDI into related industries) are relatively low.

The international garment industry *per se* thus provides the least favourable prospects for long-term industrial upgrading in developing countries of the three industries studied here. FDI in this industry is based on the exploitation of one static advantage, and can lead to sustained competitiveness as wages rise only if the country can use the finance generated and other benefits to build other capabilities. TNCs can raise local skills and capabilities to a limited extent; low sunk costs mean that the benefits of moving to new locations outweigh those of deepening in the original locations. In this the industry differs from electronics and automobiles. Meanwhile, the MFA (and the later WTO Agreement on Textiles and Clothing), which enabled the industry to spread widely across the developing world, are coming to an end. It is not clear how competitive positions will evolve once large producers like China are able to sell without quota barriers; many new entrants are certainly going to be extremely vulnerable.

This applies forcefully to the three case study countries: Morocco, Costa Rica and the Dominican Republic. They rely heavily on special market access privileges for their competitive advantage. Although foreign investors are upgrading quality and skills, these efforts are unlikely to take affiliates into a high enough market segment to survive the full force of competition after the MFA is phased out in December 2004. The two countries in Central America are already suffering from the preferential market access enjoyed by Mexico. None of them is likely to develop a local input or design base that will keep them ahead of lower-wage Asian competitors (which are also upgrading their industries). Moreover, the trade regime that attracted TNCs (for example, the United States HTS 9802) is systematically biased against local sourcing and higher value-added activities.

In sum, while FDI in garments manufacturing has launched many developing countries into the manufactured export arena, the competitive base it exploits and feeds into is largely static. Unless the countries themselves build deeper and more diverse advantages, it may prove evanescent as incomes rise. Of the three countries, only Costa Rica has been able to do this. It has emulated Singapore's strategy of targeting high-tech FDI, which is likely to provide a more lasting source of competitive advantage. More importantly, the Intel plant is expected to attract other high-technology FDI, something FDI in garment manufacture has been unable to do. It is only in the mature newly industrializing economies of Asia that leading local garment firms have diversified their edge in the industry to be able to retain a competitive position. They have used their first mover advantages and advanced capabilities to become middlemen for foreign buyers and set up their own assembly bases in lower wage locations. Later entrants that have not diversified, such as Morocco, may well find that upgrading within the garment industry is not enough to sustain future growth.

The prospects for many countries that have relied heavily on clothing to drive their manufactured export growth do not seem very bright as the industry's wage levels rise. Prospects for countries that hope to enter this activity are even less encouraging, as trade rules change and quotas are phased out. The most successful exporters of garments have been able to upgrade the quality of their products and bring local companies to the level where they can tackle design and marketing and diversify into other export-oriented activities while relocating simpler tasks to other sites. By doing this have they matched rising wages with an increased competitiveness in clothing exports. Otherwise, they would have simply lost the industry and suffered slowing export growth – a likely scenario for countries that do not succeed in raising productivity or diversifying. Garments can serve as a base for long-term competitiveness if host countries succeed in combining two approaches: upgrading the domestic economy in terms of local skills, industrial and marketing capabilities and infrastructure, and targeting complementary TNC investment into more advanced activities.

There is considerable scope for raising the quality of the garment industry itself in countries still engaged in low-segment mass production. They can strengthen training within firms (particularly in small- and medium-sized local firms) and offer specialized training in government- or industry-based institutions. Most garment industries in developing countries suffer from shortages of technicians, cutters, pattern makers, drapers and designers. They also often need more modern equipment and efficient transport and communication links with final markets. One of the most important determinants of export competitiveness in clothing is rapid and flexible response: "best practice" for high fashion clothing in Europe is around two weeks from order to delivery. At the other end are standardized, low value items like underwear that typically require a lead time of up to six months in South Asia and two to three months in South-East Asia. To come nearer to best practice levels, these exporters need to invest in a whole gamut of activities from manufacturing to information, quality control, customs clearance, transportation and delivery.

If a local textile industry exists, it tends to have few supply linkages with the export-oriented garment sector. Thus, there is often a need to improve the quality, finishing (the most capital- and skill-intensive stage) and design range of textile manufactures. Only a few developing countries have been able to sustain large and efficient domestic textile industries (such as India, Pakistan, China and Indonesia), though smaller countries do have small facilities tied to their clothing operations. Where a large textile base can be developed, however, it can provide considerable competitive advantages to garment firms in terms of cost, delivery and flexibility. This also applies to the manufacture of textile and clothing machinery. This is the most advanced backward link in the production chain, and requires advanced engineering capabilities. Where these can be developed, reaching world class supply capabilities can yield immense benefits to clothing manufacturers. The advantages lie in flexibility, specialization and quality: one of the pillars of Italian fashion "clusters" is, for example, the strength of closely related equipment manufacturers that meet the specific and changing needs of small as well as large downstream firms.

However, for most developing countries, such as those in the case studies, garment manufacturing is primarily a matter of the final assembly of imported inputs. There is little chance that they will succeed in building strong local backward linkages. What they can do is to promote the quality and delivery in their garment facilities. They may well be able to retain segments of the industry once trade is liberalized in 2005. However, they are unlikely to be able to sustain the rapid growth in exports that they had in the past – they simply do not have wage or significant quality advantages over large aggressive Asian exporters.

This does not mean that there will not be new entrants into the industry. There will always be room "at the bottom" for lower wage countries to take over simple assembly, but this does not help established exporters like Morocco or the Dominican Republic. The new entrants should also learn from them: unless they also upgrade their capabilities in the (now shorter) grace period provided, their boom in garment exports is likely to prove short-lived and limited.

7.2.3 Automobiles

Automotive production remains one of the world's most important manufacturing industries, with large employment, linkage and trade effects. Like the TV industry, it is a supplier-driven multi-tiered chain dominated by a limited and decreasing number of TNCs. Here, too, East Asian firms have challenged established European and North American producers. There have been very significant changes in product and process technologies and production organization, in particular in response to Japanese techniques that raised quality and productivity to unprecedented levels. Scale economies have always been important in the industry, but their significance has increased greatly, despite flexible production techniques and equipment. The technology, though not changing as rapidly as in electronics, is very complex and difficult to master; modern quality and precision requirements make the process even more difficult. Efficient automotive production – as opposed to simple assembly – requires a well-developed engineering industry and a diverse network of suppliers and subcontractors. Logistics and supply chain management is therefore of critical significance, as are after-sales service and brand names. All these factors conduce to greater size and spread, and have led to a wave of mergers, acquisitions and strategic alliances encompassing all major production sites in the world.

The industry has a long history of import substitution, particularly in large developing countries. Most have relied heavily on TNCs for final assembly operations, but a few, like India and the Republic of Korea, have tried to establish national industries. Given the very demanding skill, technological, scale and supply-chain needs, only the Republic of Korea has succeeded in fostering world-class national firms in the automobile industry by dint of its pervasive and coherent industrial policy. Other countries have raised their dependence on TNCs, or turned to them as national strategies have foundered. However, one of the case studies, Malaysia, provides an interesting example of a new industrial policy designed to create a national automotive company of world standard. The other cases provide examples of FDI policies based on location, market characteristics and local capabilities.

Each of the five countries studied started with an import substitution phase in this industry. Each subsequently became part of a regional group: Mexico of NAFTA, Argentina and Brazil of MERCOSUR and Thailand and Malaysia of ASEAN and AFTA. This led to changes in the trade regime, that, along with FDI liberalization, exposed the industry to strong competitive pressures and provided stronger incentives to export. However, firms were not faced with immediate exposure to full import competition; the regional schemes provided lengthy transition periods before full liberalization. Each country responded by gearing up for improved competitiveness, but in different ways and with different intensities, depending on the regime, location and TNCs involved. In general, however, the case studies show that TNCs can, under open and competitive conditions, become a major force for competitive restructuring if they integrate affiliates into their international production systems.

The main response by the automobile assemblers in the case studies was to restructure affiliate operations in various ways, to reap economies of scale, improve equipment and productivity, and raise supplier capabilities to world levels. Mexico had a head start because of its proximity to the United States market. Production integrated to North American operations became an important competitive response for United States firms to pressures from Asian TNCs. "*Maquila*" activities were greatly extended after the setting up of NAFTA. Completely new plants were established and some old ones refurbished. Intense competition in the United States market has forced all export-oriented plants and suppliers to adopt world best practice, meeting the pace of restructuring in Mexico faster than in the other countries.

In MERCOSUR and AFTA, the export orientation was still towards the regional market, though exports from Brazil to the OECD have grown significantly. There has been a strong incentive for TNCs to get a foothold ahead of competitors in the relevant regions, increasing the risk of collective over-investment. This is part of a larger problem of over-capacity in the auto industry worldwide, leading to further rationalization and restructuring in these and other countries.

The restructuring process has gone furthest in the Latin American countries. TNCs have sought larger production volumes, with affiliates specializing in fewer models or products. TNCs are limiting the number of core assembly sites, increasing the standardization of parts and components, and centralizing product design and development work in fewer centres in advanced industrial countries. They are introducing relatively simple and low-priced "developing country" models to keep costs down and to expand markets. The modernization of old plants and the establishment of new plants, along with modern organizational practices, is raising productivity dramatically. All this requires skill upgrading, and TNCs are investing in training at all levels. The effects on local technological activity are mixed. While most design and development activities are centralized in developed countries, considerable effort in the developing country sites is devoted to implementing new technologies. Not all R&D has shifted away: some Brazilian affiliates are responsible for new models for developing countries, while Mexico is starting to attract high-level development work from the United States.

Productivity is also being boosted by massive rationalization of supply chains. Assemblers are limiting the number of core first-tier suppliers, which have to meet world best-practice standards. This gives an advantage to mature, advanced companies with considerable technological and financial prowess, which are able to co-design and supply entire sub-assemblies. As a consequence, the traditional established suppliers of each TNC are rapidly internationalizing: "follow sourcing" has become an important phenomenon. Foreign suppliers have increased FDI in the three Latin American countries considerably, establishing new facilities, creating joint ventures and taking over local firms. Some local firms were technologically capable and fairly large, but have lost out to firms from developed countries because they could not establish a global presence (Barnes and Kaplinsky, 1998). Other local companies, which could not attract foreign partners, are being marginalized. In addition, there is much greater reliance on imported components by affiliates, particularly in Latin America. Greater specialization and economies of scale have ensued, and exports of intermediate components have increased.

Rationalization and restructuring have not proceeded that far in Malaysia and Thailand. Production volumes and exports remain low by international standards, and international or regional integration of production systems is not yet well developed. While some export capabilities have emerged, it is not clear that they can be sustained. For instance, in Thailand exports have been boosted by the huge drop in local demand and over-capacity created by the recent financial crisis, while in Malaysia they are facilitated by the Government and high domestic prices. The lag in restructuring is largely due to their trade and industrial regimes. Both countries offer significant protection to their auto industries. In Thailand, the level of protection has been recently raised to compensate for the phasing out of local content rules. While tariffs are due to come down in the context of ASEAN and AFTA, firms do not appear to have prepared for this. There is very little of the systematic integration and specialization evident in the three large Latin American economies. Malaysia continues to support Proton, which, while efficient as a small player, does not have the scale needed to become an independent international auto firm. The Thai supplier system is undergoing a shake-out after the crisis, with many new entries and take-overs by foreign firms, but it will only be able to reach economies of scale if the ASEAN market is unified.

Of the two, Thailand's auto industry is more advanced in terms of size and local supplier capabilities. Domestic technological capabilities are not, however, as advanced as in the TNC-dominated supply firms in Latin America. Skill levels appear to be lower, and R&D is very modest. Proton in Malaysia invests significantly in design and development, but the country's relatively small scale makes it difficult to replicate the success of national car firms in the Republic of Korea – where Hyundai, for instance, employs over three thousand engineers in automotive R&D. Pressures on both countries to liberalize imports are increasing, both as part of regional arrangements and also more generally in the WTO context. Thailand is better placed to cope with liberalization, especially if large investments planned by the major TNCs materialize. However, its supplier industry will have to undergo considerable upgrading.

The threat of over-capacity is serious in both regions, putting pressure on firms to restructure through mergers, upgrading of skills and capabilities all along the production chain, and greater specialization and integration across national boundaries. The challenge for the Asian countries is more difficult than for the Latin American ones, which have already progressed quite far in the restructuring process. Local firms will continue to be under competitive pressure as factors such as technology, scale and relations with the major TNCs continue to favour developed country investors. Local technological activity may be reduced in some areas, but it may increase in others. For instance, the growth of Fiat's design capabilities in Brazil, and of the Delphi design centre in Mexico are very promising developments in this respect. If Proton succeeds as an independent player, however, it will show that reliance on TNCs is not necessary in the industry – that the Korean example can be replicated. At the same time, some of the policies that allowed the Governments of Malaysia and the Republic of Korea to foster independent firms are being restricted under multilateral trade rules.

Can other countries learn from the experience of these five countries? The Latin American success with automotive production and internationalization suggests that an existing industry can be restructured by setting up new world-class plants, building on the skill base, engineering knowledge and infrastructure created over the years. It is not clear, therefore, that, in the future, completely new entrants in auto assembly or components manufacturing would be able to attract TNCs. Better opportunities exist for large countries with long experience of the industry to become part of global production systems. For instance, India, China, Turkey, Poland, the Czech Republic and Hungary are attracting significant automotive FDI based on existing capabilities. If they can induce the kind of investment and integration observed in Latin America, and provide the skills, incentives and infrastructure required, they may be able to experience similar restructuring.

Needless to say, for some of these economies, this would imply redesigning their current FDI regimes. They may have to use discretionary and targeted policies to induce export growth, so as to reap economies of scale. They would need to use a variety of instruments towards the promotion of FDI and of exports which is becoming more complicated, since multilateral agreements constrain instruments such as subsidies or export performance requirements. While some are being ruled out by the agreements concluded by member countries within WTO, there may be similar tools available that do not contravene the rules. Developed countries, for example, use generous grants to lure automotive TNCs, in return for understandings on local content, technological and export performance.

On the other hand, the prospects for attracting FDI into automotive manufacturing in countries without a large engineering base are fairly slim. In Africa, only South Africa has a developed automotive industry with some chance of becoming a large producer. Its more recent FDI performance has been improving, although the region in general continues to suffer from political and economic instability.

The development of global over-capacity in the industry may mean that total capacity will not expand: new investments may focus largely on relocating existing capacities, or even reducing capacities. Only a few countries seem set to benefit; some will suffer. The former are likely to be economies with large markets, or with access to large regional markets, stable FDI regimes, advanced engineering capabilities and world-class logistics and infrastructure. Low labour costs will help only if other conditions are in place and productivity and quality levels are comparable with world-class plants.

The Latin American experience also suggests that rapid trade and investment liberalization without prior strengthening of domestic capabilities can have deleterious effects on local supplier firms. A phased, gradual liberalization of the components and parts industry, backed by a coherent programme of technological and skill upgrading, would be preferable provided that the Government has the capability to mount such a programme. It is important to note that a lagging supplier industry can be a drag on the assembly segment's competitiveness and deter the integration of the industry as a whole into a dynamic global production system.

7.2.4 Resource-based FDI

Resource-based FDI can undergo the same process of restructuring and upgrading seen in the more technology-intensive manufacturing activities – if they have similar incentives and regimes. Extractive and processing technologies have advanced significantly in recent years, and many new and better quality products have emerged. As in manufacturing, advanced skills and organization, large minimum scales of production and state-of-the-art logistics are needed to compete effectively in many resource-based activities. The Chilean case shows that FDI can contribute to the successful growth of new resource-based exports like agro- and fishing-based products; it can also increase traditional mineral exports like copper and copper products. Its success owes much to export-oriented macro policies, a friendly and non-discriminatory FDI regime, a high level of skills, favourable demand conditions and the capacity to take advantage of openings in international markets.

The Chilean case stands in strong contrast to that of Zimbabwe, another resource-rich country. In Zimbabwe poor macroeconomic management, an unfavourable regional image, unstable FDI and industrial policies, and low domestic and regional demand have contributed to poor industrial performance and a lack of interest by TNCs. A relatively strong base of manufacturing capabilities has not been upgraded to cope with world competition. Domestic skills and technological activity have not been used sufficiently to diversify agro-based export activities.

However, the Chilean success with resource-based exports has a counterpart in poor performance in its manufacturing industry, particularly in dynamic, technology-based activities. Chile's competitive base remains concentrated on activities with relatively slow-growing final markets, some of which are technologically vulnerable. The spillover effects on learning are limited, and the industrial R&D base is very weak, inappropriate to the strong education base. Increased competitiveness has relied primarily on utilizing static advantages, and it is not clear how these will evolve naturally into more dynamic, sustainable advantages. In the absence of industrial policy, no restructuring has taken place in manufacturing, and a change of policy may be needed to remedy this.

On the other hand, the Chilean case shows that there is considerable growth potential in natural resources, and TNCs can be tapped to exploit this potential. This would require FDI and macroeconomic policies, combined with a strong skill base and targeted policies to support the development of resource-based activities. Countries should, however, be aware that this activity tends to be limited in terms of learning, technological spillovers and market growth (though there may be segments where rapid growth and technology development are possible, for instance by the application of biotechnology). As in the case of garments, this means that countries should not avoid developing the primary sector but should use the gains from natural resources exploitation to build more sustainable advantages within and outside the sector. A proactive strategy is recommended. Otherwise, a passive focus on resource-based exports may well lead to a neglect of the manufacturing sector, in particular of higher technology activities within manufacturing.

7.3 General policy lessons

7.3.1 Preliminaries

This study illustrates graphically that, under the right conditions, TNCs can contribute to expanding export earnings and building short-term competitiveness. It also suggests that the longer-term effects of FDI, in terms of building a sustainable competitive base, differ by industry and host country and that FDI-based competitiveness-building can have drawbacks. The nature of an industry – pace of market growth, nature of technical change, market structure and logistics – affect how and where an activity spreads internationally, which processes can be located in particular locations and how much they deepen over time. The nature of the host economy – its size, location, resource endowments, skill base, technological capabilities and policies – has a strong impact on whether and how it participates in globalization and how much benefit it draws from FDI. These differences are important for drawing general policy lessons.

The current policy climate – favouring broad-based and rapid liberalization of trade and FDI regimes – is based on the clear and simple premise that markets are the best means of allocating resources. According to this (simplified) argument, the best strategy for developing countries to benefit from globalization would therefore be to remove all policy interventions in trade and foreign entry. Governments would limit themselves to providing security and stability, good macroeconomic management, clear and transparent rules including national treatment of investors, and basic public goods (education, health and infrastructure). They would remove impediments to private enterprise and implement a strong competition policy. They would not attempt to guide resource allocation into particular activities.

However, as noted earlier, this does not rule out the need for strategic interventions since the underlying assumptions about market efficiency (and government inefficiency) do not hold. The present case studies have shown both the benefits and the costs of liberalization in the process of industrial restructuring and competitiveness.

The main findings of our studies can be summarized as follows:

- Liberal FDI policy, if combined with incentives from the trade regime (essentially strong export orientation), can lead to – and does generally not go beyond – the exploitation of *static* comparative advantages.

- FDI can build *dynamic* comparative advantage in industries in which there are complex and lengthy learning processes, and in countries where the base for such upgrading exists; otherwise the investment closes down or moves on. TNCs differ in their individual reactions, depending on their strategies and competitive positions.

- The extent of dynamism depends critically on government policies: the most important of these are building advanced skills, developing supplier capabilities among domestic enterprises, encouraging technological activity and targeting and guiding FDI.

The reasoning behind these conclusions is outlined below (and discussed in greater detail in UNCTAD's *World Investment Report 1999*, see UNCTAD, 1999a).

7.3.2 Need for policies on FDI

FDI flows – their quantity and quality – are determined increasingly by efficiency and competitiveness. Resource-based investments apart, the countries that receive most FDI in a liberalized environment are those with the immobile factors needed for the competitive facilities of TNCs. These immobile assets – skills, service and supply networks, infrastructure, and institutions – have to complement the mobile assets of TNCs. While transport costs and taste differences mean that large markets will always remain attractive to foreign investors, an important draw for FDI remains the economic base of a country: incentives to attract TNCs cannot compensate for the lack of such a base.

This being said, there remains a case for proactive policies to attract FDI. Countries may not be able to attract the volume and quality of FDI they desire, or that their economic base merits, for one or more of three reasons. These are high transaction costs; deficient information on the potential of the host economy; and insufficient coordination between the needs of TNCs, the assets of the host economy and the potential to improve those assets. As noted, this provides a case for proactive attraction and targeting strategies to increase FDI.

There is also the need for policies to build domestic capabilities, to attract higher quality FDI, induce existing investors to upgrade, increase local diffusion and add greater value to local resources. The need for such intervention arises where markets do not give the correct signals for resource allocation to economic agents or fail to coordinate their investment decisions properly. Where markets are weak and supporting institutions absent, information may not flow efficiently, risky projects may never be undertaken, costly learning may not be undergone, and externalities and linkages with other agents may result in under-investment. It then becomes necessary for development for Governments to intervene in markets to encourage specific types of investment and build or strengthen institutions.

It is important to note, however, that FDI policies require that Governments be able to formulate coherent strategies, decide on trade-offs between objectives, and design, monitor and implement policies to overcome market failures that beset these objectives. This cannot be taken for granted. Experience shows that government failure can be as costly as market failure. This does not rule out the case for intervention. Many strategies have been efficient – some, for example in East Asia, dramatically so. Moreover, government skills and capabilities are not static. Governments can learn, and the capabilities of officials can be improved with training, information and correct incentives. Policy design must reflect current (and future) government capabilities, and not require interventions that exceed those capabilities. This means that policies must be flexible and constantly monitored. They must also be coherent and consistent in addressing objectives, with coordination between different branches of government and between the Government and economic agents.

The need for coherence and coordination means that competitiveness or FDI strategy requires an overall "vision" of objectives and how they can be achieved. Such visions can differ greatly, depending on the nature of the economy and the government. In the case of the mature East Asian NIEs, one vision – pursued by Singapore – was to rely heavily on FDI, integrate the relatively small economy into TNC production networks and promote competitiveness upgrading within these networks. Another vision, that of the Republic of Korea and Taiwan Province of China, was to develop domestic enterprises and autonomous innovative capabilities, resorting to TNCs for arm's-length sources of technology. Yet another, that of the colonial administration in Hong Kong, was to leave resource allocation largely to market forces, while providing infrastructure and governance. Strategies can be made, of course, without explicit visions. They can emerge from political and social processes, inter-group and intra-governmental interactions, and other internal or external pressures. In such cases, however, there is a risk that policies are not fully coordinated, signals are unclear, difficult strategic decisions are not taken and responses to changes are slow.

This suggests that there is no *ideal* strategy related to competitiveness or FDI for all countries at all times. Any good strategy must be context specific, reflecting the level of economic development, the capabilities of the government, the resource base, the specific technological features of a country and its competitive setting. The appropriate strategy for a country with an advanced industrial and skill base and a well-developed administration must differ from that for a country with rudimentary industry, deficient skills and weak administrative structures.

7.3.3 Static and dynamic competitiveness

The case studies show that TNCs are generally effective vehicles for exploiting *static* comparative advantages in host countries, provided that host countries provide the economic conditions for such exploitation. However, the long-term impact of FDI on competitiveness depends not just on the static exploitation of factor endowments but also on the *dynamics* of skill and technology transfer by TNCs. This depends, in turn, on how much upgrading of local capabilities takes place, how far local linkages deepen, how many complex technological functions are entrusted to affiliates and how closely they integrate with the local technology system. In some cases, static advantages mature naturally into dynamic ones. In others, they do not: TNCs simply exploit existing advantages and relocate as those advantages erode. This happens particularly where the host economy's advantage is based on low-wage unskilled labour or primary resources, and the main TNC export activity is low technology assembly or simple extraction.

The extent to which TNCs dynamically upgrade their technology and skill transfer and raise local capabilities and linkages depends on the interaction of four factors. These are the trade and competition regime; government policies on TNC operations; the corporate strategy and resources of the TNC; and development and responsiveness of local factor markets and institutions.

The trade and industrial policy regime in a host economy provides the incentives that lead enterprises (local and foreign) to develop capabilities. In general, the more competitive and outward-oriented the regime, the more dynamic the restructuring and upgrading process. A highly protected regime, or one with stringent constraints on entry and exit, deters technological upgrading, isolating agents from international trends. This does not mean, however, that free trade or immediate liberalization is the best policy. The costs, risks and difficulties of learning deem that some protection be given to new activities, and that existing activities be granted a period for re-learning; both forms of protection must be complemented by improvements in factor markets, in particular skills and technology. A strongly export-oriented setting with selective trade interventions provides the best setting for upgrading where there are difficult learning processes involved. The Latin American automotive industry is a good example.

However, there is little or no need for trade intervention where local learning is rapid and relatively predictable. This is the case with simple technologies (garments or final assembly of electronic products), or where there are strong cost advantages of local production (extraction of natural resources). In this case, the promotion of competitive activity requires a free trade regime with access to world-priced inputs and inflows of skills and equipment. In economies with high protection such an environment can be provided in export processing zones or their equivalent. Once established, such activities may deepen over time as experience is accumulated, TNCs train local workers and forge local linkages. Whether this is enough to develop self-sustaining competitiveness as wages rise, and technologies or market conditions change, depends on the nature and extent of local learning. Where the activity has very limited learning potential or the local absorptive base of skills is small, the sunk costs to TNCs are manageable and it makes economic sense for them to relocate to other countries that have lower costs and/or higher levels of skill.

In the industries studied, the TNCs were involved in upgrading local capabilities. However, in simple activities like low-level garment assembly the upgrading is unlikely to offset competitive disadvantages resulting from wage differences once trade distortions are removed. In more technology-intensive activities like TV or automobile manufacture, even simple assembly activity leads over time to considerable learning, making it attractive for TNCs to stay and upgrade as wages rise and technologies change. Of these two activities, automobile manufacture is more skill and experience intensive, and its restructuring has been greatly helped by prolonged protection coupled with strong export orientation. In TVs, a free trade regime has been the right environment to promote upgrading by export-oriented TNCs.

The second is government policies on TNC operations: incentives for local training or R&D, pressures to diffuse technologies and so on. Most host countries have such policies. The automotive industry in all the case studies has been subject to local content rules at some stage. The results have been poor when they were not integrated into a wider strategy for upgrading domestic capabilities. As a result, rapid liberalization of the sector has led to local suppliers being massively displaced by foreign entrants, or by imports. Continued slow liberalization will not help if the Government does not undertake measures to raise the skill and technology levels of domestic suppliers, particularly SMEs.

However, this is not an inevitable outcome. Where countries have used local content or other rules as part of a coherent strategy, as in the mature NIEs like Taiwan Province of China or Singapore, the results have been highly beneficial. TNCs have enhanced the technology content of their activities and of their linkages to local firms, which they supported in raising their efficiency and competitiveness. Much of the effort needed by TNCs to upgrade local capabilities involves extra cost and effort; they will not undertake this effort unless persuaded or induced to do so. For the host economy, it is only worth doing so if it leads to efficient outcomes. If upgrading is forced beyond this limit it will not survive in a competitive and open environment. The use of performance requirements is now being constricted by international rules such as the TRIMs Agreement. While there are good reasons for pressing for greater market orientation and level playing fields, it is important to retain policies to correct for market failures – in this case in information, linkage, cluster formation, and learning.

The third factor is TNC strategies. Firms differ between themselves in the extent to which they assign responsibility to different affiliates and decide their position in the global value chain. For instance, Fiat in Brazil has set up an independent R&D facility to design new models for developing countries, when other automotive TNCs are centralizing design activity in the developed world. While TNC strategies are decided on their own perceptions of risk and reward, host Governments can influence some aspects of TNC location by such measures as targeting investors, inducing upgrading by specific tools and incentives and improving local factors and institutions. This requires them to have a clear understanding of TNC strategies; they cannot formulate effective strategies otherwise. An effective FDI promotion agency has to include this as a necessary input into its activities.

The fourth factor, the state and responsiveness of local factor markets and institutions, is probably the most important determinant of dynamic competitiveness. TNCs respond rationally to competitive pressures and market signals, and will upgrade their affiliates where it is cost-efficient to do so. Most firms prefer their suppliers to be nearby to minimize transaction costs and facilitate coordination. However, they deepen local linkages only if suppliers are able to respond to their demands efficiently. Both depend upon the efficacy and development of skills and technological capabilities, supplier networks and support institutions. Without improvements in factor markets, TNCs can improve the skills and capabilities of their employees, but only to a limited extent. They cannot substitute for a local education, training and technology system; in the absence of rising skills and capabilities generally, it will be too costly for them to import advanced technologies and complex, linkage-intensive operations.

Education, training and technology markets in turn may have well-known public good characteristics which lead to market failures. Individuals may invest too little in their own education because of "myopia", risk aversion, lack of information, or lack of finance. Institutions may not provide the right kinds of skills, or may not have the information to design the right courses; in many developing countries, the institutions may not be present at all. Private firms may under-invest in training and knowledge creation because they fear leakage to other firms, they are themselves unaware of the benefits of training or they lack the skills or finance to provide training. SMEs may not receive adequate technical, training and marketing support. Raising local skills and capabilities thus requires widespread policy support. Some are pure public goods that only Governments can provide. Others need Governments to catalyze private provision (including by TNCs themselves) and to regulate its quality and delivery. Whatever the nature of such improvements, there is no doubt that they are critical to realizing the dynamic benefits of foreign (and domestic) investment.

TNCs tend to be industry leaders in providing training. However, the extent of training is generally limited to their operational needs. Exposure to international competition raises these needs and so induces more training. Nevertheless, as noted, such firm-specific private training cannot substitute for public education: without a strong education base, advanced job-related training provided to workers will have its limits. Thus, government investments in general and vocational education is a prerequisite for countries to benefit from firm-specific training offered by TNCs.

At the same time, there exists the risk that TNCs inhibit technological development in the host economy. The case studies confirm that TNCs transfer the results of innovation performed in advanced industrial countries, but they are slower or reluctant in transferring the innovation process itself. With some notable exceptions, foreign affiliates tend to do relatively little R&D apart from that needed for local absorption and adaptation, and one effect of globalization may be further centralization of R&D in home economies. This may not matter for countries at low levels of industrial development, but it becomes a constraint on capability building as countries approach industrial maturity and need to develop autonomous innovative capabilities. Once host countries have built strong local capabilities, TNCs contribute by setting up R&D facilities and interacting with the research establishment. However, at the intermediate stage, the entry of powerful TNCs with ready-made technology can inhibit local technology development, especially when local competitors are too far behind to gain from their presence. Their technology spillovers may, in other words, be negative. There is evidence of this in advanced host economies such as the United Kingdom or Italy; it is even more likely to be the case with semi-industrial host economies that lack the industrial depth of advanced OECD countries.

With respect to the automobile industry, the relevance of these considerations relates to the component sector rather than the final product, where scale and technology considerations have practically ruled out a local presence. However, in Malaysia, Proton provides an exception. Nevertheless, if the firm is to reach the scales and capabilities needed for true international competitiveness, it will be necessary for the Government of Malaysia to support its R&D activity. In supplier industries, on the other hand, it remains possible and desirable to enhance the capabilities of domestic firms, and it is important for Governments to devise policies to strengthen their technological activities.

Even where a host economy adopts a proactive strategy to develop local skills and technology institutions, it is possible to induce TNCs to invest in local R&D even if there is little research capability in local firms. As with many other aspects of FDI strategy, the best example here is Singapore, which has the third highest ratio of enterprise-financed R&D to GDP in the developing world, with most of it coming from foreign affiliates. The appropriate policy response, as before, is to influence TNCs selectively so that local learning is protected and promoted. In countries that do not have technological ambitions for local firms, it is possible to induce advanced TNC technological activity by building skills and institutions.

7.3.4 *Final thoughts on managing FDI policies*

Managing effective FDI policy – in the context of a broader competitiveness strategy – is a demanding task. A passive *laissez faire* approach is inadequate because of deficiencies in markets and existing institutions. Such an approach may not attract sufficient FDI, extract the benefits it offers, or regulate it well by best practice standards. However, the feasibility of any strategy depends critically on the ability of the Government to "deliver". If administrative resources are not appropriate to the skill, information, negotiation and implementation abilities needed, it may be best to move in the direction of minimizing interventions in the market: to simply reduce obstacles in the way of FDI, minimize business costs and leave resource allocation to the market.

Such a *laissez faire* FDI strategy might yield significant short-term benefits, particularly in a host country that has under-performed in terms of competitiveness and investment attraction because of past policies. A strong signal to the investment community that the economy is "open for business" can attract FDI into areas of existing comparative advantage. However, there are two problems. First, if these areas are limited, or their use is held back by poor infrastructure or non-economic risk, there will be little FDI response. Second, even if FDI comes, its benefits are likely to be static and will run out when existing advantages are used up. To ensure that FDI is sustained over time and enters new activities necessarily requires policy intervention, both to target investors and to raise the quality of local factors. Needless to say, the form of intervention has to be very different from traditional patterns of heavy inward-orientation and market-unfriendly policies – it has to be clearly aimed at competitiveness.

Government policy has to suit the particular conditions of the country at the particular time, and evolve as its needs change and its competitive position in the world alters. Making effective policies requires vision, coherence and coordination. It also requires the ability to decide on trade-offs between different objectives of development. In a typical structure of policy making, this requires the strategy-making body to be placed near the Head of Government, so that a strategic view of national needs and priorities can be formed and enforced.

As noted repeatedly, there is no ideal universal policy on FDI and there are no general prescriptions – FDI strategy is an art, not a science.

References

Abidin, M.Z. (1996). 'The Malaysian Experience in the Automotive Industry. Some Lessons and Future Directions', paper prepared for the International Symposium on "The Asian Age of Automotive Industry" organized by the Kia Economic Research Institute (KERI) and the Institute for Economic and Social Research, Jakarta.

Abo, T. (1994). *Hybrid Factory*, Oxford University Press, New York.

Abrenica, M. (1996). 'The Philippine Automotive Industry: A Case Study in Economic Governance', Paper prepared for "Analysis and Review of Competitiveness in Selected Industries in ASEAN", ASEAN Secretariat. Thailand Development Research Institute, Bangkok.

American Chamber of Commerce in Thailand (undated). 'Position Paper – ASEAN Industrial Cooperation Scheme', Bangkok.

Andersen Consulting (1992). *Lean Enterprise Benchmarking Project*. London.

_____ (1994). *The Worldwide Manufacturing Competitiveness Study: The Second Lean Enterprise Report*. London.

Ariff, M. and S.Y. Yew (1996). 'Transnational Corporations and Industrial Restructuring in Developing Countries – The Case of Malaysia', University of Malaya, Faculty of Economics and Administration, Kuala Lumpur (draft).

ASEAN Secretariat (1996). 'Basic Agreement on the ASEAN Industrial Cooperation Scheme'.

Audet, D. (1996). 'Globalisation in the Clothing Industry', in: OECD, *Globalisation of Industry: Overview and Sector Reports*, Paris.

Australian Business Foundation (1997). *The High Road or the Low Road? Alternatives for Australia's Future*, Sydney: Australian Business Foundation Limited.

Bair, J. and G. Gereffi (1998). 'Interfirm Networks and Regional Divisions of Labour: Employment and Upgrading in the Apparel Commodity Chain', paper presented at International Workshop on "Global Production and Local Jobs", International Institute of Labour Studies, Geneva.

Baldwin, R. E. and Martin, P. (1999). 'Two waves of globalisation: superficial similarities, fundamental differences', New York, National Bureau of Economic Research, WP 6904.

Bank Negara Malaysia (various years). *Quarterly Economic Bulletin.*

Bannister, G. and P. Low (1992). 'Textiles and Apparel in NAFTA: A Case of Constrained Liberalization', World Bank Working Paper, WPS 994. Washington: The World Bank.

Barba Navaretti, G. and G. Perosino (1995). 'Re-deployment of Production, Trade Protection and Firms' Global Strategies: the case of Italy', in G. Barba Navaretti, R. Faini and A. Silberston (eds.) *Beyond the Multifibre Arrangement: Third World Competition and Restructuring in Europe's Textile Industry*, Paris: OECD Development Centre.

Barnes, J. and R. Kaplinsky (1998). 'Globalisation and Trade Policy Reform: Whither the Automobile Components Sector in South Africa?' Draft, Durban: School of Development Studies, University of Natal, and Brighton: Institute of Development Studies, University of Sussex.

Battat, J., I. Frank and X. Shen (1996). 'Suppliers to Multinationals. Linkage Programmes to Strengthen Local Companies in Developing Countries', Occasional Paper 6, Foreign Investment Advisory Service, Washington DC: International Finance Corporation and World Bank.

Bedê, M.A. (1997). 'A Política Automotiva not Anos 90', in: G. Arbix, and M. Zilbovicius (eds.) *De JK a FHC: A Reinvenção dos Carros*. Sao Paolo: Scritta, pp. 357-87.

Biggs, T., Shah, M. and Srivastava, P. (1995). *Technological Capabilities and Learning in African Enterprises*, World Bank Technical Paper Number 288, Washington, DC: World Bank.

Blömstrom, M. *Transnational Corporations and Manufacturing Exports from Developing Countries* (New York, U.N. Centre on Transnational Corporations, 1990).

Board of Investment (1993). *Investment Opportunities Study – Electronics Industries in Thailand*, Bangkok, July.

———— (1996a). 'A Guide to the Board of Investment', Bangkok, May.

———— (1996b). 'A Business Guide to Thailand', Bangkok, May.

———— (1996c). 'Key Investment Indicators in Thailand', Bangkok, May.

Bolsa de Comercio de Córdoba (1996). 'Evolución y perspectivas del sector automotriz y autopartista' Serie BCC, Number 6, 20 November

Brooker Group (1997a). 'Automotive Industry Export Promotion Project. Thailand Industry Overview. Executive Summary', prepared for the Office of Industrial Economics, Ministry of Industry, Royal Thai Government, January.

———— (1997b). 'An Overview of the Automotive Industry in the Eastern Seaboard of Thailand', mimeo.

Buckley, P. J. and Muchielli, J.L. (eds.)(1997). *Multinational Firms and International Relocation*, Cheltenham: Edward Elgar.

Bustamente, J. (1983). 'Maquiladoras: A New Face of International Capitalism on Mexico's Northern Frontier', in: J. Nash and M.P. Fernandéz-Kelly (eds.) *Women, Men and the International Division of Labour*. Albany, New York: State University of New York Press.

Carrillo, J. (Coordinator) (1991). 'Mercados de Trabajo en las Actividades In-bond Assemblers, Síntesis del Reporte de Investigación', Secretaría del Trabajo y Previsión Social y El Colegio de la Frontera Norte, Mexico.

———— (1995) 'Flexible Production in the Auto Sector: the industrial reorganisation at Ford-Mexico', *World Development*, 23 (1), pp. 87-101.

_____ (1998). 'Industrial Upgrading in Mexico: The Case of General Motors in the Maquiladora Industry', paper presented at International Workshop 'Global Production and Local Jobs', Geneva: International Institute for Labour Studies.

_____, M. Mortimore and J. Alonso (1997). 'Transnational Corporations and Industrial Restructuring in Mexico: The Auto Parts and Television Receiver Industries', El Colegio de la Frontera Norte, Tijuana, and ECLAC/UNCTAD Joint Unit Santiago.

_____ and Y. Montiel (1997). 'Ford's Hermosillo Plant: the trajectory of development of an hybrid model', in Boyer, Charron, Jurgens and Tolliday (eds.), *Between Imitation and Innovation. The transfer and hybridisation of new models of production in the automobile industry*, Oxford University Press.

Carvalho, R., S. Reis de Queiroz, F. Consoni, I. Costa and J. da Costa (1997). *Abertura Comercial e Mudança Estrutural na Indústria Automobilística Brasileira,* Campinas, Departemento de Política Científica e Tecnológica.

CBI and LBS (1994). *Competitiveness: How the Best UK Companies Are Winning*, London: Confederation of British Industry (CBI) and London Business School (LBS).

Chachage, C.S.L., M. Ericsson and P. Gibbon (1993). *Mining and Structural Adjustment. Studies on Zimbabwe and Tanzania*. Research Report no. 92, Nordiska Afrikainstitutet, Uppsala.

Chudnovsky, D. and A. López (1997). 'Las estrategías de las empresas transnacionales en Argentina y Brasil: ¿que hay de nuevo en los años noventa?', Working Paper 23, CENIT, Buenos Aires, August.

_____, A. López and F. Porta (1997). 'Market or Policy Driven? The Foreign Direct Investment Boom in Argentina' *Oxford Development Studies*, 25 (2), pp. 173-88.

Cid Passarini, G. (1997). 'Transnational Corporations, Industrial Restructuring, and Competitiveness of Developing Countries: The Chilean Case,' Report for UNCTAD Interregional Project on Transnational Corporations, Industrial Restructuring and the Competitiveness of Developing Countries, June.

Competitiveness Policy Council (1993). *Building High Performance Workplaces,* Washington, DC.

Consejo National de Zonas Francas (1994). *Annual Report*. Santo Domingo.

Dailami, M. and M. Walton (1989). 'Private Investment, Government Policy, and Foreign Capital in Zimbabwe', Policy, Planning and Research Working Papers, WPS 248, World Bank, Washington DC.

Darlin, D. (1996). 'Maquiladora-ville', *Forbes*, 6 May.

Datton, D. (1991). 'Foreign direct investment in the U.S. automotive industry', in: Department of Commerce, *Foreign Direct Investment in the United States*, Washington, August.

Department of Statistics of Malaysia (various years). *Industrial Surveys,* Kuala Lumpur.

Dicken, P. (1998). *Global Shift: Transforming the World Economy*, Third Edition, London: Paul Chapman.

Doeringer, P., A. Watson, L. Oxborrow, P. Totterdill, B. Courault and E. Parat (1998b). 'Transforming Apparel Production Channels: Lessons from the Clothing Industry in the US, UK and France', paper presented at the International Workshop on "Global Production and Local Jobs", Geneva: International Institute for Labour Studies.

Doner, R. F. (1991). *Driving a Bargain: Automobile Industrialization and Japanese Firms in Southeast Asia.* Berkeley: University of California Press.

Dunning, J. H. (1993). *The Globalization of Business*, London: Routledge.

EC (1994). 'An Industrial Competitiveness Policy for the European Union', Communication from the Commission to the Council and Parliament, *Bulletin of the European Union*, 3/94.

ECLAC (Economic Commission for Latin America and the Caribbean) (1993). *Directorio sobre Inversión Extranjera en América Latina y el Caribe 1993: Marco Legal e Información Estadística*, (Santiago).

_____ (1994). 'Centroamérica y el TLC: efectos immediatos e implicancias futuras', LC/MEX/R.494 (SEM.68/3), October.

_____ (1997). 'Integración Económica e Inversión Extranjera: La Experiencia Reciente de Argentina y Brasil' *Desarrollo Productivo*, No. 32, Santiago, Chile, July.

_____ (1998). 'Foreign Investment in Latin America and the Caribbean. 1998 Report', Santiago.

ESCAP (Economic and Social Commission for Asia and the Pacific) (1995). 'Sectoral Flows of Foreign Direct Investment in Asia and the Pacific', ESCAP Studies in Trade and Investment 5, New York: United Nations.

_____ (1998). 'Foreign Direct Investment in Selected Asian Countries: Policies, Related Institution-building and Regional Cooperation', Development Papers no. 19, ST/ESCAP/1809. New York: United Nations.

Elson, D. (1994). 'Uneven Development and the Textiles and Clothing Industry', in L. Sklair (ed.) *Capitalism and Development.* London: Routledge.

Ernst, D., T. Ganiatsos and L. Mytelka (1998). *Technological Capabilities and Export Performance: Lessons from East Asia*, New York: United Nations.

Esser, K., W. Hildebrand, D. Messner and J. Meyer-Stamer (1996), *Systemic Competitiveness: New Governance Patterns for Industrial Development*, London: Frank Cass.

Fagerberg, J. (1996). 'Technology and Competitiveness', *Oxford Review of Economic Policy*, 12 (3), pp. 39-51.

Fernandéz-Kelly, M.P. (1983). *For We Are Sold, I and My People: Women and Industry in Mexico's Frontier.* Albany (NY): Suny Press.

Ferro, J.R. (1995). 'International Competition and Globalization Challenging the Brazilian Automotive Agreement', ECLAC/IDRC Project CAN/93/S41, Santiago.

FIAS (1995). 'FDI News Sectoral Focus: the Latin American Auto Industry', *FDI News*, Volume 1, Number 1, World Bank, December.

Financial Times (1997). ' Perspective: The heart of the new world economy', by Martin Wolf, London, October 1, Special issue on *The Global Company*.

Fornengo Pent, G. (1994). 'Diferenciación de productos e innovación de procesos in la industria del vestido in Italia' in: G. van Liemt, (ed.), *La reubicación internacional de la industria: causas y consecuencias*, Geneva: International Labour Organisation.

Freeman, C. and C. Perez (1988). 'Structural Crises of Adjustment, Business Cycles and Investment Behaviour', in G. Dosi et al. (eds.), *Technical Change and Economic Theory*, London: Pinter.

Fujita, K. and R. C. Hill (1997). 'Auto Industrialization in Southeast Asia. National Strategies and Local Development', *ASEAN Economic Bulletin.* 13 (3), pp. 312-332.

Fundación Invertir Argentina (1997). 'Firmas italianas establecidas en Argentina', Buenos Aires.

Gereffi, G. (1994a). 'Capitalism, Development and Global Commodity Chains', in L. Sklair (ed.) *Capitalism and Development*. London: Routledge.

_____ (1994b). 'The Globalization of Taiwan's Garment Industry', in E. Bonacich, E., E. Cheng, N. Chinchilla, N. Hamilton and P. Ong (eds.) *Global Production: The Apparel Industry in the Pacific Rim*, Philadelphia, PA: Temple University Press.

_____ (1996). 'Global Commodity Chains: New Forms of Coordination and Control Among Nations and Firms in International Industries', *Competition and Change*, Vol. 4, 1996.

_____ (1997a). 'International Trade and Industrial Upgrading in the Apparel Commodity Chain', paper presented at the international seminar on "Successful Industrial Competitiveness Policy Experiences: Lessons for Latin American and the Caribbean", ECLAC and Ministry of Economic Affairs, Santiago, Chile.

_____ (1997b). 'Global Shifts and Regional Response: Can North America Meet the Full Package Challenge?', *Bobbin*, Nov. 1997, pp. 16-31.

_____ and M. Korzeniewicz (eds.) (1994). *Commodity Chains and Global Capitalism*, Praeger, Westport, Connecticut.

Heerden, A. van (1998). 'Export Processing Zones: The Cutting Edge of Globalization?', paper presented at the International Workshop on "Global Production and Local Jobs", Institute of Labour Studies, Geneva.

Helleiner, G. K. (1989). 'Transnational corporations and direct foreign investment', in H. B. Chenery and T.N. Srinivasan (eds.), *Handbook of Development Economics,* Amsterdam: Elsevier, pp. 1442-1480.

_____ (ed.) (1995). *Manufacturing for Export in the Developing World: Problems and Prospects*, London: Routledge.

_____ (1997). 'Chilean Copper Policy Since Allende: Mines to the Miner or El Sueldo de Chile?', Draft, Latin American Centre, St Anthony's College, Oxford.

Higashi, S. (1995). 'The Automotive Industry in Thailand: From Protective Promotion to Liberalization', IDE Spot Survey, *The Automotive Industry in Asia: The Great Leap Forward?* Tokyo: Institute of Developing Economies.

Hill, H. (1990). 'Foreign investment and East Asian economic development', *Asian-Pacific Economic Literature,* 4 (2), pp. 21-58.

Hobday, M. (1995). 'East Asian latecomers first: learning the technology of electronics', *World Development*, vol. 23, pp. 1171-1193.

Hughes, K. S. (ed.)(1993). *European Competitiveness*, Cambridge: Cambridge University Press.

Humphrey, J. (1998). 'Globalization and Supply Chain Networks in the Auto Industry: Brazil and India', paper presented at the International Workshop on "Global Production and Local Jobs" Institute of Labour Studies, Geneva, 9-10 March.

_____ (1988). 'Assembler-Supplier Relations in the Auto Industry: Globalisation and National Development', *Mimeo*, Brighton: Institute of Development Studies, University of Sussex.

Hunter, A. (1990). 'Quick Response in Apparel Manufacturing. A Survey of the American Scene', Manchester: The Textile Institute.

Instituto de Economía (UADE) (1996). 'La industria automotriz en Argentina', *Informe Sectorial*, 4.

International Labour Organisation (1984). 'Export Processing Zones and Industrial Development in Asia: Papers and Proceedings of a Technical Workshop', Singapore.

International Trade Centre - UNCTAD/GATT (1994). *Textiles y prendas de vestir: introducción a los requisitos de calidad de diversos mercados*. Geneva.

Jaffee, S., and P. Gordon (1993). 'Exporting High-value Food Commodities. Success Stories from Developing Countries', World Bank Discussion Paper no. 198, Washington, D.C.

Jenkins, C. (1996). 'Post-independence Economic Policy and Investment in Zimbabwe', WPS/97-4, Centre for the Study of African Economies, University of Oxford, Oxford.

Jomo, K.S. (1996). 'Lessons from Growth and Structural Change in the Second-tier South East Asian Newly Industrialising Countries', Study 4, Project sponsored by Government of Japan on "East Asian Development: Lessons for a New Global Environment", UNCTAD, Geneva.

Julius, DeAnne (1990). *Global Companies and Public Policy: The Growing Challenge of Foreign Direct Investment*, London: Pinter Publishers.

Kaplinsky, R. (1994). 'From Mass Production to Flexible Specialization: A Case Study of Microeconomic Change in a Semi-Industrialized. Economy', *World Development*, 22 (3), pp. 337-353.

_____ and A. Posthuma (1994). *Easternisation: The Spread of Japanese Management Techniques to Developing Countries*. Ilford: Frank Cass.

Kathuria, S. (1996). *Competing Through Technology and Manufacturing. A Study of the Indian Commercial Vehicles Industry*. Delhi: Oxford University Press.

Kato, S. (1992). 'Thailand's auto industry', *Asian Monthly Review*, October.

Kirchbach, F. von, and H. Roelofsen (1998). 'Trade in the Southern African Development Community: What is the Potential for Increasing Exports to the Republic of South Africa?', Project on Economic Development and Regional Dynamics in Africa: Lesson from the East Asian Experience, UNCTAD, GDS/MDPB/Misc.11, Geneva.

Kiyoshi Tonooka, E. (1997). 'Super Oferta de Veículos e os Investimentos na Indústria Automobilística Brasilieira', AmchamNet-Brazil Investment Link, Think Tanks.

Kolodziejski, J. (1998). *MERCOSUR's Automotive Industry: Challenges and Prospects to 2005,* Executive Summary.

Kozul-Wright, R. and R. Rowthorn (1998). 'Spoilt for Choice? Multinational Corporations and the Geography of International Production', *Oxford Review of Economic Policy*, 14 (2), 74-92.

Krugman, P. (1996). 'Making Sense of the Competitiveness Debate', *Oxford Review of Economic Policy,* 12 (3), pp. 17-25.

Krugman, P. R. (1994). 'Competitiveness: A Dangerous Obsession', *Foreign Affairs*, 73 (2), pp. 28-44.

Lall, S. (1985). *Multinationals, Technology and Exports,* London: Macmillan.

_____ (1990). *Building Industrial Competitiveness in Developing Countries*, Paris: OECD Development Centre.

_____ (1993). 'Introduction: Transnational Corporations and Economic Development', in S. Lall (ed.), *Transnational Corporations and Economic Development*, Volume 3 of The United Nations Library on Transnational Corporations, London: Routledge.

_____ (1995). 'Malaysia: Industrial Success and the Role of Government', *Journal of International Development*, 7 (5), pp. 759-774.

_____ (1996). *Learning from the Asian Tigers. Studies in Technology and Industrial Policy.* London: Macmillan.

_____ (1997.a). 'Investment, technology and international competitiveness', in J. H. Dunning and K. A. Hamdani (eds.), *The New Globalism and Developing Countries*, Tokyo: United Nations University Press, pp. 232-259.

_____ (1997b). 'Technology Policy and Competitiveness in Malaysia', in K. S. Jomo (ed.), *Industrial Technology in Malaysia*, (forthcoming).

_____ (1998). 'Exports of manufactures by developing countries: Emerging patterns of trade and location', *Oxford Review of Economic Policy*, 14 (2), pp. 54-73.

_____ (ed.). *The Technological Response to Import Liberalisation in Sub-Saharan Africa*, London: Macmillan.

_____ (forthcoming). 'Technological Change and Industrialization in the Asian NIEs: Achievements and Challenges', in R. R. Nelson and L. Kim (eds.), *Innovation and Competitiveness in Newly Industrializing Economies*, Cambridge: Cambridge University Press.

_____, Robinson, P. B. and Wignaraja, G. (1998). 'Zimbabwe: Enhancing Export Competitiveness', Report prepared for the Commonwealth Secretariat.

Lande, S. and N. Crigler (1993). 'The Caribbean and NAFTA: Opportunities and Challenges', Working Paper on Trade in the Western Hemisphere, WP-TWH-51. Inter-American Development Bank / UN Economic Commission for Latin America and the Caribbean, July.

Latsch, W.W. and P.B. Robinson (1999). 'Technology and the Responses of Firms to Adjustment in Zimbabwe', in: S. Lall (ed.), *The Technological Response to Import Liberalisation in Sub-Saharan Africa*, London: Macmillan.

Lecraw, D. J. (1992). 'TNCs and Structural Adjustment in Developing Countries', University of Western Ontario, Canada, Draft prepared for the United Nations Centre on Transnational Corporations.

McKinsey Global Institute (1993). *Manufacturing Productivity*, Washington, D.C.

Mesquita Moreira, M. (1997). 'Nota Técnica AP/DEPEC', No. 9, BNDES.

Moori-Koenig, V. and G. Yoguel (1992). 'Competitividad de la PYMEs autopartistas en el nuevo escenario de apertura e integración subregional', September , CFI-CEPAL, Buenos Aires.

Mortimore, M. (1993). 'Flying Geese or Sitting Ducks? Transnationals and Industry in Developing Countries', *CEPAL Review*, 51, December.

_____ (1995). 'Paths Towards International Competitiveness', Santiago de Chile: ECLAC/UNCTAD Joint Unit, Draft.

_____ (1997). 'The Asian Challenge to the World Automotive Industry', *Revista de Economía Contemporánea*, Number 2, July-December, pp. 67-91.

_____ (1998a). 'Mexico's TNC-centric Industrialization Process', in: R. Kozul-Wright and R. Rowthorn (eds.) *Transnational Corporations and the Global Economy*. Basingstoke: Macmillan, pp. 401-430.

_____ (1998b). 'Getting a Lift: Modernizing Industry by Way of Latin American Integration Schemes. The Example of Automobiles', *Transnational Corporations*, 7 (2), pp. 97-136.

_____ (1999). 'Corporate Strategies and Regional Integration Schemes Involving Developing Countries: The NAFTA and MERCOSUR Automobile Industries', *Journal of Science, Technology and Development*, 16 (2).

_____, J.L. Bonifaz and J.L. Duarte de Oliveira (1997). 'La competitividad internacional: un CANálisis de las experiencias de Asia en desarrollo y América Latina', Desarrollo Productivo series, No. 40, LC/G.1957, United Nations Economic Commission for Latin America and the Caribbean (ECLAC), Santiago, Chile (August).

_____ and W. Peres (1998). 'Policy Competition for Foreign Direct Investment in the Caribbean Basin: Costa Rica, The Dominican Republic and Jamaica', *Desarrollo Productivo,* No. 49, United Nations ECLAC, Santiago.

Mytelka, L. K. (1998). 'Locational Tournaments for FDI: Inward Investment into Europe in a Global World', paper prepared for the Workshop on Globalization of Multinational Enterprise Activity and Economic Development, Glasgow, 15-16 May.

Najmabadi, F. and S. Lall (1995). *Developing Industrial Technology: Lessons for Policy and Practice*, World Bank, OED Study.

Narula, R. and J. H. Dunning (1999). 'Industrial development, globalisation and multinational enterprises: new realities for developing countries', Draft, Universities of Oslo and Reading.

Nelson, R. R. (1993). *National Innovation Systems: A Comparative Analysis*, Oxford: Oxford: University Press.

Nipon, P. and T. Pawadee (1998). 'Technological Capability Building and the Sustainability of Export Success in Thailand's Textile and Electronics Industries', in D. Ernst, T. Ganiatsos and L. Mytelka (eds.), *Technological Capabilities and Export Success in Asia*, London: Routledge, pp. 157-210.

O'Brien, P. and Y. Karmokolias (1994). 'Radical Reform in the Automotive Industry: Policies in the Emerging Markets', IFC Discussion Paper Number 21, Washington DC: World Bank.

O'Keefe, T.A. (1996). 'The MERCOSUR Success Story', *Latin Finance*, p. 84.

Organisation for Economic Co-operation and Development (OECD) (1987). *Structural Adjustment and Economic Performance,* Paris: OECD.

_____ (1994). *Globalization and Competitiveness: Relevant Indicators*, Paris: OECD Directorate for Science, Technology and Industry, DSTI/EAS/IND/WP9(94)19.

_____ (1995). 'Foreign Direct Investment in Argentina. Note by the Participants from Argentina', Workshop on Foreign Direct Investment, Wellington, New Zealand, SG/DNME/CIME(95)7.

Office of Technology Assessment (1990). *Making Things Better: Competing in Manufacturing*, Washington DC: U. S. Senate.

Office of the President of the United States (1997). 'Study on the Operation and Effects of the North American Free Trade Agreement', Washington DC.

Olea, M.A. (1993). 'The Mexican Automobile Industry in NAFTA Negotiations', in C. Molot (ed.), *Driving Continentally: National Policies and the North American Auto Industry*. Ottawa: Carleton University Press.

Oliber, M. (1998). 'Productive and Technological Behaviour of Auto MNCs in Argentina before and During Globalisation and its Effects on Technological Development: The Case of Fiat', MSc Thesis, Science and Technology Research Unit (SPRU), University of Sussex.

Oman, C. (1989). *New Forms of International Investment in Developing Countries: Mining, Petrochemicals, Textiles and Food*. Paris: OECD Development Centre.

_____ (1994). *Globalisation and Regionalisation: The Challenge for Developing Countries*, Paris: OECD Development Centre.

Panchamukhi, V. R. (1996). 'WTO and Industrial Policies', East Asian Development: Lessons for A New Global Environment, Project sponsored by the Government of Japan, Study No. 7. Geneva: UNCTAD.

Pasuk, P. and C. Baker (1998). *Thailand's Boom and Bust*. Chiang Mai: Silkworm Books.

Pavitt, K. (1984). 'Sectoral Patterns of Technical Change: Towards a Taxonomy and a Theory', *Research Policy*, 13, pp. 343-73.

Peres, W. (1994). "Latin America's Experience with Technology Policies: Current Situation and Prospects", *International Journal of Technology Management*, No. 9, issues 2/3.

Perez, T. (1998). *Multinational Enterprises and Technological Spillovers*, Amsterdam: Harwood Academic Publishers.

Piatti, L. and D. Spinanger (1995). 'Re-deployment of Production, Trade Protection and Firms' Global Strategies: the case of Germany' in: G. Barba Navaretti, R. Faini and A. Silberston (eds.), *Beyond the Multifibre Arrangement: Third World Competition and Restructuring in Europe's Textile Industry*, Paris: OECD Development Centre.

Pietrobelli, C. (1998). *Industry, Competitiveness and Technological Capabilities in Chile: A New Tiger From Latin America?*, Macmillan, London.

Porter, A. L., Roessner, J. D., Newman, N. and Cauffiel, D. (1996). 'Indicators of high technology competitiveness of 28 countries', *International Journal of Technology Management*, 12 (1), pp. 1-32.

Porter, M. (1990). *The Competitive Advantage of Nations*, New York: Free Press.

Posthuma, A. C. (1995). 'Restructuring and Changing Market Conditions in the Brazilian Auto Components Industry', ECLAC/IDRC Project CAN/93/S41, Santiago.

Pyke, F. (1998). 'Networks, Development and Change', paper at the International Workshop on "Global Production and Local Jobs", International Institute of Labour Studies, Geneva.

Raffaelli, M. (1994). 'Some Considerations on the Multi-Fibre Arrangement: Past, Present and Future', in S. D. Meyanathan, *Managing Restructuring in the Textile and Garment Sector: Examples from Asia*, EDI Seminar Series, Washington DC: World Bank.

Rapp, W.V. (1995). 'Japanese Producers and the Strategic Development of Vietnam's Automobile Industry' in B. Duffield Uvic (ed.) *Vietnam and Japan*. Center for Asia-Pacific Initiatives. Victoria: University of Victoria.

Rasiah, R. (1990). 'Review of Linkage Development in the Export Processing Manufacturing Sector – Particular Focus on the Electric / Electronics and Textiles / Garment Industries', Malaysian Industrial Policy Studies and the Industrial Master Plan, UNIDO, Vienna.

_____ (1996). 'Malaysia', in A.B. Supapol (ed.) *Transnational Corporations and Backward Linkages in Asian Electronics Industries*. New York: United Nations, pp. 175-210.

Reddy, P. (1997). 'New trends in globalization of corporate R&D and implications for innovation capability in host countries: a survey from India', *World Development*, 25 (11), pp. 1821-1838.

Reinert, E. (1995). 'Competitiveness and its predecessors — A 500 year cross-national perspective', *Structural Change and Economics Dynamics*, 6, pp. 23-42.

Rodrik, D. (1996). 'Coordination failures and government policy: A model with applications to East Asia and Eastern Europe', *Journal of International Economics*, No. 40 (issues 1/2), pp. 1-22.

Ros, J. (1994). 'Mexico's Trade and Industrialization Experience Since 1960: A Reconsideration of Past Policies and Assessment of Current Reforms', in G. K. Helleiner (ed.), *Trade Policy and Industrialization in Turbulent Times*, London: Routledge.

Rowthorn, R. (1997). 'Replicating the Experience of Newly Industrializing Economies', Working Paper, Research Programme on Industrial Organisation, Competitive Strategy and Business Performance, ESRC Centre for Business Research, University of Cambridge.

Sargent, J. and L. Matthews (1997). 'Skill Development and Integrated Manufacturing in Mexico', *World Development*, 25 (10), pp. 1669-1682.

Scott, B. and Lodge, G. (1985). *US Competitiveness in the World Economy*, Boston: Harvard Business School Press.

SECOFI (1994). 'Principales proyectos de inversión extranjera', *Comercio Exterior*, 44 (5).

Selassie, H.G. (1995). *International Joint Venture Formation in the Agribusiness Sector: The Case of Sub-Saharan African Countries,* Avebury, Aldershot.

Shaiken, H. (1995). 'Technology and Work Organization in Latin American Motor Vehicle Industries', ECLAC, CEPAL/IDRC Project CAN/93/S41, Santiago.

_____ and S. Herzenberg (1987). 'Automation and Global Production: Automobile Engine Production in Mexico, the United States and Canada', Monograph Series no. 26, Center for US-Mexican Studies, University of California, San Diego

Shauki, A. (1996). 'The Indonesian Automobile Industry', ASEAN Secretariat for the project "Analysis and Review of Competitiveness in Selected Industries in ASEAN", Thailand Development Research Institute, Bangkok.

Shepherd, G. (1981). 'Textile Industry Adjustment in Developed Countries', Thames Essays, No. 31. London: Trade Policy Research Centre.

Sieh, M.L. and Yew, S.Y. (forthcoming). 'Trade and Investment Link – The Case of Malaysia', in IDRC, *Harnessing Diversity: Multinationals and East Asian Integration,* Ottawa.

Sindipeças (1994). 'Perfil do Setor'. São Paolo: Sindipeças.

Spar, D. (1998). 'Attracting High Technology Investment: INTEL's Costa Rica Plant', Foreign Investment Advisory Service, Occasional Paper No. 11, Washington DC: International Finance Corporation and the World Bank.

Spinanger, D. (1994). 'La repercusión de los cambios estructurales y tecnológicos en el empleo de la industria del vestido' in G. van Liemt, (ed.), *La reubicación internacional de la industria: causas y consecuencias*. Geneva: International Labour Organisation.

Stiglitz, J. E. (1996). 'Some Lessons from the East Asian Miracle', *The World Bank Research Observer*, 11 (2), pp. 151-177.

Supapol, A.B. (1996). 'Thailand', in A. B. Supapol (ed.) *Transnational Corporations and Backward Linkages in Asian Electronics Industries*. New York: United Nations, pp. 24-287.

Swinden, P. (1994). 'Zimbabwe: An Objective Study of Investment Conditions', Zimbabwe Country Report, Century House Information, Harare.

Takayasu, K. (1996a). 'The Outlook for the Automobile Industry in Southeast Asia', *Pacific Business and Industries*, 3 (33).

_____ (1996b). 'General Overview and Development Policies of Automobile Industry in Southeast Asia in the Era of Competition', *Pacific Business and Industries*, 3 (33).

Teitel, S. and F. E. Thoumi (1994). 'From Autarchic Import Substitution to Exports: Technology and Skills in Zimbabwe's Manufacturing', Draft report for the Regional Programme on Enterprise Development, World Bank, Washington DC.

Thailand Development Research Institute (1996). 'The Evaluation of Thailand's Tariff Reductions and their Competitiveness Impact in the World Market' (in Thai), Bangkok.

_____ (1998). *Direction for Manpower Development for Long-term Industrial Development. Executive Summary.* Submitted to the Office of Industrial Statistics, Ministry of Industry, Bangkok.

Thammavit, T. (1997). 'The Automotive Industry in Thailand', paper for ASEAN Secretariat project "Analysis and Review of Competitiveness in Selected Industries in ASEAN", Thailand Development Research Institute, Bangkok.

Torp, J.-E. (1997). 'Transnational Corporations and Industrial Restructuring in Developing Countries: Zimbabwe Case Study', Report prepared for the UNCTAD Interregional Project on Transnational Corporations, Industrial Restructuring and the Competitiveness of Developing Countries, July.

UBS Global Research (1997). 'The Automobile Industry. Toyota and Japan 1996', Zurich.

United Kingdom Cabinet Office (1996). *Competitiveness: Creating the Enterprise Centre of Europe*, London: Her Majesty's Stationery Office.

United Nations Conference on Trade and Development (UNCTAD) (1993). *World Investment Report 1993: Transnational Corporations and Integrated International Production*, New York: United Nations.

_____ (1994). *World Investment Report 1994: Transnational Corporations, Employment and the Workplace* (New York and Geneva: United Nations).

_____ (1995). *World Investment Report 1995: Transnational Corporations and Competitiveness* (New York and Geneva: United Nations).

_____ (1996). *Trade and Development Report 1996* (New York and Geneva: United Nations).

_____ (1997a). *World Investment Report 1997: Transnational Corporations, Market Structure and Competition Policy* (New York and Geneva: United Nations).

_____ (1997b). 'Diversification in Commodity-dependent Countries: The Role of Governments, Enterprises and Institutions', UNCTAD Secretariat, TD/B/COM.1/12.

_____ (1998a). *World Investment Report 1998: Trends and Determinants* (New York and Geneva: United Nations).

_____ (1998b). *Trade and Development Report 1998 Determinants* (New York and Geneva: United Nations).

_____ (1998c). *The Financial Crisis in Asia and Foreign Direct Investment: An Assessment Determinants* (New York and Geneva: United Nations).

_____ (1999a). *World Investment Report 1999: Foreign Direct Investment and the Challenge of Development Determinants* (New York and Geneva: United Nations).

_____ (1999b). *Foreign Direct Investment and Development*, UNCTAD Series on issues in international investment agreements *Determinants* (New York and Geneva: United Nations).

_____ (2000). *World Investment Report 2000: Cross-border Mergers and Acquisition and Development* (New York and Geneva: United Nations).

United Nations Development Programme (UNDP) (1995). *Human Development Report*. Oxford University Press, Oxford.

UNESCO (1995). *World Education Report*. UNESCO: Paris.

_____ (1997). *World Education Report*. UNESCO: Paris.

United Nations (1998). 'World Commodity Trends and Prospects'. New York: United Nations General Assembly, GA/A/53/319.

UNIDO (1991). *Industry and Development Global Report 1990/91*, Vienna: UNIDO.

United States International Trade Commission (1995a). 'Production Sharing: Use of US Components and Materials in Foreign Assembly Operations, 1990-1993', USITC Publication 2886, Washington DC.

_____ (1995b). 'Caribbean Basin Recovery Act: Impact on US Industries and Consumers. Tenth Report', USITC Publication 2927, Washington DC.

US Congress (1992). 'US-Mexico Trade: Pulling Together or Pulling Apart?', Office of Technology Assessment, US Government Printing Office, ITE-545, Washington DC.

US Department of Commerce (1981). *US Direct Investment Abroad: Benchmark Survey*, 1977, Washington DC.

_____ (1985). *US Direct Investment Abroad: Benchmark Survey*, 1982, Washington DC.

_____ (1991). *US Direct Investment Abroad: Benchmark Survey,* 1989, Washington DC.

US International Trade Commission (1997). 'The Impact of the North American Free Trade Agreement on the US Economy and Industries: a three-year review', Investigation No. 332-381, Washington DC.

USITC (1997a). 'Production Sharing: Use of US Components and Materials in Foreign Assembly Operations, 1992-1995', USITC Publication 3032, Washington DC.

_____ (1997b). 'The Impact of the North American Free Trade Agreement on the US Economy and Industries: A Three-year Review', Investigation No. 332-381, Washington, D.C., July.

Vickery, G. (1996). 'Globalization of the Automobile Industry', in OECD, *Globalization of Industry: Overview and Sector Reports*, Paris: OECD.

Wells, L. T. and A. G. Wint (1990). *Marketing a Country: Promotion as a Tool for Attracting Foreign Investment*, Foreign Investment Advisory Service, Washington DC: International Finance Corporation and World Bank.

Werner International Inc. (1996). *Apparel Hourly Labour Cost,* New York.

Willmore, L. (1996). 'Export Processing in the Caribbean: Lessons from Four Case Studies', Working Paper No. 42, ECLAC, Port of Spain Office, Trinidad.

Womack, J.P., D.T. Jones and D. Roos (1990). *The Machine that Changed the World. The Story of Lean Production.* New York: Rawson / Macmillan.

Wong, P-K (1997). 'Creation of a Regional Hub for Flexible Production: The Case of the Hard Disk Drive Industry in Singapore', *Industry and Innovation*, 4 (2), pp. 1-23.

Wong, S. T. (1994). 'Singapore', in: S. D. Meyanathan (ed.) *Industrial Structures and the Development of Small and Medium Enterprise Linkages: Examples from East Asia*, EDI Seminar Series, Washington DC: World Bank.

Wonnacott, P. (1996). 'The Automotive Industry in Southeast Asia: Can Protection Be Made Less Costly?' *World Economy*, 19 (1), pp. 89-112

World Bank (1992). 'Export Processing Zones', Policy and Research Series No. 20, Washington DC.

_____ (1993). *The East Asian Miracle: Economic Growth and Public Policy*, Oxford: Oxford University Press.

_____ (1996). 'Staff Appraisal Report Zimbabwe. Enterprise Development Project', Report no. 15062-ZIM, Macro, Industry and Finance Division, Africa Region, Washington DC.

_____ (1997). *Global Development Finance*, Vol. 2, Washington DC.

_____ (1999). *World Development Report 1998/99*, Oxford: Oxford University Press.

World Economic Forum (1998). *Global Competitiveness Report 1998*, Geneva.

World Trade Organization (WTO) (1995a). *Trading into the Future,* Geneva.

_____ (1995b). *Trade Policy Review, Costa Rica*, Volumes I and II, Geneva.

_____ (1996a). *Trade Policy Review, Dominican Republic*, Volumes I and II, Geneva.

_____ (1996b). *Trade Policy Review, Kingdom of Morocco*, Volumes I and II, Geneva.

World Trade Organisation (1997). *Trade Policy Review, Brazil 1996,* Geneva.

Yearbook of World Electronics Data (1994). London: Elsevier.

Yew, S.Y. (1997). 'Findings of Interviews with Malaysia-based Television Assemblers', Faculty of Economics and Administration, University of Malaya, Kuala Lumpur, mimeo.

Yukawa, T. (1995). 'Nihon no Jidosha Buhin meka no Higashi Ajia ni Okeru Katsudo Jisseki ni Tsuite (Past Activity of Japanese Automobile Parts Manufacturers in East Asia)', Japan Institute for Overseas Investment, Kaigai Toyushi, 3 (6), quoted in Higashi (1995).

Zampetti, A. B. (1996). 'Globalization in the Consumer Electronics Industry' in OECD, *Globalization of Industry: Overview and Sector Studies,* Paris.

Zapata, F., T. Hoshino and L. Hanono (1994). 'La restructuración industrial en México: el caso de la industria de autopartes', Cuadernos del CES, No. 37, El Colegio de México.

ANNEX TABLES AND ANNEX

Annex table 2.1. Fifty fastest growing manufactures in world trade, ranked by 1995 value
(Millions of dollars and per cent)

SITC Number	Product	1980	1990	1995	Average annual growth rate (per cent) 1981-1990	1991-1995	1981-1995
776	Transistors, valves, etc.	14 004.7	59 011.5	171 332.9	15.5	23.8	18.2
752	Automatic data processing equipment	12 519.6	67 365.9	126 772.8	18.3	13.5	16.7
764	Telecom eqpt, pts, acc nes	19 217.6	56 642.0	112 415.3	11.4	14.7	12.5
759	Office, adp mach pts, access.	9 062.4	47 946.6	91 072.3	18.1	13.7	16.6
778	Electrical machinery nes	14 358.4	36 646.2	76 544.0	9.8	15.9	11.8
541	Medicinal, pharm products	14 010.0	36 150.0	69 982.3	9.9	14.1	11.3
772	Switchgear etc., parts nes	12 998.1	35 277.3	63 653.0	10.5	12.5	11.2
728	Other mach for spcl industries	15 631.8	37 569.3	59 653.7	9.2	9.7	9.3
893	Articles of plastic nes	8 229.2	28 697.4	48 581.4	13.3	11.1	12.6
821	Furniture, parts thereof	10 029.0	28 914.3	45 432.8	11.2	9.5	10.6
699	Base metal mfrs. nes	10 748.1	23 737.4	37 384.5	8.2	9.5	8.7
741	Heating, cooling equip	11 245.1	22 966.2	36 721.1	7.4	9.8	8.2
598	Misc. chem. products nes	9 537.3	21 077.5	34 289.9	8.3	10.2	8.9
743	Pumps nes, centrifuges etc.	8 508.1	19 685.8	31 634.4	8.8	10.0	9.1
894	Toys, sporting goods, etc.	8 135.1	19 262.5	30 439.4	9.0	9.6	9.2
582	Prod of condensation etc.	6 976.5	16 153.5	28 150.2	8.8	11.7	9.7
773	Electr distributing equip	5 139.0	13 244.3	26 319.5	9.9	14.7	11.5
716	Rotating electric plant	6 616.9	13 090.2	23 733.4	7.1	12.6	8.9
642	Paper, etc., precut, articles	5 075.2	13 025.1	21 559.9	9.9	10.6	10.1
846	Under garments knitted	3 402.3	11 841.9	21 254.2	13.3	12.4	13.0
771	Electric power mach nes	3 397.9	10 532.8	21 191.1	12.0	15.0	13.0
533	Pigments, paints, etc.	4 540.6	11 730.8	18 845.8	10.0	9.9	10.0
657	Special textile fabric, prods	4 504.9	11 072.1	18 477.6	9.4	10.8	9.9
515	Organic-inorganic compounds	5 188.9	11 573.7	18 408.9	8.4	9.7	8.8
553	Perfumery, cosmetics, etc.	2 811.6	10 068.9	18 048.5	13.6	12.4	13.2
762	Radio broadcast receivers	5 891.2	11 311.5	17 773.5	6.7	9.5	7.6
785	Cycles, etc. motoried or not	6 033.8	9 753.4	17 167.0	4.9	12.0	7.2
513	Carboxylic acids etc.	4 406.9	9 835.3	16 934.8	8.4	11.5	9.4
783	Road motor vehicles nes	3 617.5	6 556.2	16 534.0	6.1	20.3	10.7
899	Other manufactured goods	4 395.7	10 433.9	16 481.2	9.0	9.6	9.2
872	Medical instruments nes	2 904.1	9 897.2	16 249.6	13.0	10.4	12.2
664	Glass	3 565.5	9 255.2	15 264.8	10.0	10.5	10.2
098	Edible products, preps nes	2 763.5	7 326.8	14 995.7	10.2	15.4	11.9
812	Plumbing, heating, lighting equip	3 493.5	8 702.3	13 664.0	9.6	9.4	9.5
635	Wood manufactures nes	3 216.5	7 789.9	13 295.0	9.2	11.3	9.9
512	Alcohol, phenols etc.	3 872.2	7 748.4	12 194.1	7.2	9.5	7.9
774	Electro-medical, x-ray equip	2 676.7	7 622.7	11 972.1	11.0	9.4	10.5
881	Photo apparatus, equip nes	4 334.9	7 251.6	11 391.1	5.3	9.5	6.7
844	Under garments not knit	2 219.0	6 861.5	11 344.3	12.0	10.6	11.5
554	Soap, cleansing etc. preps	3 065.9	6 939.2	10 840.8	8.5	9.3	8.8
655	Knitted, etc. fabrics	2 560.5	6 015.0	10 426.6	8.9	11.6	9.8
694	Steel, copper nails, nuts, etc.	2 944.7	6 575.9	10 408.5	8.4	9.6	8.8
831	Travel goods, handbags	2 608.7	6 298.9	10 161.6	9.2	10.0	9.5
628	Rubber articles nes	1 809.6	4 774.7	8 783.7	10.2	13.0	11.1
871	Optical instruments	1 144.4	3 809.4	7 686.6	12.8	15.1	13.5
592	Starch, insulin, gluten, etc.	1 683.4	4 620.3	7 281.9	10.6	9.5	10.3
621	Materials of rubber	1 703.2	3 971.7	6 302.3	8.8	9.7	9.1
014	Meat prepd, prsvd, nes etc.	1 961.3	3 937.9	5 827.2	7.2	8.2	7.5
712	Steam engines, turbines	1 435.5	1 577.4	2 628.6	0.9	10.8	4.1
873	Meters and counters nes	637.5	1 343.7	2 408.1	7.7	12.4	9.3
	Total 50 products	**300 833.9**	**833 493.2**	**1 539 915.7**	**10.7**	**13.1**	**11.5**
	Total world manufactured exports	**1 082 682.6**	**2 543 430.0**	**3 820 965.7**	**8.8**	**8.5**	**8.7**

Source: UNCTAD.

Annex Table 2.2. Technological classification of exports [a]

Classification	SITC Category	Product	Classification	SITC Category	Product
R	001	Live animals for food	R	233	Rubber, synthetic, reclaimed
R	011	Meat fresh, chilled, frozen	R	244	Cork, natural, raw, waste
R	012	Meat dried, salted, smoked	R	245	Fuel wood nes, charcoal
R	014	Meat prepd, prsvd, nes	R	246	Pulpwood, chips, woodwaste
R	022	Milk and cream	R	247	Other wood rough, squared
R	023	Butter	R	248	Wood shaped, sleepers
R	024	Cheese and curd	R	251	Pulp and waste paper
R	025	Eggs, birds, fresh, prsrvd	R	261	Silk
R	034	Fish, fresh, chilled, frozen	R	263	Cotton
R	035	Fish salted, dried, smoked	R	264	Jute, other tex tile based fibres
R	036	Shell fish fresh, frozen	R	265	Veg fibre, excl. Cotton, jute
R	037	Fish etc prepd, prsvd nes	R	266	Synthetic fibres to spin
R	041	Wheat etc. Unmilled	R	267	Other man-made fibres
R	042	Rice	R	268	Wool (exc tops), anml hair
R	043	Barley unmilled	R	269	Waste of textile fabrics
R	044	Maize unmilled	R	271	Fertilizers, crude
R	045	Cereals nes unmilled	R	273	Stone, sand and gravel
R	046	Wheat etc. Meal or flour	R	274	Sulphur, unrstd iron pyrte
R	047	Other cereal meals, flour	R	277	Natural abrasives nes
R	048	Cereal etc. Preparations	R	278	Other crude minerals
R	054	Veg etc. Fresh, smply prsvd	R	281	Iron ore, concentrates
R	056	Vegtbles etc. Prsvd, prepd	R	282	Iron and steel scrap
R	057	Fruit, nuts, fresh, dried	R	286	Uranium, thorium ore, conc
R	058	Fruit preserved, prepared	R	287	Base metal ores, conc nes
R	061	Sugar and honey	R	288	Nonferr metal scrap nes
R	062	Sugar candy non-chocolate	R	289	Prec mtal ores, waste nes
R	071	Coffee and substitutes	R	291	Crude animal mtrials nes
R	072	Cocoa	R	292	Crude veg materials nes
R	073	Chocolate and products	R	322	Coal, lignite and peat
R	074	Tea and mate	R	323	Briquets, coke, semi-coke
R	075	Spices	R	333	Crude petroleum
R	081	Feeding stuff for animals	R	334	Petroleum products, refin
R	091	Margarine and shortening	R	335	Residual petrlm prod nes
R	098	Edible prodcts, preps nes	R	341	Gas, natural and manufctd
R	111	Non-alcohl beverages nes	Y	351	Electric current
R	112	Alcoholic beverages	R	411	Animal oils and fats
R	121	Tobacco unmnfctrd, ref	R	423	Fixed veg oils, soft
R	122	Tobacco, manufactured	R	424	Fixed veg oil nonsoft
R	211	Hides, skins, exc furs, raw	R	431	Procesd anml veg oil, etc.
R	212	Furskins, raw	U	511	Hydrocarbons nes, derivs
R	222	Seeds for 'soft' fixed oil	U	512	Alcohols, phenols etc.
R	223	Seeds for oth fixed oils	U	513	Carboxylic acids etc.
R	232	Natural rubber, gums	U	514	Nitrogen-fnctn compounds
U	515	Org-inorg compounds etc.	U	681	Silver, platinum, etc
U	516	Other organic chemicals	U	682	Copper exc cement copper
U	522	Inorg elemnts, oxides, etc	U	683	Nickel
U	523	Othr inorg chemicals etc	U	684	Aluminium
U	524	Radioactive etc material	U	685	Lead
U	531	Synt dye, nat indgo, lakes	U	686	Zinc
U	532	Dyes nes, tanning prod	U	687	Tin
U	533	Pigments, paints, etc	U	688	Uranium, thorium, alloys
W	541	Medicinal, pharm products	U	689	Non-fer base metals nes
U	551	Essentl oils, perfume, etc	S	691	Structures and parts nes
U	553	Perfumery, cosmetics, etc	S	692	Metal tanks, boxes, etc
U	554	Soap, cleansing etc preps	S	693	Wire products non electr

Annex Table 2.2. Technological classification of exports [a] (continued)

Classification	SITC Category	Product	Classification	SITC Category	Product
U	562	Fertilizers, manufactured	S	694	Stl, coppr nails, nuts, etc
U	572	Explosives, pyrotech prod	S	695	Tools
U	582	Prod of condensation etc	S	696	Cutlery
U	583	Polymerization etc prods	S	697	Base mtl household equip
U	584	Cellulose derivativs etc	S	699	Base metal mfrs nes
U	585	Plastic material nes	U	711	Steam boilers & aux plnt
U	591	Pesticides, disinfectants	U	712	Steam engines, turbines
U	592	Starch, inulin, gluten, etc	V	713	Intrnl combus piston engines
U	598	Miscel chem products nes	U	714	Engines and motors nes
T	611	Leather	U	716	Rotating electric plant
T	612	Leather etc manufactures	U	718	Oth power generatg machy
T	613	Fur skins tanned, dressed	U	721	Agric machy, exc tractors
U	621	Materials of rubber	U	722	Tractors non-road
U	625	Rubber tyres, tubes etc	U	723	Civil engneerg equip etc
U	628	Rubber articles nes	U	724	Textile, leather machnry
S	633	Cork manufactures	U	725	Paper etc mill machinery
S	634	Veneers,plywood,etc	U	726	Printg, bkbindg machy, pts
S	635	Wood manufactures nes	U	727	Food machry non-domestic
S	641	Paper and paperboard	U	728	Oth machy for spcl indus
S	642	Paper, etc, precut, arts of	U	736	Metalworking mach-tools
T	651	Textile yarn	U	737	Metalworking machnry nes
T	652	Cotton fabrics, woven	U	741	Heating, cooling equipmnt
T	653	Woven man-made fib fabric	U	742	Pumps for liquids etc
T	654	Oth woven textile fabric	U	743	Pumps nes,centrfuges etc
T	655	Knitted, etc fabrics	U	744	Mechanical handling equ
T	656	Lace, ribbons, tulle, etc	U	745	Nonelec machy, tools nes
T	657	Special txtl fabrc, prods	U	749	Nonelec mach pts, acc nes
T	658	Textile articles nes	X	751	Office machines
T	659	Floor coverings, etc	X	752	Automtic data proc equip
S	661	Lime, cement, bldg prods	X	759	Office, adp mch pts, acces
S	662	Clay, refractory bldg prd	X	761	Television receivers
S	663	Mineral manufactures nes	X	762	Radio broadcast receivers
S	664	Glass	X	763	Sound recordrs, phonogrph
S	665	Glassware	X	764	Telecom eqpt, pts, acc nes
S	666	Pottery	W	771	Electric power machy nes
S	667	Pearl, prec-, semi-p stone	W	772	Switchgear etc, parts nes
S	671	Pig iron etc	W	773	Electr distributng equip
S	672	Iron, steel primary forms	W	774	Electro-medcl, xray equip
S	673	Iron, steel shapes etc	W	775	Household type equip nes
S	674	Iron, steel univ, plate, sheet	W	776	Transistors, valves, etc
S	675	Iron, steel hoop, strip	W	778	Electrical machinery nes
S	676	Railway rails etc iron, stl	V	781	Pass motor veh exc buses
S	677	Iron, stl wire (excl w rod)	V	782	Lorries, spcl mtr veh nes
S	678	Iron, stl tubes, pipes, etc	V	783	Road motor vehicles nes
S	679	Iron, stl castings unworkd	V	784	Motor veh prts, acces nes
V	785	Cycles, etc motrzd or not	U	881	Photo apparat, equipt nes
V	786	Trailers, nonmotr veh, nes	U	882	Photo, cinema supplies
U	791	Railway vehicles	Y	883	Developed cinema film
W	792	Aircraft etc	U	884	Optical goods nes
S	793	Ships and boats etc	U	885	Watches and clocks

Annex Table 2.2. Technological classification of exports [a] (concluded)

Classification	SITC Category	Product	Classification	SITC Category	Product
S	812	Plumbg, heatng, lightng equ	S	892	Printed matter
S	821	Furniture, parts thereof	S	893	Articles of plastic nes
T	831	Travel goods, handbags	S	894	Toys, sporting goods, etc
T	842	Mens outerwear not knit	S	895	Office supplies nes
T	843	Womens outerwear nonknit	Y	896	Works of art etc
T	844	Under garments not knit	S	897	Gold, silver ware, jewelry
T	845	Outerwear knit nonelastc	S	898	Musical instruments, pts
T	846	Under garments knitted	S	899	Other manufactured goods
T	847	Textile clothing acces nes	Y	911	Mail not classed by kind
T	848	Headgear, nontxtl clothing	Y	931	Special transactions
T	851	Footwear	Y	941	Zoo animals,pets etc
W	871	Optical instruments	Y	951	War firearms,ammunition
W	872	Medical instruments nes	Y	961	Coin nongold, noncurrent
W	873	Meters and counters nes	Y	971	Gold, non monetary nes
W	874	Measuring, controlng instr			

Source: UNCTAD, based on COMTRADE and OECD (1987).

[a] Technological classification is as follows:
R: Natural resource-intensive
S: Low-technology less textile, garment and footwear cluster
T: Textile, garment and footwear cluster
U: Medium-technology less automotive cluster
V: Automotive cluster
W: High-tech less electronics cluster
X: Electronics cluster
Y: Other transactions and products

Note: S and T correspond to the low-technology set of products referred to in box 2.1, U and V relate to medium technology, and W, X, Y to the high-technology set of products.

Annex table 4.1. Garment exports from case-study countries to major markets
(Thousands of dollars and per cent)

SITC and item	Value			Annual average rate of growth Per cent		Value			Annual average rate of growth Per cent	
	Exports to Western Europe					**Exports to OECD countries**				
Morocco	1980	1990	1995	1980-1990	1990-1995	1980	1990	1995	1980-1990	1990-1995
842 Men's outerwear not knit	36 603.2	381 953.8	615 882.6	26.4	10.0	36 884.5	383 880.5	624 629.4	26.4	10.2
843 Women's outerwear nonknit	20 798.1	376 944.6	643 712.6	33.6	11.3	21 522.9	395 274.3	675 608.8	33.8	11.3
844 Under garments not knit	19 121.4	115 675.1	193 173.6	19.7	10.8	19 140.3	116 270.4	194 187.1	19.8	10.8
845 Outerwear knit nonelastc	24 275.7	262 690.4	354 761.0	26.9	6.2	24 389.6	264 537.3	356 947.4	26.9	6.2
846 Under garments knitted	10 132.1	77 677.3	175 113.5	22.6	17.7	10 221.7	78 597.9	177 534.1	22.6	17.7
847 Textile clothing acces nes	2 586.5	10 563.5	17 712.7	15.1	10.9	2 593.9	10 634.6	17 774.8	15.2	10.8
848 Headgear, nontxtl clothing	6 743.1	46 137.1	25 560.7	21.2	-11.1	6 774.6	47 574.0	26 793.0	21.5	-10.8
Total	120 260.1	1 271 641.8	2 025 916.7	26.6	9.8	121 527.5	1 296 768.8	2 073 474.6	26.7	9.8
	Exports to United States					**Exports to OECD countries**				
Dominican Republic	1980	1990	1995	1980-1990	1990-1995	1980	1990	1995	1980-1990	1990-1995
842 Men's outerwear not knit	9 325.3	258 641.5	592 230.4	39.4	18.0	9 456.4	258 706.2	593 000.9	39.2	18.0
843 Women's outerwear nonknit	18 403.6	195 696.4	364 897.2	26.7	13.3	18 403.6	195 749.2	366 063.8	26.7	13.3
844 Under garments not knit	15 819.8	57 538.8	86 872.2	13.8	8.6	15 820.7	57 566.5	86 948.2	13.8	8.6
845 Outerwear knit nonelastc	6 079.3	90 955.7	186 781.3	31.1	15.5	6 082.5	91 777.2	19 595.5	31.2	15.9
846 Under garments knitted	39 421.6	156 630.6	423 409.4	14.8	22.0	39 496.4	156 877.3	427 214.9	14.8	22.2
847 Textile clothing acces nes	334.3	7 690.9	7 575.1	36.8	-0.3	351.8	7 701.4	7 716.2	36.2	0.0
848 Headgear, nontxtl clothing	2 647.0	39 390.0	64 418.2	31.0	10.3	2 652.6	39 444.3	66 182.9	31.0	10.9
Total	92 031.0	806 543.9	1 726 183.8	24.2	16.4	92 264.0	807 822.1	1 738 722.6	24.2	16.6
	Exports to United States					**Exports to OECD countries**				
Costa Rica	1980	1990	1995	1980-1990	1990-1995	1980	1990	1995	1980-1990	1990-1995
842 Men's outerwear not knit	2 273.7	116 005.5	233 278.0	48.2	15.0	2 273.8	116 050.4	235 342.6	48.2	15.2
843 Women's outerwear nonknit	11 917.9	81 757.5	70 470.0	21.2	-2.9	11 922.7	81 842.3	70 927.4	21.2	-2.8
844 Under garments not knit	244.9	34 862.2	91 728.0	64.2	21.3	250.3	34 884.3	91 864.7	63.8	21.4
845 Outerwear knit nonelastc	1 311.7	36 858.5	79 861.2	39.6	16.7	1 330.1	37 175.3	80 850.4	39.5	16.8
846 Under garments knitted	23 525.3	118 481.5	252 158.4	17.5	16.3	23 572.0	120 107.5	258 258.9	17.7	16.5
847 Textile clothing acces nes	4.7	3 782.0	21 480.0	95.1	41.5	4.7	3 812.9	21 915.0	95.3	41.9
848 Headgear, nontxtl clothing	3.0	6 583.8	5 909.5	115.8	-2.1	2.4	6 684.7	6 026.8	121.4	-2.1
Total	39 281.1	398 331.1	754 885.0	26.1	13.6	39 355.8	400 557.4	765 185.9	26.1	13.8

Source: CANPLUS.

Note: Export data for 1980, 1985 and 1990 are three-year averages; the figure given for 1995 is the average of 1994-1995.

Annex table 6.1. Characteristics of companies surveyed

	Sector[a]	Exports FOB ($million) (1995)	Imports CIF ($million) (1995)	Principal market	Starting year of operations in Chile	No. of persons employed	Foreign capital (per cent of total)	Total estimated investment ($ million)	Principal country of origin (per cent share in total affiliate capital)
1	M	391.2	0.8	Japan	1994	625	100	583.0	United States (80)
2	A	1.4	0.5	United States	1994	40	51	0.7	France (51)
3	Fo	273.1	7.7	Japan	1992	350	54	339.3	United States (47)
4	M	105.3	10.1	Germany	1992	330	100	293.1	Canada (100)
5	A	13.6	26.2	Japan	1982	1,000	70	37.7	United Kingdom (70)
6	M	30.0	6.0	Brazil	1967	330	90	5.5	United States (66)
7	Fo	63.9	39.3	Argentina	1994	1,200	51	57.1	United States (51)
8	M	1,110.9	213.7	Japan	1990	1,700	97	883.9	Australia (57)
9	Fo	26.6	2.3	Japan	1992	142	17	4.1	Japan (7.0)
10	Fo	53.4	0.0	Republic of Korea	1979	480	33	164.0	New Zealand (33)
11	Fo	68.8	0.2	Japan	1988	50	100	0.2	Switzerland (100)
12	Fo	24.2	0.0	Japan	1987	360	50	1.5	United States (25)
13	Fo	173.9	3.8	Belgium	1991	922	100	234.7	United Kingdom (100)
14	A	24.4	0.9	United States	1987	130	0	1,2	Chile (100)
15	M	9.1	0.2	United Kingdom	1988	45	100	76.5	United States (100)
16	A	25.1	1.1	United States	1979	100	67	5.0	Saudi Arabia (67)
17	M	166.1	71.0	United States	1955	1,778	75	65.6	Panama (48)
18	M	156.1	0.0	United States	1990	511	100	305.4	Canada (100)
19	Fo	19.8	4.9	Japan	1987	210	50	57.1	New Zealand (50)
20	M	160.7	0.0	Brazil	1988	190	90	297.0	United States (66)
21	M	31.2	2.5	United Kingdom	1988	240	100	0.8	Australia (100)
22	Fo	38.6	14.3	Argentina	1988	340	100	135.1	New Zealand (51)
23	Fi	37.9	4.7	Japan	1983	800	100	10.7	Spain (49)
24	M	125.0	3.3	Germany	1994	430	76.5	367.5	Canada (77)
25	M	38.7	4.4	United States	1984	218	100	14.1	United States (100)
26	A	3.6	0.1	United States/ Canada	1989	200	50	1.0	France (50)
27	A	29.6	0.6	United States	1991	700	100	10.2	New Zealand (100)
Total		**3,202.2**	**418.7**			**13,421**	**75**	**3,952.0**	

Source: UNCTAD.

[a]   M=Mining, Fo=Forestry, Fi=Fishing, A=Agribusiness

Annex table 6.2. Operational data for metalworking companies in the survey

Item	1	2	3	4	5	6
Owner	Local	TNC	Local	TNC	TNC	Local
No. of employees	180	100	280	750	273	400
Year of establishment	1975	1980	1897	1971	n/a	1969
Major products	Trailers;	- Mining equipment	- Mining and heavy earthmoving equipment;	- Agricultural implements;	- Power cables;	- Aluminium extrusion profiles;
	Truck bodies	- Engineering goods	- Engines and trucks;	- Spraying equipment;	- Building cables;	- Copper tubes and solids;
		- Electrical switchgear	- Electrical switchgear;	- Trailers;	- Bare copper products;	- Brass hollows and solids
				- Irrigation system;	- Flexible cords and cables	
Main export market	Regional	Regional	Regional	Regional	Regional	Regional
Export as percentage of sales:						
1989-1990	25%	Insignificant for	Insignificant for the	n/a	n/a	2%
1994	15%	the whole period	whole period	n/a	15%	n/a
1995	15%			2%	20%	5%

Source: UNCTAD.

Annex table 6.3. Operational data for agro-processing companies in the survey

	1	2	3	4	5	6	7
Owner	TNC	Local	TNC	45% foreign 55% local	TNC	TNC	49% local 51% Heinz
No. of employees	1250	1.250	130	400	1490	196	1500
Year of establishment	1963	1976	1929	1944	1943	1960	1931
Major product (s)	- Cordials-condiments - Tea, coffee	- Chips and snacks - Cereals - Canned products - Grocery products	- Cigarettes	- Wines - Spirits	- Powder - Soaps - Edible oils and margarine - Canned detergents products	- Dairy products - Malt extract - Cocoa based beverages	- Cooking oil - Soaps - Margarine - Protein meals
Export strategy	Regional	Regional	Regional & international	Regional & international	Regional	Regional	Regional
Export as percentage of sales:							
1989-1990	0%	4%	5%	n/a	n/a	n /a	30%
1994	0%	n/a	22%	n/a	na%	n/a	n/a
1995	6%	10%	41%	6%	na%	11%	10%

Source: UNCTAD.

Annex table 6.4. Operational data for garment-making companies in the survey

Item	1	2	3	4	5	6	7
Owner	Local	Local	Local	TNC	Local	Local	Local
No. of employees	900	1072	350	320	1100	500	350
Year of establishment	1949	n/a	1978	1957	1963	1957	1939
Major products	- Industrial and protective clothing - Jeans - Elastics, tales and webbing	- Ladies' and children's wear	- Ladies' casual wear - Men's wear - Children's wear	- Rainwear - Protective clothing - Safety equipment - PVC-coated products	- Formal mens wear - Jeans - Swimwear - Beachwear	- Mens wear (shirts and trousers)	- Mens wear (shirts and trousers)
Export strategy	European Union and regional	Global and regional	European Union	Regional	European Union and regional	North America and European Union	United States and regional
Export as percentage of sales:							
1989-1990	n/a	50%	n/a	n/a	n/a	40%	25-30%
1994	10%	50%	50%	n/a	n/a	n/a	n/a
1995	50%	50%	65%	5%	85%	80%	10%

Source: UNCTAD.

Annex 6.1. The survey coverage

Chile

The Chilean survey covered 27 companies (of which 26 were TNC subsidiaries and was a locally-owned firm) and was undertaken in June and July 1995. The main criteria for selection were the foreign capital share in the affiliate, the latter's relationship with the most dynamic trade sectors in the Chilean economy, and its export competitiveness over the last decade. From an initial shortlist of 50 companies, 27 were selected for an in-depth interview, of which 11 were in mining, 9 in forestry, 6 in agribusiness and 1 in fishing. Although the sample may not be strictly representative of Chile's TNC-based export sector as a whole, the companies are broadly illustrative of affiliates operating in Chilean export sectors. They represent a substantial share of foreign investment in Chile between 1974 and 1994 and of total goods exported during 1995 (see table 6.4 for details), which allows one to generalize to some extent from the survey findings. Their major export products are: copper concentrates, copper cathodes, copper wire, wine, juice concentrates, grapes, cellulose, plywood, sawn woods, wood chips, MDF boards, newspaper, cigarettes, printing services, gold, methanol, hake (fish) and lithium carbonate. Some basic characteristics of the sample companies are listed in annex table 6.1.

Zimbabwe

The Zimbabwean survey, conducted during 1995, included 20 companies, of which 6 were in metal work, 7 in agro processing and 7 in garment making. Each of the three sectors chosen represents an important aspect of the manufacturing sector and each has a substantial impact on the economy at large, for example, in the form of having a large share of total manufactured output, linkages to other sectors, or high export rates and potential. The three sectors also represent different patterns of FDI contribution. In the selection of companies within each subsector both TNCs and locally-owned companies were included, to allow some comparisons to be between the responses of local companies and those of TNCs to altered market and policy conditions. The main reasons for including each sector in the study can be briefly summarized as follows:

- The **metal industry** has traditionally been the country's leading sector, with strong linkages to other industries, and with a significant representation of foreign investment. However, in recent years the sector has stagnated and new FDI has not been substantial. It has been found useful for the purpose of this study to analyse how this formerly protected sector is dealing with new market conditions and what efforts are being made to increase competitiveness.

- The **agro-industry** has a very strong participation of TNCs and has in recent years been among the leading sectors as regards improved output and export performance: the contribution of TNCs to competitiveness can be expected to be high.

- The **garment sector** is of interest as it has high exports to both regional and OECD markets, although it is also very sensitive to any changes affecting its access to markets (tariffs, quotas, etc). The sector is dominated by locally-owned companies and thus provides a useful comparison with sectors such as food processing and metalworking where TNC participation has been pronounced.

Note on the contributors

Mohamed Ariff, President, Malaysian Institute of Economic Research (MIER), Kuala Lumpur, Malaysia.

Jorge Carrillo, Director of Social Studies Department, El Colegio de la Frontera Norte, Tijuana, Mexico.

Gonzalo Cid Passarini, Director, Iquique Free Trade Zone (ZOFRI), Iquique, Chile.

Sanjaya Lall, Professor of Development Economics at Queen Elizabeth House and Fellow of Green College, University of Oxford, Oxford, United Kingdom.

Karim Laraki, President, Klonic Mena Consultants, Rabat, Morocco.

Eddy Martinez, Executive Director, Office of Foreign Investment Promotion, Santo Domingo, Dominican Republic.

Michael Mortimore, Chief, Unit on Investment and Corporate Strategies, Division of Production, United Nations Economic Commission for Latin America and the Caribbean (ECLAC), Santiago, Chile.

Nipon Poapongsakorn, Vice President, Thailand Development Research Institute (TDRI); Professor, Faculty of Economics, Thammasat University, Bangkok, Thailand.

Henny Romijn, Lecturer in Technology and Development Studies, Faculty of Technology Management, Eindhoven University of Technology, Eindhoven, The Netherlands.

Jens Erik Torp, Associate Professor, Department for Intercultural Communication and Management, Copenhagen Business School, Copenhagen, Denmark.

Rikkert van Assouw, Economist, Development Research Institute (IVO), Tilburg University, Tilburg, The Netherlands.

Lorenzo J. Vicens, Consultant, Santo Domingo, Dominican Republic.

Yew Siew Yong, Professor of Economics, Faculty of Economics and Administration, University of Malaya Lembah Pantai, Kuala Lumpur, Malaysia.

Ronney Zamora, Director of Research and Economic Advisory Department, Chamber of Industries of Costa Rica, San José, Costa Rica.

Selected UNCTAD publications on
transnational corporations and foreign direct investment

A. Individual studies

World Investment Report 2000: Cross-border Mergers and Acquisitions and Development. 368 p. Sales No. E.99.II.D.20. $45.

World Investment Report 2000: Cross-border Mergers and Acquisitions and Development. An Overview. 75 p. Free-of-charge.

International Investment Instruments: A Compendium, vol. IV, 319 p. Sales No. E.00.II.D.13. $55, vol. V, 505 p. Sales No. E.00.II.D.14. $55.

FDI Determinants and TNCs Strategies: The Case of Brazil. 195 p. Sales No. E.00.II.D.2, $35.

World Investment Report 1999: Foreign Direct Investment and the Challenge of Development. 536 p. Sales No. E.99.II.D.3. $45.

World Investment Report 1999: Foreign Direct Investment and Challenge of Development. An Overview. 75 p. Free-of-charge.

Investment Policy Review of Uganda. 75 p. Sales No. E.99.II.D.24. $15.

Investment Policy Review of Egypt. 113 p. Sales No. E.99.II.D.20. $19.

Science, Technology and Innovation Policy Review of Colombia. 175 p. Sales No. E.99.II.D.13. $23.

Foreign Direct Invesment in Africa: Performance and Potential. 89 p. UNCTAD/ITE/IIT/Misc. 15.

Investment Policy Review of Uzbekistan. 64 p. UNCTAD/ITE/IIP/Misc. 13. Free-of-charge.

The Financial Crisis in Asia and Foreign Direct Investment: An Assessment. 101 p. Sales No. GV.E.98.0.29. $20.

Science, Technology and Innovation Policy Review of Jamaica. 172 p. Sales No. E.98.II.D.7. $42.

World Investment Report 1998: Trends and Determinants. 430 p. Sales No. E.98.II.D.5. $45.

World Investment Report 1998: Trends and Determinants. An Overview. 67 p. Free-of-charge.

Bilateral Investment Treaties in the mid-1990s. 314 p. Sales No. E.98.II.D.8. $46.

Handbook on Foreign Direct Investment by Small and Medium-sized Enterprises: Lessons from Asia. 200 p. Sales No. E.98.II.D.4. $48.

Handbook on Foreign Direct Investment by Small and Medium-sized Enterprises: Lessons from Asia. Executive Summary and Report on the Kunming Conference. 74 p. Free-of-charge.

International Investment Towards the Year 2002. 166 p. Sales No. GV.E.98.0.15. $29. (Joint publication with Invest in France Mission and Arthur Andersen, in collaboration with DATAR.)

World Investment Report 1997: Transnational Corporations, Market Structure and Competition Policy. 420 p. Sales No. E.97.II.D.10. $45.

World Investment Report 1997: Transnational Corporations, Market Structure and Competition Policy. An Overview. 70 p. Free-of-charge.
International Investment Towards the Year 2001. 81 p. Sales No. GV.E.97.0.5. $35. (Joint publication with Invest in France Mission and Arthur Andersen, in collaboration with DATAR.)

World Investment Directory. Vol. VI: West Asia 1996. 192 p. Sales No. E.97.II.A.2. $35.

World Investment Directory. Vol. V: Africa 1996. 508 p. Sales No. E.97.II.A.1. $75.

Sharing Asia's Dynamism: Asian Direct Investment in the European Union. 192 p. Sales No. E.97.II.D.1. $26.

Transnational Corporations and World Development. 656 p. ISBN 0-415-08560-8 (hardback), 0-415-08561-6 (paperback). £65 (hardback), £20.00 (paperback). (Published by International Thomson Business Press on behalf of UNCTAD.)

Companies without Borders: Transnational Corporations in the 1990s. 224 p. ISBN 0-415-12526-X. £47.50. (Published by International Thomson Business Press on behalf of UNCTAD.)

The New Globalism and Developing Countries. 336 p. ISBN 92-808-0944-X. $25. (Published by United Nations University Press.)

Investing in Asia's Dynamism: European Union Direct Investment in Asia. 124 p. ISBN 92-827-7675-1. ECU 14. (Joint publication with the European Commission.)

World Investment Report 1996: Investment, Trade and International Policy Arrangements. 332 p. Sales No. E.96.II.A.14. $45.

World Investment Report 1996: Investment, Trade and International Policy Arrangements. An Overview. 51 p. Free-of-charge.

International Investment Instruments: A Compendium. Vol. I. 371 p. Sales No. E.96.II.A.9; Vol. II. 577 p. Sales No. E.96.II.A.10; Vol. III. 389 p. Sales No. E.96.II.A.11; the 3-volume set, Sales No. E.96.II.A.12. $125.

World Investment Report 1995: Transnational Corporations and Competitiveness. 491 p. Sales No. E.95.II.A.9. $45.

World Investment Report 1995: Transnational Corporations and Competitiveness. An Overview. 51 p. Free-of-charge.

Accounting for Sustainable Forestry Management. A Case Study. 46 p. Sales No. E.94.II.A.17. $22.

Small and Medium-sized Transnational Corporations. Executive Summary and Report of the Osaka Conference. 60 p. Free-of-charge.

World Investment Report 1994: Transnational Corporations, Employment and the Workplace. 482 p. Sales No. E.94.II.A.14. $45.

World Investment Report 1994: Transnational Corporations, Employment and the Workplace. An Executive Summary. 34 p. Free-of-charge.

Liberalizing International Transactions in Services: A Handbook. 182 p. Sales No. E.94.II.A.11. $45. (Joint publication with the World Bank.)

World Investment Directory. Vol. IV: Latin America and the Caribbean. 478 p. Sales No. E.94.II.A.10. $65.

Conclusions on Accounting and Reporting by Transnational Corporations. 47 p. Sales No. E.94.II.A.9. $25.

Accounting, Valuation and Privatization. 190 p. Sales No. E.94.II.A.3. $25.

Environmental Management in Transnational Corporations: Report on the Benchmark Corporate Environment Survey. 278 p. Sales No. E.94.II.A.2. $29.95.

Management Consulting: A Survey of the Industry and Its Largest Firms. 100 p. Sales No. E.93.II.A.17. $25.

Transnational Corporations: A Selective Bibliography, 1991-1992. 736 p. Sales No. E.93.II.A.16. $75. (English/French.)

Small and Medium-sized Transnational Corporations: Role, Impact and Policy Implications. 242 p. Sales No. E.93.II.A.15. $35.

World Investment Report 1993: Transnational Corporations and Integrated International Production. 290 p. Sales No. E.93.II.A.14. $45.

World Investment Report 1993: Transnational Corporations and Integrated International Production. An Executive Summary. 31 p. ST/CTC/159. Free-of-charge.

Foreign Investment and Trade Linkages in Developing Countries. 108 p. Sales No. E.93.II.A.12. $18.

World Investment Directory 1992. Vol. III: Developed Countries. 532 p. Sales No. E.93.II.A.9. $75.

Transnational Corporations from Developing Countries: Impact on Their Home Countries. 116 p. Sales No. E.93.II.A.8. $15.

Debt-Equity Swaps and Development. 150 p. Sales No. E.93.II.A.7. $35.

From the Common Market to EC 92: Regional Economic Integration in the European Community and Transnational Corporations. 134 p. Sales No. E.93.II.A.2. $25.

World Investment Directory 1992. Vol. II: Central and Eastern Europe. 432 p. Sales No. E.93.II.A.1. $65. (Joint publication with the United Nations Economic Commission for Europe.)

The East-West Business Directory 1991/1992. 570 p. Sales No. E.92.II.A.20. $65.

World Investment Report 1992: Transnational Corporations as Engines of Growth. 356 p. Sales No. E.92.II.A.19. $45.

World Investment Report 1992: Transnational Corporations as Engines of Growth: An Executive Summary. 30 p. Sales No. E.92.II.A.24. Free-of-charge.

World Investment Directory 1992. Vol. I: Asia and the Pacific. 356 p. Sales No. E.92.II.A.11. $65.

Climate Change and Transnational Corporations: Analysis and Trends. 110 p. Sales No. E.92.II.A.7. $16.50.

Foreign Direct Investment and Transfer of Technology in India. 150 p. Sales No. E.92.II.A.3. $20.

The Determinants of Foreign Direct Investment: A Survey of the Evidence. 84 p. Sales No. E.92.II.A.2. $12.50.

The Impact of Trade-Related Investment Measures on Trade and Development: Theory, Evidence and Policy Implications. 108 p. Sales No. E.91.II.A.19. $17.50. (Joint publication with the United Nations Centre on Transnational Corporations.)

Transnational Corporations and Industrial Hazards Disclosure. 98 p. Sales No. E.91.II.A.18. $17.50.

Transnational Business Information: A Manual of Needs and Sources. 216 p. Sales No. E.91.II.A.13. $45.

World Investment Report 1991: The Triad in Foreign Direct Investment. 108 p. Sales No.E.91.II.A.12. $25.

B. IIA Issues Paper Series

Employment. *UNCTAD Series on issues in international investment agreements.* 69 p. Sales No. E.00.II.D.15. $12.

Taxation. *UNCTAD Series on issues in international investment agreements.* 111 p. Sales No. E.00.II.D.5. $12.

International Investment Agreements: Flexibility for Development. *UNCTA3D Series on issues in international investment agreements.* 185 p. Sales No. E.00.II.D.6. $12.

Taking of Property. *UNCTAD Series on issues in international investment agreements.* 83 p. Sales No. E.00.II.D.4. $12.

Trends in International Investment Agreements: An Overview. *UNCTAD Series on issues in international investment agreements.* 112 p. Sales No. E.99.II.D.23. $ 12.

Lessons from the MAI. UNCTAD Series on issues in international investment agreements. 31 p. Sales No. E.99.II.D.26. $ 12.

National Treatment. UNCTAD Series on issues in international investment agreements. 104 p. Sales No. E.99.II.D.16. $12.

Fair and Equitable Treatment. UNCTAD Series on issues in international investment agreements. 64 p. Sales No. E.99.II.D.15. $12.

Investment-Related Trade Measures. UNCTAD Series on issues in international investment agreements. 64 p. Sales No. E.99.II.D.12. $12.

Most-Favoured-Nation Treatment. UNCTAD Series on issues in international investment agreements. 72p. Sales No. E.99.II.D.11. $12.

Admission and Establishment. UNCTAD Series on issues in international investment agreements. 72p. Sales No. E.99.II.D.10. $12.

Scope and Definition. UNCTAD Series on issues in international investment agreements. 96p. Sales No. E.99.II.D.9. $12.

Transfer Pricing. UNCTAD Series on issues in international investment agreements. 72p. Sales No. E.99.II.D.8. $12.

Foreign Direct Investment and Development. UNCTAD Series on issues in international investment agreements. 88p. Sales No. E.98.II.D.15. $12.

Admission et établissement. CNUCED Collection consacrée aux problèmes relatifs aux accord internationaux d'investissements. 55 p. Sales No. F.99.II.D.10. $12.

International Investment Agreement: Flexibility for Development. UNCTAD Series on issues in international investment agreements. 88p. Sales No. E.00.II.D.6. $12.

C. Serial publications

Current Studies, Series A

No. 30. *Incentives and Foreign Direct Investment.* 98 p. Sales No. E.96.II.A.6. $30. (English/French.)

No. 29. *Foreign Direct Investment, Trade, Aid and Migration.* 100 p. Sales No. E.96.II.A.8. $25. (Joint publication with the International Organization for Migration.)

No. 28. *Foreign Direct Investment in Africa.* 119 p. Sales No. E.95.II.A.6. $20.

No. 27. *Tradability of Banking Services: Impact and Implications.* 195 p. Sales No. E.94.II.A.12. $50.

No. 26. *Explaining and Forecasting Regional Flows of Foreign Direct Investment*. 58 p. Sales No. E.94.II.A.5. $25.

No. 25. *International Tradability in Insurance Services*. 54 p. Sales No. E.93.II.A.11. $20.
No. 24. *Intellectual Property Rights and Foreign Direct Investment*. 108 p. Sales No. E.93.II.A.10. $20.

No. 23. *The Transnationalization of Service Industries: An Empirical Analysis of the Determinants of Foreign Direct Investment by Transnational Service Corporations*. 62 p. Sales No. E.93.II.A.3. $15.

No. 22. *Transnational Banks and the External Indebtedness of Developing Countries: Impact of Regulatory Changes*. 48 p. Sales No. E.92.II.A.10. $12.

No. 20. *Foreign Direct Investment, Debt and Home Country Policies*. 50 p. Sales No. E.90.II.A.16. $12.

No. 19. *New Issues in the Uruguay Round of Multilateral Trade Negotiations*. 52 p. Sales No. E.90.II.A.15. $12.50.

No. 18. *Foreign Direct Investment and Industrial Restructuring in Mexico*. 114 p. Sales No. E.92.II.A.9. $12.

No. 17. *Government Policies and Foreign Direct Investment*. 68 p. Sales No. E.91.II.A.20. $12.50.

The United Nations Library on Transnational Corporations
(Published by Routledge on behalf of the United Nations.)

Set A (Boxed set of 4 volumes. ISBN 0-415-08554-3. £350):
Volume One: *The Theory of Transnational Corporations*. 464 p.
Volume Two: *Transnational Corporations: A Historical Perspective*. 464 p.
Volume Three: *Transnational Corporations and Economic Development*. 448 p.
Volume Four: *Transnational Corporations and Business Strategy*. 416 p.

Set B (Boxed set of 4 volumes. ISBN 0-415-08555-1. £350):
Volume Five: *International Financial Management*. 400 p.
Volume Six: *Organization of Transnational Corporations*. 400 p.
Volume Seven: *Governments and Transnational Corporations*. 352 p.
Volume Eight: *Transnational Corporations and International Trade and Payments*. 320 p.

Set C (Boxed set of 4 volumes. ISBN 0-415-08556-X. £350):
Volume Nine: *Transnational Corporations and Regional Economic Integration*. 331 p.
Volume Ten: *Transnational Corporations and the Exploitation of Natural Resources*. 397 p.
Volume Eleven: *Transnational Corporations and Industrialization*. 425 p.
Volume Twelve: *Transnational Corporations in Services*. 437 p.

Set D (Boxed set of 4 volumes. ISBN 0-415-08557-8. £350):
Volume Thirteen: *Cooperative Forms of Transnational Corporation Activity*. 419 p.
Volume Fourteen: *Transnational Corporations: Transfer Pricing and Taxation*. 330 p.

Volume Fifteen: *Transnational Corporations: Market Structure and Industrial Performance*. 383 p.
Volume Sixteen: *Transnational Corporations and Human Resources*. 429 p.

Set E (Boxed set of 4 volumes. ISBN 0-415-08558-6. £350):
Volume Seventeen: *Transnational Corporations and Innovatory Activities*. 447 p.
Volume Eighteen: *Transnational Corporations and Technology Transfer to Developing Countries*. 486 p.
Volume Nineteen: *Transnational Corporations and National Law*. 322 p.
Volume Twenty: *Transnational Corporations: The International Legal Framework*. 545 p.

D. Journals

Transnational Corporations (formerly *The CTC Reporter*).

Published three times a year. Annual subscription price: $45; individual issues $20.

ProInvest, a quarterly newsletter, available free of charge.
United Nations publications may be obtained from bookstores and distributors throughout the world. Please consult your bookstore or write to:

United Nations Publications

Sales Section
United Nations Office at Geneva
Palais des Nations
CH-1211 Geneva 10
Switzerland
Tel: (41-22) 917-1234
Fax: (41-22) 917-0123
E-mail: unpubli@unorg.ch

OR
Sales Section
Room DC2-0853
United Nations Secretariat
New York, NY 10017
U.S.A.
Tel: (1-212) 963-8302 or (800) 253-9646
Fax: (1-212) 963-3489
E-mail: publications@un.org

All prices are quoted in United States dollars.

Questionnaire

The Competitiveness Challenge: Transnational Corporations and Industrial Restructuring in Developing Countries

Sales No. E.00.II.D.35

In order to improve the quality and relevance of the work of the UNCTAD Division on Investment, Technology and Enterprise Development, it would be useful to receive the views of readers on this and other similar publications. It would therefore be greatly appreciated if you could complete the following questionnaire and return to:

Readership Survey
UNCTAD Division on Investment, Technology and Enterprise Development
United Nations Office in Geneva
Palais des Nations
Room E-9123
CH-1211 Geneva 10
Switzerland

1. Name and address of respondent (optional):

    _____
    _____
    _____
    _____

2. Which of the following best describes your area of work?

Government	☐	Public enterprise	☐
Private enterprise institution	☐	Academic or research	☐
International organization	☐	Media	☐
Not-for-profit organization	☐	Other (specify)	☐

3. In which country do you work? _____

4. What is your assessment of the contents of this publication?

Excellent	☐	Adequate	☐
Good	☐	Poor	☐

5. How useful is this publication to your work?

Very useful	☐	Of some use	☐	Irrelevant	☐

6.   Please indicate the three things you liked best about this publication:

_____

_____

_____

7.   Please indicate the three things you liked least about this publication:

_____

_____

_____

8.   If you have read more than the present publication of the UNCTAD Division on Investment, Enterprise Development and Technology, what is your overall assessment of them?

Consistently good   ☐   Usually good, but with some exceptions   ☐

Generally mediocre   ☐   Poor   ☐

9.   On the average, how useful are these publications to you in your work?

Very useful   ☐   Of some use   ☐   Irrelevant   ☐

10.   Are you a regular recipient of Transnational Corporations (formerly The CTC Reporter), the Division's tri-annual refereed journal?

Yes   ☐   No   ☐

If not, please check here if you would like to receive a sample
copy sent to the name and address you have given above   ☐

Index

Printed at United Nations, Geneva
GE.00-52559—October 2000–3,775

UNCTAD/ITE/IIT/MISC.20

United Nations publication
Sales No. E.00.II.D.35

ISBN 92-1-112503-0

The Scapegrace